BONHOEFFER

A Theology of Sociality

BONHOEFFER

A Theology of Sociality

REVISED EDITION

Clifford J. Green

WILLIAM B. EERDMANS PUBLISHING COMPANY
GRAND RAPIDS, MICHIGAN / CAMBRIDGE, U.K.

First edition published 1972 under the title
The Sociality of Christ and Humanity:
Dietrich Bonhoeffer's Early Theology, 1927-1933

Revised edition published 1999 by
Wm. B. Eerdmans Publishing Co.
255 Jefferson Ave. S.E., Grand Rapids, Michigan 49503 /
P.O. Box 163, Cambridge CB3 9PU U.K.

Printed in the United States of America

05 04 03 02 01 00 99   7 6 5 4 3 2 1

ISBN 0-8028-4632-7

Contents

ABBREVIATIONS

The following abbreviations have been used. All books are those of Bonhoeffer except where another author is given. Full publication details are given in the Select Bibliography.

AB   *Act and Being.* DBWE 2, Minneapolis: Fortress Press, 1996

AS   *Akt und Sein.* DBW 2, Munich: Chr. Kaiser, 1988

CC   *Christ the Center.* New York: Harper & Row, 1966

CD   *The Cost of Discipleship.* New York: Simon & Schuster, 1995

CF   *Creation and Fall.* DBWE 3, Minneapolis: Fortress Press, 1997

CW I *No Rusty Swords. Letters, Lectures and Notes 1928-1936* from the Collected Works of Dietrich Bonhoeffer. Vol. I. New York: Harper & Row, 1965

CW II *The Way to Freedom. Letters, Lectures and Notes 1935-1939* from the Collected Works of Dietrich Bonhoeffer. Vol. II. New York: Harper & Row, 1967

DB   *Dietrich Bonhoeffer. Theologe, Christ, Zeitgenosse,* by Eberhard Bethge. Munich: Chr. Kaiser, 1967; second edn.

DB-E   *Dietrich Bonhoeffer. Theologian, Christian, Man for his Times.* By Eberhard Bethge. Second unabridged edition. Revised and edited by Victoria Barnett. Minneapolis: Fortress Press, 1999

DBW   Dietrich Bonhoeffer Werke, the critical edition of Bonhoeffer's works, 1986–1999

DBWE   Dietrich Bonhoeffer Works, English edition, 1996–

E   *Ethik.* DBW 6, Gütersloh: Chr. Kaiser, 1998 (second edn.)

E-E   *Ethics.* New York: Simon & Schuster, 1995

FP   *Fiction from Prison.* Philadelphia: Fortress Press, 1981

FT   *Fragmente aus Tegel.* DBW 7, Munich: Chr. Kaiser, 1994

GL   *Gemeinsames Leben.* DBW 5, Munich: Chr. Kaiser, 1987

GS   *Gesammelte Schriften,* vols. I-VI, ed. Eberhard Bethge. Munich: Chr. Kaiser; I 1965, second edn.; II 1965, second edn.; III 1966, second edn.; IV 1965, second edn.; V 1972; VI 1974

JS   *Jugend und Studium 1918-1927.* DBW 9, Munich: Chr. Kaiser, 1986

LPP   *Letters and Papers from Prison.* The Enlarged Edition. New York: Macmillan, 1972; Simon & Schuster, 1997

LT   *Life Together.* DBWE 5, Minneapolis: Fortress Press, 1996

MW   *Die Mündige Welt,* vols I-V, ed. Eberhard Bethge et al. Munich: Chr. Kaiser, 1955-69

N   *Nachfolge.* DBW 4, Gütersloh: Chr. Kaiser, 1994 (second edn.)

PB   *Preface to Bonhoeffer,* by John Godsey. Philadelphia: Fortress Press, 1965

SC   *Sanctorum Communio.* DBW 1, Munich: Chr. Kaiser, 1986

SC-A   *Sanctorum Communio,* original dissertation manuscript, 1927.

SC-E   *Sanctorum Communio.* DBWE 1, Minneapolis: Fortress Press, 1998

SF   *Schöpfung und Fall.* DBW 3, Munich: Chr. Kaiser, 1989

WA   *D. Martin Luthers Werke.* Kritische Gesamtausgabe, Weimar edn.

WE   *Widerstand und Ergebung.* DBW 8, Gütersloh: Chr. Kaiser, 1998

PREFACE

While it is gratifying when scholars and students call for a new edition of this book, that presents the writer with a real dilemma. The reviews certainly encourage one to agree, but what should the new edition be like? Should it be a virtually re-written and updated text, drawing on new research, new secondary literature, and responding to new theological issues? Or should one recognize that a work written nearly thirty years ago had its own integrity and appeared at a particular point in theological history, which would only be confused by later amendments and updating? Tempted as I was by the former option, the latter eventually won out, not least because of work on other projects.

There are, however, some changes to the text of the edition published by Scholars Press in 1975. The most notable of these is the addition of a new chapter on Bonhoeffer's *Ethics*. Even though the first edition focused on Bonhoeffer's early theology (its title was *The Sociality of Christ and Humanity. Dietrich Bonhoeffer's Early Theology, 1927-1933)*, the interpretation propelled the analysis into considerable discussion of works after 1933, especially *Discipleship* and the *Letters and Papers from Prison*. In light of this, Eberhard Bethge noted in his review that absence of any discussion of the *Ethics* was really a defect. I hope the new chapter remedies the situation to some extent, and in the process pays tribute to a friend in whose debt all Bonhoeffer scholars permanently stand. Adding the *Ethics* chapter further increased the discussion of post-1933 writings. The new title, *Bonhoeffer. A Theology of Sociality*, reflects both my original interpretation of the early theology (the sociality of Christ and humanity) and the examination of his later theology.

Also new in this edition is the appendix, "Letters: Dietrich Bonhoeffer, Paul Lehmann and Others, 1932-1949." This contains four letters from Bonhoeffer to Lehmann, ten letters between Lehmann and several of Bonhoeffer's family and friends, and one from Lehmann to President Samuel Press of Eden Seminary related to Bonhoeffer's visit to the United States in 1939. In preparation for the final volume of the Dietrich Bonhoeffer Werke, a search of the Lehmann papers at the Luce Library, Princeton Theological Seminary, discovered these letters in 1998. The new letters appear here in English for the first time. Of special importance are those that Bonhoeffer wrote in 1941 as part of his work for the resistance movement; one letter in particular gives insight into the thinking of Bonhoeffer's resistance circle, as they planned for a post-war government and were concerned that a victorious America might promote forms of democratic life that were premature in a defeated Nazi Germany. Some of these letters will be published in volume 17 of the Dietrich Bonhoeffer Werke, and eventually in the appropriate volume of the Dietrich Bonhoeffer Works, English Edition. Their publication here makes them available quickly, and also allows the printing of letters to and from family members which will not appear in the volumes of the Bonhoeffer works. I am grateful for the friendly cooperation of Dr. Stephen Crocco, Librarian, who authorized this search and publication, and for the help of Mr. William Harris, the archivist, and of Mr. Joe Coker who carried out the first thorough search of this important collection of papers. Thanks are also extended to Lowell Zuck who kindly provided the letter from Lehmann to Press from the Eden archives. I also wish to express very warm thanks to Dr. Reinhard Krauss, my colleague in the Dietrich Bonhoeffer Works, English Edition, for his prompt translation of several of the letters at a time we were both working under considerable pressure.

There are some other changes as well. The discussion of five works of early Bonhoeffer scholarship in the 1960s has been dropped from Chapter 1; this can be consulted in the microform version of the dissertation available from University Microfilms. (The original dissertation, incidentally, also contained five appendices and a bibliography which were not included in the Scholars Press edition.) In footnote citations of Bonhoeffer's German texts I have always used the new, critical editions of the *Dietrich Bonhoeffer Werke,* while also retaining the references to the *Gesammelte Schriften.* Four volumes of the critical edition have now been translated into English, and these translations have also been used and cited. Occasional editorial improvements have been made here and there, and very occasionally a more recent piece of secondary literature has been cited in the notes. Gender-inclusive language has been used as much as possible. An index has been added, and a Select Bibliography. Several lengthy passages quoted in German have been translated for this edition. Notwithstanding these changes, the text is largely the same, and the overall argument is unchanged since I believe that the interpretation remains sound.

The study was based on Bonhoeffer's original German texts, and in quoting I worked directly from the primary sources; the citations give both the German sources and the English translations. Deviations from published translations, above all the older editions, are frequent, but I only draw attention to these when major issues in the argument are involved. For the sake of precision and consistent exposition a good number of German terms appear throughout the text. These are only italicized to indicate emphasis, either in the original sources, or my own. I trust that even readers with little German will not have difficulty navigating through these signs of Bonhoeffer's native tongue. In one important case I have changed a translation of my own found in the previous edition: "Gemeinde" is now translated "church-community," following the usage and rationale of the new translation of *Sanctorum Communio,* as explained in my Editor's Introduction to that book. Translating "Gemeinde" in Bonhoeffer as if it always and only meant "congregation" (which it sometimes does mean!) is seriously misleading.

Previous versions of this book have acknowledged those who have helped my earlier work. For this edition I am happy to thank Teri Vaughn and Patricia Onyia of Hartford Seminary for their expertise and perseverance with the word processor; David Stassen for draft translations of several German passages; and Barrie Mosher who expertly prepared the camera-ready copy.

C.G.
North Waterford, Maine
In the season of Pentecost, 1999

ACKNOWLEDGMENTS

The author acknowledges with thanks permission to quote the following copyright texts:

Excerpts from *The Communion of Saints* by Dietrich Bonhoeffer. © 1963 by William Collins Sons & Co. (as *Sanctorum Communio*) and Harper and Row, Publishers, Inc. in the translation of *Sanctorum Communio* of the Dietrich Bonhoeffer Works, vol. 1, 1998, Fortress Press.

Excerpts from *Act and Being* by Dietrich Bonhoeffer. © 1956 by Christian Kaiser Verlag. © 1961 by William Collins Sons & Co., and Harper & Row, Publishers, Inc. in the translation of *Act and Being* of the Dietrich Bonhoeffer Works, vol. 2, 1996, Fortress Press.

Excerpts from *Christ the Center* by Dietrich Bonhoeffer. © 1966 by William Collins Sons & Co. (as *Christology*), and Harper & Row, Publishers, Inc. Reprinted by permission of the publishers.

Excerpts reprinted with permission of SCM Press Ltd. and Macmillan Publishing Company from *Creation and Fall. Temptation* by Dietrich Bonhoeffer. © 1959 SCM Press, Ltd. in the translation of *Creation and Fall* of the Dietrich Bonhoeffer Works, vol. 3, 1997, Fortress Press.

Excerpts reprinted with permission of SCM Press Ltd. and Macmillan Publishing Company from *The Cost of Discipleship* by Dietrich Bonhoeffer. © 1959 SCM Press, Ltd.

Chapter 1

INTERPRETING BONHOEFFER'S THEOLOGY

In the Preface to *Sanctorum Communio*, his doctoral dissertation and first published work, Bonhoeffer states:

> The more this investigation has considered the significance of the sociological category for theology, the more clearly has emerged the social intention of all the basic Christian concepts. "Person," "primal state," "sin," and "revelation" can be fully comprehended only in reference to sociality.[1]

This study, which concentrates on Bonhoeffer's early theology, argues that this is a programmatic statement. It is programmatic for the work it introduces, and for all Bonhoeffer's early theology up to the Christology lectures of 1933. Bonhoeffer's early theology must be understood as a "theology of sociality." Indeed, without diminishing later developments and new insights, the following argument shows that the concepts and concerns of his early theology continue to be formative for his whole thought.

In arguing this thesis a crucial but surprisingly neglected concern of Bonhoeffer's theology comes to light: his theological anthropology and soteriology. If it has long been recognized that Christology is central to Bonhoeffer's thought, his anthropology has been strikingly neglected. However, only when his Christology is seen in the closest relationship

---

[1] SC 13, SC-E 21. (Bonhoeffer's major works, and other frequently mentioned texts, are cited according to the list of Abbreviations.)

with his theological anthropology can the Christology itself be fully understood, and the development of his theology as a whole be shown to have an intrinsic intelligibility. "The sociality of Christ and humanity," therefore, is the hermeneutical rubric for this interpretation of Bonhoeffer's theology.

Bonhoeffer's theological anthropology has a clear and consistent set of categories which articulate the meaning of sociality. Further, within the anthropology, the soteriological problem has a quite particular historical and social specificity in Bonhoeffer's theology. This is the problem of *power* in both its personal and social forms. Bonhoeffer diagnoses the power of the ego and prevalent forms of social power as the crisis of sociality. The powerful ego dominates others and is isolated from others; the mutual love which should characterize authentic human community is fragmented into the anti–social solidarity of egocentricity. Chapter 4 analyzes seven identical passages which recur like a chorus throughout the writings from 1927–1933, all making this same point.

Bonhoeffer's critique of destructive power in the corporate life of society accompanies his diagnosis of dominating power in the individual ego. He was particularly concerned with the destructive power evident in war, in anti–Semitism and racism generally, in the ruthless competition of capitalist economics, in the dehumanizing uses of technology, and so on; above all, he theologically and personally confronted the demonic synthesis of all these destructive forms of power in Nazism. For Bonhoeffer, power as a social and political problem was as important a part of soteriology as the perverse forms of power in the individual person.

The soteriological problem of power, then, is intrinsic to the theology of sociality, in that dominating power violates both the interpersonal relations and the corporate operations of human communities and institutions. But the resolution of the problem is also given in sociality. In Bonhoeffer's theology, the presence of Christ is described in a very deliberate and comprehensive phenomenology of sociality. Revelation is an inherently social event, which occurs in a human community of persons; it is inseparable from, and is directed to, the concrete modes of being in human personal, communal, institutional, and political life. The outcome of revelation, consequently, is a new social form of humanity in which love liberates people from dominating and exploitative power over others to the freedom of being with and for others.

Analysis of these central motifs—Christology, anthropology, sociality, soteriology—brings out another new insight into the character of Bonhoeffer's theological development: the *autobiographical dimension* of his theology. The analysis of his own theological texts in the company of Bethge's masterly biography enables us to see, for the first time, that a deep, personal concern is at work along with the theological, philosophical, exegetical, ecclesiastical, and political factors which informed his thinking. The problem of the powerful ego—a term used deliberately—was an existential concern for the young Bonhoeffer. In 1932, as Bethge has documented, a personal liberation occurred which illuminates the theological path he had already travelled as it directed the course upon which he then embarked. Without a knowledge of this autobiographical dimension, understanding of Bonhoeffer's theological development would be darkened by inner obscurity or externally imposed speculation, or both.

The book *Discipleship* is the direct theological expression of Bonhoeffer's personal liberation in 1932. Beneath its exegetical, ecclesiastical, and political concerns runs a deep, personal concern of the theologian himself. It is impossible properly to understand the book without knowing this fact, and seeing how it influences the theology, exegesis, and the portrait of Luther. Yet when we recognize that Bonhoeffer's existential commitment to faith and the church in 1932 gives an autobiographical dimension to the theology of this book, we also see how the new theme of discipleship is related to the theology of sociality which preceded it: discipleship does not replace the theology of sociality; it *adds* to it and *presupposes* it. Bethge has shown that while *Discipleship* was not fully articulated or published until 1937, its basic themes were all present *in nuce* in an address Bonhoeffer gave in November, 1932, shortly after his experience of "becoming a Christian" in the summer. Existentially and theologically, therefore, the essence of *Discipleship* belongs in the 1927–1933 period.

To understand that there is an autobiographical relationship, as well as a theological connection, between his formative writings and his book on discipleship is also to illuminate Bonhoeffer's prison writings. That justly famous theological celebration of human strength and "adulthood" must be understood in the light of Bonhoeffer's earlier concern with the soteriological problem of power. In the 1930s Bonhoeffer does not clearly distinguish between human strength as a good to be positively affirmed, and dominating power which is the root of the soteriological problem. There is also a Christological counterpart to this unresolved issue in the anthropology: in various writings, including *Discipleship*, there is an unresolved tension between Bonhoeffer's distinctive appropriation of the Lutheran theme of the weakness of Christ in his freedom for humanity, and the portrait of Christ as a domineering power figure. Both the anthropological and Christological tensions are resolved in the prison theology.

Simultaneous with the argument on this soteriological point in Chapter 6, I will demonstrate that the Christology and anthropology presented in terms of sociality in the early theology is indispensable for understanding the content and method of Bonhoeffer's prison theology. While this study concentrates on the early theology from 1927–1933, both the motifs and the dynamics of this theology press forward to the writings of the later 1930s and the mid 1940s; this makes it both natural and necessary to give some selective consideration to material beyond the early period.

At the end of this chapter I will briefly relate these fundamental contentions to the insights and issues which emerge from several major works of Bonhoeffer research. Before doing so, the rationale for selecting this period and designating it as Bonhoeffer's early theology must be indicated.

A. The Rationale for a Study of Bonhoeffer's Early Theology

There are several compelling reasons for taking the years 1927–1933, bounded by *Sanctorum Communio* at the beginning and *Christology* at the end, as the formative period of Bonhoeffer's theological career.

First, this period has a professional and vocational unity. It can be described as Bonhoeffer's academic period. The period of his early theology covers his years as a university theologian, first as a student and then as a professor. By "academic" I do not suggest that Bonhoeffer was an ivory tower intellectual whose thought was quite unrelated to personal and social concerns; indeed, the opposite was the case. Nor do I overlook the year that he spent as a pastor with the German congregation in Barcelona (1928–1929), or the fact that he was ordained in November, 1931 and had preaching, parish, and chaplaincy responsibilities. Nor do I forget that he assumed leadership in ecumenical activities during this time. I mean rather to emphasize that his primary professional activity was academic—as a graduate student, a post–doctoral scholar at Union

Theological Seminary, and a teacher at the University of Berlin. Although he did not resign his university position in 1933, he put aside this academic work after his Christology lectures in the summer of that year to throw himself into the Kirchenkampf as a leader of the Confessing Church. Shortly thereafter he took up his pastorate with the German congregations in London, which he turned into a bastion of church opposition to Hitler. This academic period, then, covers the years in which Bonhoeffer laid systematic foundations in his books and lectures, foundations which, while supporting later creative building, continued to shape and characterize his theology to the end.

Second, the years 1932 and 1933, with their respective personal and political significance for Bonhoeffer, brought new theological questions and new responsibilities. This does not mean that Bonhoeffer put his early theology in cold storage and began again *de novo*. On the contrary, many direct impulses and continuities relate the pre–1933 theology to that of the years of church struggle. But his personal, exegetical, ecclesiastical, and political concerns during the mid–1930s were most clearly expressed in *Discipleship* which is acknowledged by Bonhoeffer himself as marking a further stage of theological development.[2] His move from the university to the London pastorate in October, 1933 thus signals the transition from the initial to the middle period of his work, and the *terminus ad quem* of his early theology.

Third, and related to the previous point, this early period includes a personal liberation in Bonhoeffer's life which is directly related to his theology. In the biography Bethge speaks of "transition from theologian to Christian."[3] This will be discussed in Chapter 4 under the heading of Bonhoeffer's own formulation: the turn "from the phraseological to the real."[4] This deep, and largely hidden, personal experience, was intimately connected with his theology of sociality and particularly its soteriological problem. It therefore illuminates his previous writings in retrospect. At the same time it was a major impetus in the theology of *Discipleship*. Since this experience and the initial writing on *Discipleship* occur toward the end of the 1927–33 period, light can be shed on

---

2 For Bonhoeffer's own observation that *Discipleship* marked the end of the second stage of his work, see LPP 369; see also Chapter 4 below.

3 DB 246–250, DB-E 202ff.

4 LPP 275.

5 Initial formulations, including the well–known phrase "cheap grace," first appear in the summer of 1932; cf. DB-E 208ff.

the much discussed nature of the change which is apparent when comparing *Discipleship* to the early theology.[5] Some interpreters, such as Müller and Phillips, have argued that *Discipleship* represents a detour or even a regression in Bonhoeffer's theological development. The argument will demonstrate its intrinsic and intelligible connection with his previous theology. Indeed, I contend, it is only in light of the theology of sociality, and the soteriological problem within it, that indispensable theological and autobiographical keys for opening the door of *Discipleship* can be found.

A further advantage which accrues from the fact that *Discipleship* has its beginnings in 1932 is being able to show that this book by no means dispenses with the theology of sociality. Even those who cannot see this in *Discipleship* itself cannot fail to recognize that *Creation and Fall* and the 1933 *Christology* are among the best examples of Bonhoeffer's theology of sociality. These were both written *after* the personal and conceptual foundations of *Discipleship* were laid down in 1932.

That *Discipleship* does not cancel, but presupposes, the theology of sociality makes it possible to uncover the integrity of Bonhoeffer's whole theological development. In Chapter 6 I will argue that a full appreciation of fundamental convictions, and even linguistic formulations, in Bonhoeffer's prison writings about "religionless Christianity" in a "world come of age" requires an understanding of both the early theology of sociality and the insights and problems of *Discipleship*. Without an exact knowledge of the early theology it is not possible to appreciate the developments in both *Discipleship* and the *Letters*. The beauty of the early period is that its achievements and problems point forward to the two following stages.

Finally, if a study of Bonhoeffer's early theology needs external support beyond the reasons internal to his own theological development, it is given in the bias of previous research. So great has been the impact of the prison letters that the bulk of Bonhoeffer scholarship has concentrated on, or been directed to, the interpretation of those seminal but incomplete writings. This has led either to neglect, or to highly selective

---

6   It has also misled reputable theologians into making strange judgments. John Macquarrie, for example, writes: "There has been a tendency to overrate Bonhoeffer as a theologian. His work is too fragmentary for him to stand in the first rank in that respect. But it would be impossible to overrate his importance as a disciple..."; and again: "His enduring significance is better explored in a biography than in an analysis of this theology" *(The New York Times Book Review,* June 21, 1970, 31, 5).

study, of the early writings.[6] It is small wonder, then, that no persuasive interpretation of these writings has yet appeared. This study intends to rectify the situation and, in so doing, to show the indispensable insights which the early theology gives for understanding Bonhoeffer's theological pilgrimage as a whole.

B. PROBLEMS IN BONHOEFFER INTERPRETATION

From 1956 to 1970 more than thirty extensive studies of Bonhoeffer's theology were written; these appeared as dissertations and books in German, French, English, and Dutch.[7] By far the greatest number of these were written in the 1960s, an indication of the wide impact made by Bonhoeffer in theological circles at that time.

The most striking fact is that by far the largest number of studies have focused on the prison writings. Next in order come studies on Bonhoeffer's ethics. This means that more than half of the earlier research concentrated on Bonhoeffer's writings from the last five years of his work. Even studies which discuss the whole Bonhoeffer corpus frequently consider the earlier writings from the perspective of his last years. While it is of course necessary to study the later theology, this is very problematic when it functions as a hermeneutical key to the earlier work.

Here we encounter the first and most severe problem of methodology in Bonhoeffer interpretation, namely a teleological bias which obscures the intrinsic purpose and integrity of the early theology, and inhibits the discovery there of insights which authentically illuminate the later writings.[8] Probably the most vexing example of this severe methodological problem is found in John A. Phillips' *Christ for Us in the Theology of Dietrich Bonhoeffer.*[9] Phillips makes no secret of his view that the prison

---

[7]   Details of these works, including unpublished dissertations, are given in the bibliography of the dissertation microfilm.

[8]   Müller was the first to exemplify this; see his *Von der Kirche zur Welt. Ein Beitrag zu der Beziehung des Wort Gottes auf die societas in Dietrich Bonhoeffers theologischer Entwicklung.* Leipzig: Köhler & Amelang; Hamburg–Bergstedt: Herbert Reich Evang. Verlag, 1961. A second edition, unchanged except for the addition of another *Nachwort,* was issued in 1966. Müller's work was originally a dissertation at Humboldt University in 1956, and was the first comprehensive work on Bonhoeffer to be written.

[9]   New York: Harper & Row, 1967; British title *The Form of Christ in the World. A Study of Bonhoeffer's Christology* (London: Collins, 1967). The work originated as a doctoral dissertation at the University of Glasgow under Ronald Gregor Smith, the author being a former student of William Hamilton.

letters and *Ethics* are Bonhoeffer's "most productive" theology; that the ecclesiology of the early theology is a virtual prison from which Bonhoeffer spends most of his life trying to escape; that *Discipleship* was a regressive achievement which imposed restrictions that "proved disastrous for his future course"; and that Bonhoeffer finally "broke free from his intractable ecclesiological theory" to explore the reality of the revelation in Christ in secular, worldly life.[10]

Phillips' preoccupation with the later writings directly affects his interpretation of the writings from the previous decade. He is candid about the fact that, in discussing the early theology, "it is systematically necessary that [he] anticipate themes which will occur in Bonhoeffer's later work."[11] The hermeneutical problem here is acute. To read the early theology—if only partially, in fairness to Phillips—from the standpoint of the latter is a hermeneutical method which is historically impermissible. It is self–evident that such a method prevents the early works from being read in their own context and in terms of the primary issues to which they were directed. This teleological method eventually begs the question of the continuities and discontinuities between the early and later writings. This is especially so when Phillips concentrates on the *novel* elements in the prison letters; this circumscribes the hermeneutical pre–understanding all the more. Such teleological bias must be studiously avoided.

Two other methodological problems are common in the earlier literature of Bonhoeffer research. One is the thematic approach. This analyzes a particular subject by tracing it thematically though Bonhoeffer's writings, or by giving special attention to a text where that subject is most prominent. Resulting from this are many studies on subjects such as: secularity, religion, preaching, ecclesiology, social philosophy, personalism, epistemology, the resistance movement, and so on. Many of these studies, by their intensive investigation of a particular subject have yielded useful insights and clarified important details. One example is Rasmussen's work, which includes a careful analysis of the nature and course of Bonhoeffer's pacifism, and has illuminated some connections between his resistance activities and his writings in the *Ethics* and the prison letters.[12]

---

10   Phillips, 30, 74f., 28.

11   Ibid., 58; cf. 58ff., 200ff.

12   Larry Rasmussen, *Dietrich Bonhoeffer: Reality and Resistance* (Nashville: Abingdon, 1972)

Despite such contributions, this method cannot, by definition, directly concern itself with the question: what are the distinctive marks and developments which characterize Bonhoeffer's theology *as a whole*, within the framework of which a particular theme or subject is to be investigated? Yet a thematic study must inevitably make assumptions about the theology as a whole; some of the commonest assumptions are that Christology is the "clue" to Bonhoeffer's theological development, and that ecclesiology is the primary concern of his early theology. A second limitation of the thematic method is that it must make assumptions about the characteristic themes and inner movement of Bonhoeffer's whole thought before these have been securely established, assumptions that may be false, limited, or distracting. While research advances by an interaction of detailed examinations and general hypotheses, a major problem of the earlier stage of Bonhoeffer studies is that this interaction proceeded largely by accident and without the rigorous historical analysis necessary to establish the distinguishing characteristics and inner movement of Bonhoeffer's theology as a whole.

A third methodological problem is found in comparative studies, which include works comparing Bonhoeffer and Friedrich Gogarten on secularity; studies of selfhood comparing Bonhoeffer with Harry Stack Sullivan, and with C.G. Jung; studies of ethics comparing Bonhoeffer with Emil Brunner, Werner Elert, Reinhold Niebuhr, and H. Richard Niebuhr; a study comparing preaching in Bonhoeffer and Bultmann; a study comparing the concept of religion in Barth, Bonhoeffer, and Tillich; and various others. While such comparisons can help our understanding of Bonhoeffer by showing similarities and differences with his contemporaries, they share the basic problem of the thematic method; they, too, cannot address the issue of the distinctive marks and developments of Bonhoeffer's theology viewed as a whole.

In distinction from these methods this study is historical. The plan is to follow Bonhoeffer's theological course, examining the main works in the contexts in which they were written. Thus the next chapter analyzes *Sanctorum Communio*, Bonhoeffer's doctoral dissertation, examining it in detail, and interpreting its argument in terms of itself, not as an anticipation of later writings. When the following chapter focuses on *Act and Being* we must, indeed, decide how it is connected to *Sanctorum Communio;* but we can only do this when we are sure *what* the argument of *Sanctorum Communio* is, and, further, what is the fundamental concern of *Act and Being* itself. By this procedure we can interpret the development of Bonhoeffer's theology with some confidence. The interpretive argument will thus arise out of the textual analysis which will proceed historically and contextually.

Using this method limits the amount of the Bonhoeffer corpus which can be considered. If there were more articles and monographs giving special studies of Bonhoeffer's major writings, one might be more ambitious. But since this is not the case, the relatively conspicuous neglect of the early theology in previous research requires us to begin at the beginning.

However, the early theology will be related to two writings completed later than 1933, namely *Discipleship* and the *Letters*. But this will be done within strict limits—they will be discussed only in terms of those aspects which can be demonstrably connected to the early theology; the aim here is not a comprehensive interpretation of the later works. Such an interpretation can only follow upon a comprehensive study of their theological foundations.

The primary purpose, then, is to expound Bonhoeffer's early theology. But some incidental comparison can aid this purpose. The intellectual resources upon which Bonhoeffer drew, including Luther, Barth, Hegel, Scheler, Dilthey, Tönnies, Seeberg, and others will be considered from time to time.[13] Similarly, some occasional comparisons with Bonhoeffer's theological contemporaries—Barth, Bultmann, Tillich, Gogarten, and others—can serve to highlight his own distinctive position. But such comparisons will be limited to selected points, and will usually be brief. It will obviously be fruitful in the future to have more thorough and comprehensive comparisons between Bonhoeffer and his predecessors and contemporaries, especially Luther and Barth, Bultmann and Tillich.

As indicated above, several themes will consistently occupy our attention: sociality, Christology, anthropology, and soteriology. These themes, however, have not been selected for the convenience of limiting the scope of the study or of comparison with another theologian. Rather, they have emerged from the texts themselves, and command attention because they are central to Bonhoeffer's theological work and development.

---

[13] By 1971 two studies had begun to examine Bonhoeffer's intellectual background: see David T. R. Wilcox, *Bonhoeffers Anfänge und seine Wurzeln im 19. Jahrhundert,* doctoral dissertation, Tübingen, 1969; Carl–Jürgen Kaltenborn, *Adolf von Harnack als Lehrer Dietrich Bonhoeffers,* doctoral dissertation, Humboldt University, Berlin 1969.

A final comment on the meaning of the word "contextual" in a "historical–contextual" method is necessary. "Historical" points to the examination of Bonhoeffer's writings which takes each work, in order, in its own right, and builds up the coherent development of his thought by analyzing continuities, innovations, and revisions as his thinking proceeds. "Contextual" points to the personal and social matrix in which this thinking was done. Almost all interpreters of Bonhoeffer's theology have repeatedly emphasized the close connection between Bonhoeffer's theology and his life experience. This connection has been most obvious with respect to Bonhoeffer's later writings: the *Ethics* and prison writings are clearly related to his experience in the resistance movement, as *Discipleship* is evidently related to the Kirchenkampf. But even such obvious connections could only be partially understood until Eberhard Bethge's biography, first published in 1967, made its rich resources available. Not only does it confirm and illuminate more brightly the contextual character of Bonhoeffer's later writings. It also makes possible, for the first time, a true appreciation of the contextual character of the early theology. Bethge's biographical work has been indispensable for discovering some basic insights which this study presents, especially the autobiographical dimension of Bonhoeffer's theology.

The first edition of this book contained at this point a detailed review and critique of five major Bonhoeffer studies written between 1956 and 1968: Hanfried Müller, *Von der Kirche zur Welt*;[14] John D. Godsey, *The Theology of Dietrich Bonhoeffer*,[15] originally written in 1958 as a dissertation under Karl Barth; John Phillips, *Christ for Us in the Theology of Dietrich Bonhoeffer*;[16] Heinrich Ott, *Reality and Faith: The Theological Legacy of Dietrich Bonhoeffer*;[17] and André Dumas, *Dietrich Bonhoeffer. Theologian of Reality*.[18] I will not repeat that

---

[14] See above, note 13. An English translation of an article which epitomizes Müller's approach to Bonhoeffer, written just after he completed the dissertation, is "Concerning the Reception and Interpretation of Dietrich Bonhoeffer," in *World Come of Age* (Philadelphia: Fortress Press, 1967) ed. Ronald Gregor Smith, 182–214.

[15] Philadelphia: Westminster Press, 1960.

[16] See above, note 9.

[17] Philadelphia: Fortress Press, 1972. The German original, *Wirklichkeit und Glaube I: Zum theologischen Erbe Dietrich Bonhoeffers* (Zurich: Vandenhoek & Ruprecht), was published in 1966.

[18] New York: Macmillan, 1971. The French original, *Une Théologie de la Réalité: Dietrich Bonhoeffer* (Geneva: Labor et Fides), was published in 1968.

analysis here,[19] but simply note that beyond the detailed questions posed
to the several interpreters, it showed that major disagreements were
more evident than agreements at that stage of Bonhoeffer studies.
However, it is relevant to summarize the major issues which emerged
from the review of those works, and to show how the argument of the
following chapters will deal with them.

(1) Can *Sanctorum Communio*—and, according to some interpreters,
all the early writings prior to *Discipleship*—be understood primarily as "ecclesiology"?

(2) What, indeed, is the main subject of the next book on "act" and
"being," and how does it relate to the prior *Sanctorum Communio*
and to the 1930–32 writings which follow it?

(3) What accounts for the transition from the first two academic
treatises to *Discipleship*, and how is this book—with its intense
stress on obedience—related both to Bonhoeffer's own personal
experience and the church–political context of the *Kirchenkampf?*

(4) Granted that Christology is central to Bonhoeffer's theology, are
there tensions and changes within it, or is it essentially unchanging? What role does the *theologia crucis* play in the Christology?
Does Christology per se render intelligible Bonhoeffer's theological development—whether an expanding Christology, a Christology
of many tensions, or a Christology which remains essentially the
same?

(5) Is the Christology also a soteriology, and does it deal with any
identifiable anthropological problems which make sense in the
contemporary, historical context?

(6) In relation to this, does theological anthropology have any significance in Bonhoeffer's early theology, or is the anthropological
insight of *Mündigkeit* in the *Letters* a *creatio ex nihilo?* Is the

---

19 It may be consulted on pages 12–37 of the Scholars Press edition. The
discussion of Phillips is based on my review "Sociality and Church in Bonhoeffer's
1933 Christology," *Scottish Journal of Theology* 21.4 (December, 1968), 416–
34; for Ott and Dumas, see my review article "Interpreting Bonhoeffer: Reality
or Phraseology?" *Journal of Religion* 55.2 (April, 1975), 270–75. For my review
of David Hopper, *A Dissent on Bonhoeffer* (Philadelphia: Westminster, 1975),
see *Union Seminary Quarterly Review* XXXII.3–4 (Summer, 1976), 183–86.

question of *Mündigkeit* related to previous anthropological concerns in the first writings and in *Discipleship*?

(7) What are the main factors affecting Bonhoeffer's theological development—ideas alone, ideas and external events in society, or an interaction of thought, social events and the personal life of the theologian himself? To what extent and in what way do the biographical and social factors influence his theology?

(8) Given Bonhoeffer's frequent references to Luther, the acknowledgment by all interpreters of Luther's significance for him, and the attempt of Lutheran interpreters to understand Bonhoeffer in traditional Lutheran categories, what does a comparison of the two theologians reveal about their similarities and differences?

(9) Finally, what is the theological importance of sociality, which Müller, Ott, and Moltmann have seen to be quite significant in Bonhoeffer? Is his early statement about the "social intention of all the basic Christian concepts" a formative point of departure, or a passing remark of little meaning?

C. THE ARGUMENT AHEAD

The basic position I will argue on these issues was summarized at the beginning of this chapter. This will be amplified and documented as follows. Chapter 2 will demonstrate that Bonhoeffer's "theology of sociality" is the comprehensive context in which the ecclesiology of *Sanctorum Communio* is set. His Christology will be seen in intrinsic relationship to his anthropology in his understanding of creation, sin, and the "new humanity" in the Christian community. There is a clear and consistently used set of anthropological concepts which extend from the first work throughout the early theology. Moreover, we see emerging in his first work a distinctive and modern soteriological problem in this anthropology which is clearly related to the Christology: human power in both its personal form (the power of the ego) and its social form.

Chapter 3 argues that theological anthropology is the primary locus for the question of "act" and "being." This work not only corrects an unduly actualistic theology in *Sanctorum Communio;* in addressing the transcendentalist–idealist and the ontological traditions in philosophy and theology current at the time, Bonhoeffer especially sharpens his phenomenology of the soteriological problem on its personal side, namely, the power of the ego. His opening critique of philosophical anthropology is much more than a dispassionate analysis of the relative merits of the two schools of thought. It is a fundamental, and sometimes even passionate, attack on the intellectual, philosophical self: the unlimited and dominating "knowing I" in its power violates both personal and social being with others. The Christology of Christ's "being free for" humanity is directly correlated to this soteriological problem, continuing the understanding of Christ as *Stellvertreter* in *Sanctorum Communio*. In integrating the rightful claims of actualistic and ontological schools of philosophy and theology, Bonhoeffer employs and refines the basic conceptuality of sociality developed in the first book; he develops it further on the ontological side, but this is a personal and communal ontology concerned with concrete human relationships and with the role of "consciousness" and "conscience" within them. These are the germinal ideas from which the book develops, and they are an intrinsic part of the soteriological problem mentioned above.

In both of these works, then, we see that Bonhoeffer's basic conceptuality is the theology of sociality; that within it there is a close correlation between Christology and anthropology, and that the relation between the two focuses on a quite specific and clearly defined soteriological problem. His discussions of the church and of actualism and ontology, and the connection of the first two books, are shown to be clear and intelligible within this perspective. Moreover, Bonhoeffer's divergence from Luther already becomes apparent in these two works, particularly in the discussion of conscience in *Act and Being*.

Chapter 4 focuses on the theological significance of Bonhoeffer's personal experience which culminates, in 1932, in "the theologian becoming a Christian," as Bethge describes it. This chapter illumines Bonhoeffer's theological development both retrospectively and prospectively. In the first part I demonstrate that Bonhoeffer's soteriology focuses on the problem of power in self and society. Most revealing is the fact that the personal problem of power is the power of the ego, and that this constitutes an existential crisis for the theologian himself. We see how his intellectual work and brilliantly successful achievements in academic theology are deeply rooted in his personal history, and how his autobiographical memoirs and letters describe his own personal problem in terms identical to his analysis of sin in many theological texts up to 1932. From several quarters come influences which result in his turning "from the phraseological to the real," the most important of them being his response to the Sermon on the Mount. This leads to the new understanding of faith as personal "discipleship" in obedience to the authority and command of Christ in the church. For the first time Bonhoeffer becomes a committed, practicing church member and Christian. The book *Discipleship* is above all the expression of this existential struggle and profound change: its theology of discipleship was outlined in an address Bonhoeffer gave in November, 1932, proving conclusively that not the external events of opposition to Hitler in the *Kirchenkampf* but Bonhoeffer's own spiritual struggle is the formative impulse for the book; what he discovered in his own life, he then expressed when Hitler came to power.

Relevant to both the Confessing Church and the political struggle against Nazism, *Discipleship* is theology profoundly influenced by Bonhoeffer's personal history. The analysis documents how the book's teaching on becoming a disciple, its exegesis, and its portrait of Luther are heavily informed by an "autobiographical dimension." Comparison of Bonhoeffer with Luther, and analysis of his portrait of the Reformer, show clearly that the soteriological problems in Luther and Bonhoeffer are quite distinct, and differ both historically and in their psycho–social dynamics: in Luther the negative conscience, in Bonhoeffer the power of the ego which destroys human sociality.

Seen in this light, tensions and even contradictions appear in Bonhoeffer's theology. While the exposition shows that the previously developed theology of sociality is indispensable for Bonhoeffer's argument about obedient discipleship in the church, his Christology now presents Christ as predominantly a power figure whom the disciple must obey, forfeiting his own autonomy and attempting to suppress his own ego strengths in obeying Christ. The issue of power is not resolved in either the anthropology or the Christology of *Discipleship*. The power Christ does not fit with the Christology of the theology of sociality; yet at the same time there is a form of *theologia crucis* in *Discipleship* which builds on the theology of sociality. Here we see that the close correlation of Christology and anthropology, which previously was a conceptual connection, is now an existential one in Bonhoeffer himself. Furthermore, while obedient discipleship freed Bonhoeffer from autonomous ambition, his personal need to be mastered directly informs his presentation of the power Christ. Corresponding to the Christological contradictions are anthropological conflicts, all centering on the relationships of power, strength, and weakness. Neither in his personal experience, nor in the Christology and anthropology of his theology does Bonhoeffer adequately clarify these crucial matters. The context of Nazism and the

Kirchenkampf further complicates the whole problem. I conclude, therefore, that in the experience and the theology informed by the turning "from the phraseological to the real" in 1932, only a partial resolution of the soteriological problems is to be found.

Chapter 5 focuses on Bonhoeffer's theology in 1932–33, his last year as a teacher at the University of Berlin, and the year immediately following his 1932 experience. The two main writings from this year are *Creation and Fall* and the 1933 *Christology* lectures. Here I argue: (1) the clear continuation of his theology of sociality, thus reinforcing the argument in Chapter 4 that the theology of discipleship (which grew from 1932 to 1937, the year of its publication) necessarily presupposes the formative theology of sociality; (2) the continued use of the basic anthropological categories; (3) the continued correlation of Christology and anthropology; (4) Bonhoeffer's continued preoccupation with the personal and corporate aspects of the problem of power, the latter with particular reference to Nazism; (5) the influence of his 1932 experience on the immediately following theology; and (6) the ambivalence about the relations of power, strength, and weakness in this period which are so strong in the later–published *Discipleship*.

The sixth and final chapter selectively examines the *Letters* insofar as they relate to the early theology and retrospectively confirm the preceding argument. There, a striking consummation of the Christology and anthropology of the theology of sociality and the free practice of discipleship is given. At the same time the contradictions in *Discipleship* are overcome. The impetus for this is the combination of personal experience in the resistance movement and historical and theological reflection in the ensuing imprisonment. In the resistance movement Bonhoeffer was united with people, significantly including his secular, humanist brothers, who combined strong, healthy egos and free, responsible action on behalf of others. In their company he, now freed of both the initial ambition of the powerful ego and the attempt to suppress the autonomous ego, came to a personal and theological affirmation of human autonomy and *Mündigkeit*. This was confirmed as a historical and cultural phenomenon by his prison reading (especially of Dilthey) and by personal observation. By contrast, he diagnoses "religion" as rooted in human weakness and dependency upon a power God. The anthropological insight of *Mündigkeit* reopens the Christological question in such a way as to allow the Christology of the earliest writings on sociality and Bonhoeffer's *theologia crucis* from the 1933 *Christology* and *Discipleship* to come to fruition. In place of the power Christ who requires ego suppression in *Discipleship*, and the illusory power God of religion who reinforces weakness and dependence, we have the weak Christ, "the one for others." In this original form of *theologia crucis*, Bonhoeffer sees the possibility both of affirming human strengths and transforming human existence by Christ so that such strengths will be freely and responsibly used in the service of co–humanity. In this context we can see that Bonhoeffer's theological development has a larger historical significance than he could realize, both as regards the relation of theology to Freud's critique of religion and his views on self and society, and as regards Bonhoeffer's fundamental transformation of the Lutheran tradition.

Chapter 2

HUMAN SOCIALITY AND THE NEW HUMANITY OF CHRIST: *SANCTORUM COMMUNIO*

Bonhoeffer, we have already seen, makes the following statement in his Preface to *Sanctorum Communio:*

> The more this investigation has considered the significance of the sociological category for theology, the more clearly has emerged the social intention of all the basic Christian concepts . 'Person,' 'primal state,' 'sin' and 'revelation' can be fully comprehended only in reference to sociality.[1]

This chapter argues that this is a programmatic statement for Bonhoeffer's first work; later chapters will show that it is also programmatic for the whole of his early theology and, furthermore, that sociality continues to inform all Bonhoeffer's theological writing, including *Discipleship* and the prison letters. Here, then, is set out the distinctive conceptuality which is formative for Bonhoeffer's whole theological development. I call this conceptuality his theology of sociality.

To demonstrate that *Sanctorum Communio* lays the foundation of Bonhoeffer's theology of sociality is to challenge an unquestioned orthodoxy of Bonhoeffer studies: that the complex argument of *Sanctorum Communio* can be adequately subsumed under the rubric of ecclesiology. This orthodoxy embraces a wide range of interpreters, and is the more

---

[1]   SC 13, SC-E 21.

striking because they agree on this matter despite their disagreement on
many major issues. The orthodoxy thus encompasses those who, on the
one hand, regard Bonhoeffer's first book as merely preliminary, or even
an obstacle, to the theological development which led to the so-called
secular theology of the prison letters; this view is held by writers such as
Hanfried Müller and John Phillips. On the other hand, it includes those
who, like Eberhard Bethge and John Godsey, argue for a much more
integral relation between the thought of the young and the mature
Bonhoeffer.

The consensus of this orthodoxy is premature. *Sanctorum Communio*
is Bonhoeffer's most complex and most demanding book. Even Reinhold
Seeberg (the adviser for the dissertation), it is said, had difficulty with its
sophisticated conceptuality and intricate argument.[2] It is also, sharing this
dubious distinction with *Act and Being,* Bonhoeffer's most neglected book.
No monographs have presented a thorough analysis and interpretation of
its argument. Furthermore, all the published texts were incomplete until
the critical edition appeared in 1986; this made it even more difficult to
comprehend the complex conceptuality which had become increasingly
esoteric with the passage of many years. Fortunately, through the generosity of Eberhard Bethge, this study was based on the original manuscript
of the work.[3]

To challenge this orthodoxy, however, is not to deny that *Sanctorum
Communio* deals with ecclesiology. To dispute this would be fly in the face
of its very title, and to ignore the conspicuous size and detail of its
culminating fifth chapter on the church. The orthodoxy must be criticized

---

[2]   Reported by Fritz Figur in *I Knew Dietrich Bonhoeffer,* ed. Wolf-Dieter
Zimmermann and Ronald Gregor Smith (New York: Harper & Row, 1966), 55.

[3]   The full text is now available in the critical German text of the Dietrich
Bonhoeffer Werke, and as volume 1 in the Dietrich Bonhoeffer Works English
edition. References to the manuscript in the first edition of this book will now
normally be given to the new German edition. The textual history of *Sanctorum
Communio* is given in the Editor's Introduction to the new translation, and can
be summarized as follows: the first German edition (1930) lacked some twenty
to twenty-five percent of the original manuscript; the third and fourth German
editions (1960, 1969) included in an appendix selections amounting to about half
of the unpublished material; about one tenth of the original text therefore
remained unpublished; and the first English translation (London: Collins, 1963,
as *Sanctorum Communio;* New York: Harper & Row, 1963, as *The Communion
of Saints*) is a distinct fourth redaction which in parts confusingly and erroneously conflates material from the various German texts—it was made from the
published German texts, not the original manuscript.

and corrected, then, not for what it asserts but for what it ignores or minimizes: the setting of the ecclesiology in Bonhoeffer's much more comprehensive and ambitious *theology of sociality*. His introductory statement about "the significance of the sociological category for theology" and "the social intention of all the basic Christian concepts" cannot be ignored.

'Sociality' is a complex category, embracing a number of particular concepts. These concepts will be explained in the course of the argument, and in this way a clear understanding of sociality as a category will be built up. A definition offered at this point would be so complicated, and so overloaded with terms themselves requiring explanation, as to be unwieldy and scarcely intelligible. Suffice it for the present to say that Bonhoeffer sees all human life as essentially social, that he develops a theological phenomenology of the human person in relation to other persons and to various types of corporate communities and institutions, and that he interprets the Christian gospel within this matrix. Later in the chapter a more detailed summary will be given.

This chapter has three sections. Section A introduces the argument of the book by presenting initial evidence showing that sociality is the comprehensive framework in which the ecclesiology must be understood, and by examining briefly how Bonhoeffer relates theology, social philosophy, and sociology. Section B shows that the four main concepts (person, creation, sin, revelation) are articulated as a theology of sociality. Section C concludes the chapter with a discussion of "the sociality of Christ and humanity" as the appropriate description of Bonhoeffer's formative theological work, and a consideration of its significance for his theological development.

A. INTRODUCTION TO THE ARGUMENT OF *SANCTORUM COMMUNIO*

1. SOCIALITY AS THE CONTEXT OF ECCLESIOLOGY

There are several clear indications that a theology of sociality is Bonhoeffer's more comprehensive concern and thus the context for the ecclesiology. When he identifies in the Preface *"person, primal state, sin* and *revelation"* as basic Christian concepts which are fully understood only in terms of sociality, this is not a passing statement mentioning a random selection of admittedly important theological terms. It is, rather, a precise identification of the main theological subjects treated throughout the book under the rubric of sociality. Accordingly, Chapter 2 sets forth Bonhoeffer's view of the Christian concept of person. This is the pivotal notion of the whole work, being fundamental to his interpretation of both individual and corporate life. Chapter 2 thus serves as the foundation of all that follows. Chapters 3 through 5 deal, respectively, with the primal state, i.e., creation, with sin, and with revelation. In each case these doctrines are treated in terms of sociality. Creation is discussed in terms of the primal community, sin in terms of the broken community, and revelation as the restoration of human sociality in the new humanity of the Christian community.

This structure of the work shows that the statement in the Preface is programmatic for the whole argument. Bonhoeffer's concern with sociality involves the whole range of theological subjects. Ecclesiology is set within a much more comprehensive theological framework. If it would be claiming too much to call the work a little summa, it is not an overstatement to describe it as an introduction to a Christian theology of sociality.

The Foreword to the original manuscript supports this reading. Bonhoeffer begins by saying that the work is an interdisciplinary one which seeks to make the insights of social philosophy and sociology fruitful for the theological consideration of the church. He continues: "Thus the basic problem can be defined as the problem of a *specifically Christian social philosophy and sociology.*"[4] Now, a Christian social philosophy which builds upon the basic theological concepts, and which sets forth the social intention of these concepts, will certainly have to give a major place to a consideration of the Christian community, the church. But this does not mean that its sole and exclusive concern is ecclesiology. It is because Bonhoeffer has this wider purpose that his argument in *Sanctorum Communio* is by no means restricted to traditional questions in ecclesiology, such as worship, preaching, sacraments, ministry, church authority, pastoral care, and so on. On the contrary, it treats a wide range of theological topics: doctrines of God, creation, sin, Christ, revelation, and Spirit; and it discusses many anthropological subjects, such as the Christian understanding of person, community, society, ethics, and history.

4　SC 200, SC-E 22, italics mine; the next paragraph in the manuscript continues with the statement quoted about the social intention of theological concepts.

If ecclesiology is taken as the exclusive concern of *Sanctorum Communio*, one cannot adequately explain the detailed discussion of so many subjects which fall outside the doctrine of the church, nor the elaborate and sophisticated conceptuality which is developed to deal with them in "a Christian social philosophy and sociology." If, however, we see that sociality is the category which informs the whole discussion, then we can understand both the discussion of these subjects and the reason why the Christian community has a central place in this theology of sociality.

A further indication of Bonhoeffer's overall concern with a theology of sociality comes early in the text when he locates his own endeavor by reference to a quite specific philosophical tradition. He states that he intends to set forth "a Christian philosophy of Geist" [spirit] which will give direction to a "Christian social philosophy" and thereby "overcome the idealist philosophy of immanent Geist."[5] This ambitious statement confirms his concern with sociality as the comprehensive framework for his interpretation of the Christian community. It follows a critical analysis of several schemata of philosophical anthropology and culminates a sharp critique of German idealism.[6] Idealism in its various forms, Bonhoeffer argues, is a philosophy of "immanent Geist"; it understands the human person as an instance of universal reason, and its epistemological preoccupation with the subject-object relation informs its whole anthropology. However, he contends, the epistemological subject-object relation is not a sociological category, and therefore idealism can neither give essential value to the individual person nor adequately understand human community. Some other relationship must therefore be considered basic in a Christian social philosophy which seeks to overcome idealism's philosophy of immanent Geist.[7]

Even Bonhoeffer's critique of idealistic social philosophy, however, serves further to relate him to a philosophical tradition much concerned with human social experience. His very use of the term Geist, and his critique of idealism, remind us that Reinhold Seeberg and Hegel both stand in the near and distant background of Bonhoeffer's dissertation. 'Sociality'

---

5 SC 215, n. 29, SC-E 44.

6 These four philosophical viewpoints—Aristotelian, Stoic-Christian, Epicurean and Enlightenment, German idealism—are discussed at greater length in the original manuscript than in the pre-DBW texts.

7 SC 23-25; SC-E 41-45.

was an explicit and significant category in Seeberg's theology.[8] Hegel, who had influenced Seeberg, is well known for what John Hermann Randall calls his "fundamental socializing of all the concepts for dealing with human experience," thus overthrowing the individualism and social atomism of the Enlightenment.[9] Indeed, one of Bonhoeffer's chief criticisms of Hegel is that he made the individual person an 'accident' to the 'substance' of social process. But at the same time Bonhoeffer borrows and transforms concepts from Hegel, and is not reluctant to acknowledge his contribution to social theory.

The critique of idealism, incidentally, helps to locate Bonhoeffer's theological approach in the history of modern theology. Aware of the theological problems that derive from the impact of Kant and post-Kantian epistemology, he does not seek a breakthrough via an alliance with neo-Kantianism or existentialism, as his older contemporaries in the dialectical theology of the 1920s were doing at the time.[10] It is rather with sociological categories that he tries to develop a new conceptuality for dealing with theological subjects such as transcendence, Christology, faith, justification, and so on. Not the context of epistemology, but human sociality, holds theological promise. The 'social basic-relation' is not the subject-object relation but the I-You relation.

That a theology of sociality is the comprehensive concern and therefore the context for the ecclesiology of *Sanctorum Communio* is initially demonstrated, then, by at least the following evidence: the programmatic statement in the Preface; the direct and explicit correlation of this statement to the structure of the whole book; the wide range of theological and anthropological subjects discussed in the argument under the rubric of sociality; the sophisticated and complex conceptuality appropriated from social theory to develop the argument; and Bonhoeffer's explicit desire to

---

8   Cf. his *Christliche Dogmatik* (Leipzig, 1924-25) I: pp. 505f., 507ff.; II: pp. 327f., 350. The origins of Bonhoeffer's interest in sociality, however, are much more complicated than the fact that he was Seeberg's student. The complex set of concepts he uses to explicate sociality was not simply taken over from Seeberg, but hammered out in debate with others; not least among these was Max Scheler, from whom the idea of Gesamtperson was appropriated and modified; cf. AB 112 n. 38.

9   *The Career of Philosophy*, vol. II (New York: Columbia University Press, 1965), p. 315.

10   See his criticisms in *Act and Being* of efforts along these lines by Barth, Bultmann, and Gogarten.

overcome the idealist philosophy of Geist with a Christian social philosophy of Geist.

2. THEOLOGY, SOCIAL PHILOSOPHY AND SOCIOLOGY

While aligning himself more with the systematic than the historical school of sociology in Germany early in the century, Bonhoeffer strikes out independently. He finds the systematic school defective in its view of the human person, leading to an inadequate definition of the subject matter and the method of sociology; he argues that this *sociology* is, perhaps unwittingly, informed by a *social philosophy* which understands the human person atomistically and individualistically.[11] Accordingly, he proposes his own definitions of the subject matter and method of social philosophy and sociology.

Both social philosophy and sociology are Geisteswissenschaften (humanities disciplines) employing a phenomenological method. The two disciplines, however, are to be clearly distinguished. Social philosophy seeks "insights... into the nature of person and community."[12]

> Social philosophy deals with fundamental social relationships that are *presupposed by* all knowledge of, and will for, empirical community. It deals with the 'origins' of sociality in the human spirit [Geistigkeit], and the intrinsic connection of sociality and spirit. It is the study of the primoridal mode-of-being of sociality per se.[13]

"Sociology," in distinction from social philosophy, "is the study of the structures of empirical communities."[14] Its purpose is a systematic presentation of the laws constitutive for the structure of social groups. 'Structure' here refers not only to relations and interactions within a given social form, but to persons as centers of action and also to the whole group as a unified system [Gebilde].[15]

---

[11] SC-E 27.

[12] SC-E 28. Here 'Gemeinschaft,' as often in Bonhoeffer's text, is a general term referring generically to the whole range of social structures in human corporate life; the more specific, technical use of Gemeinschaft is discussed below.

[13] SC 16, SC-E 28f.

[14] SC 16, SC-E 30.

[15] SC 16.

Social philosophy and sociology are related to each other in that the former provides the 'norm' for the latter, and the latter builds upon the former as its basis. Social philosophy, in other words, provides certain fundamental anthropological presuppositions about human social existence, and about the human person as Geist, with which to understand the structures of empirical communities.[16] Conversely, sociology traces back the manifold interactions in a given social structure to those constitutive acts of Geist which give that social structure its characteristic individuality.[17]

The relation of theology to social philosophy and sociology must now be clarified. Indeed, if Bonhoeffer wants to develop "a Christian philosophy of Geist" to "supersede idealism's philosophy of immanent Geist," and if social philosophy investigates the basis of empirical social structures in the acts and relationships of human Geist, then the relationship between theology and social philosophy is especially important. It is intensified by the introductory statement in the manuscript that the fundamental problem in the work can be designated as that of "a specifically Christian social philosophy and sociology."

The clarification of the relationship between theology and the other two disciplines has two parts. On the one hand, social philosophy and sociology have a relative autonomy; they are independent of theology. They pursue their investigations and develop their own theories and concepts. Theology may borrow philosophical concepts such as Geist, and sociological concepts such as 'Gemeinschaft' and 'Gesellschaft.' Bonhoeffer borrows the latter terms from Tönnies, just as he appropriates the former from the German philosophical tradition. Furthermore, these appropriations can frequently allow philosophical definitions to stand unchanged. For example, he accepts the "general metaphysical concept of person as Geist," following Seeberg, which understands the human person as "self-conscious and spontaneously acting."[18] This definition can also be applied to God as absolute Geist.[19] On the other hand, theology will often need to qualify and transform these borrowed concepts, and sometimes to reject their presuppositions in order to replace them with theological foundations. Thus Bonhoeffer rejects the possibility that the "general metaphysical" view of Geist can even

---

16 SC 15ff., SC-E 24ff.
17 SC 16, SC-E 30; cf. SC 52.
18 SC 221, SC-E 59.
19 SC 218, SC-E 53.

approach the Christian understanding of person; but having first established the latter on independent theological grounds, he finds that the metaphysical understanding of Geist has validity when placed *within* the Christian theological understanding of person. Likewise he denies the possibility that the church is amenable to classification in a pre-established sociological typology. Its essential nature must be understood from within, on the basis of revelation; then it is possible to see what sociological forms are adequate to describe it.

The interdisciplinary method in *Sanctorum Communio*, then, is identical with that employed in the next work, *Act and Being*. Bonhoeffer appreciates and appropriates insights found in non-theological disciplines. But he is perfectly clear and confident about his method as a theologian. The ultimate criterion is the revelation in Christ. This combination of theological confidence, which manifests his indebtedness to Barth, and intellectual openness, which reflects his Berlin upbringing and education, is refreshing indeed in the theological scene of the late 1920s in Germany.

It would distract from the study of Bonhoeffer's theology to undertake a lengthy analysis of his choice of social theorists and sociological schools as his discussion partners. Discussions of this may be found elsewhere.[20] But this is a suitable occasion briefly to mention some weaknesses. It is consistent with Bonhoeffer's preference for a systematic sociology of social structures, for example, that virtually no empirical data on the actual, social role of the church appears in his ecclesiology. Nor does he seriously raise the question of how his *theological description* of the Christian community relates to the *actual religious institution* existing around him. Again, even if we willingly grant the necessity for sophisticated academic works in theology, we may still ask how the major intellectual contributions of theorists like Marx, Weber, and Troeltsch can be left out of Bonhoeffer's discussion.

Such weaknesses notwithstanding, the significance of *Sanctorum Communio* is that it laid down the conceptual framework for Bonhoeffer's theology of sociality. In so doing it signaled a completely new context

---

[20] See, for example, Peter Berger's "Sociology and Ecclesiology" in *The Place of Bonhoeffer* (New York: Association Press, 1962), ed. Martin E. Marty, 53-79. While many of Berger's criticisms are pertinent, his exposition is marred by misinterpretations on several major points.

and approach for theological thinking.[21] While aligning himself with the new theological movement of Barth and his early colleagues, Bonhoeffer criticized and went beyond them. He saw their theological renovation inhibited by a preoccupation with *epistemology* characteristic of modern European philosophy. Growing out of philosophical reflection which was more or less directly tied to the scientific world of objects, the influence of epistemologically-oriented philosophy in theology was more effective in polemics than in new constructive thinking. Bonhoeffer, consequently, wanted to move theology to a world of persons, communities, historical decisions, and ethical relationships. In *Sanctorum Communio* he turned to "the significance of the sociological category for theology," and set out to develop a conceptuality suitable to this endeavor.[22] The content of this theology of sociality must now be set out.

B. THEOLOGICAL CONCEPTS ARTICULATED AS A THEOLOGY OF SOCIALITY

When Bonhoeffer said that "'person,' 'primal state,' 'sin,' and 'revelation' are fully understandable only in relation to sociality," he was

---

[21] About three years later, in John Baillie's seminar on philosophical theology at Union Theological Seminary, Bonhoeffer again discussed the question of an appropriate conceptuality for Christian theology (DBW 10 434ff.; GS III 110ff.; as shown below, Bonhoeffer was as much expounding his own position as presenting Barth's "theology of crisis"). "The history of theology was to a large extent a permanent seeking for more adequate forms of thinking in order to express the facts of the revelation" (441). "Even now ...Protestantism lacks its own proper philosophical terminology" (442). While Luther made a start with an "essentially dynamic-voluntaristic" form of thought, he, and Orthodox Protestantism after him, fell back into a "substantial form of thinking" which Kant then rejected (ibid). "Substantial thinking," Bonhoeffer argues, is prone to contradictions, and runs "a great danger of making revelation static and depriving it of its actual liveliness" (441). What is needed, he suggests, is "a dynamic-voluntaristic thinking" (441). Bonhoeffer's own voluntarism is perfectly clear in *Sanctorum Communio* and *Act and Being,* both written prior to this New York paper. The conceptuality alluded to in the shorthand phrase "dynamic-voluntaristic thinking" is, in fact, nothing other than his own theology of sociality. He first articulates it in *Sanctorum Communio,* and then develops it further, in debate with two main post-Kantian philosophical traditions, in *Act and Being.*

[22] In his Foreword to the Gregor Smith translation, Bethge refers to Bonhoeffer's point of departure as two conflicting bases, the sociological school

clearly referring to the four chapters of his book in a programmatic statement. By considering them in order we may grasp the full range of theological meaning in the term sociality.

1. 'PERSON' AS RELATIONAL AND CORPORATE

The whole argument of *Sanctorum Communio* is built around the Christian concept of person. Indeed, this concept of person recurs unchanged in each text of Bonhoeffer's early theology;[23] it is also found in essentially the same interpretation in his theology of 'non-religious Christianity.' Furthermore, it is the concept of person which Bonhoeffer uses to achieve his goal of establishing a Christian social philosophy in place of the idealist philosophy of immanent Geist. This is done not by a cavalier dismissal of the idealist emphasis on Geist qua consciousness and reason, but by setting the latter *within* the Christian understanding of the human person. Person, in other words, is used to interpret Geist, not vice versa. This procedure is followed through all stages of Bonhoeffer's argument in *Sanctorum Communio.*

Bonhoeffer's interpretation of person, it is imperative to understand, is a concept which is corporate as well as individual. This clearly distinguishes his position from philosophers and theologians such as Martin Buber, Eberhard Grisebach, Friedrich Gogarten, and Emil Brunner. These thinkers made much of the concept of person, and of the I–You relation—which Bonhoeffer also uses. But the concept of the person in their work remains an individual concept, since its locus is in the relation

---

of Troeltsch and the dialectical theology of Barth (cf. DB-E 83); Peter Berger (*op. cit.,* 55ff.) has a similar view. This is problematic. If this was Bonhoeffer's main concern we would certainly have expected much more detailed discussion of both Troeltsch and Barth than the incidental references the book actually contains. In a personal conversation (July, 1969) Bethge clarified his statement by saying that the naming of Troeltsch was meant to refer to the general atmosphere in Berlin; the Barthian approach was certainly in conflict with this. I think this polarity has only a general significance for this book; Bonhoeffer's purpose was more specific than mediation or synthesis. His own statements about "the social intentions of all the basic Christian concepts," and his desire to "overcome and supersede idealism's philosophy of immanent Geist" point to his own programmatic concern with a theology of sociality.

23 See below, Chapters 3 and 5. In *Act and Being,* Dasein replaces Geist as the main anthropological category; Dasein, nevertheless, is interpreted as *person.* In the 1933 Christology, the main anthropological category is Existenz; it is still understood as *person.*

between individuals as I and You; therefore their positions could be described as inter-personal personalism. Bonhoeffer goes beyond this usage in a quite original way to show that the concept of the person is fruitful for understanding corporate human communities, and the relation of individuals to them. A major impetus in this direction comes from the fact that Hegel had used Geist as a concept applying to both corporate and individual life; since Bonhoeffer interprets Geist by means of person, he does so in corporate as well as individual life.

Aware now of what is to come, the most clear procedure is the one Bonhoeffer himself followed. First, the concept of person as *relational,* the individual self relating to others in social life, will be expounded; then Bonhoeffer's use of the concept of person to interpret the *corporate,* or collective, dimension of social life will be discussed. But it is already apparent why he begins the substantive argument of *Sanctorum Communio* with "the Christian concept of person"; it is the central concept of the book, integrating the whole argument.

'Person' as a relational concept In Bonhoeffer's interpretation, person means the *socio-ethical, historical person.* The definition makes ethical *will* fundamental in its anthropological and theological presuppositions.[24] Bonhoeffer insists equally on the irreducible, independent integrity of the individual person, and on the fact that this person exists *essentially* in relation to others and in corporate human structures. His paradigm is not "cogito, ergo sum," but "I relate ethically to others, ergo sum."

---

[24] The voluntarism of Seeberg, and of others such as Dilthey, is clearly influential here. The discussion of Dilthey in *Act and Being* illuminates Bonhoeffer's position in *Sanctorum Communio.* "Dilthey had already attempted to deal with the problem of transcendence in terms of the historical problem of the encounter [Begegnung] of two personal wills.... But even this attempt can succeed only when its sets out from the person of God who encounters human beings in revelation" (AS 125, AB 127f.). "W. Dilthey's inquiry into the reality of the external world *[Beiträge zur lösung der Frage vom Ursprung unseres Glaubens an die Realität der Aussenwelt und seinem Recht,* 1890, *Ges. Schrift.* V, 1. Hälfte, S. 90ff.]* is based in the experience of the will and the resistance [Widerstand] it offers, and attempts fundamentally to overcome the whole of the idealistic theory of knowledge in favor of a philosophy of life [Philosophie des Lebens] shaped by history. Thus interpreted, Dilthey's work is of decisive significance for the current philosophy of history, especially as it has recently acquired influence on theology" (AS 48f. n. 26, AB 55 n. 26).

The human person always exists in relation to an 'other.' *"For the individual to exist, 'others' must necessarily be there."*[25] From an ethical viewpoint human beings do not exist 'immediately' through themselves qua Geist; human existence, rather, is mediated, for we exist in responsibility as we encounter an 'other.'[26] Human being is therefore essentially relational and social; to be human is to be a person related to others in human communities. Granted that the person is an individual, who lives as an independent unity of willing, feeling and knowing, nevertheless one only realizes his or her full humanity as a person essentially related to others in human communities.

It is upon this presupposition of the person as a willing socio-ethical subject in relations with others that Bonhoeffer accepts the general, metaphysical understanding of Geist, which understands human beings as self-conscious and spontaneously acting. Geist, therefore, is interpreted by his theological concept of the person in the historical decisions of social-ethical relationships. Within social life people encounter one another with ethical claims which must be answered by responsible decision.

Crucial for this anthropology is the notion that persons, as independent and individual willing beings, constitute limits, boundaries, or 'barriers' [Schranke, Grenze] for each other.[27] The 'other,' as 'You,' stands over against the self, related to the self as a whole person, yet independent of the self. Negatively, this means that the egotism and dominating pretensions of people are checked and halted as they run up against the countering wills of others. This cannot happen in the function of Geist as reason, since reason is in principle limitless and unbounded; but it does happen in the confrontation of ethical wills. Positively, encounter with the other as thou constitutes a person as a distinct, ethical self; in contemporary parlance, the encounter contributes to the formation of one's ethical identity. Furthermore, when the other person wills and affirms the self in love, that is a creative source of life for the self; it contributes human resources to the self from 'outside,' thus 'limiting' and helping to overcome the dehumanizing forms of self-will which the self can never resolve by itself in isolation.

---

25 SC 30, SC-E 51.

26 SC 30, SC-E 50: "From the ethical perspective, human beings do not exist 'unmediated' qua spirit in and of themselves, but only in responsibility vis-à-vis an 'other'."

27 SC 29ff., SC-E 49ff.

Bonhoeffer's point that the independent will of the other person is a Schranke, or Grenze, to the will of the self is an explicit part of his critique of idealism, especially its attempt to treat anthropological questions with presuppositions from epistemology. *"The attempt to derive the social from th epistemological category must be rejected as a μετάβασις εἰς ἄλλο γένος."*[28] On the basis of the subject-object relationship, the other person never really attains the status of an independent subject. By definition, the relationship of knowing does not bring the knowing subject into the social sphere; knowing does not involve the whole being of the knower as person. Moreover, in the relationship of knowing, any 'resistance' encountered in the object can be overcome by the powers of the knowing subject.[29] Furthermore, genuine individuality is lost in idealism, since the individual is ultimately an instance of universal Geist.[30] In opposition to idealistic-epistemological thinking Bonhoeffer asserts that *human reality* is encountered in the social sphere.

> The You as a reality-form [Wirklichkeitsform] is by definition independent in encountering the I in this sphere. In contrast to the idealist object-form, it is not immanent to the mind [Geist] of the subject. The You sets the limit [Schranke] for the subject and by its own accord activates a will that impinges on the other in such a way that this other will becomes a You for the I.... *The transcendence of the You says nothing at all about epistemological transcendence [erkenntnistheoretische-gegenständliche Transzendenz].* This is a purely ethical transcendence experienced only by those facing a decision....[31]

By defining the person in terms of *decisions* in socio-ethical encounters with others, the *historicity* of human life becomes fundamental for Bonhoeffer's anthropology.[32] The 'moment' is the time of ethical respon-

---

[28] SC 25, SC-E 45; cf. SC 218, SC-E 53: "two qualitatively different spheres."

[29] SC-E 41f., 45f., 51f., 53.

[30] SC-E 40f., 45.

[31] SC 31, SC-E 51f.; the word gegenständliche in the second last sentence is taken from SC-A 42f., cf. SC 217 n. 65. In the prison letters Bonhoeffer repeats this distinction of socio-ethical and epistemological transcendence almost verbatim; cf. LPP 379, 282, 381.

[32] In fact the *social,* the *historical,* and the *natural* are the three fundamental and inter-related anthropological categories in his theology. Further discussion of all of them is found at several points in the following chapters.

sibility. 'Reality,' ethically defined, is not timeless; it is essential to the being of ethical persons that they live in responsible decision in time.

> At the moment [Augenblick] of being addressed, the person enters a state of *responsibility* or, in other words, of decision. By person I do not mean at this point the idealists' person of mind or reason, but the person in concrete, living individuality. This is not the person internally divided, but the one addressed as a whole person.... *In the concept of the moment, the concept of time and its value-relatedness [Wertbezogenheit] are co-posited.* The moment is not the shortest span of time, a mechanically conceived atom, as it were. The 'moment' is the time of responsibility, value-related time, or, let us say, time related to God; and, most essentially, it is concrete time. Only in concrete time is the real claim of ethics effectual; and only when I am fully responsible am I conscious of being bound to time....

> Thus there follows from our concept of time an idea that is quite meaningless for idealism, that *the person ever and again arises and passes away in time.* The person does not exist timelessly; a person is not static, but dynamic. The person exists always and only in ethical responsibility; the person is re-created again and again in the perpetual flux of life. ... In the last analysis the reason why idealist philosophy fails to understand the concept of person is that it has no *voluntaristic* concept of God....[33]

I quote this passage at length since it vividly illustrates Bonhoeffer's view of the historical nature of the person, and also because it has wider implications. One is that it shows how he rooted the historicity of the self in its social and ethical nature; on both points this clearly distinguishes his anthropology from an existentialist version of human historicity, with its individualism and its underdeveloped ethical sense, as seen, for example, in Bultmann. The other is that it raises a serious anthropological question to which Bonhoeffer returns in *Act and Being.* To say that "the person ever and again arises and passes away in time" is excellent polemics, but it makes the point at the expense of fragmenting human existence, rendering any real continuity and unity of human being quite problematic. Nevertheless, for the present the very overstatement

---

[33] SC 28, SC-E 48. Since he mentions the idea of value, and since he elsewhere draws upon Scheler, note that for Bonhoeffer 'value' is constituted by 'person' and not vice versa, as in Scheler; cf. SC 29. Also, Bonhoeffer appreciated Kierkegaard's critique of the idealist view of time and reality, but disagreed with his view that the I established itself in ethical decision; this means that the I has no necessary connection with a concrete You, and so Bonhoeffer found in Kierkegaard an extreme individualism (SC 34, n. 12, SC-E 56, n. 12).

serves to document the importance of historicity as an essential aspect of human sociality.[34]

Given this concept of the person whose individual existence essentially consists of historical, socio-ethical relations with others, Bonhoeffer concludes that for Christian theology the relation of I and You is the 'social basic-relation.'[35] 'You' is the specific designation for 'other' in Christian thought. By 'social basic-relation' he means that fundamental perspective in which relations between individual persons, between individuals and groups, and between corporate bodies are all to be envisaged.[36] To choose the I-You relation as the social basic-relation is not to deny the mutations, so to speak, which are involved in the contexts of creation, sin, and redemption. It is rather to decide the basic perspective in which these several human 'states' are to be viewed.

The theological basis for this relational anthropology of self and other is given, Bonhoeffer argues, in the Christian view that to be human is always to be a creature before God as 'Other,' as the divine 'You.' As created, as sinner, and as redeemed, the human person is always in relation to God, encountered by the Word of God. Even the individual person is never alone, isolated, or self-sufficient. The theological basis of the anthropology is apparent in the following passage:

> It is a Christian insight that the person as a conscious being is created in the moment of being moved—in the situation of responsibility, passionate ethical struggle...; thus the real person grows out of the concrete situation. Here, too, the encounter [Begegnung] lies entirely in the spirit [Geist], as in idealism. Spirit here, however, has a different meaning from idealism. *For Christian philosophy, the*

---

[34] A nice statement which shows the 'reciprocity' of the personal and corporate dimensions of life in relation to historicity is found at SC-E 119: *"When peoples are called God's will for their purpose in history is at work,* just as when individuals are called they experience their history." Here, also, the link between the divine Word and human historicity is quite plain.

[35] SC 32ff., SC-E 52ff. The interchangeable German terms 'soziale Grundbeziehung' and 'soziale Grundverhältnis' should be translated 'social basic-relation,' not 'basic social relation' as in the Gregor Smith translation. The latter suggests that there is *a* basic social relation. Bonhoeffer shows that in the history of philosophy a number of models of social basic-relation have been put forth: the subject-object model from epistemology, atomistic individualism, forms of collectivism, and utilitarian-contractual views (cf. SC-A 17-26, and now SC 209-14, and the much abbreviated version in SC 20-22). It is the I-You relation which he chooses as appropriate for the Christian 'social basic-relation.'

[36] SC-E 78

> *human person originates only in relation to the divine; the divine*
> *person transcends the human person....* Idealist individualism's
> notion of spirit as being-for-itself [Fürsichsein] is unchristian.... The
> Christian person originates only in the absolute duality of God and
> humanity; only in experiencing the barrier does the awareness of
> oneself as an ethical person arise.[37]

This passage is crucial. Not only does it disclose the theological basis for
the anthropology. *It is the first expression of that characteristic social-*
ethical-historical understanding of transcendence which remains
essentially unchanged throughout Bonhoeffer's theological career. It is
a cardinal instance of the programmatic statement: "all the basic Christian concepts...are fully understandable only in relation to sociality."

The socio-ethical relation to the human 'other' is precisely the form
in which people encounter the divine 'Other.'

> *God or the Holy Spirit joins the concrete You; only through God's*
> *active working does the other become a You to me from whom my I*
> *arises. In other words, every human You is an image [Abbild] of the*
> *divine You.* You-character is in fact the essential form [Form] in which
> the divine is experienced; every human You bears its You-character
> only by virtue of the divine. This is not to say that it [the human You]
> is a borrowed attribute of God, and not really a You. Rather, the divine
> You creates the human You. And since the human You is created and
> willed by God, it is a *real, absolute, and holy You,* like the divine You....
> Since, however, one person's becoming You for an other fundamen-
> tally alters nothing about the You as person, that person as I is not holy;
> what is holy is *the You of God, the absolute will, who here becomes*
> *visible in the You of social life* [italics mine]. The other person is only
> a You insofar as God brings it about. But God can make every human
> being a You for us. *The claim of the other rests in God alone; for this*
> *very reason it remains the claim of the other.*[38]

Here, as in the previous passage, transcendence is interpreted in terms of
sociality. *"The concepts of person, community, and God* are inseparably
and essentially interrelated."[39]

Two fundamental assertions are being made in this theological view
of human social relationships. First, God is the one who establishes the
other as You in relation to the self, thus constituting the self as a person.
Second, God is the divine You who encounters the self in the ethical limit

---

37 SC 29f., SC-E 49.
38 SC 33, SC-E 54f.
39 SC 19, SC-E 34.

and claim of the human 'other.' "God is a You for us, that is, active will standing over against us."[40] These two assertions cannot really be separated; since transcendence is to be understood in terms of sociality, they are two aspects of the one relationship. Therefore, Bonhoeffer boldly states: *"the You of the other person is the divine You."* [41] God is not *immanent in* us, but is *present to* us in the social relationship. The transcendence of God means God's presence as 'Other.' God is distinct from but not absent from us; God's otherness is a transforming presence, and not an eternal elusiveness. We do not deal with an invisible God in an invisible world of our wishful fantasies; God is met and heard only in the real world where human, personal wills encounter one another; God is to be sought in the real experience of historical, social, ethical existence. Furthermore, as we shall see, the purpose of the divine presence is precisely to renew the personal and corporate life of human sociality. Human personal being, then, derives ultimately from the personal being of God. If God has been philosophically described as absolute Geist, Bonhoeffer insists that God, as well as human beings, must be fundamentally understood as Person.

To summarize: person refers to the human being who is at once an individual, willed to be such by God, and essentially related to others in social relationships. Specifically in ethical encounters with the other person as You is one's own personal being constituted; in such encounters the transcendent divine You is present. A person's will constitutes a 'limit' for others, and participates in human 'reality' in encountering their wills. The essence of a person is to will in responsible decision in ethical relationships, and such decision manifests the historicity of human life. In short, the person is a social-ethical-historical being before God.

'Person' as a corporate concept Particularly in Hegel, the philosophical tradition had used the concept of Geist to interpret corporate life as well as individual existence. Bonhoeffer, consistent with his procedure of understanding Geist in individual life by means of his Christian concept of the person, does the same when he interprets Geist in its corporate, social formations. 'Person' is not a concept limited only to individuals. It is rather a model, which, while first expounded in terms of individuals in the relationship of I and You, is fundamental to his interpretation of

---

[40] SC-A 45, SC 218; the earlier printed text and translation which omit the "Du," are corrupt at this point.

[41] SC 33f., SC-E 55.

corporate life. A social community—family, people, nation, church—and its 'objective Geist,' therefore, is considered as a 'collective person.' In its most universal use the concept of person is even applied to humanity as a whole, which is described as the 'Menschheitsperson.' Indeed, this application is crucial to Bonhoeffer's whole discussion of creation, sin, Christ, and the church. Adam, as created and fallen, and Christ 'personify' and represent modes of being of all humanity; each is regarded as a 'Kollektivperson' in the most universal sense.[42]

It follows that, in distinction from the representatives of 'interpersonal personalism,' Bonhoeffer regards the I-You relation as fundamental not only to relations between individual persons, but also to relations between individuals and social groups, to relations between one social group and another, and ultimately to the relation between God and humanity as a whole.[43] This section examines how Bonhoeffer builds up his argument to the position where humanity as a whole is the 'I' standing before God as the 'You.' Adam 'represents' and 'personifies' created and fallen humanity before God; Christ represents and personifies God before humanity and the 'new humanity' before God. As the argument unfolds, the remaining components of the category 'sociality' become clear.

Human persons are not only essentially related to others; these relationships always occur within various forms of human community. These communities, like individual persons, are constituted by conscious and deliberate human willing.[44] When people will in the same *direction,* willing has a mutual or reciprocal character; each must will and intend the person of the other, and themselves be willed and intended by the other. From this willing together, corporate social forms arise. From different types of willing, Bonhoeffer develops a typology of social forms. The two most important social forms in this typology are 'community'

---

[42] 'Person' is also applied to God, of course. Since idealism had described God as absolute Geist, Bonhoeffer interprets this with the view of God as "Allperson," "universal person of God" (SC 50, SC-E 79).

[43] In a 1932 address on "Christ and Peace" Bonhoeffer stated "that the relations between two peoples [Völker] have a deep analogy to the relations between two individual persons"; cf. Jørgen Glenthøj, ed., MW V, *Dokumente zur Bonhoeffer-Forschung 1928-1945,* 71, and now DBW 12 234.

[44] SC 51ff., SC-E 80ff.

[Gemeinschaft] and 'society' [Gesellschaft]; here Bonhoeffer appropriates and modifies the well-known distinction of Ferdinand Tönnies.[45]

Typologically considered, in a Gemeinschaft people will one another and their common life as ends in themselves, thus constituting a 'structure of meaning.' Examples of such communities are families, friendships, peoples and nations, right up to humanity as a whole; the church, in a special sense, is also a Gemeinschaft. In a Gesellschaft people will one another and their common life as means to a rational end, as in business corporations, political organizations, and so forth; such willing constitutes the society as a 'structure of purpose.'[46]

When people will together in communities and societies they give rise to the phenomenon of 'objective Geist,' that is, social Geist, in distinction from individual or subjective Geist.[47] Here Bonhoeffer is appropriating from Hegel, and in so doing is perhaps likely to arouse

---

[45] SC 55ff., SC-E 86ff. First published in 1886, Tönnies' very influential *Gemeinschaft und Gesellschaft* had reached its sixth edition by 1926. Bonhoeffer, as usual, changed the concepts which he took over; this is why he says, though it is omitted in the Gregor Smith translation, that he uses Gemeinschaft "in a special sense." For Tönnies a Gemeinschaft was a social group which had 'grown' organically, while a Gesellschaft was one that had been 'made' artificially; a certain romantic nostalgia may be detected in this distinction. Bonhoeffer also sees a confusion between a historical and a systematic phenomenological method in Tönnies' definitions. Consistent with his preference for the latter method, Bonhoeffer defines them according to the nature of their constitutive acts of will ('will to meaning,' 'will to rational purpose') and their structure ('structure of meaning,' 'structure of purpose'), not according to their origin. Furthermore, he places both types in the 'primal state,' thereby dismissing the possibility of viewing a Gesellschaft merely as a sinful Gemeinschaft (SC 247, SC-E 117f.).

[46] SC 56, SC-E 88; see also SC 59ff., SC-E 91f. If the analysis of the *direction* of willing yields the Gemeinschaft-Gesellschaft types, the analysis of the *strength of wills* yields the distinction between a Herrschaftsverband and a Gewaltverband. In the latter the stronger will activates the weaker by imposing itself mechanically, as it were, whereas in a Herrschaftsverband the will which obeys the stronger does so from an understanding of the meaning of what is commanded. Hence a *Herrschaftsverband,* because it presupposes *meaning,* is compatible with both Gemeinschaft and Gesellschaft, whereas a Gewaltverband is incompatible with Gemeinschaft. Ultimately Bonhoeffer argues that the structural, sociological distinctiveness of the church consists in the fact that it *combines* characteristics of Gemeinschaft, Gesellschaft, and Herrschaftsverband. In this community, the divine lordship [Herrschaft] is such as to create a genuine unity and equality among its members.

[47] SC 62ff., SC-E 97ff.

prejudice against his position. Yet common parlance, albeit non–technically and without the Hegelian apparatus, points toward the phenomenon Hegel described. If we describe the 'spirit' of a social group by speaking of its 'mentality,' 'culture,' or 'mood' (as in phrases such as 'the suburban mentality,' 'African–American culture,' or 'youth culture'), we are referring to the social phenomenon which Hegel called 'objective Geist.' Discussing Hegel's view of this concept, a noted historian of philosophy writes:

> It is 'objective spirit' that displays both Hegel's grasp of fact and his originality of insight at their highest. Objective spirit is the direct ancestor of the 'cultural heritage' and 'social process' of our own social science. Though it fits neatly into the dialectical scheme it is hardly a dialectical or speculative notion.... It is Hegel's most suggestive and fertile idea, his major philosophical discovery. It signalized the definite overthrow of eighteenth-century individualism, and made it impossible for nineteenth-century social science to take seriously the atomism of the Enlightenment.[48]

Bonhoeffer, whose appreciation for Hegel could on occasion match his vehement polemics against him, would agree with Randall's evaluation.[49] While rejecting Hegel's subordination of the individual person to the social process, he supported Hegel's perception that human life is inescapably social.

> The tragedy of all idealist philosophy was that it never ultimately broke through to personal spirit [Geist]. However, its monumental perception, especially in Hegel, was that the principle of spirit is something

---

[48] John Herman Randall, *The Career of Philosophy,* vol. II (New York: Columbia University Press, 1965), pp. 314f.

[49] The relationship of Bonhoeffer and Hegel needs much more research. The opinion of D. Böhler, at one time a student of Helmut Gollwitzer, cited by Bethge (DB 112 n. 80, DB-E 952 n. 110) that Bonhoeffer only knew Hegel in a secondhand and popular way is certainly problematic, if not downright erroneous. Böhler wrote to Bethge: "At the time of *Sanctorum Communio* Bonhoeffer had appropriated the bourgeois Hegel renaissance but scarcely Hegel himself." When this footnote was published Bonhoeffer's cousin and fellow student, Hans Christoph von Hase, wrote to Bethge: "I think note 80 is a lot of nonsense. Among others, Dietrich had read the philosophy of religion and the phenomenology very carefully and discussed them extensively. This was self-evident in Seeberg's seminar. He also knew Kant's critiques very thoroughly, and definitely as early as that.... I regard this note as superfluous" (letter to Bethge, 28.7.1967). Franz Hildebrandt, Bonhoeffer's closest friend in the late twenties and early thirties, had many lively discussions with him about Hegel. He confirms the

objective, extending beyond everything individual—that there is an objective spirit, the spirit of sociality, which is distinct in itself from all individual spirit. Out task is to affirm the latter without denying the former, to retain the perception without committing the error.[50]

Here, at last, idealism gets its due.

Bonhoeffer insists that the 'spirit' of a social structure (family, university, corporation, nation) is a reality sui generis. While it arises from the interaction of the individual wills of the members of the corporate group, and is real and operative *only in those individual persons,* it nevertheless has a distinctive character and identity which is not identical with any given individual. It is trans-individual, a reality sui generis, and not simply reducible to the aggregate of the individual wills from which it arises. The willing of every individual contributes to the character of the objective Geist; reciprocally, individual willing is itself affected by the objective Geist of the particular social structure. Illustrations of the point can easily be found when one considers the life of a family, a college, an ethnic group, or a congregation.

Now, having appropriated the Hegelian concept of objective Geist, Bonhoeffer makes a *crucial transformation.* He asks: by what conceptual model should we interpret the social spirit of *communities?*[51] What is an appropriate concept to understand theologically the social life of families, ethnic communities, nations, churches, and so on? Shall we regard the social life of these communities fundamentally in terms of the

---

view of von Hase: "Of course, von Hase is absolutely right against the sheer nonsense of Böhler. I do not remember the details of our ...discussion on the subject" (Hildebrandt to Green, December 8, 1970). This is strong circumstantial evidence. One must nevertheless dispute, on the other hand, the premature and probably misleading view of Dumas "that Hegel gave Bonhoeffer his basic stimulus when he was a student ... and when he was a young professor, after which he went on to work out his own point of view" (*op. cit.,* p. 217); it is more than misleading of Dumas to argue that Bonhoeffer was so thoroughly Hegelian that his *Letters* run the risk of dissolving all transcendence in immanence—the most serious of the few criticisms Dumas makes of Bonhoeffer. Further study of the question would need to examine not only Bonhoeffer's published writings, but also his library; as of 1969, most of the library was in Bethge's possession, but some of it was in Berlin. A set of student notes from the seminar Bonhoeffer gave on Hegel's philosophy of religion in the summer semester of 1933 (cf. DB 257, 266f.) was first published in 1988; see *Dietrich Bonhoeffers Hegel Seminar 1933,* ed. Ilse Tödt (Munich: Chr. Kaiser, 1988).

50 SC 46, SC-E 74.

51 Here Gemeinschaft, in the specific sense defined above.

dynamics of consciousness whereby mind comes to self-realization? Bonhoeffer rejects this Hegelian option, for which the subject-object schema would constitute the social basic-relation. Or does the notion of class struggle, as in Marx, provide the key? Is the familial model, with its basic parent-child relationship, the most suitable? What of the clan, or tribe, with its internal cohesiveness and its friend-foe distinction between insiders and outsiders?[52] Bonhoeffer answers by taking his idea of person, in the social basic-relation of I and You, as the conceptual model most appropriate for a theological understanding of the life of communities. The objective Geist of communities—family, people, nation, church, humanity as a whole—is to be interpreted as a Kollektivperson.[53]

---

52 While I have provided most of these illustrations, Bonhoeffer does, of course, explicitly dismiss the subject-object schema; in another text he refers to the "friend-foe" distinction.

53 Bonhoeffer took the 'Kollektivperson' notion from Max Scheler (cf. AS 108 n. 38, AB 112 n. 38). Scheler, who actually used the term 'Gesamtperson,' developed the theory in his *Der Formalismus in der Ethik und die materiale Wertethik. Neuer Versuch der Grundlegung eines ethischen Personalismus.* Scheler appears not to have used the term 'Kollektivperson.' Bonhoeffer normally uses 'Kollektivperson,' though several times he uses 'Gesamtperson' as its equivalent (cf. SC 50, 65 n. 2, 153, 194. On occasion Bonhoeffer will use 'Gesamt' in combination words to signify universality as distinct from particular or local communities, cf. Gesamtgemeinde, Gesamtkirche and Lokalgemeinde [SC 152f., 255], where the meaning is similar to Gesamtgemeinschaft. But Kollektivperson and Gesamtperson are used interchangeably in both universal and more particular contexts; no technical distinction is involved in the two words). That Bonhoeffer intends his 'Kollektivperson' to be generally equivalent to Scheler's 'Gesamtperson' is seen when he cites Scheler's discussion of the latter in relation to his own consideration of the former (cf. SC 48f. and n. 15). But I do not want to press terminological similarities to suggest identity of meaning, for Bonhoeffer exercised a sovereign freedom in his borrowings, and he is critical of Scheler at many points. A study of similarities and differences, however, would be significant. Bonhoeffer refers to him quite frequently in his own early writings, and possessed a number of Scheler's books; in particular, he had the 1921 and 1926 editions of the *Formalismus,* and the copy of the 1921 edition in his personal library is carefully worked through and annotated. Bonhoeffer also found Scheler helpful in showing the relation of individual and corporate life to be a reciprocal one in contrast to atomistic and collectivist alternatives. A passage in the manuscript [SC-A 81f.] unpublished until the critical edition (SC-E 76) reads: "This problem has been in constant dialectical movement since the Enlightenment or, if you will, since the beginning of all philosophical thought, and it has still not been settled. The 'either-or' alternative was all one ever saw; one was unable to grasp that the intrinsic dialectical

Here the objection is likely to be raised that treating a community's spirit as a Kollektivperson is a piece of social magic, and dangerous at that; it is an hypostatization of the social spirit into a 'superperson,' which elevates it to a superior status autonomous of individual wills, and confers on it an authority divorced from the concrete responsibilities of particular persons. The objection completely misses the point. It ignores that *reciprocity* between individual and corporate life which is *essential* in Bonhoeffer's understanding of sociality; it forgets that the *ethical is intrinsic* to the definition of 'person.'[54] The very reason he applies to communities his own model of the human person is *to guarantee that they are understood to have the same ethical-historical character as the individual person.* The ethical sphere is not confined to the private moral questions of individuals. Corporate communities as such, *pace* still prevalent ideologies, are not ethically neutral; they are ethical 'bodies' as much as the individual person. Accordingly, this corporate use of the concept of person insists that individuals are not private persons but people who have responsibility for the socio-ethical life of their communities; to use 'person' also as a corporate concept is to remind individuals that their personal life essentially includes a corporate dimension. Thus, far from detaching corporate responsibility from the individual, the idea of the Kollektivperson simultaneously confers it upon the individual and the community. Indeed, since there can be no Kollektivperson apart from a community of individual persons, it is *in individual persons* that the call to corporate, ethical responsibility is heard. In responding to this ethical claim these persons act on behalf of the whole community. Bonhoeffer gives as an illustration the prophets of Israel who both speak the Word of Yahweh's justice and judgement *to the people as a whole* and in themselves repent on behalf of the whole community.[55]

---

movement of the subject matter entailed 'both-and'.... Only recently has this possibility been thought through theoretically and, in my view, a solution approached via this route. The way as prepared by the investigations about the problem of understanding [Verstehen], to my knowledge first pursued systematically by Scheler, taken up by the students of the phenomenological school, and then with Theodor Litt extended by discoveries of basic principles and modified. The discipline of sociology proper played little role here." This reciprocity is of course deliberately reflected in Bonhoeffer's very title, *Sanctorum Communio*.

[54] Cf. SC-E 120, where Bonhoeffer explicitly says that individuals must struggle to a decision of their own wills and not blindly submit to the particular claims of the Kollektivperson.

[55] Retrospectively, Bonhoeffer's own life provides another excellent example. His response to the national crisis in Hitler's Germany can certainly be

It is not only individuals, then, but communities *as such* in their corporate activities which must hear the Word of God in their own historical situations. The community as such is an 'I' addressed by the divine 'You.'[56] Through persons who act in the name of and for the sake of the corporate body, the community must respond in ethical responsibility.

> God does not desire a history of individual human beings, but the history of the human *community [Gemeinschaft]*. However, God does not want a community that absorbs the individual into itself, but a community of *human beings*. In God's eyes, community and individual exist in the same moment and rest in one another.[57]

----

understood as personal practice of his own theology of sociality in this aspect; indeed, his theology was an impulse to his action. It is not accidental that those with other theologies acted quite differently, whether in support of Hitler, or with an apolitical policy informed by a two-kingdoms ethic that was quite inadequate to the situation.

[56] SC-E 118ff.

[57] SC 51, SC-E 80. Here one must note the problem of the concept of person being corporately applied to a Gemeinschaft but not to a Gesellschaft. The reason for this is that Bonhoeffer defines a Gemeinschaft as an end in itself and a Gesellschaft as a means to an end. Since persons can never be regarded as means to an end, his theory cannot treat societies as 'ethical collective persons.' But the problem which ensues is that precisely the most powerful social institutions—of business, government, education, labor, communications, etc.—are not constituted as ethically responsible in their very essence. To be sure, all their members are ethically defined, as individuals and as members of Gemeinschaften. Yet the problem remains in a most important area of corporate life, even though one may allow the need for a distinction between the two social types. Since a great deal of the life of any person consists of instrumental, rational-purposive activities—without thereby diminishing one's status as an ethical agent—Bonhoeffer might have found a way to apply his concept of person in its corporate sense to Gesellschaften. After all, personal and corporate life is not ethically neutral simply because it is instrumental and rationally purposive; nor does a Gesellschaft ethically neutralize itself because it has loose personal bonds, is predicated on individual self-interest, and its members are more impersonal, reserved, conventional and cautious toward each other—cf. SC 58f., SC-E 91. While Bonhoeffer himself did not raise the question in precisely this form, he tried to deal with it both in his doctrine of 'orders of preservation' (see Chapter 5, below) and in his doctrine of the 'mandates' in the *Ethics;* these ideas include corporate social forms of both the Gemeinschaft and the Gesellschaft types. (Incidentally, his interest in various corporate social forms in *Sanctorum Communio* is clearly the intellectual matrix from which these later ideas were born.) In making this criticism it should be recalled that Bonhoeffer is not, as noted above, simply following Tönnies'

In order to move to the center of his theological argument, Bonhoeffer universalizes his concepts of community and person. Every community, understood as a Kollektivperson, is embraced in a more comprehensive one. Ultimately, therefore, "humanity is the comprehensive community [Gesamtgemeinschaft] that embraces all communities."[58] Humanity—the human race as a whole—is the Menschheitsperson.[59] Here Bonhoeffer moves into a form of universal argument consciously analogous to Paul and reminiscent of Irenaeus' doctrine of recapitulation: Adam and Christ are seen as prototypes; they are 'representatives' who 'personify' two fundamental styles of human being throughout humanity as a whole. Around these two universal 'collective persons' Bonhoeffer articulates the Christian drama of creation, fall and redemption.

One might well ask how these all-embracing concepts—universal community, Menschheitsperson, Adam, Christ—are related to the personal life of individuals and the specific social communities in which people actually live their concrete history. People live, indeed, in their specific communities, each having its own distinctive ethos, or 'spirit' [objective Geist]; these communities range all the way from the most direct and intimate communities such as families and friendships, through wider communities such as people and nation, to the most universal community—humanity as a whole. Bonhoeffer acknowledges the great variety of character and culture which distinguishes these communities, varying from place to place, nation to nation, culture to culture, and all changing during successive, historical periods. Yet throughout this rich and changing diversity of human spirit manifested in these distinctive ways, common dynamics are evident. Theologically understood, these dynamics are mutations, so to speak, of the social basic-relation of I and You; these are manifested in creation and the 'primal community,' in sin and the 'broken community,' and in redemption and the community of the new humanity. Adam 'personifies,' as prototype and representative, both the created person and community, and the isolated person and fragmented solidarity of humanity in sin. Christ 'personifies' the new human being in the new humanity. In other

---

position; he is deliberately moving away from the conservative and romantic elements of Tönnies' theory. But he did not go far enough at this point, and so the problem remains.

58 SC 75, SC-E 120.

59 SC 76, SC-E 120f.

words, Adam, created and fallen, represents a fundamental and universal mode of human being which is operative in all the individual and corporate life of humanity, pervading all its diversity and changes. Christ, likewise, is a mode of personal and corporate being in which all people may be restored to their authentic humanity. The diversities of human experience exhibit the universal dilemma and promise of our common humanity as disclosed in these two primal names.

A summary of the main concepts in the category of sociality prepares for their theological use in interpreting creation, sin, and revelation. The individual social-ethical-historical person described previously exists not only in relations with other individual persons but also in corporate social structures. These social structures, of both the Gemeinschaft and Gesellschaft types, are constituted by the direction of human willing. They are corporate unities, not just agglomerations. The relationship between the individual and the corporate structure is one of mutual reciprocity, each acting upon the other. *Individual persons* and *communities* are equally willed by God, so that both individualism and collectivism are ruled out. People willing together give rise to the phenomenon of objective Geist. The objective Geist of a community [Gemeinschaft] is interpreted as an 'ethical collective person'; this constitutes every Gemeinschaft per se as an ethical reality. As an ethical Kollektivperson each Gemeinschaft is an 'I' standing before God as the ultimate 'You.' Since a community and its individual members exist reciprocally, the individual person is called upon to act in ethical responsibility for the community as such. The most universal community is humanity as a whole, embracing all other communities. Adam is the Kollektivperson who personifies humanity as created and fallen, thus being the prototype of the life of every individual and every community before God; Christ is the Kollektivperson of the new humanity, overcoming the sin of the old humanity of Adam; he is the reality of a new personal and corporate life for every human being. The social form of Christ as the Kollektivperson of the new humanity is the church.

2. Creation: The 'Primal State'

Bonhoeffer treats creation under the rubric of the primal state.[60] As he said in the programmatic statement, "'primal state' ...can be fully

---

[60] SC 36-39 summarizes SC-A 55-65. The summary is not found in the Gregor Smith version since it followed the fuller original version found in the

comprehended only in reference to sociality."[61] Therefore his chapter on this subject is a discussion of various aspects of human social life 'before the fall.'[62] It need hardly be said that he is not engaged in speculation about a literal, pre-historical paradise; 'primal state' is an ontological concept, not a chronological condition. Analogous to eschatology, the primal state is "hope projected backwards," as Bonhoeffer puts it.[63] The discussion of "the original unbroken community"[64] considers the human situation prior to sin by looking at phenomena of personal and corporate life from the perspective of the revelation of Christ.[65] The purpose of this is to distinguish, particularly against idealism, human being as created, as sinful, and as redeemed in the new humanity of Christ.[66] "It makes the

---

appendix of the third German edition; see now SC 220ff. and SC-E 58ff. The summary, however, adds some clarifying sentences. Furthermore, when it alters the heading from "Das theologische Problem: Die ursprüngliche ungebrochene Gemeinschaft" to "Das methodische Problem: Die ursprüngliche ungebrochene Gesellschaft [sic! typographical error] an important clarification is made. The original heading, contrary to statements in the text, gives the impression that only this section of the chapter is theological, whereas Bonhoeffer intends that the whole chapter be understood theologically.

[61] A formerly unpublished statement in the manuscript reads, characteristically: "There has always been reflection about justice, sanctity, piety, and even intelligence and science in the case of Adam. But for a long time no thought at all has been given to the fact that these concepts belong together with that of social community" (SC-E 64).

[62] This exposition concentrates on the interpretation of creation in terms of sociality. But another fundamental anthropological category which Bonhoeffer consistently uses throughout his early theology should be noted: 'Natur.' All the discussion about 'Geist' should not lead us to ignore Natur as essential to human being. For human existence, Natur is especially, though not exclusively, the *body*. The relations between Geist and Natur are reciprocal, though Geist has the priority. "In the Christian [understanding of] person, soul and body are bound together in an indissoluble unity" (SC 195, SC-E 285f.). Between them "there is such a close bond that Geist is no more conceivable without Natur than human Natur without social Geist" (SC 42f.); cf. SC 66f., 70ff., 241f., and also AB 172, 174, 180f. Discussion of Natur as a major anthropological category is reserved for Chapter 5, since *Creation and Fall* contains a much more detailed treatment.

[63] SC 36.

[64] SC-A i; cf. SC 69. Until the 1970 German edition of *Sanctorum Communio,* all the printed editions erroneously read "Gesellschaft" instead of "Gemeinschaft" at this point.

[65] SC 36; SC-E 58ff.

[66] Ibid.

real movement of things from unity through break to unity concretely vivid."[67] This presentation presupposes all that has gone before in the discussion of 'person,' except where sin was implied: the ethical concept of person, human being as equally individual and relational-corporate, as self-conscious and willing Geist, as historical, the ideas of objective Geist and Kollektivperson, and, in all this, the view that God is related to humanity in this social fabric of existence.

While the 'primal community' is related to the later presentation of the church, Bonhoeffer is concerned with human nature as such. Creation is not just an ideal religious prelude, so to speak, for ecclesiology. By definition, human being is social being; creation is a social reality. If the specifically Christian concept of person emphasizes that human being is social, ethical, and historical, Bonhoeffer argues that even the general, metaphysical view of Geist presupposes sociality. Human sociality as conscious being is documented in our thinking, understanding, and communicating—especially as seen in language; in our willing; and in our feeling.[68] Various forms of Gesellschaft, whose essential purpose is human self-preservation, have their place in creation. Bonhoeffer also agrees with the view, which he finds in patristic writings and Thomas Aquinas, that the state, as an agency of order and well-being, belongs to creation.[69] Sociality, therefore, is not a privileged Christian domain but belongs to humanity as such. In all aspects of life "human beings as spirit [Geist] are necessarily created in a community."[70]

If theology makes such assertions, it nevertheless wants to point to the spirit which informs the whole of creation. In the original, unbroken community [Gemeinschaft], the human creature lives in community with God and with others. Understood from the revelation in Christ, the primal community is a community of *mutual love.*[71] It is constituted by the divine love, and *the divine love rules by its serving.* (It is crucial to note how the divine rule is defined here as loving service; this has great implications for Bonhoeffer's later theology.)[72] In community with God as with one

---

[67] SC 36.

[68] SC-E 65ff.

[69] SC 236ff., SC-E 96ff. Here he seems to depart from the predominant Lutheran view of the state as a restrainer of sin; see further discussion on this point in Chapter 5.

[70] SC 39, SC-E 65.

[71] SC-E 60f.

[72] SC-E 60. This statement that God's love rules by serving anticipates, I believe, a similar one in *Act and Being:* the freedom of God is "freedom for

another, people serve by their loving; divine and human wills relate to others by loving; there is an identity of direction and purpose in God's willing and human willing.

Human community with God is actual and real in the community people have with one another; the creature loves and serves the Creator by the common service of mutual love in the human community. Love and service of God in community with God is not an individualistic possibility; the divine community takes form in human sociality, in the human community where people relate both to other individual persons and to the community as a whole. Without using the actual language of his later formulation, Bonhoeffer clearly means here that God's being and human being in the primal community is always a 'being-for' one another.

Adam is the Kollektivperson who personifies the individual person and the objective Geist of the primal community. He 'stands for' the person and community whose spirit is one of service to God by living in mutual human love.[73]

The *anthropological* concentration in this discussion of creation is characteristic of Bonhoeffer. To be sure, the human person is understood as the *creature of God* known in the revelation of Christ. The primal community of human beings with one another is simultaneously their being in community with God. But there is no treatment—as found in Barth, for example—of subjects like creation as the work appropriated to the Father, the relation of the Father to the other 'persons' of the Trinity, creation and election, and so on. His discussion of the Creator is always in relation to the human creature; it is in the anthropological sphere that a comprehensive and sophisticated set of categories is articulated. More discussion of this point follows later.

3. SIN: ADAM AND THE 'BROKEN COMMUNITY

As with creation, "'sin'... can be fully comprehended only in reference to sociality." Bonhoeffer's discussion of the personal and corporate

---

humanity"; this, in turn, points forward to the formulation of the 'non-religious' Christology in the *Letters:* Jesus is "the one for others."

[73] In discussing the primal community, Bonhoeffer refers to the Genesis creation narratives, saying that the meaning of the creation of man *and* woman is "life in sociality"; cf. SC 224, SC-E 61. "God created man and woman with a bias towards one another" (SC 51: "aufeinander angelegt"). This anticipates the discussion in *Creation and Fall* of this relationship of man and woman as *imago Dei* understood as *analogia relationis;* see below, Chapter 5.

dimensions of sin is concerned with the social nature and consequences of sin.

"Sin [is]... the will that in principle affirms as valuable only itself, and not the other, and that acknowledges the other only on its own terms."[74] More specifically, sin is a self-seeking in which demanding replaces giving, and the self uses, instead of loving, the other; mutual love is perverted into an isolated self-love.[75]

> Instead of being directed to the other, both to God and to other human beings, love is now extended only to the self. Everything becomes a means of self-seeking.[76]

Sin, to invert one of Bonhoeffer's later expressions, is a 'being-for-self.' Fallen Adam is "extremely egocentric."[77] Above all, and this is crucial for my later argument, sin is the exercise of a self-serving *power* over others. "The other will is not ignored or negated; rather, *one seeks to force it into one's own will and thus overcome it.*"[78]

If this description points more to sin in personal relationships, Bonhoeffer sees the same phenomenon in corporate life. Gemeinschaft is now willed not as a meaningful end in itself, but as a means for the ends of the self. The Gesellschaft is similarly distorted. It is not, as we have seen, a sinning Gemeinschaft; Bonhoeffer rejects this sort of romantic accusation. Sin, rather, perverts the purposive character of instrumental associations, so that by the evil will operative in them they become "an institution for the systematic exploitation of one by the other."[79]

Given the centrality of power, dominance, and exploitation in this description of sin, the importance of the concept of 'barrier' [Grenze, Schranke] in Bonhoeffer's understanding of the ethical person is quite apparent. The countering and resisting wills of others check and limit the inordinate pretensions of the self; the same goes for relations between corporate groups.[80]

---

74 SC 248, SC-E 118.

75 SC-E 109f., 117; cf. 98, 180.

76 SC-A 128.

77 SC-E 146; cf. SC-E 167.

78 SC 54, SC-E 86; italics mine; cf. SC 26, SC-E 4-5, where the critique of 'dominance' is applied to the idealist concept of Geist as mind.

79 SC 248, SC-E 118.

80 At this point one is naturally reminded of Reinhold Niebuhr's analysis of the relation between the will to live and the will to power. Bonhoeffer,

When these anthropological dynamics are analyzed theologically Bonhoeffer focuses on sin as a disobedient *"ethical act of rebellion [Auflehnung] against God's rule."* [81] The sinner rebels against God and climbs to the highest summit—of isolation.[82] Here is that Promethean strain which is so typical in Bonhoeffer's account of sin, and which I later examine in the context of his soteriology.

If this is the nature of sin, its consequence is to 'break' and fragment the primal community of people with God and with one another. This does not mean that people become asocial, but rather that created sociality is torn by a profound inner contradiction. Sin is a "divisive power [Macht]"[83] which comes between human beings and God, and between human beings themselves. Consequently, the individual person, still inescapably related to others and bound up in corporate life, is afflicted by a deep isolation,[84] while corporate existence is a contradictory solidarity of egocentric individualism.

Consistent with this account of the way sin disintegrates the created sociality of people with God, with themselves, and with each other, is the interpretation of original sin in a *social conceptuality.* In the theological tradition this doctrine sought to deal with the social significance of sin.[85] The problem of the doctrine is: how can theology simultaneously express the individual's responsibility in sin, and the universality of sin among all people, without formulating the latter in a way that contradicts the

---

however, developed this idea in relation to Dilthey, Grisebach, and Gogarten, prior to reading Niebuhr.

[81] SC 224, SC-E 61; italics Bonhoeffer's.

[82] SC 72, SC-E 115.

[83] SC 224, SC-E 61.

[84] SC-E 108; cf. SC-E 147ff., 166. Here Bonhoeffer introduces another consistent and characteristic motif of his thinking: *conscience* is a result of the fall, manifesting inner division. There was no conscience in the primal state. Furthermore, he introduces a critical revision of the Lutheran view of conscience in saying that conscience is just as likely to be an instrument of self-justification, as of Christ's Anfechtung [spiritual attack] through the law. It is extremely doubtful if he ever realized how far the revision begun here was to take him, not only from a decadent Protestantism, but also from Luther himself. Substantial comparison of Bonhoeffer and Luther on this point is found below in Chapter 4. There I also analyze systematically the syndrome of power, dominance, isolation, and conscience which constitutes the soteriological problem in Bonhoeffer's theology. The same phenomenon is even more clearly evident in the analysis of *Act and Being* in the next chapter.

[85] SC 70, SC-E 109.

individual ethical responsibility intrinsic to the former? In Augustine's classical approach Bonhoeffer finds an inappropriate biological category to express the universality of sin; this severely compromises human ethical responsibility, for sin virtually becomes a biologically given destiny. Ritschl, on the other hand, overcame the biological bias of the tradition, but could make no sense of universal sin except as the sum of individual sins. Augustine has an inappropriate form of universality which undermines personal responsibility, and Ritschl has a form of individual responsibility which cannot do justice to the corporate universality of sin.[86] Bonhoeffer believes that his conceptuality of sociality can go beyond this impasse.

A human being, Bonhoeffer has argued, is an individual ethical person. People are also corporate beings, responsible for their communities, and each community is construed as an 'ethical Kollektivperson'; humanity is the most universal community, and fallen Adam embodies and 'personifies' this Kollektivperson. Sin is therefore simultaneously an act of the highest individual responsibility and a prototypical deed of humanity universally. Each person who sins acts no differently from Adam. In the sin of every individual the common sinfulness of humanity is awakened again. Everyone simultaneously does their own sinful deed, and the deed of sinful humanity. The act of the individual person and the Kollektivperson is one and the same. In the deepest isolation of sin we find ourselves in utmost solidarity with all humanity. Fallen Adam 'personifies' the humanity of the broken community; everyone is Adam. Here the dimensions of individual responsibility and universality in sin are linked; but the universality is not made an excuse for the individual sin, and the individuality of sin does not deny its corporate, universal character.[87]

With regard to the empirical spread of sin, Bonhoeffer also argues that this is to be understood in terms of sociality, not sexuality. To be sure, the psychological matrix of sin cannot be used to explain away the personal responsibility which sin entails. But, given the situation of 'broken community,' the mutuality of love has been replaced by egocen-

---

[86] SC-E 109ff. This analysis of the Augustinian and Ritschlian positions is a form of the 'act' and 'being' question which Bonhoeffer takes up in his *Habilitationsschrift*. It is no accident, therefore, that original sin is discussed again in his next book, and treated again in terms of sociality.

[87] SC 70ff., SC-E 109ff.

tricity. This means that the people's initiatives toward love are not reciprocated, so they direct their own love to self-seeking.[88]

Adam, then, is the Kollektivperson of the old humanity. He embodies, 'represents,' and 'personifies' the universal sin of humanity corporately, and the sin of every individual person. Personal and corporate life in sociality is 'broken' in the old humanity of Adam. To this world Christ comes as the Kollektivperson of the new humanity.[89]

4. REVELATION: CHRIST AND THE NEW HUMANITY

"'Revelation'... [is] fully understandable only in relation to sociality." It is only after he has articulated this whole, complex conceptuality of sociality, and employed it theologically to interpret the Christian drama, that Bonhoeffer comes to speak explicitly of revelation and the *sanctorum communio*.[90] The ecclesiology is set within the broadest horizon, and the idea of revelation addresses the universal dilemma of all humanity. Far from the sort of exclusivity suggested by Phillips, for example, Bonhoeffer presents the most catholic of ecclesiologies. Those who know little of Bonhoeffer usually associate *Sanctorum Communio* with the phrase, "Christus als Gemeinde existierend";[91] few have realized that this ecclesiological phrase can only be properly understood after they have appreciated the prior statement: *Christ is the Kollektivperson of the new humanity.*[92]

The main theses of the book's culmination in Christ, revelation and the new humanity will first be presented; then some important details will be considered.

---

[88] SC 247f., SC-E 117f. Such egocentric self-seeking is not to be confused with self-preservation.

[89] The German Menschheit has similar connotations to the English words 'humankind' and 'humanity.' The latter, in addition to being inclusive, not only expresses the corporate sense of the whole human species, but also better suggests Bonhoeffer's theological argument that Christ restores the *true* humanity of human beings.

[90] Of course, the whole argument presupposes this revelation, but now its full import is disclosed.

[91] This is Bonhoeffer's Christological-social transformation of Hegel's phrase, "Gott als Gemeinde existierend."

[92] See the sixth proposition in the theses for doctoral graduation: "Die Kirche ist Christus 'als Gemeinde existierend' und als Kollektivperson zu verstehen"; GS III 47 and DBW 9 477.

As the revelation and the reconciling act of God, Christ is the Kollektivperson of the new humanity. In his person he embodies and inaugurates a new social basic-relation between God and humanity, and therefore among human beings. This new humanity is no mere potentiality, dependent on humanity for its realization; it is a *reality* in the person of Christ, and the reality of the new humanity in Christ is *actualized* among people by the Holy Spirit.[93]

The new humanity of Christ, socially concrete in the church, is presented in the third act of the drama of all humanity from creation (primal community), through fall (broken community), to reconciliation. This Christology and ecclesiology, therefore, is concerned with the rehabilitation and renovation of genuine humanity for all people. Christ is the Kollektivperson of the new humanity, superseding Adam as the Kollektivperson of the old humanity. Bonhoeffer's thinking is the very opposite of sectarian exclusivism; it moves, like Paul and Irenaeus, on the level of universal humanity. So the Word of Christ is not only a word to the church. Rather, his presence in and as the church creates a new social reality of human existence, and this is a paradigm, a promise, and a challenge which encounters humanity in all human life. The presence of Christ as Kollektivperson of the new humanity is the divine 'You' encountering the 'I' of the old humanity of Adam. Thus, when Bonhoeffer describes Christ in the social form of the church as the Kollektivperson of the new humanity, this is a deliberate way of relating Christ and the church to humanity as a whole; it is not a way of confining Christ to the church, or of sanctifying any complacent and self-righteous ecclesiastical self-preoccupation. Accordingly he states, as he does again in the 1933 Christology lectures, that the history of the church is the hidden center of world history.[94]

Revelation, that is, the person of Christ, exists in a *social form:* the church. Revelation is not an idea, a past historical happening, a doctrine, or an entity. It is a *person,* and since person and community are inseparable, the revelation of Christ is present in a personal-communal form: "Christus als Gemeinde existierend."[95]

---

[93] SC 89ff.; SC-E 143ff., 157ff.

[94] SC-E 211.

[95] SC 76, 87; SC-E 121, 141. "Gemeinde" in this edition is translated "church-community," as in the Dietrich Bonhoeffer Works translation of *Sanctorum Communio;* a full discussion of its meaning is found in the Editor's Introduction of that text (cf. SC-E 14-17). "Gemeinde" is Bonhoeffer's preferred theological term for the church, and is Christologically defined as in the axiom

Like all human social structures, the church has its distinctive social spirit, or 'objective Geist.' Since it is a special form of Gemeinschaft, this is to be regarded as an 'ethical Kollektivperson.' How are these, as human phenomena, related to the Holy Spirit (divine Geist) and Christ as the Kollektivperson of the new humanity? This question needs a clear answer, in view of those interpreters who see Bonhoeffer in danger of identifying the church with Christ. The objective Geist of the church is not identical with the Holy Spirit, but is the "bearer" of the Spirit;[96] the divine Spirit creates and makes effective its own forms (Word and sacrament) in the social life and spirit of the empirical, human community of the church. Similarly, as an ethical Kollektivperson, the church is not equivalent to Christ himself. He is present in and as the church-community in Word and sacrament, but freely and creatively present. The person of Christ, the divine You, encounters the 'I' of the church; the Word of the cross and resurrection encounters the church, breaking it up and building it up in a dynamic, historical relationship.[97]

The presence of Christ is not the essence of the church at human disposal; Christ is not a possessed attribute of his human community, frozen into a static being. Understood on the model of the ethical person in social relations, the life and spirit of the church is continually in historical encounter with the person and Spirit of Christ.[98] In this encounter the old humanity of Adam, the *peccatorum communio*, is being transformed by the dynamics of justification and sanctification. The *sanctorum communio* is the *peccatorum communio*, the old humanity, being transformed, renewed, and reconciled by the reality of the new humanity of Christ.

"The church is Christ existing as church-community [Gemeinde]." The theological term Gemeinde also shares a common root with Gemeinschaft, one of Bonhoeffer's sociological terms for the church. While in some contexts Gemeinde can naturally refer to individual congregations, the latter are "local actualisations of the unity of God's church-community [Gemeinde]," to use the language of Hofmann which Bonhoeffer quotes (SC-E 223; cf. 226).

[96] SC-E 1215ff.; cf. SC-E 136.

[97] SC 144, SC-E 213f.

[98] SC 146, SC-E 215f. For other statements expressly denying the equivalence and interchangeability of the church and Christ see: SC-E 136, 139, 145f., 210, 213f., 288, etc. If further confirmation of this distinction between Christ and the church is desired, see the very Barthian critique of the church and religion in Bonhoeffer's Barcelona lecture, "Jesus Christus und vom Wesen des Christentums"; the text is published in GS V 134-156 and DBW 10 302ff.; cf. DB 149ff., DB-E 116f.

This encounter and these dynamics create, Bonhoeffer contends, a distinctive sociological form. This can only be appreciated when one understands the essence of the church theologically from the inside, on the basis of the revelation which discloses what the church really is. The church is a Spirit-community [Geistgemeinschaft] as a community of love [Liebesgemeinschaft]. From the viewpoint of its members, this is not the simple, unambiguous love of the primal community, nor is it the perfected love of the eschatological community. Yet, created by the serving of the divine love, the Christian church community is a genuine actualization of the divine love, such as to overcome the egocentricity, dominance, and isolation which marked and marred the old humanity. The signs of Christ's presence are the transformation of sin into the co-humanity of love which actively wills, affirms, serves, and bears the other; sin is overcome in "active being-for-one another" [tätige Füreinander][99] where love voluntarily and vicariously identifies with and suffers for others, intercedes for others, and forgives others.[100]

With this life, the church is clearly an end in itself, thereby having characteristics of a Gemeinschaft. But it is also an instrument of God's will for humanity, and this purposive dimension gives it characteristics of a Gesellschaft. Furthermore, as constituted by the lordship of Christ's love as Stellvertreter the church has characteristics of a Herrschaftsverband. In its essential sociological structure, the church is a distinctive social form: it is a Geistgemeinschaft as Liebesgemeinschaft.[101] It is grounded in the activity of the Holy Spirit who *actualizes* the community of the new humanity which is real in Christ's lordship of love. Under this lordship the human act of love combines willing as an end in itself and purposive willing. The human *purpose* is to will what God wills; but God wills the *community* of people who love one another as an *end in itself*.[102] This analysis of the structure of the Christian community

---

[99] SC 120; this formulation unmistakably anticipates the description of Christian existence as 'being-for-others' in the *Letters*.

[100] SC 117ff., 120ff., SC-E 178ff., 182ff.

[101] The seventh graduation thesis sums this up neatly: "In its sociological structure the church incorporates all potential types of social organization in itself and supersedes them in the 'community of spirit' [Geistgemeinschaft]; this rests on the fundamental sociological law of vicarious representative action [Stellvertretung]"; GS III 47, DBW 9 477f.

[102] SC 112ff., SC-E 172ff.; SC 180ff., 288ff., SC-E 260ff., 265ff. (It is perhaps not without biographical interest when Bonhoeffer says that the only other social form which approximates the structure of the church is the patriar-

exhibits Bonhoeffer's theological premise: as a social reality the church can only be understood from within, that is, on the basis of revelation.

Within this overall position are several ideas basic to Bonhoeffer's whole theological development. Fundamental is the idea of Stellvertretung: it is the central Christological concept and has far-reaching anthropological significance. To translate 'Stellvertreter' as 'deputy,' 'substitute,' or 'proxy,' would barely approach Bonhoeffer's meaning; the English terms have rather formal, legal connotations, and they suggest a secondary role. For Bonhoeffer, Christ the Stellvertreter is the *initiator* and *reality* of the new humanity. The person and action of Christ is 'vicarious' in that he does for human beings what they cannot possibly do for themselves. Herein lies his distinctive difference, as Kollektivperson, from Adam; every member of humanity sins in the same way as Adam, but only Christ overcomes the 'broken community' of sin. "In Christ... humanity has been brought once and for all–this is essential for *real* vicarious representative action [Stellvertretung]–into community with God [Gottesgemeinschaft]."[103] With this Christological foundation, the anthropological corollary is obvious: "Stellvertretung is the life-principle of the new humanity."[104] The Christian principle of Stellvertretung constitutes the new humanity; it is the distinguishing characteristic of the Christian social basic–relation [Grundbeziehung].[105]

Christ the Stellvertreter *is* the *love* of God for humanity; in essence, Christ's Stellvertretung is his loving-action-for-humanity. In this context the abstract noun 'revelation' is unsatisfactory. For this reason Bonhoeffer does not use it very much; when he does he usually puts it in the form of a verb describing personal *self-giving*. What the sin of Adam severs, God's love unites

> by revealing God's own love in Christ, by no longer approaching us in demand and summons, purely as You, but instead by *giving God's own self as an I, opening God's heart. The church is founded on the revelation of God's heart.*[106]

---

chal family; cf. SC-E 289 on God as Father, and also SC-E 228, 230, 241 on the congregation as mother.)

[103] SC 92, SC-E 146f.

[104] Ibid.

[105] SC 99f., SC-E 156f.

[106] SC 91, SC-E 145. The image of God opening his loving heart was, of course, a favorite with Luther.

Revelation, then is the personal self-communication of God's love for humanity. Already this points to the social emphasis in Bonhoeffer's interpretation of revelation.

In the fullness of his love, Christ the Stellvertreter first fulfills the law vicariously for all people; he thereby exposes that self-centeredness and isolation which, Bonhoeffer contends, was typical of humanity's relation to the law before Christ.[107] Then, in the same love, Christ goes in loneliness to the cross. In his death he also acts vicariously for humanity, bearing God's judgement upon everybody whose self-seeking [Ichsucht] had misinterpreted the law.[108] The resurrection is the triumph of vicarious love over misused law, of life over death, of the new humanity over the old humanity of Adam, of community over isolation.[109]

The divine love, which is a personal reality active among and for people in Christ, creates the community of the new humanity. When God's love is 'revealed' this *recreates* the community of humanity with God and the *community* of human beings with one another,[110] for God's Word is always simultaneously God's deed.[111]

> The preaching of God's love speaks of the community into which God *has* entered with each and every person—with all those who in utter solitude know themselves separated from God and other human beings and who believe this message.[112]

> The crucified and risen Christ is recognized by the church-community as God's incarnate love for us—as God's will to renew the covenant, to establish God's rule, and thus to create community [Gemeinschaft].[113]

---

[107] SC-E 147f; cf. SC-E 175. Bonhoeffer clearly accommodates his interpretation of law here to his own version of the soteriological problem. In isolation the sinner disposes over, or dominates the law, using it to make claims upon God (SC 93, SC-E 148). While this is related to the Pauline criticism of 'boasting' in the law, for Paul the problem of law was not so much individualistic isolation as its dividing communities of people, especially Jews and Gentiles; Bonhoeffer does not mention this. Nor does he here view the law problem in terms of the negative conscience, as in Luther; see the comparison on this point in Chapter 4.

[108] SC 95, SC-E 150.

[109] SC-E 151ff.

[110] SC-E 145.

[111] SC-E 142.

[112] SC 94, SC-E 149.

[113] SC 98, SC-E 154.

In Christ God loves human beings and opens the divine heart; and in giving God's own self to sinful human beings God renews them at the same time and thus makes the new community real and possible; but this means that *God's love wills community.*[114]

Most concretely, the Spirit through the Word actualizes the divine love in human hearts. Faith acknowledges the lordship of God's love, and the love of people for each other makes this lordship a social reality; "God's *will to rule* is the *will to love* God's church-community."[115] Christ gives people the certainty that they are loved, enabling them to love others. The love of Christ frees people from their self-imprisonment [Ichgebundenheit] and lets them love others; Christian existence is "unrestrictedly surrendering [Hingabe] to the other."[116] The other in the I-You relationship is now seen not as a claim, but as a gift.[117] Others, further, are loved *for their own sakes;* one does not love God in the neighbor, nor are neighbors loved to make them Christian—neighbors are loved for their own sake, and in *this* love of the human companions one serves the will of God.[118]

In this way, Stellvertretung, grounded in Christ, "is the life-principle of the new humanity." It is the Christological basis of that "being with one another" [Miteinander] and "active being for one another" [tätige Füreinander] which are the constitutive social acts of the Liebesgemeinschaft.[119] The sociality of Christ in his love for humanity personifies and creates the sociality of the new humanity.

Word and sacrament are the two specific forms in which Christ is present in the Spirit.[120]

Decisive is the social significance of Christ, who is present only in the church, that is, where the Christian church-community is united by preaching and the Lord's Supper in mutual Christian love.[121]

---

[114] SC 112, SC-E 173.

[115] SC 116, SC-E 177; italics mine.

[116] SC 113, SC-E 173.

[117] SC 107, SC-E 166.

[118] SC-E 169f.

[119] SC 117ff., SC-E 178ff. For more detail on the Geistgemeinschaft as Liebesgemeinschaft, see SC-E 167ff.

[120] SC-E 216, 226f., 260.

[121] SC 258, SC-E 138.

These two forms are *social* forms of the *Christus praesens,* and this
means more than the fact that they are events in and of the congregation;
it means that the form of *transcendence* is defined by Bonhoeffer's
socio-ethical understanding of *person.* Christ as the Kollektivperson of
the new humanity is present in the relations and encounters of human
persons who 'embody' Christ as independent, willing subjects. "In the
Word the most profound social nexus is established from the beginning.
The Word is social in character, not only in its origin but also in its
aim."[122] As an event in personal-communal relationships the Word
places the human person before "the ethical decision: 'for or against'.
The Protestant church addressed by preaching will always remain a
church of ethical personalism."[123] But beyond the ethical encounter of
wills which limit and check one another in the state of sin, the Word in
the 'other' person now communicates the divine love: when the other
declares God's grace and forgiveness, from 'outside' the self, the gospel
overcomes the isolation and illusions of the old self and conveys an
incomparable, 'objective' certainty.[124]

The sacraments, both eucharist and baptism, have the same social
character and intention as the Word;[125] they also, of course, have the
same content, purpose, and function as the Word. But the sacraments
have a distinct status. This is clarified by Bonhoeffer's correlation of
theological-Christological concepts with anthropological concepts; the
correlation is clearly present in *Sanctorum Communio,* but not developed in the detail found in the 1933 Christology lectures (as shown in
Chapter 5 below). Within the basic, social concept of person, Bonhoeffer identifies Geist and Natur (especially the body) as his two major
anthropological categories. There is a mutual reciprocity and interaction of the two, with Geist having the priority. On the theological side,
Bonhoeffer presents Christ as Person and the Holy Spirit as Geist, the
former 'embracing' and interpreting the latter. His view of Word and
sacrament unites the divine personal being with human personal being:
Christ in the Spirit is present as Word and sacrament corresponding to
Geist and Natur as the two basic anthropological concepts.

---

[122] SC 101, SC-E 158.
[123] SC 281, SC-E 237.
[124] SC-E 148f.; cf. SC-E 165f.
[125] SC-E 240ff.

Bonhoeffer does not have a perfectionist view of the Christian community. The *peccatorum communio* lives on in the *sanctorum communio*; the church is the kingdom of Christ in history, not the eschatological kingdom of God.[126] So the Spirit cannot be identified with the objective Geist of the church, nor Christ with the Kollektivperson of the church; Christ is indeed present in and as the church, but in a form which continually encounters it, breaking it up and building it up. *In* the visible, empirical church the *sanctorum communio*, as the communal presence of Christ, must be believed.[127] Bonhoeffer is not identifying Christ and church but describing their dialectical relationship. He wants to express the dynamics of *transformation* when the new humanity of Christ encounters and embraces the old humanity of Adam. The church, consequently, is not the consummated eschatological kingdom, nor the consecration of the *status quo ante,* but an actual anticipation of the eschatological reality of Christ in which real personal and social change occurs.

A related observation concerns the universal character of the Christology and ecclesiology within the theology of sociality. This absence of sectarianism must be stressed against the tendency of interpreters to read *Discipleship,* a decade later, as the logical outcome of *Sanctorum Communio.* But if *Discipleship* does polarize Christ and the church from the life of a secular world, this is *not* a direct continuation of the ecclesiology of *Sanctorum Communio;* Chapter 4 will show the new elements in Bonhoeffer's theology, personal experience and church-political situation which account for this polarization. In his first work, however, Bonhoeffer has a very catholic vision of Christ, humanity and the church. When he speaks of "Christus als Gemeinde existierend," he is insisting on the 'social intention' of the Christian doctrine of God, the social character of revelation in Christ, and the communal nature of the Christian life.[128] Of course, because it is a communal form of revelation, the church has its distinct life within the world. But when Bonhoeffer says that "Christ... is present [gegenwärtig] only in the church," this is the second half of the sentence which begins: "the social

---

[126] Cf. SC-E 288.

[127] SC-E 280.

[128] This is the meaning of the statements that the concept of God is only comprehensible when joined to the church (SC 85, SC-E 134), and that relation to Christ necessarily presupposes one's relation to the church (SC 81, SC-E 127; cf. SC-E 130, 137f.).

significance of Christ is decisive."[129] These statements cannot be taken out of context. Christ is the *reality of the new humanity,* superseding the old humanity of Adam. Christ, who is revealed in the life of the community of the new humanity, is therefore intrinsically related to *every person,* and to the corporate life of society.

Of course, in *Sanctorum Communio* Bonhoeffer is not yet asking about the relation of Christ to 'secular' people who may also be outside the church institution. But he does explicitly say that it would be wrong to regard the empirical church and the world as ultimate antagonists; the line of encounter and decision is found *within* the church itself, since the church is the world of Adam being encountered and transformed by the presence of the new humanity of Christ.[130] If faith means incorporation into the community of Christ, it is Christ who requires his community not only to preach, but also responsibly to speak to contemporary events in the world at large,[131] and to concern itself, as Bonhoeffer did, with questions such as "church and proletariat."[132] *Sanctorum Communio,* then, describes a relative distinction and a dialectical relationship between church and world; its Christology of Christ as the Stellvertreter of the new humanity has a catholic thrust which prevents an ecclesiological exclusivity.

In *Sanctorum Communio* Bonhoeffer's Christology, which interprets the kerygma of cross and resurrection by the vicarious love of the Stellvertreter, is intrinsically soteriological. To describe Christ as Stellvertreter is to describe his person and work in one; there is no separation of person and work.[133] Consistently, this Christology is intrinsically linked to the anthropology. If true human nature is to be for

---

[129] SC 258, SC-E 138; cf. SC-E 158f., where Bonhoeffer is explicitly criticizing *individualism.*

[130] SC 193, SC-E 283. Consistent with this are the statements that Christ, the Kollektivperson of the new humanity, means the reconciliation and justification of the *world* (SC-E 144), and that Christian eschatology is not only an eschatology of the church but also an eschatology of *Kultur* and *Natur* (SC 194, SC-E 283).

[131] SC 172, SC-E 251.

[132] SC-E 271ff. Seeberg objected in a marginal comment: "Does this really belong in the framework of this study? If so, only brief or rewrite" (SC-A 324, SC 290, SC-E 271). The first published version, partially subsidized by the Seeberg Foundation, omitted the section!

[133] Nor is the Chalcedonian question of the two natures discussed, though the classical formulation is implicit in the understanding of Christ as both God's love for humanity and the representative of human beings before God.

others in the mutuality of love in social existence, Christ embodies this true humanity.[134] And if human beings have forsaken their true personal and corporate being for an isolated, self-serving, domination of others, then Christ the Stellvertreter reverses this condition; Christ's freedom in love overcomes human self-imprisonment. The Christology is therefore a soteriology which is intrinsically correlated to the human condition which Bonhoeffer delineates. He has obviously thought out this relationship fairly clearly in the process of his theological innovation. The wider significance of this is that in his first book Bonhoeffer not only began to focus the soteriological problem which is distinctive of his theology,[135] but he also anticipated the main theme which appears in the Christology of the *Letters:* Christ as "the man for others" is directly developed from Christ the Stellvertreter who is the Kollektivperson of the true humanity.[136]

Having presented the church as the new humanity of Christ, and theologically described its life and structure in relation to human sociality in the primal and broken communities, Bonhoeffer then applies his comprehensive theological position to a number of specific ecclesiological questions.[137] These discussions are fairly brief, and altogether comprise a relatively small portion of the book; indeed, Bonhoeffer used much more space developing his social conceptuality than discussing these specific ecclesiological subjects. The application of the theology of sociality in these discussions is by no means unimportant; but it adds no new material to the basic conceptuality we have presented. Therefore the significance of *Sanctorum Communio* as the foundation of Bonhoeffer's theological development can now be summarized.

---

[134] This is why Bonhoeffer said that the primal state can only be understood "backwards" from the revelation in Christ.

[135] See further discussion on this in Chapter 3 and especially in Chapter 4.

[136] To be sure, the theme of the weakness of Christ in the *Letters* has special significance for the critique of religion; but even this, as later argument will demonstrate, is related to the soteriological problem which appears in his earliest works.

[137] The subjects discussed are: the worshipping congregation, the local congregation and house churches, preaching and Scripture, the preacher and personal faith, baptism and eucharist, *ecclesiolae in ecclesia,* the care of souls, impersonal urban churches, authority and freedom, councils and synods, and church and proletariat; cf. SC-E 226ff.

C. THE SOCIALITY OF CHRIST AND HUMANITY

The programmatic character of Bonhoeffer's statement about "the significance of the sociological category for theology" and "the social intention of all the basic Christian concepts" is indisputable. In *Sanctorum Communio* he develops a theological phenomenology of the personal-social character of human existence rooted in a social interpretation of God's relation to humanity in Christ. The exposition above yields several major conclusions about *Sanctorum Communio* as Bonhoeffer's first and formative theological work.

First, it is beyond any doubt that the ecclesiology is set within the more comprehensive context of Bonhoeffer's theology of sociality. When he states that he intends to develop a Christian social philosophy in place of the idealist social philosophy of immanent Geist, this includes much more than a doctrine of the church; it also involves more than his argument that the church is a distinctive social structure when analyzed from a theological perspective. It means, as the programmatic statement in the Preface plainly indicates, that the whole of theology and all its central concepts are interpreted in a social conceptuality.

It follows, secondly, that sociality informs Bonhoeffer's discussion of *all* the basic Christian concepts: person, creation, sin, and revelation. Here it is not necessary either to summarize again the complex of ideas which together comprise the category 'sociality,' or to review how these are employed in expounding central theological subjects. There are two aspects of Bonhoeffer's argument, however, which should be emphasized, because they are so important for his future theology and, indeed, his own life.

The first, of course, is the fundamental theme of this study: *the sociality of Christ and humanity*. Bonhoeffer understands human persons as social beings, their personal life bound up in a network of relations with others and with corporate communities. But human sociality is grounded in the social being and activity of God as seen in the revelation in Christ. God creates and wills simultaneously both individual persons in their uniqueness and corporate human communities. The Word of God encounters both individuals and corporate structures, and in these encounters of God and human beings history is made. God is involved in the historical life of humanity; indeed, one may say that God not only speaks to human beings in their history, but that God has a history in and with humanity. Concretely, the human person is created to live a personal-social existence in community with

God and other human beings. Sin disrupts the created primal community, with contradictory consequences for both individual and corporate
life. In Christ, God reveals that love which is the basis and bond of all
community, so creating the 'new humanity' in which the true life of
Christ and humanity is actualized in the world, transforming human life
so that its created origin and its eschatological goal are the realities
which shape human life in the world.

The second aspect that must be highlighted is Bonhoeffer's treatment of *transcendence*. This, too, is interpreted in terms of sociality.
Transcendence is not God's otherness beyond humanity and above the
world; the holy, creating, sustaining, and reconciling love of God which
is revealed in Christ is God's lordship *in* the world *among human beings*.
To be sure, Bonhoeffer is never in danger of identifying God and
humanity, any more than of confusing Christ and the church. But that
relational duality which characterizes the life of human persons is a
reflection of God's relatedness to humanity. In other words, God is
present in the encounter of individuals and their communities as
Kollektivpersonen. The 'other,' as individual person and corporate
person, is the 'form' in which God is really present as the divine 'Other'
in the world. Transcendence in Bonhoeffer's theology of sociality, then,
is *socio-ethical transcendence*. Its form is the social form of human
personal life, and its content and goal is to create and redeem community
between human beings and Christ and among human beings themselves.

A third conclusion is that already in *Sanctorum Communio* Bonhoeffer demonstrates that *anthropology* is inseparable from his Christology
and has a fundamental role in his theology. There are several indications
of this. One is the character of the Christology itself: as Stellvertreter,
Christ is the reality of the *new humanity*; his transcendence is his
presence as lord in human form; his saving work is to transform the
community of sin into the community of the Spirit of love, and this
community with God only exists *as community with other human
beings*. Another sign is the *methodological* importance of anthropology.
In his foundation chapter on the Christian idea of person, for example,
Bonhoeffer states that the concepts of person, community, and God have
an essential and indissoluble relation to each other; while acknowledging that one can reach a Christian view of community either from the
concept of God or from that of the human person, he chooses to begin
from the anthropological end, and then proceeds to a lengthy analysis of
concepts of person and community in four philosophical anthropolo-

gies.[138] Other instances of this methodological procedure could be given. Again, the elaborate and highly sophisticated conceptuality of sociality is basically an *anthropological phenomenology.* To be sure, it is repeatedly informed by theological criteria, but it remains an anthropological schema. It is quite significant, and typical of Bonhoeffer, that he draws theological concepts into this anthropological conceptuality rather than, as Barth tended to do, establishing all community and relationships in the inner-Trinitarian life and then deducing the anthropological sphere from them; consequently Bonhoeffer spends far more time in intricate discussion with contemporary philosophers and sociologists than with the dogmatic concepts of the classical theological tradition. Finally, the significance of anthropology in his theology is demonstrated by the clear set of concepts which he articulates and which recur in his following works. Within the comprehensive conceptuality of sociality and its central idea of person, the two basic anthropological concepts are Geist and Natur; though the latter is not treated at length in his first book, it is clearly present. Geist, interpreted by person, refers to the human person as a self-conscious and spontaneously willing being. The voluntarism, which links person and Geist, also includes human historicity; historicity, further, is intrinsic to Bonhoeffer's *ethical* definition of the person. (While *Sanctorum Communio* contains little discussion of specific ethical issues, it provides the conceptual basis in the anthropology which moves Bonhoeffer into concrete ethical thinking and action in the 1930s.)

The fourth and final conclusion concerns *soteriology.* In *Sanctorum Communio* Bonhoeffer gives a fairly clear indication of the specific anthropological problem which pervades his early theology. His account of sin is specific, not vague; this specificity involves clearly delineated anthropological dynamics: power, egocentric self-seeking, domination and exploitation, and individual isolation and corporate fragmentation. This is the syndrome which stands in contrast to the love and mutual self-giving of the primal community. This is the syndrome which the love of Christ the Stellvertreter overcomes, thereby inaugurating the new humanity and talking up the *peccatorum communio* into the transforming life of the *sanctorum communio.* This soteriological problem becomes prominent in Bonhoeffer's next book, *Act and Being.*

---

[138] SC 19ff., SC-E 35ff.

Chapter 3

CHRISTIAN ANTHROPOLOGY AND SOCIAL ONTOLOGY IN *ACT AND BEING*

With *Sanctorum Communio* complete, Bonhoeffer had laid down the foundation of his thought with the impressive conceptuality of his theology of sociality. Though he was obliged by university custom to write an Habilitationsschrift to secure a teaching position, there is a more intrinsic connection between his first and second works than external requirement. But the connection takes some discovering.

From February 1928 to February 1929 Bonhoeffer served as assistant pastor to the German congregation in Barcelona. There he prepared *Sanctorum Communio* for publication, and began work on the second book. Reinhold Seeberg advised Bonhoeffer, following the classical German approach to the training of a systematic theologian, to gain more expertise with the methods and problems of biblical and historical scholarship. He suggested, accordingly, that an historical study of the problem of ethics in scholasticism might be appropriate; this could lead eventually to a career as an historian of Christian ethics, and a work on the history of ethics from the Sermon on the Mount to the contemporary period.[1] While it is interesting to observe Seeberg encouraging him in the direction of ethics, Bonhoeffer, with characteristic independence, had his own ideas. During 1929 he wrote to Seeberg, and to his friend Rössler, that he was planning a systematic work on the question of *consciousness*

---

[1] Letter of October 19, 1928, GS III 17f., DBW 10 105.

[Bewusstsein] and *conscience* [Gewissen]; he related these to some current reading in Luther, and to an interest in the "problem of the child in theology."[2] Certainly the concerns with consciousness in philosophy and theology and with conscience are central to *Act and Being*, while Luther and "the child" appear at important points in the argument. Noting well that consciousness and conscience are questions which fall naturally in the area of theological anthropology, we ask: what is the real subject matter of this book on *"act and being"?*

A. THE SUBJECT OF *ACT AND BEING:* THEOLOGICAL ANTHROPOLOGY

How does an essay on "transcendental philosophy and ontology in systematic theology"[3] fit into Bonhoeffer's theological development? The secondary literature gives a bewildering variety of answers to this question. One line of interpretation puts the emphasis on theological epistemology: Bethge, Godsey, Marty and others favor this view.[4] A second, related view suggests that the book is chiefly concerned with the nature of revelation: Phillips, Sherman, and Woelfel, for example, share this judgement.[5] Heinrich Ott gives a third view, combining the first two in his own way: the basic issue is the "mode of the knowledge of God," pursued via a new ontological interpretation of revelation which leads to a new theological epistemology; Ott stresses the importance of Bonhoeffer's "sociological category" (understood to be the church as a

---

2   To Seeberg, July 20, 1928 and October 10, 1928: GS III 15ff., DBW 10 81ff., 102 ff.; to Rössler, August 7, 1928: GS I 53, DBW 10 90ff.

3   The subtitle of the book, not printed in the first English translation.

4   Bethge, DB-E 122, 133f.; Godsey, *op. cit.,* 55; Marty, *The Place of Bonhoeffer* (New York: Association Press, 1962), 82. Bethge sees epistemology related to ecclesiology as a way of pursuing the concreteness of revelation. Godsey speaks of the epistemology of revelation in the context of two competing philosophical traditions informing the theology at the time. Marty, none too clearly, refers to "a sociology of epistemology."

5   Phillips, consistent with his overall thesis, stresses revelation in the form of ecclesiology (*op. cit.,* 57). Sherman sees the question of revelation posed by competing types of theology (*The Place of Bonhoeffer,* 87). Woelfel, in his book *Bonhoeffer's Theology: Classical and Revolutionary* (Nashville: Abingdon Press, 1970), sees as the "key issue ... the relationship between philosophy and theology" as this is concentrated in "the resolution of the problem of revelation in the concept of the church" (55, 283).

personal community) for the ontological–existential being of revelation, with the consequence that theological thinking and knowing have a fundamentally communal–dialogical character.[6] Fourth, and closely related to Ott's position (though ignoring sociality), is the view of Dumas. He sees the book as methodological, with Bonhoeffer taking his ontological approach (as Dumas interprets it) to deal with the reality of revelation in the church as this bears on philosophical and theological epistemology.[7] Moltmann's view is a fifth, generally related to these though not spelled out in detail: *Act and Being* is a work on "theological ontology" which continues Bonhoeffer's interest with sociality in the previous book and relates it here to the interpretation of revelation.[8] Müller gives a sixth option: *Act and Being* is basically an ecclesiological work, the partner of *Sanctorum Communio*. It deals with the theological foundation of the church, showing how the nature of revelation— understood as a dialectical unity of act and being—requires the church Gemeinschaft; the social reality of the church is necessarily grounded in the nature of revelation.[9] Finally, another view considers theological methodology, especially the relation between philosophy and theology, as the official subject matter; however, this writer says, Bonhoeffer perhaps "is more interested in exploring the nature of the church than in pursuing the original argument of the book."[10]

This is an impressive range of disagreement. Yet each of these views manages to highlight one or more aspects of Bonhoeffer's discussion; epistemology, revelation, philosophy and theology, sociality, ontology, ecclesiology, and theological schools and methods are all present in the book. Even though these divergent views overlap considerably, the various interpretations are even less successful in relating the themes they highlight to other aspects of Bonhoeffer's discussion. This lack of agreement and clarity over so fundamental a matter as the central subject of *Act and Being* suggests that a major component of Bonhoeffer's early theology has not been recognized by these interpreters. Consequently, they cannot agree on the book's central subject nor show how the several

---

[6] Ott, *Wirklichkeit und Glaube* I, 200–208.

[7] Dumas, *op. cit.,* 97ff.; cf. 112, 114, 116.

[8] Moltmann, "The Lordship of Christ and Human Society," in Moltmann and Weissbach, *Two Studies in the Theology of Bonhoeffer* (New York: Charles Scribner's Sons, 1967), 21, 47ff.

[9] Müller, *Von der Kirche zur Welt,* pp. 117ff., 147f., 151f., 36f.

[10] William Kuhns, *In Pursuit of Dietrich Bonhoeffer* (Dayton, Ohio: Pflaum Press, 1967), 27, 29.

aspects of the discussion relate to this. An additional problem is this: how one identifies the concern of *Act and Being* will largely determine how its connection to *Sanctorum Communio* is understood.

Bonhoeffer himself is partly responsible for this confusion. The book is a tour de force. Furthermore, its various statements of purpose do not always clearly reveal what he is actually doing. Indeed, one may say that he was not totally aware of a basic concern which occupied him as he wrote the book. Seen within the wider context of his writings and the movement of his thought over several years, however, his actual preoccupation in *Act and Being* is unmistakable. Continuing to approach theology in terms of sociality, he now concentrates on *theological anthropology.* Theological anthropology, in fact, is the missing link which the secondary literature overlooks. This judgement will be substantiated in a moment.

Given theological anthropology as the central focus of *Act and Being*, there are three interrelated concerns which intrinsically link *Sanctorum Communio* and the Habilitationsschrift. These concerns are more deeply rooted in Bonhoeffer's own thinking than the fact that 'actualist' and ontological positions in philosophy and theology were vying with each other in the early decades of the century, though this was indeed true. These issues are predominantly, though not exclusively, anthropological; they are handled with the conceptuality of sociality, which itself is somewhat modified in the process.

First, the issue of 'act' and 'being' is implicitly present in *Sanctorum Communio* in the way the individual, ethical person is related to corporate life. One both wills, decides, and *acts* as an individual, responsible person at the same time as living in basic modes of corporate *being.* People have a 'being' in both Adam and Christ which they *actualize* and make their own by their decisions. (The analysis of the problem of original sin, as pointed out in the previous chapter, clearly anticipates the more deliberate treatment of the act–being dialectic in *Act and Being.*) Christ, also, has a 'being' with and for humanity in his social presence which simultaneously encounters people with revelation and transforms human life in the community of the new humanity; Christian existence, accordingly, is an interaction of personal faith and being–in–a–community.

Secondly, while this implicit act–being dialectic is found in *Sanctorum Communio*, the main emphasis in the central concept of person is *actualistic.* This is more evident in the anthropology than the Christology. The ethical decision and responsibility of the person is stressed to the point where Bonhoeffer says that "the person ever and again arises and passes away in time." But this polemic against his view of the metaphysics and anthropology of idealism really involves an extreme *fragmentation* of personal life: it cannot, as such, give an adequate alternative account of the *continuity* of human life, that is, of the *being* of a person who is involved in the drama of creation, sin, and salvation. This is a sharp, unresolved issue in *Sanctorum Communio* which is explicitly taken up in *Act and Being*.

Third, and at the deepest level, Bonhoeffer brings to the fore in *Act and Being* the soteriological problem—already adumbrated in *Sanctorum Communio*—at the heart of his theological anthropology. This is the problem of the powerful, dominant self who, particularly in his[11] intellectual activity, adopts an autonomous, self–referring, isolated and self–enclosed attitude to reality. This problem is crucial to Bonhoeffer's attack on philosophical anthropology in *Act and Being*, and its centrality explains why a preoccupation with 'consciousness' is a starting point for the book. Not only does concern with this soteriological problem pervade the whole book; it does so because the academic treatise had great existential significance for Bonhoeffer himself. The next chapter will show conclusively that the posture of this powerful self corresponded to Bonhoeffer's own personal attitude, and that this was a problem agitating him existentially even at the time he was *intellectually* offering a theological resolution of it in this book. In *Act and Being*, then, we find Bonhoeffer indirectly working at the central anthropological problem in his early theology. He articulates it in this book, and continues the formulation with the same dynamics and the same terminology for several years. This consistency will later require us to designate it as *the* soteriological problem in his theology. It is the problem of power, which, in its personal dimension, is best understood specifically as the *power of the ego*.[12] I refer here to the later argument because it clarifies the following analysis of *Act and Being*.

These three issues lead Bonhoeffer from his first to his second book. Their predominantly anthropological character results in his treating the relation of 'act' and 'being' under the rubric of theological anthropology. That theological anthropology is the main subject of *Act and Being* will become fully evident in the exposition of its argument. Initially, however, this is confirmed by other pieces of internal and external

---

[11] See note 36 below.

[12] Definition of the term 'ego' is reserved for the beginning of Chapter 4.

evidence: the structure of the work itself, the essential recapitulation of its content in Bonhoeffer's anthropological inaugural lecture five months later, and the repetition of the same teaching in a 1932–33 seminar on theological anthropology.

To understand the structure of the book I designate the two leading motifs of the argument as the *anthropological question* and the *anthropological problem.*[13] The question is concerned with the 'act' and 'being' dimensions of human existence, that is, with existential and ontological perspectives on human life. The anthropological–soteriological *problem* is concerned with the autonomous self, particularly as found in the cognitive activities of the dominant, isolated ego imprisoned in itself.

The structure and argument of the work may now be briefly indicated.[14] The work is simply designed, having three parts. Part A deals with the *"autonomous understanding of Dasein in philosophy."*[15] Philosophical epistemologies are examined as a way to disclose the presuppositions of philosophical anthropologies. In analyzing philosophical anthropology through epistemology, Bonhoeffer is not just recognizing a major preoccupation of modern philosophy. His more fundamental reason is that "the meaning of epistemology is anthropology";[16] in the last analysis "epistemology is the attempt of the I to understand itself."[17] With this premise he examines both transcendentalist–idealist (act) and ontological (being) traditions. In doing so, the *anthropological problem* quickly comes to the fore.[18] Common to both

---

[13] Only a terminological alteration of Bonhoeffer's language is involved in this distinction; his formulation, "das Akt–Sein Problem," in the titles of the three parts could just as properly have used the word "Frage."

[14] Appendix D in the original manuscript of this book, available from University Microfilms, gives a more detailed commentary on the structure of *Akt und Sein* and the movement of its argument, showing how these disclose theological anthropology as its main subject. Reference to the table of contents of the German text is helpful while reading the following pages.

[15] AB 33, italics mine.

[16] AB 25, AB 30.

[17] AS 27, AB 33.

[18] For this reason the anthropological question of the 'act' and 'being' dimensions of human life receives little discussion in Part A. His exposition of Heidegger's combination of being and decision in Dasein (AB 71f.), and of Pryzwara's attempt to establish a continuity of human being qua creature (AB 73f.), are the main discussions of this question. The discussion of the anthropological question is found in detail in Part B, sections 1 and 2. Here Bonhoeffer examines the theological anthropologies which are correlated to the actualistic

philosophical traditions Bonhoeffer diagnoses the problem of the autonomous I trying to understand itself from itself. But a theology of revelation holds that an understanding of Dasein is impossible on this basis. This presupposition of autonomous philosophical anthropology is a fundamental *mis*understanding. Truly to understand human existence, an independent starting point must be found from which this problem can be overcome.

Part B, accordingly, offers revelation in Christ as the premise for human self–understanding. Both revelation and human life are personal realities which therefore must be comprehended in terms of sociality. Hence the hinge of the book is Part B, section 3, where the Christian community is presented as the place for understanding Dasein, because here revelation encounters human beings in a socio–personal mode of being. From this vantage point, a proper understanding of human being, both in the church-community and generally, may be gained. The church-community is the place where the anthropological problem of the autonomous I can be overcome, and where the anthropological question of act and being can be answered. Both the problem and the question are treated in terms of the sociality of revelation and of human existence. Only in the context of a community of persons grounded in and encountered by the self–revealing Christ can the self be freed from its autonomous, isolated, knowing I which violates reality by understanding everything from itself. Again, only because the present Christ reveals in his own person the unity of act and being can human beings be understood as a unity of act and being, whether the concrete human existence is a 'being in Adam' or a 'being in Christ.'

Having established the main lines of a Christian anthropology on the basis of revelation, Bonhoeffer can then develop in Part C "the concrete doctrine of humanity 'in Adam' and 'in Christ.'" Its central category is the 'creature,' both as fallen and as restored in Christ. This is described as "the concrete doctrine of humanity" because it gives much more detailed treatment to issues such as: individual responsible acts in relation to 'being–in' a determinate mode of human existence (Adam or Christ); flight from the loss of one's true self; the conscience of the sinner and of the Christian person; justification; the continuity of human existence; creation as history and nature; and the roles of the past and the eschatological future

---

and ontological concepts of revelation, which in turn are informed by the two philosophical traditions.

as determinants of the creatureliness of the Christian person. The diagnosis and overcoming of the *anthropological problem* and the answer to the anthropological question, previously given at the end of Part B, inform the discussion of all these topics in Part C.

This brief outline makes it plain that *Act and Being* begins with a critique of philosophical anthropology, proceeds to interpret revelation—in a social ontology—as the foundation for a Christian understanding of human existence, and concludes by building on this foundation a more concrete Christian anthropology. There are, to be sure, various other themes woven into this subtle, tightly reasoned, and somewhat repetitious book. Its main subject, however, is theological anthropology.

Further confirmation of this subject matter is given by Bonhoeffer himself. His inaugural lecture removes any lingering doubt. Its title, "The Anthropological Question in Contemporary Philosophy and Theology," and explicit phrases within it, clearly identify theological anthropology as its subject.[19] The lecture was delivered on July 31, 1930, six months after the Habilitationsschrift was completed.[20] The inaugural lecture, in fact, is nothing less than a summary of the argument of *Act and Being*. Once this identity of content is recognized, we realize that nothing is more natural than a newly appointed professor giving an inaugural lecture on the subject of his current work and the issues foremost in his mind.[21]

The conceptuality of the lecture is equivalent to that in the book.[22] The movement of the argument is the same. The lecture discusses the same philosophers and theologians in the same groupings as the book, and Bonhoeffer makes the same identification of their several contributions and weaknesses.[23] Most significantly, the same basic problem is diagnosed: the knowing I which dominates a violated world of its own construing in the solitariness of self–imprisonment.[24] The same issues

---

[19] GS III 62–84, DBW 10 357ff., CW I 50–69. Note that the exact words of the first half of the lecture title, "die Frage nach dem Menschen," occur in the introduction to *Akt und Sein;* cf. AS 25.

[20] DB-E 135.

[21] Bethge also recognizes the identity of subject matter in the book and the lecture when he uses *Akt und Sein* to suggest the content of the missing second last page of the lecture manuscript; cf. GS III 83; cf. DBW 10 377, n. 53.

[22] The lecture concepts of 'limit' [Grenze] and 'possibility' [Möglichkeit] are analogous to the categories of 'act' and 'being' in the treatise.

[23] Scheler, Heidegger, Grisebach; Tillich, Barth, Holl, Bultmann, Gogarten.

[24] GS III 81f., DBW 10 375f., CW I 66f.

are discussed,[25] and treated with the same theological conceptuality and propositions.[26] The inaugural lecture, then, confirms what the structure of *Act and Being* shows: its main subject is theological anthropology.

Yet a third confirmation of theological anthropology as the central subject of *Act and Being* is found in the notes from Bonhoeffer's seminar given in the winter semester of 1932–33: "Dogmatische Übungen: Probleme einer theologischen Anthropologie." Bethge indicates that he formulated the second half of the title from the contents, in order to supplement the formal, official title;[27] there can be no doubt, however, after studying the seminar notes, that this formulation is correct.[28] The issues discussed not only fall within the area of theological anthropology; they had all been previously discussed in the Habilitationsschrift and the inaugural lecture.[29] There is, to be sure, a new element in the seminar. This is the emphasis on the discipline of the Christian life in worship, reading the Bible, meditation, and prayer. It clearly derives from Bonhoeffer's commitment to a personal faith in the summer of 1932, discussed below in Chapter 4. But the new element does not

---

[25] The proper context for gaining genuine human self–understanding; the unity of human existence which includes both continuity of being and historical–existential encounter and change; the effectual Grenze which liberates as it limits a person; and so on.

[26] Christ present in the church-community liberating people from their dominating self–isolation, and from relating to their neighbors as things rather than persons; revelation as the point of reference for true human self–understanding; the concrete determination of human existence 'in Adam' and 'in Christ'; human life 'in bezug auf' Christ as Grenze; the dialectic of future and past in the Christian life; and the overcoming of conscience in faith.

[27] DB 264f., 1091 n. 17.

[28] DB 1091–95, DBW 12 178-199.

[29] The main seminar topics are: the Christian self–understanding is gained not by reflection on the self but by looking away from the self to Christ who is present in the 'other'; the human person does not exist as an object but as an historical Existenz in relations with others; human being is always either a 'being in sin' or 'being in Christ'; the unity, wholeness, and continuity of the self in light of the theological distinction between the 'old I' and the 'new I,' and his criticism of Barth's treatment of this issue; the wholeness of the 'new I' in light of the doctrine of justification; the relation of Glaube and Glaubigkeit ("religious experience"; cf. GS III 97, DBW 10 421) in Christian existence; the personal community of the church where the continuity of the self is established through God and the neighbor; being–in–the–church and the freedom of grace and revelation in faith *(act);* the problem of conscience; and, finally, Christian existence as ultimately determined not by the past but by the future.

contradict the fact that the seminar concentrated on the basic issues earlier treated most fully in *Act and Being*; these are issues of theological anthropology. Bethge is quite right in pointing to the intimate connection with Bonhoeffer's earlier writings, especially the "anthropological inaugural lecture" and *Act and Being*.[30]

Having established that theological anthropology is the primary concern of *Act and Being*, we proceed to Bonhoeffer's critique of, and appropriation from, philosophical anthropology. Because the critique is predominant, and because the anthropological problem raises the theological question of human liberation from an "autonomous understanding of Dasein," this part of the argument is treated under the rubric of soteriology.

B. PHILOSOPHICAL ANTHROPOLOGY AND THE SOTERIOLOGICAL PROBLEM

If the focus of *Act and Being* is on theological anthropology, there is an even more specific concern within the anthropological focus. This is soteriology. The discussion of philosophical anthropology poses the problem of the self turned in upon itself, seeking to place itself in the truth, individualistically isolated, adopting a mastering attitude to the world through its knowing—in short, making the self God, and putting human companions, nature, and God under its power. Given this problem, the theological answer articulated in the second and third parts of the book must necessarily relate Christ, revelation and grace to this anthropological problem. In Part C Bonhoeffer argues that human being can only be concretely understood, in light of revelation, in one of two modes: 'being in Adam,' i.e., in sin, or 'being in Christ.'[31] Since he allows only these two options, and since he argues that the anthropological problem is only exposed and overcome by the revelation of Christ, this justifies describing the central anthropological problem as a *soteriologi-*

---

30 DB 264; cf. also the two fragments of Bonhoeffer's own notes for the seminar, GS III 162–165, DBW 12 192-97, including the explicit references to the question of "Sein und... Akt." Several issues, concepts, and assertions of *Act and Being* may also be found in a text contemporaneous with the seminar on theological anthropology, namely Bonhoeffer's lengthy review article on Karl Heim's *Glaube und Denken;* cf. GS III 138–159, DBW 12 213-31.

31 Each of these determinate modes of being involves an interaction of 'act' and 'being.'

cal problem. Soteriology, in its simplest definition, deals with the saving activity of Christ among human beings who are alienated from God, from each other, and themselves.[32] The question of 'act' and 'being,' then, must be seen in relation to the soteriological problem which permeates the book. Failure to do so would violate the cardinal premise of Part C: theologically understood, human being (including its 'act' dimension) is concretely always either a being–in–sin or a being–in–faith.

Bonhoeffer's critique of philosophical anthropologies consistently drives to the diagnosis of one crucial problem. Hence it is unnecessary to review his analysis of all the philosophers discussed.[33] His diagnosis and his objection to the anthropological premise in both transcendental-ist–idealist and ontological traditions is this:

> The offense against Christian thinking in any autonomous self-under-standing is that it believes human beings to be capable of giving truth to themselves.... But here [in Bonhoeffer's theology] truth means only that reference to God which Christian theology does not hold possible save in the *word* of God that is spoken to about and to human beings in the revelation of law and gospel....
>
> Thinking is as little able as good works to deliver the *cor curvum in se* from itself.[34]

This summary judgement, which should not be isolated from his appreciation for the constructive philosophical insights discussed shortly, is reiterated and spelled out by innumerable statements throughout the book. They are so frequent, and so consistent with the passages on the soteriological problem throughout his early theology, that we must conclude: in *Act and Being* the soteriological problem characteristic of Bonhoeffer's thought is urgently pressing to the fore. (This is not to minimize, however, the analysis of various issues in philosophy and theology which he certainly undertakes in the book.) A concise review of the statements spelling out the summary just quoted confirms the importance of the soteriological problem, and shows that more is in-volved than a dispassionate analysis of types of philosophy.[35] The

---

[32] For a fuller consideration of this, see the discussion in Chapter 4, "Power as a soteriological problem."

[33] A summary of his critical exposition of the main philosophers is given in Appendix D; see note 14 above.

[34] AS 73f., AB 79f.

[35] It may be argued with considerable plausibility that Bonhoeffer does not always do justice to the philosophers he discusses, and that he sometimes pays

composite portrait which emerges informs the criticism of all philosophers and theologians treated in the book.

The man[36] with the 'autonomous self–understanding' who considers himself capable, by his own knowing, of finding the truth about human existence and placing himself in that truth, has the following characteristics. His is an autonomous I, understanding himself from himself and by his own power.[37] His existence, consequently, is isolated and individualistic.[38] His being and thinking are imprisoned, caught in his own system, closed in upon himself; his fundamental orientation is that of the *cor curvum in se*.[39] Yet his knowing I regards itself as the source of self–understanding, as the point of departure for philosophy, and, indeed, as the point of reference for the world and reality itself.[40] He has, in fact, assumed the role of God, as a creator and lord over all.[41] He thereby subjects everything to his own authority and power, dominating and violating reality; he 'masters' other people, nature, and even God.[42]

The next chapter contains a systematic analysis of several such portraits throughout Bonhoeffer's early theology. Here the question

---

insufficient attention to their specific contexts and concerns. This is a complex question, however, and to pursue it now would lead us far astray. But two brief notes are pertinent: first, the philosophers who reviewed the book were very critical, especially of Bonhoeffer's oversimplification in consistently forcing the epistemological problem back to idealism (cf. DB 172, 169; DB-E 100, 97); second, Bonhoeffer's own almost subterranean personal involvement in the anthropological problem of the book is largely responsible for this distortion (cf. Bethge's observation on this point, quoted below).

36 Because of the autobiographical reference in this passage, discussed below and especially in Chapter 4, I have deliberately used masculine language in this passage.

37 AB 31, 36, 45f., 49f., 66, 72, 76, 90, 137, 141f., 147f.

38 AB 42, 45, 80, 87, 126, 138f., 142, 147ff., 161.

39 AB 36, 39, 42f., 46, 58, 72, 75, 76, 80, 89, 137, 144, 146f., 150, 157, 161.

40 AB 35, 39, 72, 87.

41 AB 42f., 44f., 45, 50f., 53, 64, 66, 76ff., 88, 137, 141, 150.

42 AS 32, AB 39 (thought as "Herr"); AS 36, AB 43 (bearing in himself the possibility of "overpowering" [Bewältigung] the world); AS 39, AB 46 ("Vollmacht" of the I); AS 58, AB 64 ("das Absolute... zu bewältigung"); AS 61, AB 67 ("die Bewältigung des Seins durch das erkennende Ich"); AS 71, AB 76 (being falls under "die Gewalt des denkenden Ich"); AS 89f., AB 94; AS 136, AB 137f. (sin is the "Vergewaltigung des Daseins (Geschöpfseins)"; AS 140, AB 141 ("'sich als Herrn seiner Welt wissende Denken'" corresponds to isolation); AS 144f., AB 146; AS 149, AB 150 ("Gewalt des Ich"); AS 152, AB 153 (the creation for fallen humanity is "seine eigene, vergewaltigte, "gedeutete, Welt").

arises: how are we to explain the striking recurrence of these statements throughout the book? Subsequent argument will show that the composite picture which emerges from them has a double significance: it is identical with the description of the soteriological problem which permeates the first decade of Bonhoeffer's theology; it is also to a large degree a self–portrait of the theologian himself, whose urgent existential concern is expressed in this theology. Bethge, without providing the documentation given here, points to this phenomenon in *Act and Being*, acknowledging that its theology has what I call an 'autobiographical dimension.'

> However, behind the highly abstract discourse, which the uninitiated can scarcely follow, hides a *passionate personal involvement*. Bonhoeffer's most characteristic concern was at stake in the insistence upon the *extra nos* and *pro nobis* of salvation. His own difficulties sharpened his sensitivity to every breach in the system through which deadly self–reflection might enter and establish its secret mastery.[43]

But to the reader who is not a novice, this "passionate personal involvement" is not even barely concealed; it is conspicuously evident. Indeed, it is a major part of the explanation for the composite portrait which these recurrent statements sketch.

Bethge's observation puts the emphasis on a self–reflection which is contrary to the faith which looks directly to Christ and away from the self. Self–reflection, Bethge continues, corresponds to solitude, whereas faith (in Bonhoeffer's understanding of Christ's presence in sociality) involves community.[44] This is certainly a crucial part of Bonhoeffer's argument. But it is not the whole picture. We must understand this self–imprisoned self–reflection (the attempt of the isolated I to understand itself from itself) in light of Bonhoeffer's repeated references to the *power* of the knowing and interpreting I. Thought is a "lord," "almighty" in its power. The "thinking" and "knowing I" is described as "overpowering" and "violating" all reality. Under the limitless power of intellect and reason, the creation becomes for the fallen man "his own, violated, 'interpreted' world."[45] Such intellectual aggressiveness allows

---

[43] DB 170, DB-E 134, italics mine. A full consideration of this autobiographical dimension is given in Chapter 4.

[44] DB 170, DB-E 134f.

[45] The notion of the 'interpreted' world of the fallen person's knowing and thinking recurs in other crucial passages presented below. In contrasting this with the 'reality' in which a person may live with God and others, Bonhoeffer means to point to the use of intellectual pursuits in the interest of selfish self–advancement and as a form of power people may gain over others; he also wants

one to conceive a God in one's own image, or to imagine that one can seize God in some intellectual system.[46] This preoccupation with intellectual power is an essential part of the soteriological problem in Bonhoeffer's theology. The isolated self–reflection Bethge mentions must be seen in this context.

Bonhoeffer's analysis of philosophical anthropologies, then, is heavily informed by a concern with a particular soteriological problem which has profound import that extends far beyond the explicit issues of 'act' and 'being.' This concern, furthermore, is deeply rooted in the struggles of the theologian's own inner life. Consequently, while particular criticisms are often penetrating, his polemical generalizations about philosophy need to be viewed with considerable critical caution. Their tendency to reduce all philosophy in the direction of an absolute idealism derives from the overriding urgency, for the theologian himself, of the soterio-logical problem. In other words: the problem which agitated Bonhoeffer personally, and on which he concentrated theologically, was—to put it briefly—the omnicompetence of the knowing mind; this fits better with an absolute idealism than with Kant's critical philosophy, for example; but since all philosophy represents, to a greater or lesser degree, a confidence in the human intellect, and since Bonhoeffer found this intellectual power problematic in himself, he attacks all philosophy; he does so by tending to reduce it to the form he found most problematic, namely, an absolute idealism. If this existential involvement with his subject matter produces problems, his typological analysis of actualistic and ontological traditions is nevertheless on safer ground. In both of these traditions he sees insights which, with suitable reinterpretation, are theologically valuable. They are heuristically helpful for understanding both revelation and human being.

Philosophies of act are best represented by genuine transcendental-ism which Kant most closely approaches. Here thought is understood as always in–relation–to [in bezug auf] transcendence, but never as having disposal over the transcendent. In such philosophy the object transcends thought, standing over against it. There is a resistance [Widerstand] of transcendence to domination by the thinking and

---

to suggest the difference between an epistemological, subject–object, 'scien-tific,' and technical mentality, and a humanistic, personal, social and ethical mentality as two fundamentally different approaches to anthropology.

[46] Cf., e.g., AB 53, 104, and other statements on the point cited above.

knowing I.[47] Genuinely free thought, precisely in order to remain free, is satisfied with being in relation to transcendence; it does not ascribe to the I power over, but remains "in relation to" [in bezug auf], transcendence.[48] The true sense of act is pure intentionality, *actus directus,* Dasein being directed permanently to transcendence;[49] truth "is" only in the relation–to–transcendence of the act itself.[50] At its best, transcendentalism expresses the fact that consciousness and transcendent being are related to one another[51] in a way that neither puts being under the disposal of consciousness nor leaves the knowing I imprisoned within its own autonomous interpretation.

This epistemology presupposes an anthropology. Human beings in their existentiality are always "in relation to" something beyond themselves.[52]

> Such people see themselves placed in a *contingent* here-and-there [situation]. As people who are questioning, thinking, and acting, they have to find their way in the midst of it, and have to relate every given situation to themselves so that they can decide 'in reference to it'. And the violation [Vergewaltigung] that people thereby themselves do suffer at being *'in relation to' an other,* at being in reference to a transcendent which 'is already there', is something fundamentally different from the certainty of bearing within themselves the possibility of mastering [Bewältigung] the world. In other words, in the purely transcendental understanding of Dasein even the character of the act is expressed more purely than in the conflation of act and being in idealism. Only where Dasein, *continually being directed to the transcendent,* cannot understand itself, or, to put it another way, is able to understand that it does not understand itself, is the true meaning of act brought to expression: act as an 'in relation to' that never comes to rest, as intentionality pure and simple, as evident in psychic process but as understandable only on the far side of it, act as 'direct' consciousness *(actus directus).* Here philosophizing itself is essentially related to Dasein, because it places itself within the responsibilities of human Dasein and raises its questions only from within that context. Accordingly, the questions themselves belong to Dasein and so do not

---

47 AS 28, AB 34.

48 AS 33, AB 40.

49 AS 36, AB 43; cf. the concept of "direction of will" in *Sanctorum Communio.*

50 AS 38, AB 44.

51 AS 41, AB 48: "the relatedness of consciousness and being-that-is-transcendent" to one another.

52 AS 40, AB 47.

involve the answer in advance. Thus philosophizing partakes of the
act-character of Dasein and does not speak from such a having [Haben]
as would be grounded in a being [Sein].

A human being in relation to the transcendent, a contingent, deciding,
responsible, relating person, whose thinking is dependent upon his or her
willing—this person is very similar to the one we have already met in
Bonhoeffer's anthropology. It is not surprising that Bonhoeffer finds the
anthropology of a "pure" transcendentalism appealing. He points out,
however, that whether a person will in fact remain 'in relation to'
transcendence, and not assume that the I can understand itself from itself,
is no theoretical question of epistemology but a decision of practical
reason, i.e., of the ethical person.[54] But for Bonhoeffer, the ethical person
and transcendence are related to each other in human sociality. If the
Kantian anthropology was unable to protect its pure intention, this was
because of its obscure and ineffective version of the transcendent.[55]

On the other hand, *philosophies of being*—with varying degrees of
success—uphold the primacy of being over consciousness. "It is the
concern of *true* ontology to demonstrate the primacy of being over against
consciousness and to uncover this being."[56] If effective, they do not
absorb being into consciousness or place it at the disposal of the knowing
I. Nor do they annul knowing, but endeavor properly to express the
relation of being and thought—the way in which thought is, as Bonhoeffer
puts it, "suspended" [aufgehoben] in being.[57] Bonhoeffer found in
Heidegger both of these characteristics of a genuine ontology, yet judged
his achievement to be vitiated by the fact that Heidegger understands
Dasein as self–contained finitude.

The *ontological perspective,* appropriated by theology, also contributes to understanding both revelation and anthropology. By stressing
the priority of being over the individual subject, ontology can express
God as prior to and independent of human faith. It can also speak of a
unity and continuity of reality, without falling into a static and reified
form of metaphysics. In this way, God can be emphasized as really 'over
against' human beings, 'external' to their grasping efforts, in short,

---

53   AS 35f., AB 42f., italics mine, translation altered.
54   AS 33, AB 40; cf. AB 45.
55   AB 50; cf. 45, 46f.
56   AS 53, AB 59.
57   AS 54, AB 60.

genuinely transcendent. At the same time, by pointing to being as having a "given" continuity, it is possible to speak of God and revelation as really related to us, rather than continually eluding us. Similarly, an ontological perspective on anthropology can stress the fact that we live in a concrete, determinate mode of existence, and that we have—along with all changes in our lives—a real continuity of existence. The theological and anthropological aspects are both best understood, Bonhoeffer argues, by understanding human existence in terms of 'being in' social communities.

The *transcendental,* or act, *perspective* also has important theological significance. With respect to revelation, it stresses the freedom of God who, as transcendent, genuinely encounters humanity. Anthropologically, this tradition emphasizes the importance of human responsibility, existential decision, human being always in relation to, and accountable to, the transcendent God. Faith is not a possession or *habitus,* and is not derived from self–reflection, but is an alert and historically alive "looking to" Christ. Again, it is in terms of human social relationships that Bonhoeffer hopes to do justice to these insights derived from the tradition of transcendental philosophy.

C. CHRISTIAN ANTHROPOLOGY: A SOCIAL ONTOLOGY

In moving to Bonhoeffer's constructive presentation, there are four main questions which must be treated. (1) How does he understand the nature of revelation, which constitutes the premise of Christian anthropology? (2) What is his social ontology? (3) In both his Christology and anthropology, how are the claims of 'act' and 'being' united in this ontology? (4) What resolution is proposed to the anthropological problem which, in this theological context, must now be seen as a soteriological problem? These four questions are all interrelated, and will be discussed under three headings: "Revelation in Christ"; "Humanity 'in Adam'"; and "Humanity 'in Christ.'"

1. REVELATION IN CHRIST

Bonhoeffer's critique of the philosophical efforts to gain "autonomous Daseinverständnis" rests on the theological premise that not only God but also humanity must be understood in relation to revelation. It is Christ, as *extra nos* and *pro nobis,* who lets people understand them-

selves not as self–established, self–imprisoned, isolated, and dominating "lords of the world," but as creatures of God.

Revelation is a social reality. God cannot be understood in isolation
from humanity, and human beings cannot be understood individualistically. (Individualism, of course, was one of the fundamental components
in Bonhoeffer's criticism of an 'autonomous Daseinsverständnis.') In
reality, human beings, precisely as individual persons, are always in
human communities. Revelation, likewise, is and occurs communally,
that is, in the church.[58]

> Revelation should be thought of only in reference to the concept of the
> church [Kirche], where the church is understood to be constituted by
> the present proclamation of Christ's death and resurrection–within, on
> the part of, and for the community of faith [Gemeinde].[59]

Being drawn into the revelation event must be understood in a theological–sociological category, that is, in terms of a person's
being–in–the–church.[60]

Bonhoeffer continues to think of Christ as the Kollektivperson of the
new humanity, and his view of the church-community must be read in this
universal light. The congregation, as a specific and localized social
community within the whole church, is created by Christ as a "new
humanity." It does not arise from human needs and wishes, or by
modifying existing human communities. Christ is, then, the
Kollektivperson of the church-community in which God's revelation is
and occurs.[61]

> God reveals God's own self as person. The community of faith is
> God's final revelation as "Christ existing as church-community
> [Gemeinde]" ordained for the end time of the world until the return of
> Christ. Here Christ has come the very nearest to humanity. Here Christ
> has given Christ's own self to the new humanity in Christ. The person
> of Christ draws together in itself all whom Christ has won, binding and
> committing Christ to them and them to one another. The 'church' is
> . . . the community of faith created by and founded upon Christ, in

---

[58] AS 109, AB 113.

[59] AS 107, AB 110. Proclamation takes place in Word and sacrament as
communal forms; cf. AS 108, AB 111, and AB 92f., 129. Both Word and
sacrament proclaim the one Christ of the cross and resurrection; cf. AS 107, AB
110, and *passim*.

[60] AS 107, AB 110f.

[61] AS 108, AB 111.

which Christ is revealed as the δεύτερος ἄνθρωπος, as the new human being, or rather, as the new humanity itself.[62]

First created by Christ's revelation, the church-community is the presence of Christ, the self–revealing God. He is present as person, and his community of persons is "Christus als Gemeinde existierend."

Since revelation has this personal–communal mode of being, revelation can never be thought of as an entity. Here Bonhoeffer agrees with Barth and other theologians of the early dialectical theology who appropriated from the philosophical 'act' tradition, especially Neo–Kantianism. Revelation does have the contingency and freedom of 'act'; we are always 'in relation to' the transcendent, and never have it under our control as an entity. The *freedom* of God in revelation is a sine qua non. However, this freedom must *not* be understood formally and abstractly. Here Bonhoeffer criticizes Barth's teaching up to the *Christliche Dogmatik* (1927) as a purely formal and inadequate version of the freedom of God in revelation.[63] Barth, rightly wanting to preserve the contingency of revelation, and to assert that it encounters us 'from outside' and not from any human possibilities, did not base his view of God's freedom upon the actual *content* of that revelation, but upon an abstract and formal concept of freedom heavily influenced by Neo–Kantianism. Consequently, Barth presents God's freedom in a polemical and negative way: God is free *from* human disposal.[64]

---

[62] AS 109, AB 112, trans. altered.

[63] AB 90.

[64] Pertinent to this Bonhoeffer–Barth debate is a comment by T.F. Torrance. Torrance's accusation that Bonhoeffer betrays "a distinct element of epistemological Apollinarianism" would strike terror into the heart of any theologian—except that it follows from an unhappy mistake. To substantiate this frightening charge, Torrance quotes Bonhoeffer where Bonhoeffer is expounding the early Barth (AB 92)! When, as Torrance says, Barth sought to correct just such an error "by making the *humanity* of Christ so central to theological epistemology," it was the error of Barth's own previous work which he was correcting. Mercifully, Bonhoeffer never came near the dread heresy for which Torrance reproached him, nor did he need any tutoring on this point of orthodoxy. For Bonhoeffer the true humanity of Christ was never in question, and he saw the importance of this for theological epistemology earlier than Barth; his argument in *Act and Being* that God's freedom is a freedom of full self–giving and self–binding to humanity is as far from Apollinarianism as from the elusiveness characteristic of the early Barth's dialectic. For Torrance's comment, see his *Theological Science* (London: Oxford University Press, 1969), p. 292 n. 1.

Bonhoeffer agrees with Barth that there is a contingency in revelation, and that it encounters one 'from outside.' But he rejects the formal
understanding of God's freedom in revelation. He deliberately replaces
dialectical theology's purely actualistic view of revelation with an
ontological or, more precisely, *socio–ontological* interpretation. The
theological presupposition for this is his understanding of the divine
freedom. In the Word, God discloses that divine freedom is precisely
freedom for humanity. God's free self–revelation discloses that divine
being is a "being for humanity." In one of the classical passages of the
book, Bonhoeffer writes:

> In revelation it is not so much a question of the freedom of God on the
> other side of revelation–i.e., God's aseity, God who eternally remains
> within God's own self–as it is of God coming out of God's own self.
> It is a matter of God's *given* word, of the covenant in which God is
> bound by God's own action. The freedom of God finds its strongest
> evidence precisely in that *God freely chose to be bound to historical
> human beings*, and to be placed at the disposal of human beings. God
> is not free from humanity but is *free for humanity. Christ is the word
> of God's freedom.* God *is* present…. 'haveable', graspable in the Word
> within the church.[65]

This passage, which Bethge rightly sees as the original matrix for the
Christological formulation of Jesus as "the man for others" in the
Letters,[66] is fundamental to Bonhoeffer's theological development. It
demonstrates the *sociality of God as the prototype and possibility of
human sociality:* if Christ is God–being–free–for–humanity, then human beings in Christ can find their true humanity in being free for one
another and for their communities. This leads into Bonhoeffer's social
ontology, and his proposal for dialectically integrating 'act' and 'being'
in a theology of sociality. From this view of God's given, present, and
available being–free–for–humanity, it follows that there is a *being of*

---

[65] AS 85, AB 90f., trans. altered, italics mine; cf. AS 109, AB 112, and AB
124. In this passage the free being of God is understood not formally but from
its specific content, "substantially" as Bonhoeffer puts it. In exactly the same
way he insists that no statements about the being of God may be merely formal.
Theology must always speak in terms of God's concrete way of being. God is
the personal name of One whose being is always "being–just," "being–holy,"
"being–love" (AB 75). For Bonhoeffer's continued insistence that "God" is a
personal name, not an abstract noun or general concept, see his 1944 prison essay
on "The First Table of the Ten Commandments," trans. John Godsey, *Preface to
Bonhoeffer* (Philadelphia: Fortress Press, 1965), pp. 60ff.

[66] DB 171, DB-E 135.

revelation. Specifically, and here we meet again a familiar conceptuality, this being of revelation has the *social* form of the church-community.[67] The church-community is the communal way of being [Seinsart] of the present Christ. God is freely bound to the personal church-community, and precisely *this self–giving* and binding proves that it *is God's freedom.* Because God has freely given and bound himself, because Christ is present in the church-community, it follows that revelation is

> somehow held fast here.... The community of faith really does have the word of forgiveness at its disposal.... As the Christian church, the congregation may declare in sermon and sacrament that 'you are forgiven'.[68]

> The being of revelation 'is', rather, the being of the community of persons that is constituted and formed by the person of Christ....[69]

That the being of revelation is the being of Christ in the church-community as a community of persons expresses two points: its *continuity of being* as *transcendent* to the individual, and its *contingent freedom* which engages a person in existential encounter. Affirming the ontological thesis of being as prior to one's response to being, Bonhoeffer proposes the social category as a way to integrate dialectically the 'being' and 'act' dimensions of revelation in Christ.

First, there is a *priority* and *continuity* of the being of revelation which is *transcendent* to the individual's acts of faith. Without diminishing the encountering, existential character of the Word, it is constantly present and transcendent to the individual by its being in and as the

---

[67] Bernard Noble consistently translated "Gemeinde" in his rendition of *Act and Being* as "communion." This English word has a variety of meanings which detract from Bonhoeffer's precise usage. (On p. 119, n. 1, Noble admits the potential confusion but compounds it by saying that "Gemeinde" never means eucharist; while semantically true, this comment distracts the reader from Bonhoeffer's view that the eucharist is a form of revelation which is constitutive for the Gemeinde.) "Communion" also has individualistic, subjective, and pietistic associations which contradict Bonhoeffer's meaning. For Bonhoeffer, "Gemeinde" is the theological–ecclesiastical category, and "Gemeinschaft" the sociological category; they should be kept distinct. "Gemeinde" here is translated with the basic meaning "church-community" as explained in the Editor's Introduction to *Sanctorum Communio,* SC 14ff.

[68] AS 109, AB 112f.

[69] AS 110, AB 113. Christ is the subject of the church-community's proclamation (Word and sacrament) and its believing, and the ground of its communal life; cf. AB 111, 112, 114.

church-community. While revelation is never present apart from faith, it can be present in a community apart from an act of faith of any single individual; even if, at any given time, I do not hear in faith, there are others who do, and so the Word of Christ is always present and active. Its continuity of being present is not institutionally guaranteed, as in Catholic ecclesiology, in the doctrine of orthodoxy, or the bibliolatry of fundamentalism. Its being present is "trans–subjectively guaranteed" in the congregation as a personal community.[70] Its presence in the community guarantees its *continuity of being* because it is "outside" of me and *transcendent* to my particular acts. In the community of persons, the other person who ever and again encounters me *ab extra* with the Word is the guarantee of the continuity of revelation.[71]

Second, if the *communal* nature of revelation present in and as the church-community guarantees its being transcendent to me and its continuity *extra me,* the *personal* character of the church-community assures that I will be *existentially encountered* by the revelation; its *extra me* is simultaneously its *pro me,* its *freedom* for me is precisely its freedom to encounter me. The sociological concept of the person, as before, remains decisive for Bonhoeffer's ideas of God, Christ, the congregation, and its members. Therefore revelation can never be understood as entity [Seiend] or thing, whether that be a single, past event,[72] or a present entity—institution, dogma, or Bible. ("Einen Gott, den 'es gibt,' gibt es nicht; Gott 'ist' im Personbezug, und das Sein ist sein Personsein.")[73] Yet nor can revelation be interpreted merely as non–entity and non–objective.[74] Revelation, rather, is interpreted by the category of the person, for person is neither entity nor non–objective. Interpreted by the category of person, revelation's continuity of being is one that always encounters the existence of the hearer.[75]

Only in the relation and encounter of persons is Christ really revealed and present. A person is not an entity, but is genuinely 'objective' to the self; the 'other' concretely stands independently 'outside of' and 'over against' the self. The other person thus embodies revelation as genuinely 'outside' the self. In the sociological category of the person as 'other' in community, "revelation presents itself *in correlation to my whole*

---

70 AS 110, AB 113f.

71 AS 110f., AB 114.

72 AB 113.

73 AS 112.

74 Nichtseiend, nichtgegenständlich: AS 110, AB 113.

75 AS 110f., AB 114.

Existenz."[76] Revelation is present in personal encounter. The other person is a real Grenze to the I, a limit to the dominating ambitions of the self; the other person is also, as embodying the Word of forgiveness *ab extra,* the promise and possibility of the self's liberation into a new existence. The other person in the congregation, however, can only have this role as a "mode" of revelation present and encountering the self because Christ is present in and as the church-community. It is only because Christ is present as person that the self acknowledges the other as a genuine person and not as an entity or merely extant thing.[77]

> The existence of the person who ever and again hears [the Word] is vitally affected by this community.... This is founded on the personal character of the church-community, whose subject is Christ. For only through the person of Christ can the existence of human beings be encountered, placed into truth, and transformed into a new way of existence. But as the person of Christ has been revealed in the church-community, the existence of human beings can be encountered only through the church-community. It is from the person of Christ that every other person first received their personal character for other human beings. So they themselves even become Christ for us in demand and promise, in being existential limits on us *ab extra*, and, as such, also guarantors of the continuity of revelation.[78]

Therefore, since the revealing Christ is present in the personal form of the social community of faith, revelation has both a transcendence and continuity of being, and simultaneously encounters the whole existence of the members of the community. Within the church-community the being of revelation always includes its being a contingent event, which comes from outside the self. The concerns of act and being are dialectically integrated in this social understanding of revelation.

In this exposition Bonhoeffer is moving into an ontological interpretation of revelation by the continued use of his theology of sociality. By thinking in social rather than epistemological categories, he is able to present a dialectical integration of act and being in the interpretation of revelation.[79]

---

[76] AS 112, AB 115, italics mine.

[77] AS 112, AB 115; for this whole paragraph, cf. AS 110ff., AB 113ff.

[78] AS 110f., AB 114, trans. altered.

[79] Here we have a particularly clear elaboration of the meaning of Bonhoeffer's introductory statement:

> The concept of revelation has to be thought about within the concreteness of the concept of the church, that is to say, in terms of a socio-

Revelation is the premise for Christian anthropology. Since the Christian community is the social presence in and through which Christ encounters people, we understand why this section of his argument recalls us to the original issue at the beginning of the inquiry: in contrast to the "autonomous Daseinsverständnis" in philosophy Bonhoeffer sets "the church as the place where Dasein is understood." We therefore turn to his theological anthropology, examining how he deals with both the anthropological *question* of 'act' and 'being' and the *soteriological problem* of the powerful, autonomous, self–imprisoned I. The two issues are inseparable, since the act–being dialectic is present in both sinner and person of faith.

2. HUMANITY 'IN ADAM'

In Christ we see that God's being is not formal and abstract, but concrete: for example, God's freedom is being free for humanity; always we should speak of God's being–holy, being–just, and so on. Accordingly, we must always see human being concretely. We exist in a determinate mode of being, and theologically there is no neutral or formal human being. Therefore, while it is possible, in a general way, to describe human being as being God's creature,[80] the creature must be concretely understood as either being in sin or being in faith, "being in Adam," or "being in Christ."

---

logical category in which the interpretation of act and of being meet and are drawn together into one. . . . The theological concepts of object [Gegenstand] and knowledge are shown to be determined by the sociological concept of person, and must be recast accordingly. *The sphere* of the entity [des Seienden], of the 'extant' ['es gibt'], *of static concepts of being, is set in motion through the sociological category* (AS 26, AB 31, italics mine, trans. altered).

This passage, incidentally, reminds us that "church" is not the only concept implied when Bonhoeffer speaks of "the sociological category."

[80] "A creature is Dasein through and for God in faith, i.e., in being encountered by revelation" (AS 151, AB 152). This most general theological definition is as critical of Catholic ontology and natural theology as of attempts in philosophical anthropology to give general ontological definitions independent of ontic existence, and ignoring the human creature in relation to God. It may be noted that even this general definition transforms and integrates the perspective of philosophical ontology (here God is the creature's Seinsgrund and Lord) and transcendentalism (here Dasein is "in relation to" an encountering transcendence); cf. AS 149f., AB 151.

Humanity "in Adam" means fallen humanity. This applies personally to each individual and corporately to all human communities, up to and including humanity as a whole. Being in Adam involves the dialectical interaction of being and act, as does being in Christ. Bonhoeffer here builds upon the understanding of the human being as individual and humanity which he first presented in his discussion of original sin in *Sanctorum Communio*. In the light of revelation each person is shown to be already "in" a mode of being characterized by self–seeking, willful self–assertion at the expense of others, and the attempt to dominate others as much as to be a solitary "lord" as an individual self. Concretely this means that human communities and institutions are, from the smallest to the greatest of them, pervaded and perverted by this 'spirit.' Adam, as we have seen, is the Kollektivperson of this sinful mode of being, the 'personification' of the sinful being of humanity universally. But to say that each person is already found to "be" in corporate human associations which are determined by this posture is not to allow any lessening of individual, personal responsibility. On the contrary, the individual wills, decides, and acts in accordance with the posture of fallen Adam. Individuals repeatedly make themselves responsible by their own acts for the sin which pervades all humanity. *Being* in sin, the individual also '*act*ivates' and perpetuates the sin of a humanity which refuses to be God's creature.[81] The individual thereby becomes culpable. Since the individual's acts repeat and confirm the sinful life of the old humanity of Adam, this establishes personal responsibility; the individual person is thus 'in Adam,' indeed, is Adam. Individual people cannot shift the responsibility to their corporate communities. As Bonhoeffer puts it, "in Adam, act is as constitutive for being as being is for act."[82]

I have already shown how a fundamental anthropological problem, which is correlated to a profound, personal concern of the theologian himself, permeates the whole discussion of *Act and Being*. I have suggested that this anthropological problem is, in fact, nothing less than *the* distinctive soteriological problem which is fundamental to Bonhoeffer's early theology. Full documentation of this judgement will be given in the next chapter. Here one passage may be quoted which shows that when Bonhoeffer describes human sin "in Adam" he has a quite distinct form of sin in mind.

---

[81] AS 143ff., AB 144ff.
[82] AS 145, AB 146.

"In Adam" means: being in untruth, i.e., in culpable *perversion of the will* (i.e. one's essence) *inwards to the self, cor curvum in se.* The individual has torn himself out of community with God, and thus also with other people, and now stands alone, which is in untruth. Because he is alone the world is 'his' world, *the neighbor has sunk into the world of things...* and *God has become a religious object;* but *he himself has become his own creator, his own master and property.* That in his knowing he must now begin and end with himself corresponds to this situation, for *he is now utterly 'by himself' in the falsehood of naked self–lordship.*

...*Human thought and philosophy in sin is self-glorifying...; all knowledge,* including and above all the γνῶθι σεαυτόν, *is ultimately intent on human self–justification.* But eventually, under the colossal burden of being creator and bearer of a world, in the cold silence of his eternal solitude, he becomes anxious about himself and begins to dread. Now, elevating himself to be the final judge of himself he indicts himself—in the voice of conscience. But the answer of the indicted person is remorse *(contritio activa!). The conscience and remorse of a person in Adam are his ultimate grasp for himself, the confirmation and justification of his autocratic solitude. He impeaches himself and summons his better self. Yet the cry of conscience only disguises the mute loneliness of a bleak isolation and sounds without echo in the self–dominated and self–interpreted world....* Only when Christ breaks a person's solitude does he know himself placed in the truth.[83]

This passage succinctly recapitulates those many statements which built up the composite portrait presented earlier. That portrait is identical to this one of humanity "in Adam."

There are four interrelated themes in the above passage and in the other statements previously gathered together in the composite portrait. The first is the *power of the knowing and "interpreting" I;* this man glorifies and justifies himself by his thought and intellectual activity, he is "his own creator [and] master," and by his thought and self–knowledge he believes he can establish himself in the truth. Second, *his attitude is one of domination;* "the world is 'his' world, the neighbor has sunk into the world of things... and God has become a religious object," he lives in "the self–dominated and self–interpreted world." Third, *he is isolated;* "he has torn himself out of community with God, and thus

---

[83] AS 136–40, AB 137–41, italics mine, trans. altered; cf. especially AB 28, noting the passionate language and many metaphors identical with, or very similar to, those in this passage. (On the masculine pronouns in the quotation and commentary upon it, see note 36 above.)

also with other people, and now he stands alone, which is in untruth."
Finally, he accuses himself in *conscience*. His conscience accuses him
particularly at the point of his isolated, self–sufficient autonomy; he
indicts himself, that is, for the way he has violated the true sociality in
which people were created to live together. In summoning "his better
self" he is trying by his own power to restore himself to his true being
and responsibility with and for others. But this *self*–exhortation only
manifests his self–imprisoned condition. Only Christ can break the
solitude and place him in the truth, that is, in his true being with others
where the sociality of Christ and humanity is a community of persons,
not a dominion of things.

In the next chapter I will analyze no less than seven major passages,
from the years 1927 to 1932, which are all virtually identical to this one;
they certainly repeat the same four themes identified here. Subsequent
discussion will examine power as a soteriological problem in Bonhoeffer's
early theology, and this passage from *Act and Being* will be treated under
the rubric, "the power of the ego." That will be the appropriate context
to introduce a more precise analytical conceptuality. For the present it
suffices to note that this epitome of Bonhoeffer's soteriological problem
gives great prominence to exactly those two concerns he mentioned when
commencing the work: *consciousness* and *conscience*.[84] It locates them
right in the center of the crisis of sociality which is the human lot "in
Adam." This calls for further examination later, which will show that the
"passionate personal involvement" which Bethge perceptively discerns
in this "highly abstract discourse" plays a decisive role in the development of Bonhoeffer's theology. For the present it is necessary to see how
Christ breaks the solitude so that people can know themselves as
creatures of God who have been placed in the truth.

3. HUMANITY 'IN CHRIST'

Revelation is the theological foundation for seeing human being–in–
Adam as a being–in–sin. Likewise, the relationship of Christ's revelation
and human faith, both understood in the social relationships of the
Christian community, is the presupposition for discussing the dialectic of
being and act in Adam. By considering humanity's "being in Christ" we

---

84 A "Note on 'Conscience' in *Akt und Sein,*" is contained in Appendix D,
part B; see note 14 above.

see how that presupposition is theologically established in its positive form rather than its negative expression.

The church-community, as the communal *Christus praesens,* is the place of genuine Daseinsverständnis, for here people understand themselves from revelation, not out of their own autonomous self–understanding.[85] This new understanding, furthermore, discloses human existence as a dialectic of being and act. Most specifically this is a dialectic of "being in the church-community" and faith (act). "In the concept of the human being the dialectic of faith and 'being in...' is concretely interpreted afresh in the sociological category."[86]

To be in Christ is to be in the Gemeinde. Being-in-the-church-community is being-in-Christ; this is being-in-the-truth, being-in-revelation. This *being* involves, of necessity, faith as *act.* Faith, as a gift of God, is being directed to Christ *(actus directus)* and being drawn into the community of his person. The human act of decision responds and answers to the Word which, in the church-community, encounters one *ab extra.* By faith one becomes a member of the church,[87] and "the *being of* revelation, the being of the church-community of Christ, 'is' only in *faith.*"[88] Thus faith as personal act recognizes itself as the "being-mode" of its being in the church.[89] Just as the being of revelation in the form of personal community includes its characteristic of encountering a person existentially, so the act of faith simultaneously involves being in the church. For the believer, act is act-presupposing-being (or: act-in-relation-to-being), and being is being-including-act. This, in fact, is the dialectic of *sola fide, sola gratia.*

Faith therefore presupposes a being which is independent of and outside the believing self: that is, transcendence is Christ's-being-present-in-the-church-community. Faith discovers itself always as already in the church-community; there it encounters a being which is both present and

---

85   AB 109f.

86   AS 116, AB 119; cf. AB 31f. It would be a grave mistake to restrict "sociological category" to the church-community. In *Act and Being* it continues to mean that whole conceptuality developed in *Sanctorum Communio*: person, socio-ethical encounter, Adam and Christ as Kollektivpersonen, human beings as both corporate and individual, and so on; all of these notions are involved in the sentence quoted, but the emphasis is on the community of faith as the concrete social form of revelation.

87   AB 117.

88   AS 115, AB 118, italics mine.

89   Ibid.: Seinweise seines Sein in der Kirche.

prior to the act, and it acknowledges that this being is quite independent of the human act of faith.[90]

Understood in terms of sociality, being and act are dialectically integrated in Christ's revelation and the life of the person of faith. The human person is act in being, self in community, individual in humanity. What this means for the actual understanding of the Christian life in the community of faith is stated by Bonhoeffer this way.

> In the historical reality [Wirklichkeit] of the congregation of Christ to which I belong I hear another person really proclaim the gospel to me; he offers me the sacrament: 'you are forgiven.' He and the congregation pray for me, and I hear the gospel and pray with them. I know myself bound into the Word, sacrament and prayer of the congregation of Christ, the new humanity.... I know myself borne by the congregation, and bearing it. Here I, the historical, whole human being (individual and humanity) am encountered and I believe, i.e. I know myself borne. I am borne *(pati)*, therefore, I am *(esse)*, therefore I believe *(agere)*. Here the circle closes, for here even *agere* is *pati*.[91]

In passing we must observe that Bonhoeffer's repetition of his basic proposition that the church is the *new humanity* enables his references to the congregation to be understood in proper perspective. By no stretch of the imagination is he promoting a sort of sectarian congregationalism.[92] The universal church of Christ exists, to be sure, in historical, empirical, spatially–localized communities.[93] But since Christ is the Kollektivperson of the new humanity, these congregations are therefore spatially localized forms of this new humanity of Christ.

---

[90] AS 114, AB 117f.

[91] AS 118, AB 120f., trans. mine; cf. AB 116, and the reference to Luther on the *nova nativitas*.

[92] Bonhoeffer's leadership in the ecumenical movement should be seen as an expression of his theological understanding of the church as the new humanity. His commitment was no mere enthusiasm for a current ecclesiastical fashion, nor simply a pragmatic concern for national and international problems; nor was it just an ad hoc, though admittedly serious, desire that the ecumenical movement recognize the Confessing Church as the legitimate evangelical church in Germany. In his theology, rather, Christ is the Kollektivperson of the church as the new humanity. Therefore the Oekumene must simultaneously clarify its theological status as *church* and precisely as church speak and act for the peace, justice, truth, and freedom of humanity. (See Bonhoeffer's ecumenical addresses and writings, and the account of his ecumenical work in Bethge's biography.)

[93] AS 118, AB 121. It also exists in other forms as well.

As part of the being–act dialectic, an issue of particular concern to Bonhoeffer in this social ontology is the continuity and unity of the self in Christian existence. Because of their actualistic doctrines of revelation informed by Neo–Kantianism, theologians like Bultmann and the early Barth could not do justice to this anthropological issue.[94] For a Christian anthropology, furthermore, the issue has a special sharpness because of the distinction made between the 'old self' who dies to sin and the 'new self' who rises in faith to new life. But clearly, since he insists on a 'being' of revelation, as well as its freedom and contingency, Bonhoeffer also wants to understand the being of the Christian in faith so that the continuity and unity of the self is not fragmented into a succession of isolated moments.

No more than the being of revelation is human being that of an entity [Seiendes], any more than the existentiality of revelation and human existence means the discontinuity of repeatedly evaporating into non–entity.[95] The continuity, as well as the existentiality, of human being must be understood in the *social concept of person.*[96]

Nor can the question of the continuity and unity of human being be answered by positing creaturehood as the substratum, or essence, which underlies both being in sin and being in Christ. No such neutral or formal depth of being is accessible behind or below the concrete human way of being; essence cannot be isolated from existence in this fashion. So it is only the person of faith who may say that the sinner is also God's creature.[97] In other words, to speak concretely of the continuity and unity of the self, the past must be taken just as seriously as the present and the future; one's past "being in Adam" is just as significant as one's present being in Christ and one's ultimate eschatological destiny. This means that the present always has two determinants, the past and the future. Conscience is the determinant from the past, the past of the sinful self "in Adam"; the child is the eschatological determinant from the future, a future of simple and unreflecting faith.[98] What do these determinants mean for the continuity of Christian existence in the community?

---

[94]   AB 97–102.

[95]   Nichtsein, here a synonym for Nicht–Seiendes and a partner of Nichtgegenständlichkeit; cf. AS 117, AB 130.

[96]   Cf., e.g., AB 151f.

[97]   AS 149f., AB 151; cf. AS 136, AB 137f.

[98]   Recalling that "the theological problem of the child" was a subject mentioned along with "consciousness" and "conscience" in Bonhoeffer's germinal ideas for the book, we now see the connection. If the self's consciousness—the

In Bonhoeffer's theology, it is crucial to note, conscience is in no way the voice of Christ. It is the voice of sinful self–reflection. Conscience is the opposite of the faith which looks solely to Christ *(actus directus)* and away from the self. Nevertheless, the person in Christ is a forgiven sinner, who has a continuity with a past which is expressed in conscience.[99] So it can happen that even in one's new being in Christ (in the church-community) the old conscience as accusing self–reflection can intrude itself between the believer and Christ; this deflects the Christian from looking directly to Christ to reflecting instead on the self. How is this overcome? How does Christ kill this conscience, and re*act*ivate one's faith as *actus directus?* The answer is not as complete as one might wish, but in terms of the whole argument it appears to be this:[100] while self–reflection indeed distracts faith, insofar as it occurs in the context of the Christian's being in the Gemeinde, there Christ is present to kill conscience; specifically, Christ is present in the other person and can speak the Word, "von aussen," which simultaneously forgives the defection from faith and reorients the person out of self and into Christ. When restored to faith the Christian finds once more that he or she already "is" in the community of Christ.[101] Thus one's past, speaking in conscience, is continually being overcome through being in the Gemeinde. This means that Christian conscience is transformed conscience, in which self–reflection is embraced by Christ, so that people see themselves only as forgiven by Christ. The continuity of the self, vis–à–vis the past, is that of continually being transformed by Christ 'present' in the community of faith.[102]

But Christ is not present as an entity. He is present as person in the Christian companion. At the same time as Christ is "outside" the self and "coming to" the self through the other, he comes from the future. What can be possessed and imprisoned in the self is, Bonhoeffer argues, in a

---

self–referring, self–imprisoned, self–asserting, and self–justifying activity of the knowing intellect—is central to the problem, and if *conscience* is yet another mode of self–reflection, self–assertion, and self–justification, the *child* is the theological sign of eschatological salvation. (In relation to this see Bonhoeffer's interpretation of infant baptism, AS 159f., AB 159f.) It is also at this stage of his argument that he brings in the quotations from Luther's commentary on Galatians, also mentioned in the group of germinal ideas; cf. AB 150.

[99] AS 154, AB 155.

[100] See especially AB 100f., 102, 113f., 118–122.

[101] AS 154f., AB 155.

[102] AS 155f., AB 155f.

real sense already past; another person, and Christ in that person, can never be possessed in this way. The free and contingent revelation comes from the future because it comes to the Christian *ab extra* in the other person.[103]

In the new being as being–in–the–congregation, Christians receive Christ who "comes to" them from their neighbors. Looking away from themselves, they see only Christ, in whom they see only life; there is no sin and death in Christ. "To see Christ in Word and sacrament means to see, all in one act, the resurrected Crucified One in the neighbor and in creation. Here alone does that future reveal itself which in faith determines the present."[104] This is the vision of the eschatological consummation. The child, being open to the coming future, is free to live in the present. Theologically, therefore, "the child is neighbor to the *eschata.*"[105]

For the Christian, then, the transformation of the past in the present depends ultimately upon the eschaton. In the life of the congregation the presence of Christ brings the eschaton into the present and overcomes the past. In so doing the unity and continuity of the Christian person is guaranteed.

One final but fundamental matter must be discussed in this consideration of the Christian's 'being in Christ.' If this account of Christian existence gives answers to several issues in Bonhoeffer's explicit concern with 'act' and 'being,' we are more than curious to see what theological resolution he offers to the book's soteriological problem which is so closely woven into the fabric of the official agenda. This is no idle

---

[103] AS 157ff., AB 157ff.; cf. AS 107f., AB 110f., AB 113f. Bonhoeffer makes his point with a play on "zukommende" and "zukünftige." If revelation did not have this characteristic of coming from the future it could never be "present"; it would always be past, therefore entity, therefore not personal event, therefore not revelation. Its characteristic of coming from the future enables it to resurrect, as it were, the past event of revelation to a living presence. Hence "in the concept of the contingent happening which comes to us [zukommenden] the present is determined through the future [Zukunft]." In this context, recall the proposition in *Sanctorum Communio* and his graduation theses (GS III 47, DBW 9 477) on the dialectic in Paul's concept of Christ both present in the congregation and in heaven.

[104] AS 158, AB 158f. Note here the unity of act and being: the future has a *being* in the present (presence) in the *act* of faith in the congregation; also, since faith is the 'Seinsart' of the future, faith is 'suspended' in the being of the future, and the believer has a being in the future of Christ.

[105] AS 159f., AB 160.

curiosity since the soteriological problem which comes into sharp focus in *Act and Being* is the characteristic soteriological problem of his early theology. Since the next chapter will demonstrate that in 1932 Bonhoeffer comes to an existential decision which directly informs his soteriology in the mid 1930s with an emphasis on *radical obedience,* the intriguing question is: what resolution does he offer early in 1930, more than two years prior to his own existential breakthrough?

The transition from 'being in Adam' to 'being in Christ' is a movement which involves several themes: from autonomous self–understanding to understanding oneself from revelation; from trying to be a lord and creator to finding oneself as God's creature under the lordship of Christ; from isolated self–imprisonment to community; from the domination of others and of nature to the love of others; from self–seeking to freedom for others; and from conscience as self–reflection and self–accusation to faith and forgiveness in Christ.

This is a movement which occurs because of Christ's presence in the matrix of human sociality; Christ is the reality of the new humanity in the corporate and individual dimensions of personal life. As such, it is a movement which restores people to their authentic sociality with Christ and with one another. If isolated autonomy loses reality [Wirklichkeit] and transcendence,[106] the presence of the transcendent Christ restores people to reality, placing them in the truth; here truth is not simply an idea, but a new existence of the whole person with and for others. Theologically, human truth must be understood as *personal* and *social,* corresponding to the *communal* nature of the revelation of Christ as *person.*

The Christology on which this soteriological movement depends has two dimensions. In one dimension Bonhoeffer repeatedly speaks of Christ in terms of the kerygma: as Christ is the resurrected Crucified One, so one dies to the old life in Adam and is resurrected into the new life in Christ, that is, in the community of Christ's presence. But this dimension depends for its articulation on the other: Christ is *person,* present in the relationships of sociality in the community of faith. It is this latter dimension which provides the specific content, so typical of Bonhoeffer's theology, for interpreting the kerygma.

The fundamental soteriological movement found in *Act and Being* is one which frees people from their self–imposed isolation into genuine

---

[106] AS 32, AB 39.

community and authentic selfhood. The classical soteriological passage
quoted above concludes with the statement that Christ breaks the
solitude of false being in the "self–dominated and self–interpreted
world." Consequently, the idea of the totally autonomous, self–contained and self–sufficient individual is an empty abstraction.[107] To be
encountered by the judgement and grace of revelation is to be directed
to humanity. This, of course, quite alters one's relation with others:
"Through the Christusperson the other human being is rescued from the
world of things [Dingwelt] ... into the social sphere of persons."[108] The
cor curvum in se becomes a person in community with others; individualistic self–seeking is overcome. To be in the new humanity of Christ
is to be in a community whose "behavior is believing and loving."[109]

   The reader familiar with the theology of the *Letters* cannot miss the
similarity between these Christological and anthropological statements
and the later formulations: Christ, "the one for others," and Christian
existence as "being for others." To be sure, the precise formulations of
the mature Bonhoeffer do not occur here. But their spirit is present. His
concern here, as well as his conceptuality, is "the sociality of Christ and
humanity." The striking passage on God's freedom in Christ being God's
freedom for humanity is fundamental to the resolution of the soteriological problem in *Act and Being*. Negatively, it diagnoses sin as imprisonment
in self through isolation from and domination of others; to be 'in Adam'
is not to be free from self or for others—such being is precisely a
"Beisichselbstbleiben." Positively, it presents Christ as the free and
liberating God who restores a person to true being in community with
others; in Christ God is free for humanity, setting people free to participate in the community of the new humanity of which he is the prototype
and personification.

D. BONHOEFFER'S THEOLOGICAL SITUATION, 1930–31

Completed in February, 1930, *Act and Being* was Bonhoeffer's most
important work between the writing of *Sanctorum Communio* in 1927 and
the theology he produced after taking up his university position in the

---

107 AS 117, AB 120.
108 AS 124, AB 127.
109 AS 111, AB 115.

winter semester of 1931–32.[110] Analysis of this complex work yields several conclusions about the continuities and developments in his theology up to 1930–31.

First, it is perfectly evident that his concern with "the significance of the sociological category for theology" and "the social intention of all the basic Christian concepts" is as programmatic in *Act and Being* as it was in *Sanctorum Communio*. All the major concepts minted in the first work are taken over into the second. "Person," as a Christological and anthropological concept personal life as involving relations of historical decision vis–à–vis the "other" as "Grenze," the mutual iteration of individual and corporate–communal life, Adam and Christ as the Kollektivpersonen of the old and new humanities, the personal–communal presence of Christ in revelation and the concomitant socio–ethical interpretation of transcendence—this whole conceptuality is indispensable for the argument of *Act and Being*.

Moreover, it is this understanding of the sociality of Christ and humanity which ultimately informs Bonhoeffer's critique of philosophical anthropology as much as it constitutes the point of departure for his treatment of the specific act–being question. Allowing the problems in his reading of various philosophers, his critique undoubtedly reveals his *own* concern: the isolated, individualistic, knowing I which interprets reality from itself as the center. This anthropological paradigm is so vigorously and consistently criticized because it is quite at variance with anthropology of Bonhoeffer's theology of sociality. More is at stake than the purely theoretical question of different philosophical approaches to the act–being dimensions of a given anthropology. The knowing I alone with itself in a violated world, or, the human community of persons whose center and life is Christ: this is the alternative Bonhoeffer poses.

Second, a new emphasis appears in Bonhoeffer's theology of sociality in his desire to develop a social ontology. The anthropology of *Sanctorum Communio*, particularly in its presentations of Adam and Christ, pointed toward the concern with human *being* in communities and the continuity and unity of the self which are explicit in *Act and Being*; but the first book was chiefly 'actualistic' in its views of revelation and human being. In *Sanctorum Communio* Bonhoeffer could say that in encounter with the divine Word present in the other, "the person arises and passes away in time." This was fine polemics against idealism, but

---

[110] During the academic year 1930–31 Bonhoeffer was a post–doctoral fellow at Union Theological Seminary, New York.

hardly an adequate answer to the question about the continuity and unity of human existence vis–à–vis the kerygma which challenges people to relinquish an old life and receive a new life. Bonhoeffer therefore addressed a problem in his own theology, as well as in the theologies of others, when he took up the question of act and being. His first book had been significantly influenced by the 'actualism' of the early dialectical theology. Now he undertook a correction, and he did it with the tools of sociality. Consistent with his critique of the anthropological problems attending a starting point in epistemology, he did not approach ontology as a meta–*physics,* as did Aristotle. He tried, rather, to approach ontology as a phenomenology of the being of God and human beings in the social relationships of historical, human communities. In so doing he stressed the necessity for concrete anthropological concepts in theology (being 'in Adam' or 'in Christ') against formal and neutral interpretations. More significantly still, he perceived the being of Christ with the same concreteness: his freedom is that freedom in which his *being is with and for* humanity; this formulation was to lead to the Christological formula, "Christ, the man for others," so crucial in the prison letters.

Third, *Act and Being* confirms the contention that theological anthropology is a fundamental aspect of Bonhoeffer's theology. The book arises out of the anthropological issues of consciousness and conscience, and the treatment of the act–being question moves from the critical analysis of philosophical anthropology to a constructive treatment of precisely these issues in its theological conclusion. Unless the anthropological issues of the book are acknowledged, the treatment of revelation and Christology is not intelligible.

This leads to the fourth conclusion. In *Act and Being* Bonhoeffer *clearly* articulates for the first time the distinctive soteriological problem in his theological anthropology. The following chapter will present evidence from other texts in 1930–31, and beyond, which give identical accounts of the particular human problem to which he returns again and again. His inaugural lecture and seminar papers from his year at Union Seminary continue to paint the portrait of the isolated, self–imprisoned I, violating social relationships in its knowing and its intellectual power. Showing this to be an existential problem for the theologian explains why the argument of *Act and Being* moves on two levels; obviously and avowedly, Bonhoeffer is dealing with the act–being question; just as obviously, though not as clearly acknowledged by him, he is formulating and grappling with this soteriological problem which has a particular theological urgency because of its existential dimension.[111] Consciousness and conscience, the germinal ideas, lead to this soteriological problem in the heart of the anthropology.

The articulation of this soteriological problem is the most significant new element which appears when *Act and Being* is compared with *Sanctorum Communio*. Retrospectively, to be sure, we can see it is adumbrated in the first book. Here it appears in clear focus. This insight leads to the next chapter, which will give a comprehensive anlysis of the soteriological problem in Bonhoeffer's theology, document its autobiographical dimension, and examine its theological and personal resolution in 1932 when Bonhoeffer made a turning "from the phraseological to the real" and laid the foundations for *The Cost of Discipleship*.

---

[111] These two levels, or the double agenda as we might put it, partly explain the uncertainty found in the secondary literature, and also problems in the attitude to philosophy in the primary text.

Chapter 4

FROM THE PHRASEOLOGICAL TO THE REAL: 1932

There is a noble lineage in Christian theology in which an intimate relationship obtains between the thinking of theologians and their personal experience as Christians. Simply to name Augustine, Luther, and Kierkegaard amply demonstrates this fact. Bonhoeffer belongs to this lineage. This is not to deny significant connections between the theological and personal concerns of Bonhoeffer's older contemporaries in Protestant theology, such as Barth, Bultmann, and Tillich. Among these leaders of modern theology, however, Bonhoeffer is the only one who is a child of this century, and it may be that the distinctive character of his own particular concerns as a theologian and a Christian illuminates the remarkably catholic appeal of his life and writings.

The year 1932 was decisive for Bonhoeffer. In the two previous years, several experiences and deep, personal concerns had affected him profoundly. These came to fruition in the summer of 1932. He described the change in words taken for the title of this chapter: "a turning away from the phraseological to the real." Looking back on the 1932 experience twelve years later, he wrote to Bethge, with typical restraint:

> There are people who change, and many who can scarcely change at all. I don't think I have ever changed very much, except perhaps at the time of my first impressions abroad and under the first conscious influence of Papa's personality. Then a *turning away from the phraseological to the real ensued.*[1] Furthermore, I don't think that you

---

[1] This German sentence reads: "Damals ist eine Abkehr vom Phraseologischen zum Wirklichen erfolgt." The English translation ("It was

105

have altered much yourself. ...Neither of us have really experienced
a break [Bruch][2] in our lives. Certainly we have deliberately broken
[gebrochen] with a good deal, but even that is again something quite
different. (Even the time we both experience now does not mean a
break in the passive sense.)[3] Earlier I often used to long for such a
break myself. Now I think differently about it. Continuity with one's
past is also a great gift. Paul wrote I Tim. 1:13 ["I formerly blasphemed..."] as well as II Tim. 1:3a [I thank God whom I serve with a
clear conscience..."]. Everything seems to me to have been guided
inevitably, necessarily, and straightforwardly by Providence.[4]

then that I turned from phraseology to reality." [LPP 275]) suggests an almost
causal sequence of overseas experience, his father's personality, and the ensuing
personal 'turning.' Without contending that these influences are unrelated to his
"turning away from the phraseological," I find two difficulties with the English
rendering. First, it is misleading not to differentiate the ensuing personal
experience more carefully from the earlier influences. As we shall see, many
years prior to the 1944 statement Bonhoeffer had explicitly identified the *Bible*
as the most decisive factor in this 'turning,' not his travels or his father. Second,
careful differentiation is required by the fact that this statement in the letter can
hardly be read as a simple chronological sequence. Such a reading would require
the assumption that his father's personality had no conscious influence upon him
until after his travels in Spain and America, i.e., when, in 1932, he was twenty–
six years of age; this assumption, I think, would be very difficult to sustain. Even
if it were proved, however, the first reason would not be invalidated.

2   But see the discussion below where the word 'Bruch' is precisely the
term Bonhoeffer uses in *Nachfolge* to describe the disciple's step into obedience,
and his own "turning away from the phraseological to the real."

3   My parentheses. By "passive" break Bonhoeffer means, as the context
indicates, one that has not been made by deliberate, personal choice.

4   Letter of 22.4.1944: WE 397f., LPP 275f; italics mine. It is pertinent
briefly to observe that this reflection on the course of his life was written at a
time when he had passed beyond the *Nachfolge* period; Bonhoeffer articulates
this explicitly three months later in the letter of July 21, 1944 (WE 542f., LPP
369f.). In *Nachfolge* the theological, autobiographical, and political–ethical
stress is on the "break," though it is a break in the form of a "turning away"
which brings to reality what had previously been words. At that time the
"break" is more emphasized than the continuity. At the end of his life the
emphasis is on continuity, though this integration includes the "turning." In the
letter of July 21, 1944, Bonhoeffer plainly says that he could only have reached
his present position "along the road I have travelled." Bethge confirms this
interpretation: "You are quite right that Bonhoeffer's perspective in the early
30s was naturally different since he was really after something else, while
towards the end he looked back and then emphasized the continuity" (letter of
January 23, 1971). (It is quite relevant to recall here Bonhoeffer's concern in
Act and Being for continuity of personal being, especially his desire to integrate
the *whole* life of the self—including the "old self" in the "new self"—within the
dynamics of revelation, faith and the Christian community with its Word of
judgment and grace.)

This "turning," Bethge has shown in his biography, was completed during 1932.[5] In the same year the foundations for *Discipleship,* eventually published in 1937, were laid.[6] This illuminating experience must be related to the theology which preceded and issued from it.

This chapter is complex. Its soteriological focus draws together several major themes. Section A concentrates on *power* as the specific soteriological problem in Bonhoeffer's early theology, analyzing his writings in two sections: the power of the ego, and the problem of power in society. The passages on the power of the ego disclose the important fact that Bonhoeffer's theological writings on this problem have an autobiographical dimension; his autobiographical memoirs show a detailed correlation between the problem of the power of the ego in his theology and in his own personal life. This section concludes by discussing why the problem of power, in its personal and corporate forms, may properly be regarded as a genuine soteriological problem in theology. Section B examines Bonhoeffer's commitment to personal faith and the church in 1932 against the background of his adolescent decision to become a theologian. The insights provided by his biographer further illumine the personal problem of the power of the ego, and they detail the nature of the change in 1932 and its immediate theological effects. This naturally leads to Section C, where the analysis of *Discipleship* shows that its theology is a direct result of the personal 'turning' in 1932. The discussion of *Discipleship* establishes that its theology of discipleship *presupposes* the theology of sociality, adding the element of *obedience* to it; that the book is pervaded by an 'autobiographical dimension' which must be recognized in order fully to understand its text; and that it contains unresolved theological and personal problems which grow out of the 1932 experience and point forward to their resolution in the prison letters. Section D, finally, sets out the influence of personal discipleship on Bonhoeffer's theological development during the 1930s, showing new interests and ideas, and signs of his way ahead.

A caveat must be entered before continuing. I speak advisedly of the "autobiographical *dimension*" of Bonhoeffer's theology. The argument which follows shows that a full understanding of Bonhoeffer's theological development requires an acknowledgment of this dimension, especially in *Discipleship.* But I oppose the use of this insight in any form of psychological reductionism. Bonhoeffer's theology is not, to paraphrase Schleiermacher, "personal psychological affections set forth in speech."

---

5 DB 246ff., DB-E 202ff.
6 DB 515ff., DB-E 450ff.

If we recall the major influences of Barth's theology on Bonhoeffer's thought, his responsibility to the classical theological tradition, his running debate with his Lutheran heritage, and his attention to contemporary philosophical developments and to cultural and political movements, and particularly his exegetical basis in *Discipleship*, then such reductionism must be ruled out. My purpose, therefore, is to illuminate Bonhoeffer's theology by showing its autobiographical dimension, not to make a side excursion into biography.

The first topic, then, is the soteriological problem of power in Bonhoeffer's early theology.

A. The Soteriological Problem: Human Power

Bonhoeffer does not explicitly announce that power is the soteriological problem on which he intends to concentrate. Therefore his various discussions of sin and the human problematic in the early writings must be gathered to show that it is indeed accurate to designate power as the central soteriological issue which concerns him.

A working definition of power is necessary to make this analysis. Power is a concept with a long, complex history. The modern term has a rich set of connotations which, in addition to the general use, includes special meanings in political, legal, military, mathematical, and technological usage. Throughout this wide range of meaning two main themes can be distinguished. The one refers to capacity, ability, capability, and efficacy; it stresses potency in contrast to impotence. Webster summarizes this theme as "capability of acting or of producing an effect." The other, which Webster describes as "a position of ascendancy, ability to compel obedience," has synonyms like authority, dominion, control, command, might, and force. In a shorthand formulation the former is "power as capacity necessary for self–fulfillment" and the latter "power as dominance." It is the latter theme, "power as dominance," which is basic to this analysis of the soteriological problem in Bonhoeffer. Indeed, if dominating power constitutes a grave problem in personal and social life, it is equally true that there can be no life if it is devoid of, or denied, capacity and effectiveness, that is, power of being.[7] I will argue that it is precisely by dealing with *dominating power* in his theological and

---

[7]   In this positive sense Tillich consistently regarded power as an essential component in the dynamics of all being.

personal pilgrimage that Bonhoeffer is able to arrive at that Christian celebration of human *strength* and *maturity* which is so conspicuous in the prison writings.

This preliminary definition leads to analysis of the soteriological problem of power. The evidence will be presented in two parts, the first considering the individual person under the rubric "the power of the ego," and the second analyzing the corporate aspect in a discussion of "the problem of power in society." This procedure accords well with Bonhoeffer's contention that individual, personal life is always set in a corporate, social matrix; it also follows the movement of his thinking, first seen in *Sanctorum Communio,* from the interpersonal to the corporate relations of human sociality. Further, it permits a distinction between Bonhoeffer's existential concern with the power of the ego, and the forms of power prevalent in his society.

1. THE POWER OF THE EGO

The term 'ego' is used deliberately, though without digressing into all the complexities of conflicting psychological theories.[8] In light of the psychoanalytic tradition of Freud and the post–Freudians, however, the term 'ego' does point to a particular aspect of the human self. For the present purpose it is sufficient to say that 'ego' is used in a general sense to refer to the following activities of the unified and conscious self: rational analysis and organization of the natural world and the human social environment, as in science, technology, social and personal planning; deliberate willing toward specified goals; reflection on past and present experience, and mental projection of future activities; calculating the consequences of behavior; conscious regulation of emotional and instinctual self–expression; problem solving; intellectual activities throughout the range of human experience; synthesizing perceptions and data; conscious decision–making, judgment, and evaluation. I group these activities of the self under the concept of *ego.* All these activities contribute to autonomy, competence, and mastery in personal life.

---

8   Cf. George S. Klein, "Psychoanalysis II: Ego Psychology," *International Encyclopedia of the Social Sciences,* ed. David L. Sills (New York: Macmillan Company and the Free Press, 1968), vol 13, pp. 11–31. In particular the present discussion cannot go into the issue of whether 'ego' implies independent energy motivated to competence (e.g., Heinz Hartman, Robert W. White, and others) or whether it draws its energy from the id as Freud contended; Klein's article presents these views and evaluates the state of ego theory.

This discussion of personal power is further clarified by relating the definition of 'ego' to the concept of 'self'. The working definition of ego does not identify *ego* with *self*.[9] 'Self' is the term used here to refer to the whole personality, including, together with the ego, those unconscious aspects designated in psychological theory as id and superego. Nor do I imply that the ego is the sole seat of power, as it were, in the self. The power of instinctual drives, on the one hand, and the power of the superego, on the other is obvious; with respect to the superego, it is evident that both the pressure of an accusing conscience (negative superego) and the claim of the positive conscience (superego as ego–ideal) can generate great energy and power for good and ill. The argument here simply contends that it is the power of that aspect of the self described as ego which is central to the soteriological problem in Bonhoeffer's theology and personal experience. Again, I do not wish arbitrarily to isolate ego from id and superego, as if they were unconnected; rather, the analysis concentrates on that aspect of the self with which Bonhoeffer was most concerned: the ego.[10]

----

9   'Self' is commonly used as the comprehensive term in psychological literature. Some theorists use it as virtually equivalent to other integrative concepts like personality and identity. Some differentiate self and ego, as I do here in line with the psychoanalytic tradition, regarding self as the comprehensive category and ego as a sub–category; others use self and ego interchangeably. Cf. Muzafer Sherif, "Self Concept," *International Encyclopedia of the Social Sciences.,* ed. David L. Sills (New York: Macmillan Company and the Free Press, 1968), vol. 14, pp. 151–59.

10   Bonhoeffer, of course, no more provides us with this analytical conceptuality than he explicitly announces power as the focus for his soteriology. But the evidence will show that the conceptuality is appropriate and elucidating. In reply to the possible objection that the use of certain categories from the psychoanalytic tradition is quite alien to Bonhoeffer himself and also to the psychiatric approach of his father, the following observations are pertinent. First, the reader is referred to Appendix E (in the microfilm version of this work), "Preliminary Note on Karl Bonhoeffer's Attitude to Psychoanalysis"; this corrects the common but erroneous view that his attitude was "antagonistic"; see also my "Two Bonhoeffers on Psychoanalysis" in A. J. Klassen ed., *A Bonhoeffer Legacy* (Grand Rapids: Eerdmans, 1981), 58–75. Second, Chapter 6 includes discussion of the similarities between Dietrich Bonhoeffer's critique of religion and that of Freud. Further, the discussion shows that, all unbeknown to Bonhoeffer himself, his theology has considerable significance for problems in Freud's anthropology and views of human society. These similarities and differences are uncovered and illuminated by the use of certain psychoanalytic concepts. Third, it is quite legitimate methodologically to use, for heuristic purposes, categories not employed by a given thinker, so long as his writings contain evidence demonstrating the appropriateness of the categories.

Given this working definition of 'ego,' within the dynamics of the whole self, I contend that for Bonhoeffer the soteriological problem is centered on the *power* of the dominating ego.[11] The capacities of the ego are used to advance and serve the self and as power to dominate others; this destroys the mutuality of love and freedom which should characterize human sociality, and so people are alienated from one another and isolated in their self–centered egotism.

This focus on the power of the ego in Bonhoeffer's thought is sharpened by seeing it in a broad, historical perspective. Speaking generally, we can consider the asceticism of the classical Christian tradition as related to the id in psychological theory, and Luther's preoccupation with the problem of conscience as related to the superego, especially in its negative, accusing function. By referring to the power of the *ego,* I intend to locate elsewhere the heart of the soteriological problem in Bonhoeffer's thought. For him neither instinctual drives nor the guilty conscience with its repressed anger and compulsive works occupy the center of the stage. The issue for Bonhoeffer is whether the powers of the ego will be used for the service of others, or whether they will function in a dominating and egocentric way.

The case that the soteriological problem in Bonhoeffer's theology is focused on the power of the ego is documented by a most striking phenomenon in his early writings. This is the regular recurrence of seven passages which, often formulated in identical phrases, consistently identify the soteriological problem from 1927 to 1932. These formulations recur in quite diverse discussions: the effect of sin on the primal community, the presuppositions of philosophical anthropology, the critique of idealism, and the exegesis of Genesis 3. There are four major themes in these passages: the *power* of the ego, its *dominance* of others, the *violation of created sociality,* and the function of *conscience* in accusing the isolated self and exhorting one to the "better self."

These passages are crucial, and must be quoted at length. The first one is found in *Sanctorum Communio*; it adumbrates the recurrent themes, although not as completely or as compactly as the later passages. The problem is indicated in several statements throughout the book.

> Sin [is] . . . the will that in principle affirms as valuable only itself, and not the other, and that acknowledges the other only on its own terms.[12]

---

[11] The relation between Bonhoeffer's writing on the problem of the dominating ego and his own behavior in personal relationships is discussed later.

[12] SC 248, SC-E 118. See also: the description of unholy conflict as that in which one will forces itself upon and subjects another (SC 54, SC-E 86); the

Fallen Adam, accordingly, personifies the whole of sinful humanity in being "extremely egocentric."[13] Therefore, while the primal community

> grew up on the basis of love, with the fall its place is taken by *Selbstsucht.* This led to the break in unmediated *community with God,* as likewise in the unmediated *human community....*

> Whereas the primal relation of people to one another is one of giving, in the state of sin it is *purely demanding.* Every person exists in complete, voluntary isolation, no longer sharing with others the same life in God. Now everyone has his own conscience. There was no conscience in the primal state.... *Conscience* can just...as well be *the ultimate prop of human self–justification* as the place where Christ strikes home at people through the law.[14]

The second passage is from *Act and Being*, completed in February, 1930. Here the four themes appear in sharp definition.[15]

> 'In Adam' means: being in untruth, i.e. in culpable *perversion of the will* (i.e., one's essence) *inwards to the self, cor curvum in se. The individual has torn himself out of the community with God, and thus also with other people,* and now he *stands alone,* which is in untruth. Because he is alone the world is 'his' world, *the neighbor has sunk into the world of things...,* and *God has become a religious object;* but *he himself has become his own creator,* his own master and property. That in his knowing he must now begin and end with himself corresponds to his situation, for now he is utterly *'by himself' in the falsehood of naked self–lordship.*[16]

---

proclivity of Geist qua reason to serve as an instrument of domination especially by predicating human relations on a subject–object relation, rather than an I–You relation, thereby opening the way to treating other persons as objects and things (SC 26f., SC-E 45f.); the interpretation of the empirical spread of sin because one's movement to love in community meets egocentricity in others rather than mutuality (SC-E 117); the sharp distinction between a Herrschaftsverband— applicable to the Christian community in terms of the serving of the divine love—and a Gewaltverband, constituted by a relation of power, which requires mechanical obedience and precludes community (SC 59f., SC-E 91f.; SC-E 261).

13 SC 91, SC-E 146; cf. SC-E 150.

14 SC 69f., SC-E 107f., italics mine.

15 I noted in Chapter 3 that Bonhoeffer wrote to Seeberg and Rössler in the summer of 1928 about his current work on the problem of *consciousness* and *conscience;* cf. DBW 10 81ff., 90ff., 102f., 105, GS III 15ff., GS I 53. This suggests that his thinking on the soteriological problem was being further pursued and clarified; indeed, when he finished *Act and Being* he had formulated the problem in terms he was to repeat, almost verbatim, in the following three years.

16 Selbstherrlichkeit, selbstherrlich. The German terms have the dual connotation of lordship and glorification; see below where, in a paper written in

Human thought and philosophy in sin is self–glorifying...; all knowledge, including and above all the γνῶθι σεαυτόν, is ultimately intent on human self–justification. But eventually, under the colossal burden of being creator and bearer of a world, in the *cold silence of his eternal solitude,* he becomes anxious about himself and begins to dread. Now, elevating himself to be the final judge of himself he indicts himself— in the voice of *conscience.* But the answer of indicted person is remorse *(contritio activa!).* The *conscience* and remorse of a person in Adam are his *ultimate grasp for himself, the confirmation and justification of his autocratic* [selbstherrlich] *solitude.* He impeaches himself and *summons his better self.* Yet *the cry of conscience* only disguises the mute loneliness of a bleak isolation ['Bei–sich'] and sounds without echo *in the self–dominated and self–interpreted world....* Only when Christ breaks a person's solitude does he know himself placed in the truth.[17]

Systematic shape can be given to the four major themes involved in the problem of the power of the ego as they appear in this passage; in doing so, some phrases and nuances of passages which follow will be anticipated. Then the other five passages will be quoted to confirm and add detail to the systematic analysis given here.

The person described by Bonhoeffer in the passage is a man of *power.* He is a "creator and lord," ruling over all he surveys. A godlike figure, he is the "creator and bearer of a world." Bonhoeffer emphasizes particularly the role of this autonomous man's thought and philosophy in his power; this emphasis pervades *Act and Being.* He thereby draws attention to the aspect of the self I have defined as the *ego.* "Human thought and philosophy in sin is self–glorifying"; intellectual activity serves the glory of the self. By the powers of his ego this man exists in and as the center of a "self–interpreted world." Reality and truth are

---

English, Bonhoeffer makes the identical point, speaking of the "autocracy and self–glorification...in philosophy."

[17] AS 136–140, AB 137-141, italics mine. Compare the numerous other statements in *Act and Being* which repeat throughout the book the themes gathered together in this passage; these have been noted in Chapter 3. Recall especially the following, its vivid and passionate language occasioned by a critique of Hegel: "The concrete person, including the philosopher, is not in full possession of Geist; to imagine that he needs only to come to himself in order to be in God must lead to horrible disillusionment in experiencing the total self–introversion [In–sich–selbst–gekehrt–Seins], the self–confinement and isolation of the very loneliest solitude with its tormenting desolation and sterility" (AS 35, AB 42). (Where masculine language appears in these quotations, it appropriately indicates the autobiographical reference, though without denying the wider import of the analysis.)

grounded in his own interpretation and knowledge; his knowing must "begin and end with himself." Moral self–knowledge also serves self–justification. This effort, furthermore, is ultimately successful. To be sure, this powerful man is not totally free from remorse and Angst. Yet it is imperative to note that conscience is described as an instrument of his power, not as the means of his defeat; it is "the confirmation and justification of his autocratic" attitude. In the following passages Bonhoeffer will describe this man of powerful ego as heroic and conquering, as a "despot" and "autocrat." His credo is: "God is man himself." He is the man who overcomes his few small weaknesses to become God's self–appointed defender and victorious champion.

Next, this self with the powerful ego *dominates* others. Because his lordship is false, he rules over others as "things." God, too, is regarded as "a religious object." In the egocentricity of this powerful man, demanding replaces giving and competition excludes mutuality, as the *Sanctorum Communio* passage stated. The "self–interpreted world" is a "self–dominated" world.

The corollary follows: *created sociality is violated.* In dominating others one is torn "out of community with God, and thus also with other people." This is inevitable when others are "things" and God a "religious object." Having made himself a creator and lord by the powers of his own ego, neither God nor his neighbors are regarded as a genuine boundary [Grenze]. God and neighbor are subordinated to the powerful ego of the self; they are not genuine "others" to be loved and served in mutuality, but things to be used. Power, not mutual love, characterizes the self–other relationships. Just as true social relations with others are violated, so the true social existence of the individual is lost. To be sure, people still live in social relations and corporate structures, but these are everywhere torn apart by an egocentric and isolated individualism. One lives in "bleak isolation," in the "cold silence of his eternal solitude," "utterly by himself." The one enclosed in the "self–interpreted world" of his own intellectual achievement cannot enter into 'real' relations with others, in Bonhoeffer's definition of human reality. He lives from, by, and for himself, his will directed to himself; his "being in untruth" is this isolated self–sufficiency which thinks that the other person is not needed.

Finally, *conscience*—as the conscience of the self with the powerful ego—gives voice to the plight of this man, not least in dramatizing the dilemma of conscience itself. Conscience, according to this *Act and Being* passage, has two aspects: "he impeaches himself and summons his better self." This accusation and exhortation arise out of his situation of isolated lordship, ruling over a world made by his own interpretation and cut off from the others whom he dominates in his power. The conscience which "disguises the mute loneliness...in the self–dominated and self–interpreted world" is, as Bonhoeffer puts it in other passages, the attempt to "take the place of the missing other," to "feign the presence and reality of an other in his life." Negatively, conscience is the self–accusation which arises from violated sociality. Positively, conscience is also one's self–exhortation to live up to his "better self," that is, to relate freely to others in love and service. In this way he could be freed from the attempt to live alone in the self–imposed isolation which accompanies dominating and self–sufficient power. He would then be reunited with God, his neighbors, and the other creatures. But in his present isolated condition he can neither relate freely to others nor really find himself. The dilemma of conscience in Bonhoeffer's phenomenology, however, is that it is a self–serving instrument. It is "the ultimate grasp of a person for himself, the confirmation and justification of his autocratic solitude." As *self*–accusation and *self*–exhortation, it is a powerful means of self–assertion and self–justification. Conscience does not defeat or transform this man, but is co–opted by his powerful self–will; it "sounds without echo," and, as another passage puts its, "its call fades away into the silent, dominated world of the ego." The tragic circle is closed. "Only when Christ breaks a person's solitude does he know himself placed in the truth."

Additional passages on this soteriological problem confirm our analysis with striking consistency of thought and language, and finally reveal the autobiographical dimension within Bonhoeffer's formulation of the problem. The third of the seven passages occurs in the inaugural lecture on "The Anthropological Question in Contemporary Philosophy and Theology," delivered on July 31, 1930.

> The sinful person...finds himself in a humanity which has *fallen away from God because it wanted to be like him,* and now stands under his judgment. He sees himself condemned as an individual and as everyman.... The spirit of sin has torn him away from the Spirit *of God and from his neighbor. Now his spirit circles continually around itself. Now he is lord of the world,* but only of just that world *which his ego interprets for itself; he is lord in his self–enclosed, violated world. He sees his fellow man as a thing,* and God as the one who satisfies his *religious needs.* Now he seeks to establish himself eternally in this world; he does not wish to die, he wants to justify himself and live eternally. But in searching for this...*he begins to feel a frightful loneliness.* He becomes anxious about his *lordship over a dead world,* and in his Angst he breaks the *fearful silence* of his loneliness; he breaks loose from himself, *encounters himself in order to take the place of the*

missing other and indicts himself. That is *conscience.* But since he is accuser, defendant, and judge all in one, *the call of conscience proves itself to be nothing other than the ultimate grasp of the ego for itself. And its call fades away in the silent, dominated world of the ego.*[18]

The fourth and fifth passages on the soteriological problem came several months later in two papers which he wrote in English at Union Theological Seminary. So deeply is this concern embedded in his mind, that his exposition of Barth to John Baillie's seminar finds Bonhoeffer, as one scholar has already observed, quoting himself![19] Bonhoeffer's subject[20] obliged him to present the soteriological problem in a theological analysis of philosophy. In this fourth passage, comprised of several sentences from the Barth paper, the discussion refers first to idealism, and then to realism; but the analysis soon pushes beyond all philosophies to the anthropological problem in general.

> Here [in idealism] the ego is found not only as reflecting, but even a creative ego. It creates its world itself. *The ego stands in the center of the world, which is created, ruled, overpowered by the ego.* The identification of the ego with the ground of everything which as been called God is inevitable. *There are no limits for the ego; its claim and its power are boundless;* it is its own standard. *Here all transcendence is pulled into the circle of the creative ego....* Man knows himself immediately by the act of the coming of the ego to itself, and knows through himself essentially everything, even God. *God is in man;* God is man himself....

> [Realism] claims to leave room for transcendent reality [but cannot prove] that its definition of reality is not its own interpretation of it. As long as realism fails here, transcendent reality has to be referred to *the interpreting ego,* which constitutes reality and which, even though it

---

18   DBW 10 375f., GS III 81f., CW I 66f., italics mine.

19   Hans Pfeifer, *Das Kirchenverständnis Dietrich Bonhoeffers. Ein Beitrag zur theologischen Prinzipienlehre,* unpublished doctoral dissertation, Heidelberg, 1964, p. 74, cited DB 196 n. 38, DB-E 959 n. 37. Pfeifer does not draw attention to our passage, but to another. The biographer suggests that it was zeal as Barth's advocate which explains Bonhoeffer's quoting himself. While this may be a factor, the explanation must surely include the fact that Bonhoeffer is here dealing with a fundamental problem in his theology of sociality which is also a decisive existential concern for himself. These self–quotations are evidence of the extent to which he is presenting his own theology together with his exposition of Karl Barth. (The phenomenon also shows that Bonhoeffer had identified with Barth's theology to a significant degree.)

20   "The Theology of Crisis and its Attitude towards Philosophy and Science."

denies it, *remains the center of reality.* The ego knows reality and it knows itself. *It is essentially autonomous.*

Man in *statu corruptionis* is indeed alone, he is *his own creator and lord, he is indeed the center of his world of sin. He made himself God and God his creature....* The world of man is the world of *egocentricity,* of godlessness.

Man must remain alone in his overpowered and misinterpreted world.

Away from Christ we live in our own overpowered and egocentric world.[21]

The fifth passage, also from early 1931, states more clearly than the fourth the point stressed before, namely the dominance of the powerful, egocentric man over his neighbors, and thus the perversion of created sociality.

Conceived reality is not reality any longer.[22] The reason for this is that *thinking is in itself a closed circle, with the ego as the center....* Thinking does violence to reality, pulling it into *the circle of the ego,* taking away from it its original 'objectivity'. Thinking always means system, and system excludes reality. Therefore, it has to call *itself* [Bonhoeffer's italics] the ultimate reality, and *in this system the thinking ego rules.*

It follows that not only his fellow man but also God is subordinated to the ego. That is the strict consequence of the idealistic, and, as far as I see, of all exact philosophical thinking which tries to be *autonomous.* This fact of the *captivity of human thinking within* itself, that is to say, of *its inevitable autocracy and self–glorification* as it is found in philosophy, can be interpreted theologically as the corruption of the mind, which is caused by the first fall. *Man 'before' the fall must be thought of as being able to think of 'reality,' that means to think of God and the fellow man as realities. Man 'in' and 'after' the fall refers everything to himself, puts himself in the center of the world, does violence to reality, makes himself God, and God and the other man his creature.*[23]

---

21   DBW 10 434ff., GS III 119f., 122f., 126, italics mine. Some of the same themes are repeated in a discussion of "The Religious Experience of Grace and the Ethical Life," GS III 91ff., esp. 92, 97ff.; cf. DBW 10 416ff.

22   'Reality' here clearly refers to that socio–ethical definition of reality first set forth in *Sanctorum Communio,* i.e., social relationships of love, freedom, ethical responsibility, and mutuality among people in the community created by the serving rule of the divine love.

23   DBW 10 424f.; GS III 101; Bonhoeffer's English, italics mine. (See the following pages for the continuing use of the concepts: person, transcen-

The sixth passage is located in the lectures on "Creation and Sin" given during the 1932–33 winter semester. Bonhoeffer presents a theological interpretation of Adam's fall narrated in Genesis 3. Adam

> is *sicut deus*. He gets his own way. He is himself creator, source of life, and origin of the knowledge of good and evil. *He is only for himself, he lives out of himself, he no longer needs others; he is lord of his world, but now of course the solitary lord and despot of the mute, violated, silenced, dead ego–world.*

> But as man *sicut deus* he really *cannot live...without God, without the other persons or without the other creatures.* In *conscience* and remorse *he always seeks to feign the presence and the reality of another in his life.* He accuses and torments himself; and he *glorifies himself— all in order to escape, through lying, from the dreadful loneliness of an echo–less solitude.*[24]

The seventh, and final, passage comes from the summer of 1932.[25] It is in a quite different literary genre, and was unpublished for many years; yet it makes the same points, and does so with similar imagery.

> Solemnly he stood there in the presence of his God, in the presence of his class. He was the *center of attention*. Did he look as he had wanted to look, serious and determined? ...The moment swelled into endless pleasure, the classroom expanded into the infinite. There he stood in *the center of the world as the herald and teacher of his knowledge and his ideals*; now they all had to listen to him in silence, and the blessing of the Eternal rested on his words and on his head. And again he felt ashamed. For he knew about his pitiful vanity.

> How often he had tried to master it....

---

dence, Grenze, reality, *actus directus,* and the historicity of both revelation and human existence.)

[24] SF 131f., CF 142. See also the consistent formulation in the 1932 summer–semester lectures on the church: "Der mensch in Adam herrscht über seine Welt und kann doch sein echoloses Alleinsein nicht überwinden. Jede Sünde ist erst Sünde, das heisst: Bruch der Gemeinschaft" (DB 1061, DBW 11 263f.). See too the repetition of the critique of reason in the same terms as given above in a review, written at this time, of Robert Jelke's *Vernunft und Offenbarung* (Gütersloh, 1932), DBW 12 200ff., GS III 136f. See also the consistent repetition of the basic soteriological problem in *Nachfolge;* fallen Adam is described exactly as before: "Adam became 'like God'—*sicut deus*— in his own way. But now that he had made himself god he no longer had a God. He ruled in solitude as a creator-god in a God-forsaken, subjected world" (N 298, CD 299).

[25] DB 63ff., DB-E 38ff.

It had made a tremendous impression on him when he had read in Schiller that one needed only to rid himself of a few small weaknesses *to be like the gods.* Since then he had been on the watch. *He would emerge from this struggle like a hero...*

[Seeing the distrust of the class he questions himself.] Didn't they think him capable of it? Didn't they believe in the sincerity of his intentions? Did they know something about him that he did not know himself?

Why are you all looking at me like that? . . . Denounce me as a mendacious, conceited person who *does not believe what he says!* Don't keep so considerately silent, as if you understood me! . . .

There is the throng. *He stands in the center and speaks,* fervently, passionately. He corrects himself. A leaden silence lies over the throng, a dreadful, silent mockery. No, it cannot be. He is not the man they take him to be. He really is in earnest. They have no right to scorn me. They are doing him wrong, all of them. He prays.

God, say yourself whether I am in earnest about you. Destroy me now if I am lying. Or punish them all; they are my enemies, and yours. They do not believe me. I know myself that I am not good. But I know it myself—and you, God, know it too. *I do not need the others. I, I, I shall triumph.* Do you see how I triumph? Do you see how they retreat? Their consternation? *I am with you!* I am strong. God, I am with you.

Do you hear me? Or do you not? To whom am I speaking? To myself? To you? To those others here?

Who is it that is speaking? My faith or my vanity?

God, I want to study theology. Yes, I have said so, and they all heard it. There is no more retreat.[26]

This last passage is autobiography. Bonhoeffer wrote it in a period of personal upheaval in 1932, reflecting upon and interpreting an experience he had as a high school student.[27] Few theologians have bared their souls with such candor as this. The memoir, as Bethge observes, shows the extent to which ambitiousness was involved in Bonhoeffer's adolescent decision to be a theologian. It also shows a remarkable congruity with the six theological passages from 1927 to 1932–33 quoted previously. The power of the ego, with its achievements of knowledge, ideals,

---

[26] DB 65f., DB-E 40f., following Victoria Barnett's version in the unabridged and revised translation; italics mine.

[27] DB 64f., DB-E 39f.

understanding, impressive speech, determination, and will power; the superiority over others, leading to the scene of glorious victory, defeating the enemies of self and God; the violation of sociality in dominant self–assertion and rejection of the unneeded others; and the internal self–accusations of conscience whose voice is subordinated to self–assertion and self–justification, finally to die away. Even the metaphors—especially the ego in the center, the silence of solitariness—are identical to those recurring in the theological writings. Here is a man with godlike power, ostensibly God's conquering hero on earth but in actuality an egocentric student of Schiller's advice.

This autobiographical memoir should be compared with, and its central points confirmed by, another from the same period. In it Bonhoeffer recalls his imagining himself, as a child, on his deathbed. He is the center of family attention, saying his last words to them all. Having secretly prepared this utterance many times, he will die an impressive, devout death—the boy, who, in the moment of death, is the advocate of God before his elder brothers and father.[28]

Another revealing piece of evidence throws additional light on Bonhoeffer's personal attitude to power, namely, his attraction to Michelangelo's statue, "The Victor." His sister, Susanne Dress, has reported that the Bonhoeffer children became acquainted with this statue from the picture and text of Romain Rolland's *Das Leben Michelangelos* (translated from French to German in 1920) which their father read them. As adolescents, Susanne and Dietrich discussed the statue at length. That it had more than passing significance for Bonhoeffer is shown by the fact that his sister later took him the book during his imprisonment. At that time the statue of "The Victor" expressed the feelings of a man who, with the members of his family, was obliged to resort to violent power in the effort to resist even more destructive violence.

Rolland begins his book with a paragraph on this statue—the picture follows immediately in the German edition.

> In the National Museum in Florence is a marble statue which Michael Angelo called "The Victor." It represents the beautiful nude figure of a young man, with curly hair over a low forehead. Standing erect, he has placed his knee on the back of the bearded prisoner, who bends and,

---

28   DB 62ff., DB-E 38f. This way of thinking about death perhaps casts in a different light the memories of Bonhoeffer's twin sister Sabine; cf. DB-E 38. Whether her brother's meditations had the same pious purity as her own may be doubted.

like an ox, stretches his neck forward. But the victor looks not upon him. When about to strike he stays his hand, and turns away his sad mouth and irresolute eyes. His arm falls back toward his shoulder. He throws himself backward. A desire for victory no longer fills his heart—it is repulsive to him. Though he has conquered, he in turn is vanquished.[29]

Larry Rasmussen, who secured the information about this book from Frau Dress, recounts her interpretation as follows:

> Here is the picture of the reluctant conspirator, the exerciser of violence who can find no pride in this practice, but who nonetheless must be "The Victor," who nonetheless must subdue the beast Hitler.... Michelangelo's "The Victor" is the embodiment of the way the Bonhoeffer family viewed their active resistance—a necessary, violent venture which must not be regarded as normative behavior, a matter of painful necessity in near apocalyptic times which must not be applauded as proud, militarist heroism.[30]

This is fair commentary on the attitude of Bonhoeffer during his imprisonment. However, it is likely (especially in view of some opinions Bonhoeffer expressed in Barcelona, found below) that in his younger days Bonhoeffer had other feelings about the statue. It is difficult to read about "the victor" described in the 1932 autobiographical memoir without concluding that Bonhoeffer at one time admired and identified with the figure of the conquering hero; he certainly describes himself in such images in his own writing. Yet precisely that memoir, and other autobiographical reflections, show that even as a young boy and an adolescent he had, to put it mildly, ambivalent attitudes toward conquest, competition, and domination. He knew the isolation and self–accusation which was the victor's bitter reward.

This problem occupied him, theologically and personally in the years from about 1929 to 1932. The resolution he reached in 1932 freed him, now purged of personal ambition, for that service of deputyship for others which his resistance activity embodied—even freed him for the necessary deed of violent power in spite of the guilt and abhorrence it then entailed. The autobiographical dimension of Bonhoeffer's theology, and

---

29 Romain Rolland, *The Life of Michael Angelo* (London: William Heinemann, 1922), translated from the French by Frederic Lees, p. v.

30 Rasmussen, *Dietrich Bonhoeffer: Reality and Resistance, Christology and Conspiracy,* Th.D. dissertation, Union Theological Seminary, New York, 1970, note on pp. 51–53. This note in not included in the published version of Rasmussen's work.

his personal attempt to resolve the soteriological problem, will be discussed in more detail later in the chapter.

This presentation has clearly identified the soteriological problem in Bonhoeffer's theology of sociality, especially as regards the individual person. In view of Bonhoeffer's Lutheran heritage, and the beginning of his modification of it already apparent in his discussions of conscience, a comparison with Luther highlights the specific forms of soteriology in the two theologians, thereby further clarifying Bonhoeffer's position.

At many points in his writings Bonhoeffer uses Luther's phrase, *cor curvum in se*, to summarize sin and the soteriological problem. Luther, Bonhoeffer implies, was saying exactly the same thing as himself. Yet while there are important similarities, there are decisive differences. Comparison highlights the distinctive, modern soteriological problem with which Bonhoeffer was concerned. It also indicates, as later comparisons further support, that Bonhoeffer appropriated insights from Luther which were fruitful for dealing with the problem of power in his own theology of sociality;[31] he is also highly selective in his reading of Luther, straining his interpretation to a virtual breaking point, in the effort to make the Reformer speak to a new problem.

The soteriological problem in Luther, theologically and personally, centers on the guilty conscience. This is such a well established point that lengthy documentation is not required. Ample quotations illustrating this may conveniently be found in the writings of Gordon Rupp and Gerhard Ebeling.[32] The following well–known passage from the 1545 Preface to his Latin writings is, as Rupp says,[33] a "most important piece of evidence" where Luther makes his point very clearly.

> Though I lived as a monk without reproach, I felt that I was a sinner before God with an extremely disturbed conscience. I could not believe that he was placated by my satisfaction. I did not love, yes, I hated the righteous God who punishes sinners, and secretly...I was

---

[31] See the discussion below of Bonhoeffer's portrait of Luther in *Nachfolge,* and the comparison of the *theologia crucis* in Bonhoeffer and Luther which is found in Chapter 5.

[32] See Rupp's *Luther's Progress to the Diet of Worms* (New York: Harper & Row, 1964), especially Chapter II, "Mr. Fearing," and *The Righteousness of God* (London: Hodder and Stoughton, 1953), especially Chapter 5, "The Bruised Conscience." In Ebeling's writings see particularly "Theological Reflexions on Conscience," and "The Necessity of the Doctrine of the Two Kingdoms," *Word and Faith* (Philadelphia: Fortress Press, 1963).

[33] *Luther's Progress to the Diet of Worms,* 33.

angry with God, and said, 'As if, indeed, it is not enough, that miserable sinners, eternally lost through original sin, are crushed by every kind of calamity by the law of the decalogue, without having God add pain to pain by the gospel and also by the gospel threatening us with his righteousness and wrath?' Thus I raged with a fierce and troubled conscience.[34]

Guilty conscience, works to placate the righteous God, hatred of God who demanded satisfaction by works, and full circle back to the guilty conscience—that was Luther's treadmill. The frontier which Luther crossed is deftly described by Erik Erikson in his perceptive study of the Reformer.

Luther accepted for his life work the unconquered frontier of tragic conscience, defined as it was by his personal needs and his superlative gifts. *'Locus noster,'* he said in the lectures on the Psalms, *'in quo nos cum Deo, sponsas cum sponsa, habitare debet...est conscientia.'* Conscience is that inner ground where we and God have to learn to live with each other as man and wife. Psychologically speaking, it is where

---

34 "Preface to the Complete Edition of Luther's Latin Writings," *Luther's Works*, vol. 34, *Career of the Reformer: IV*, ed. and trans. by Lewis W. Spitz (Philadelphia: Muhlenberg Press, 1960), pp. 336f. The theological resolution of the Reformer's personal crisis was, of course, his doctrine of justification with its strict distinction between law and gospel. The resolute exclusion of law from the conscience is beautifully expressed in Luther's 1531 lectures on Galatians. "Now we have said before, that the law in a Christian ought not to pass his bounds, but ought to have dominion only over the flesh, which is in subjection unto it, and remaineth under the same. When it is thus, the law is kept within his bounds. But if it shall seek to creep into thy conscience, and there seek to reign, see thou play the cunning logician and make the true division. Give no more to the law than belongeth unto it, but say thou: O Law, thou wouldest climb up into the kingdom of my conscience, and there reign and reprove it of sin, and wouldest take from me the joy of my heart, which I have by faith in Christ, and drive me to desperation, that I might be without all hope, and utterly perish. This thou dost besides thine office: keep thyself within thy bounds, and exercise thy power upon the flesh, but touch not my conscience; for I am baptized, and by the Gospel am called to the partaking of righteousness and everlasting life, to the kingdom of Christ, wherein my conscience is at rest, where no law is, but altogether forgiveness of sins, peace, quietness, joy, health and everlasting life. Trouble me not in these matters, for I will not suffer thee, so intolerable a tyrant and cruel tormenter, to reign in my conscience, for it is the seat and temple of Christ the Son of God, who is the king of righteousness and peace, and my most sweet saviour and mediator; he shall keep my conscience joyful and quiet in the sound and pure doctrine of the Gospel, and in the knowledge of this passive and heavenly righteousness." (*A Commentary on St. Paul's Epistle to the Galatians*, ed. Philip S. Watson; London: James Clarke & Co., 1953, 28.)

the ego meets the superego, that is where our self can either live in wedded harmony with a positive conscience or is estranged from a negative one.

Hans' son was made for a job on this frontier. But he did not create the job; it originated in the hypertrophy of the negative conscience inherent in our whole Judaeo–Christian heritage in which, as Luther put it: 'Christ becomes more formidable a tyrant and a judge than was Moses.'[35]

Despite similarities in the two men, Luther clearly was a late medieval theologian dealing with "the hypertrophy of the negative conscience" in the Catholic penitential piety; Bonhoeffer is a modern theologian dealing with the problematic of power in human social relations. A comparison shows similarities: forms of self–preoccupation and egotism lead both to speak of the *cor corvum in se;* both want to expose the futility of salvation by works, whether penitential and monastic works in Luther's case, or secular and academic achievements in the case of Bonhoeffer; and both give conscience a significant role in the soteriological problem.

But these similarities are expressions of a different problematic in each case; they arise in quite distinct historical, ecclesiastical, theological, and psycho–social contexts. Bonhoeffer does not begin with guilt, but with the *power* of the dominating and accomplished ego. Negative conscience is not the beginning and primary locus of his problem; conscience, as the attempt of the self "to replace the missing other," is the *consequence* of the isolation of the self in a violated sociality. Accordingly, while in Luther conscience as the accusation of the law prepares

---

35   *Young Man Luther* (New York: W. W. Norton, 1962), p. 195; the Luther quotations are from WA 3, 593 and WA 40 I, 562. Erikson overstates his historical generalization about "the negative conscience inherent in our Judaeo–Christian heritage"; see the highly instructive comparison of Paul, Augustine, and Luther in Krister Stendahl, "The Apostle Paul and the Introspective Conscience of the West," *Harvard Theological Review,* vol. 56, 1963, pp. 199–215; see also, for the shift from early Christian to medieval Catholic piety, George Hunston Williams, *Anselm: Communion and Atonement* (Saint Louis, Missouri: Concordia Publishing House, 1960). Paul Lehmann also questions whether Erikson, notwithstanding his distinction of positive and negative conscience, has sufficiently stressed Luther's accomplishment beyond the frontier of negative conscience, e.g., in his new concepts of person and society; cf. *Ethics in a Christian Context* (New York: Harper & Row, 1963), p. 365 n. 1, citing Karl Holl. Beyond these questions, however, Erikson's discussion of superego functioning as negative conscience in Luther is illuminating for our comparison with Bonhoeffer.

the way for the gospel, in Bonhoeffer it cannot serve this function; for if conscience is treated as the ultimate self–assertion of the powerful ego, it does not bring people to their knees but very successfully serves their own self–justification—hence its call always "dies away."[36] Again, while in Luther grace frees a person to serve and love the neighbor, as in Bonhoeffer, for Luther it is nevertheless not violated sociality per se, with its isolated loneliness, which constitutes the heart of the problem; but in Bonhoeffer the question is precisely how one can be free for others in a genuine mutuality of love and service, how the dominating and overpowering ego can be freed from itself into an authentic sociality. Not internal guilt with its hatred of God and self, and its compulsive, unsatisfying works, but power over others and the loss of mutual love in community—that is the crux of Bonhoeffer's soteriological problem. For this reason, the main Christological and anthropological answer, which runs from the earliest writings to the theology of the prison letters, develops the theme of God's freedom for humanity and Christ's freedom as "the one for others" who liberates people into service and vicarious action in free responsibility for others. Bonhoeffer's fallen Adam is a powerful, godlike figure, not a medieval penitent at his wit's end. Dominance, not guilt; power, not self–doubt; self–congratulation and vanity, not despair; God's self–appointed champion, not the hater of the heavenly Father with inordinate demands—these are the attributes of Bonhoeffer's fallen Adam. To follow Rupp's lead, we are dealing not with "Mr. Fearing," but with "Mr. Success," "Mr. Self–Made Man."[37]

Two major points have been sufficiently documented: first, in his early theology Bonhoeffer consistently defines the personal side of the soteriological problem as that of the powerful ego and its violation of the essential sociality of a person with others and with God; second, this was an existential problem for the theologian himself, as proved by the correlation of the theological passages and the autobiographical mate-

---

[36]　Already in *Sanctorum Communio* Bonhoeffer indicated his divergence from the traditional role of the law in Lutheran soteriology: "Conscience can just as well be the ultimate prop of human self–justification as the place where Christ strikes home at a person through the law' (SC 69f., SC-E 108). By *Nachfolge* this skepticism led to a reversal of the Lutheran schema (see below), and in the *Letters and Papers from Prison* the idea of "making every person a sinner first" was completely rejected.

[37]　See Bonhoeffer's 1934 sermon on this very subject, DBW 10 404-12, GS IV 174–79. It is quite autobiographical, and is discussed below in Chapter 6.

rial.[38] Now writings must be examined on the corporate side of the soteriological problem, to show Bonhoeffer's concern with destructive power as a problem in the life of society.

2. THE PROBLEM OF POWER IN SOCIETY

To what extent do we find in Bonhoeffer's early theology a concern with the problem of power in society which parallels his writings on the problem of the powerful ego? Certainly we have seen that in his discussions of the sin of the self he always considers the human person set in a social matrix, to the extent of according "general egotism" a large part in the empirical spread of sin, and describing Adam (the Kollektivperson of fallen humanity) as personifying the "extreme ego-centricity" of the whole human race. A closer examination of various writings shows that a concern with destructive power in society parallels his preoccupation with the dominating power of the individual ego.

Once again, *Sanctorum Communio* is indicative. Bonhoeffer has no problems with personal or social conflict in the 'primal creation'; indeed, it serves to generate strength [Kraft] of will.[39] Nor is the collective will to self–preservation problematic; indeed, that is the proper purpose of many human institutions.[40] The problem arises with sin, which perverts the original function of rational, purposive associations [Gesellschaft]. When the evil will is operative, such an association becomes *"an institution for the systematic exploitation of one by the other."*[41]

Seven years later Bonhoeffer makes this point in an even more forceful way, supporting it by references to philosophical tradition and to particular instances of social exploitation. He inveighs in a London sermon, written in English, against "an aristocratic philosophy of life which glorified strength and power and violence as the ultimate ideals of humanity." He indicts the church for having "adjusted itself far too easily to the worship of power," and asserts that "Christianity stands or falls with its *revolutionary protest against violence, arbitrariness and pride of power and with its plea for the weak.*"[42] Concretely he is

---

[38] See further the letters cited later in this chapter which amplify the autobiographical dimension.

[39] SC-E 84f.

[40] SC-E 118.

[41] SC 248, SC-E 118, italics mine.

[42] DBW 13 410, GS IV 180f., italics mine. The whole passage contains a clear allusion to Nietzsche: "Christianity is a religion of slaves, of people with

thinking of the poor, the aged, the insane, the untouchables of India, and black people in America— *"a man exploited by society, a coloured man in a white country."*[43]

It would impose an undue limitation on the range of Bonhoeffer's concern with social issues to suggest that he was interested only in those problems which manifest exploitative power. But it is not misleading to say that his concern with power in society is a central and recurrent theme in his early theological writings. His sensitivity to this problem led him to be one of the earliest and most uncompromising opponents of Nazi tyranny with its elaborate mythology of power worship, its grandiose program of conquest, and its dehumanized social vision. The same sensitivity made him an advocate of the Jews within Germany, and a tireless worker in the ecumenical movement for international peace. A study of some additional texts will confirm the recurrence of this leading theme.

The first passage comes from a lecture on Christian ethics in Barcelona.[44] It shows that initially Bonhoeffer himself was significantly involved in "the worship of power."[45] Discussing the problem of war, Bonhoeffer describes it as sinful and murderous, yet he justifies it in the name of the love concretely owed to one's own Volk. The Christian knows that his enemy is also fighting for his own Volk, and will attempt to love him as a Christian should. "Nevertheless I will do something to him which love and gratitude to my Volk, in which God lets me be born, commands me to do." Bonhoeffer traces back the question of whether war is justifiable in Christian ethics to the question of history, Volk, and God. In discussing this he presents the following piece of patent Lebensraum philosophy which is highly revealing; it should be compared with the autobiographical memoir quoted above.

> *Völker are like men.* They are immature and need leadership; they grow to the bloom of youth, to manhood, and they die. In this there is nothing which is either good or evil in itself. Yet profound questions

---

inferiority complexes." Bonhoeffer had read Nietzsche thoroughly in his youth.

43 Ibid.

44 "Grundfragen einer christlichen Ethik," February 8, 1929, now published in DBW 10 323-45, GS V 156–180, formerly published in part, not including the sections quoted here, in GS III 48–58, CW I 39–49; cf. DB 153f., DB-E 119.

45 After he had existentially come to terms with the problem of power in the personal "turning" of 1932, his attitude is quite different; the later passages discussed document this change of attitude.

are involved here, for growth requires expansion, and the increase of power [Kraft] involves pushing the other aside. This is the same in personal life and in the life of a Volk. But every Volk has a call of God in itself to make history, *to enter into the contest of the life of Völker.* It is valid to hear this call out of the growing and becoming of the Volk as it occurs in the sight of God. *God calls the Volk to manliness, to battle [Kampf], and to victory. The strength and the power [Macht] and the victory is from God who creates youth in individual and Volk. God loves youth, for God himself is eternally young and strong [stark] and victorious. Anxiety and weakness should be defeated by courage and strength.* Should not a Volk which has experienced the call of God to its own life, to its own youth and its own strength, should not such a Volk follow this call, *even if this means treating as unimportant the life of other Völker?* God is the Lord of history. If a Volk humbly bows before this holy will which guides history, then in its youth and strength it can, with God, overcome the weak and the cowardly; for God will be with it.[46]

Bethge rightly observes that Bonhoeffer never spoke in this "titanic" manner again.[47] The description of the manly, powerful, heroic, conquering figure—God's ally—in the autobiographical memoir exposes the vanity, ambitiousness, competitiveness, and God–forsaken solitude of such an attitude.

In his address of July, 1932 to an ecumenical youth peace conference in Czechoslovakia, Bonhoeffer discussed "The Theological Basis of the World Alliance." Arguing that the church must proclaim concrete ethical commands, he rejects the view that the doctrine of "orders of creation" could be an adequate theological foundation for Christian ethics. This

---

[46]   GS V 173, DBW 10 339f., italics mine. (This passage expands the very brief mention of a Volk making its history by war which is found in *Sanctorum Communio*; cf. SC 74, SC-E 119.) The passage continues in the same vein about individual life. "If our inner growth and youthfulness and our strength lead us to surpass other people, that is, if we are inwardly required by what God does to us to separate ourselves from friends, then there must be no sentimentalities; for God wants the courageous decision to move on, leaving the other behind even if it causes pain. God wants strength of life, not fear. And God knows how to richly heal the wounds that he inflicts through us, that we inflict on God's behalf." In the same way he speaks of economic life. "In short, the situation is that today we have been placed in an economic and business world *where the weaker must be ruined by the stronger,* and that, if we want to participate in business life, it is necessary to go along with it in this sense." Rejecting a double standard of personal and business ethics, Bonhoeffer justifies cutthroat capitalism by invoking the greater good of the Volk, and the duty of the Christian to help the victims of society.

[47]   DB 153, DB-E 119.

doctrine, very popular at the time, can justify any existing social practices as expressions of the will of God. Bonhoeffer singles out for special mention several forms of prevalent power struggle: the exploitation of the weak by the strong,[48] the life and death competition of economics, war, the class struggle, nationalism, and strife [Kampf] within nations.[49]

In the same address the question of modern war receives particular attention. Modern war, in comparison with wars of earlier centuries, has become so destructive of the outward and inner life of all combatants that it is the gravest obstacle to revelation and therefore should be outlawed by the church. Significantly, Bonhoeffer refers to Bismarck, as symbolic of the demonic development found in modern warfare. Despite efforts late in his career to out–flank and repress socialists with sweeping social reforms, Bismarck deservedly earned the name of "iron chancellor." He was a symbol of Prussian miliary imperialism, constitutional arbitrariness, and reactionary military elitism—in short, militarist power–politics.[50]

In August, 1932 Bonhoeffer addressed another ecumenical conference in Switzerland on the subject, "The Church is Dead."[51] In order to hear the Word of Christ in another Christian and then be responsible to the world, it is imperative, Bonhoeffer argues, that the Bible be taken more seriously. The church will then encounter the nations with the message of peace. The nations are torn within and without by power struggles: in economic life, in political life, in ideological battles, in patriotism fueled by hate, in the world scene bristling with weapons, in nations like Germany seeking to compensate for humiliation by a new titanism, in the desperate hunger of millions of people. In all this he sees

---

48 Bonhoeffer displays his concern for minority groups early in the address, a concern he showed in his actions on behalf of the Jews, and which he also relates to caste in India and race in America in the 1934 sermon quoted above.

49 DBW 11 336, GS I 149, CW I 165; cf. the reference earlier in the address to the political upsurge of nationalism among German youth.

50 DBW 11 341, GS I 155, CW I 170. Barth's comment on Bismarck is apt: "Bismarck—not to mention Hitler—was (in spite of the *Daily Bible Readings* on his bedside table) no model statesman because he wanted to establish and develop his work on naked power." ("The Christian Community and the Civil Community," in *Against the Stream,* ed. R. Gregor Smith [London: S.C.M. Press, 1954], p. 40.)

51 DBW 11 350-57, GS I 162–70, CW I 182–89. The perceptive reader will notice several autobiographical allusions, as well as fundamental themes characteristic of Bonhoeffer's theology of sociality, in this address. August was, of course, just a very short time after his liberating experience of that summer.

a "lust for power" driving humanity to the point where it lays violent hands on itself.[52] Christ encounters the demonic powers of the world with the judgment of the cross upon hatred, and the proclamation of peace— not a peace which represses conflict nor a peace which preserves falsehood and injustice, but a peace of truth and justice.

In November, 1932 Bonhoeffer wrote a piece on the church, discussing at the end the question of the church's responsibility in politics. Departing from Lutheran tradition, he argues that the church must at the right times make quite specific commands for political life. In doing so, however, the Christian community must be alert to a serious danger which was particularly acute at that time in Germany, namely, that the church itself might unwittingly be exploited in the political power struggle.[53] If its political word is to be effective, the church cannot afford to replicate the very problem which it seeks to address; peace, truth, and justice—not a position of power and privilege—is what the church should seek in society. The inner life in which the church is to hear the concrete command, and from which it is to speak, is a life of brotherly love in community; here people are freed from loneliness, they belong to one another, give themselves to one another, and know their responsibility. The life of this community is one of service, prayer, and forgiveness, in which people are truly with and for one another [Füreinander].[54]

Another aspect of the problem of power is discussed in the important address on "The Führer and the Individual in the Younger Generation"; it was first given as a radio talk on February 1, 1933, published in abbreviated form later that month, and then given again in its fullest form in March. The younger generation, Bonhoeffer argues, achieved several insights as it faced the shaking of the foundations brought by World War I. The first he mentions is the destructive and meaningless use of technology in warfare.

> One discerned in the collapse people experienced the triumph of things over human beings, the victory of the machine over its maker. The

---

52 DBW 11 354, GS I 166f.

53 DBW 12 238f., GS III 290, CW I 157.

54 DBW 12 237, GS III 287, CW I 54f. This passage clearly echoes the essence of the church first described in *Sanctorum Communio*. Note Bonhoeffer's repetition of his initial contention that the church is not a sacred sanctuary, but the world transformed by the present Christ; DBW 12 235ff., GS III 286ff., CW I 153ff.

technology intended to serve humanity in controlling nature had been turned against it; humanity was defenseless and technology deprived of its essential meaning.[55]

Technical power is put at the service of misguided political power and its consequence is destruction and meaninglessness.

In the same address Bonhoeffer attacks the new German Führer concept because it oversteps the limits involved in the definition of an office to become a cult of the supremacy of the leader's person. The problem is not that the Führer has authority and power, while an office does not; both are related to the people in a "Machtverhältnis."[56] The problem is the unlimited and arbitrary character of the power which follows when Führer supersedes office, for the function of the office is precisely to secure a limited and rational leadership. With the advent of the political Führer in the person of Hitler a new social and psychic possibility emerges for the nation. The political Führer concept is messianic, eliciting a perverse form of faith. Since the person of the Führer is by definition without the limits of office, law, and constitution, this makes possible a collective drive for power by the identification of the people with him. The totalitarianism of the individual Führer is the vehicle for the collective egotism of the people; the unlimited power of the leader is the instrument for the wishes and ambitions of the people.[57] Here Bonhoeffer astutely diagnosed the inner logic that led to the outbreak of militaristic imperialism which unleashed its fury several years later.

---

[55] DBW 12 246, GS II 25, CW I 193. At this time Bonhoeffer was giving his lectures on "Schöpfung und Sunde," and it is in light of the context illuminated by this address that we should understand his criticism of technology there; cf. CF 48, 67. In the *Letters* a much more positive estimate of the possibilities of technology is found.

[56] See later on Christ as a power figure in *Discipleship*; subsequent discussion evaluates the political and personal significance of this.

[57] DBW 12 242-60, esp. 253ff., GS II 22–38, esp. 31ff.; CW I 190–204, esp. 198ff. It is important to note that Bonhoeffer describes this transference of individual wishes and ambitions to the leader not as the action of strong, mature people, but as compensation for feelings of weakness and inadequacy. In light of this one should not simply regard as two sides of the same coin Bonhoeffer's version of the problem of power in the dominant individual ego, and the social manifestations of the problem of power; see further discussion below. (In this address, incidentally, almost all the basic concepts of sociality—responsible person, I and You, Grenze, individual and community, objective Geist, Stellvertretung, etc.—are employed.)

In light of the problem of power, the title of a February, 1932 lecture attracts immediate interest: "The Right of Self–Assertion [Selbstbehauptung]."[58] Bonhoeffer sketches the struggle [Kampf] for life in work, education, social classes, and nations. Then he compares a quite romantic and schematized view of the East, represented especially by Gandhi, with the West. India symbolized Eastern resignation: it is better to suffer and die than to live by a self–assertion which does violence to life. European and American civilization, by contrast, symbolizes its approach to the struggle for life in two things: "the machine and war are the two forms of the Western solution to our problem."[59] That humanity should rule over nature by the machine is the fundamental motivation of Western history. But this is then applied to human relations and social life.

> The European must fight for his right to life first against nature, yet not only against nature, but also against other people. His life means in the strictest sense 'killing.' That has never been so horribly clear as in the past decade and a half.[60]

In place of this violent, competitive, and destructive assertion of life through the will for power, Bonhoeffer offers an alternative. A man first becomes human and first rightly asserts himself

> when he understands himself not as the lord over his own life, but when he understands his life as responsible to the brother: [the other] human being. Then he does not live alone, but he lives essentially through and for the other, co–ordinated to him in responsibility.[61]

The right of self–assertion is not a self–serving right, but the right to serve others, including the ultimate possibility of responsibly dying for others. This applies as much to communities and nations as to individuals.[62] The basis of self–assertion as the right to serve others is

---

58 DBW 11 215-26, GS III 258–69. This address employs, explicitly or implicitly, all Bonhoeffer's concepts of sociality.

59 DBW 11 220, GS III 263.

60 DBW 11 221, GS III 264.

61 DBW 11 222f., GS III 265.

62 "Every community, even the great community of the nation, does not live for itself but for the other. It lives in responsibility for the kindred community [Bruder], the kindred nation. For the nation there is absolutely no isolated life... Only because it is ready to die for the other may it live. As means of the self-assertion of the community, war and machinery require sacrifices of individuals, but have their sole justification from the community's readiness for sacrificial

the cross of Jesus the Christ, "his death for the brother."[63] Not the domination and destruction of others in the power struggles of the world, but the free and responsible service of others (even, if need be, to death)—that is Christian and human self–assertion.

The contrast between this attitude and that of the Barcelona address is dramatic. That Bonhoeffer could speak like this even before he had fully resolved the problem of power in his own existence is remarkable evidence of the degree to which his theology had a freedom which transcended his own person. This passage, in fact, even goes beyond the position of *Discipleship*. Its understanding of Christ's "death for the brothers," and the mature responsibility in which a person "lives...for the other," could be quotations from the *Letters and Papers from Prison;* indeed, these key formulations are virtually identical with the later expressions where Christ is "the one for others," and the Christian life as "existing for others."

The passages examined here are sufficient proof that Bonhoeffer's concern with destructive forms of power in society are parallel to his theological preoccupation with the power of the ego. Power, in Bonhoeffer's theology, is the crucial soteriological issue. The next chapter will consider additional material on the problem of social power when discussing Christ as the Mediator of political history. At this point, however, an important distinction must be made with respect to the parallel concerns of power in the ego and in society.

I deliberately describe these concerns as "parallel." They are related but not identical. The distinction derives from the different dynamics involved in the forms of power operating in the ego and the society in the particular personal and social context of Bonhoeffer's historical situation. The distinction, briefly, is between a power of the ego which is grounded in basic strengths, and types of social power which are rooted in basic weaknesses—humiliation, frustration, repressed aggressiveness, deprivation, and so on. The former presupposes achievement and competence, whereas the latter tries to compensate for lack of self–esteem and fulfillment.

---

death for the other, yes, [even] for the enemy brother. They may never be means of self-seeking and self-deification, and if they are reduced to this it is time to protest" (DBW 11 223f., GS III 266f). Contrast this with Bonhoeffer's description of more familiar forms of nationalism, based on the 'might makes right' philosophy (DBW 11 218, GS III 261).

63 DBW 11 226, GS III 269.

The ego described by Bonhoeffer and embodied in himself, is strong. Knowledge, education, intellectual acuteness, strength and confidence of will, creativity, mastery—these are the salient qualities in the picture he draws. They obviously presuppose the secure status and impressive achievements of the cultured German intelligentsia to which he and his family belonged, and whose philosophical tradition Bonhoeffer engaged in his writings. That he consciously stood within this distinguished tradition, and that he admired its strengths as fully as he acknowledged its weaknesses, is absolutely clear from the people portrayed and sentiments expressed in his literary efforts in prison.[64] Bonhoeffer needed no tutoring on the dangers and corruptions of power based upon great personal strengths. But he was conscious of the difference between such power, and the power which is rooted in frustration and weakness that was such a conspicuous phenomenon in the German society of his time.

In distinguishing the problem of ego power grounded in basic strengths from expressions of social power rooted in weakness, there is an obvious risk. It is difficult to make generalizations about the mentality and motivations of a whole nation, as is done when the distinction points to the social misuse of power rooted in weaknesses which seeks compensation for unfulfilled wishes. In many individual cases the generalization would be subject to exceptions. Nevertheless, one does have to account for the response of the German people to Hitler as an exceptional social phenomenon. In his address on the Führerbegriff, Bonhoeffer argued that the "law of transference [Übertragung]"[65] was at work. By this means the people sought to compensate for the humiliation and suffering which they experienced in their defeat in World War I, the imposition of the Treaty of Versailles, and the economic

---

64   See the "Dramenfragment" and "Romanversuch." Excerpts were originally published in GS III 478–512; the full texts were published in 1978 as *Fragmente aus Tegel* (Munich: Christian Kaiser) and translated as *Fiction from Prison. Gathering Up the Past* (Philadelphia: Fortress, 1981). The critical edition of *Fragmente aus Tegel* (DBW 7) was published in 1994, English translation 1999. Bonhoeffer himself acknowledged that these contained "a good deal of autobiography"; LPP 94, 129f. What is particularly instructive for the distinction made here is the contrast between the aristocratic figures and the "petty power wielders." Neither group is portrayed as immune to the temptations of power. But the former are strong, proud, responsible and courageous; the petty tyrants are motivated by revenge for what they have suffered at the hands of other petty tyrants, and so are like a contagious disease which infects a whole nation. The allusion to the Nazi psychology is transparent.

65   DBW 12 256, GS II 34, CW I 200

privation of the Depression.[66] The compensation argument is plausible. Of Hitler's *Mein Kampf,* and particularly its confused and irrational style, Ralph Manheim states: "the logic is purely psychological: Hitler is fighting his persecutors, magnifying his person, creating a dream world in which he can be an important figure."[67] Millions of German citizens came to share his dream, and Hitler's personal struggle from insignificance to dictatorship supplied the specters for a national nightmare. The display of destructive power which emerged from these demonic depths is far removed from the creative strengths of the tradition which nourished Dietrich Bonhoeffer. It is no accident that Bonhoeffer stood as a servant of Christ, and a member of a distinguished family tradition, against Hitler, the Antichrist.

3. POWER AS A SOTERIOLOGICAL PROBLEM

Having established the problem of power as the central anthropological problem in Bonhoeffer's early writings, and having demonstrated the autobiographical dimension of his theology, the questions must be posed: in what specific sense is power a soteriological problem? Briefly stated, soteriology deals with the saving work of Christ as reconciling people to God and delivering them from sin. Barth, for example, introduces his doctrine of reconciliation with the following general statement of his thesis.

> The subject–matter, origin and content of the message received and proclaimed by the Christian community is at its heart the free act of the faithfulness of God in which he takes the lost cause of humanity, who have denied him as Creator and in so doing ruined themselves as creatures, and makes it his own in Jesus Christ, carrying it through to its goal and in that way maintaining and manifesting his own glory in the world.[68]

To describe power as a soteriological problem is to speak concretely and historically about the context where God's "free act of faithfulness" is performed in Jesus Christ in whom "he takes the lost cause of humanity...

---

[66] See also the 1930 address in New York, DBW 10 576ff., GS I 66ff., CW I 76ff.

[67] "Translator's Note" to Adolf Hitler, *Mein Kampf* (Boston: Houghton Mifflin Company, 1943), p. xii.

[68] *Church Dogmatics* IV/1 (Edinburgh: T. & T. Clark, 1956), trans. G.W. Bromiley, 3.

and makes it his own"; it is to focus on a specific way, highly characteristic of our own times, in which humanity has denied their Creator and
thereby "ruined themselves as creatures." To focus soteriology in this
way is both faithful to Bonhoeffer himself and consistent with findings
of modern theological scholarship.

Contemporary theological research makes it increasingly clear that
if the theologian speaks of the Christian gospel delivering people from
sin this is, at best, an extremely general statement; at worst, it can be a
highly abstract, unhistorical and therefore almost meaningless statement. Throughout the history of the church, however, theologians have
always sought to give concrete meaning to the concepts of sin and
salvation, and to relate the saving work of Christ to the specific concerns
of their contemporaries.[69] In different epochs, consequently, certain
aspects of human existence have been more urgent existential problems
than others. Here it is not my purpose to judge, with secure retrospective wisdom, whether the crucial issues were always correctly identified.
One could, however, examine Athanasius, Augustine, or Anselm, for
example, to show that the specific focus of their soteriologies varies
with the different theologians in their changing historical situations.
Likewise, one could explore the characteristic concerns of Barth,
Bultmann, or Tillich to make the same point in our own century. But this
would lead us far away from the present argument, so I proceed to the
discussion of Bonhoeffer, recalling in the process the earlier comparison
with Luther.

In Luther, conscience, as negative superego, is the anthropological
locus of soteriology. Faced with the demanding law and threatening
wrath of God, Luther felt condemned. He was not at peace, but punished

---

[69]   On the historical character of theological work, including soteriology,
see, for example: Krister Stendahl, "The Apostle Paul and the Introspective
Conscience of the West," *Harvard Theological Review,* vol. 56, 1963, pp. 199–
215; George Hunston Williams, *Anselm: Communion and Atonement* (Saint
Louis, Missouri: Concordia Publishing House, 1960); Etienne Gilson, "St.
Thomas Aquinas," in *The Wisdom of Catholicism* (London: Michael Joseph,
1950), comp. by Anton C. Pegis, pp. 860ff.; Erik Erikson, *Young Man Luther*
(New York: W. W. Norton, 1962); Karl Barth—on the question of natural
theology in his own work in relation to the central theological concerns of the
Reformers—"No" in *Natural Theology* by Emil Brunner and Karl Barth, trans.
Peter Fraenkel (London: Centenary Press, 1946), esp. pp. 101ff.; Paul Tillich, in
many of his writings, e.g., *The Courage to Be* (New Haven: Yale University
Press, 1952), pp. 57ff.; Herbert Richardson, *Toward an American Theology*
(New York: Harper & Row, 1967), esp. 1–49.

himself with penitential works. He did not love, but hated God, thereby compounding his guilt. His heart was turned in upon himself, and so his self–preoccupation prevented him from properly loving his neighbors. He was thus at odds with the great commandment at every point: he did not love God, or his neighbors, or himself.

His new understanding of justification by faith revealed the merciful heart of God to Luther. Loved without works, Luther was simultaneously able to love God and to accept himself. Conscience became the seat of Christ, and law was cast out. 'Passive righteousness' replaced the fruitless effort of penitential works. Luther was freed from guilt. Freed to love God, freed to accept himself, the self–preoccupation of the *cor curvum in se* was overcome, and Luther was now also free to love and serve his neighbors. "A Christian is a perfectly free lord of all, subject to none. A Christian is a perfectly dutiful servant of all, subject to all."[70]

In this soteriology, then, the grace of Christ meets the sinner at the point of conscience qua negative superego. In enabling people to love the God whose forgiving mercy accepts them without preconditions, they are saved from guilty self–accusation and hatred of God, from futile penitential works, and from a self–preoccupation which prevents the love and service of others. By grace people are healed from being at odds with God, with themselves, and with others. Luther's soteriology, then, has a quite specific set of anthropological dynamics, apart from which justification by Christ cannot be truly understood.

I have argued that Bonhoeffer's soteriological problem, while resembling certain aspects of Luther's problem, has a quite distinctive character and set of dynamics of its own. The components of Bonhoeffer's problem have their locus not in negative conscience but in the power of the ego. The powerful ego is at odds with God, self, and others. The successful achievements of the ego have been won at the cost of violating the essential created sociality of human beings with each other. In making the self the center of reality, one usurps the place of God, and is isolated from others. Instead of freely loving and serving others in mutuality, they are dominated, dehumanized into 'things.' Since such power violates their true being with others, and their own being as creatures of God set in community with their neighbors, they are also at odds with themselves. The emphasis with Bonhoeffer, however, is not

---

70 "Martin Luther's Treatise on Christian Liberty," *Luther's Works*, vol. 31, *Career of the Reformer:* I, ed. Harold J. Grimm (Philadelphia: Muhlenberg Press, 1957), 344.

on guilt, self–rejection and self–punishment; neither is the problem manifest in hatred of God and self, nor in angry frustration with futile works. Bonhoeffer's emphasis falls on the discrepancy between the achievements of the powerful ego and the claim of positive conscience ("better self": ego–ideal). People whose power leads them to dominate others and isolate themselves are at variance with the true nature of human beings as God's creatures, namely, to be with and for others in the personal relationships and corporate responsibilities of human sociality.[71]

Characteristic of Bonhoeffer, and also distinguishing him significantly from Luther, is the fact that his concern with power as a problem in the corporate life of society parallels his concern with the personal power of the ego. His writings, and his personal commitment to political action as a Christian commitment, show that collective and institutionalized power is as much a part of the human problematic, and therefore a proper concern for soteriology, as personal power; had this not been so, it would have meant that he jettisoned half of his whole theology of sociality. He did not do this, of course, and so we find theological analysis of, and active involvement in, several crucial problems of destructive social power: institutional exploitation, as in the ruthless competition of capitalist economics; class oppression, as seen in caste systems, antisemitism, and racism generally, and in the neglect and despising of poor, aged, and insane people; war, arms races, and the patriotism of hatred, especially as manifestations of the Nazi "master race" mythology and the destructive political messianism it fostered; and the inhuman use of technological power in warfare. These destructive forms of social power are just as much manifestations of sin, and therefore to be encountered with the gospel of salvation, as the forms of sin which beset the life of any individual person. Christ is as much the Mediator of society's history as of the personal existence of the individual person; Christ is as much the 'center' of the state as of the individual person.[72]

Bonhoeffer, however, unlike Luther, did not come by one step to formulate clearly his Christological answer to the soteriological problem of power. The predominant strain in the Christology of *Discipleship* is the power and *authority* of Christ. This is in conflict with a form of

---

[71] For Bonhoeffer personally, I will argue, this discrepancy was the hiatus between his professed vocation as a Christian, and the ambition, vanity, and self–congratulation which pervaded his intellectual work as a theologian in the early years of his career.

[72] See the discussion of the 1933 Christology lectures in Chapter 5.

theologia crucis which emphasizes the weakness of Christ. The latter is predominant in the Christology lectures, in the address on "The Right of Self–Assertion" and other occasional pieces we have discussed and, of course, in the prison letters; it is also present in *Discipleship,* but in a subordinate role. Corresponding to this predominant emphasis on the power of Christ in the major writings of the 1930s, and the weakness of Christ in the prison letters, is an anthropological movement: from the attempt to suppress ego autonomy in *Discipleship*, to the affirmation of ego autonomy in the prison letters.

Subsequent analysis will document this Christological and anthropological movement, thereby clarifying the soteriology. Here it suffices to say that Bonhoeffer's concern with both individual and corporate forms of dehumanizing power is as genuine a soteriological problem as those faced by Luther and other theologians before him. His problem is not identical with that of Luther, or of Augustine. That human life is historical and God a living God, are presuppositions in Bonhoeffer's theology from beginning to end. Before he was fully aware of it, Bonhoeffer was theologically and existentially concerned with a crucial, modern problem: power. If any form of power serves to set people at odds with Christ, with their neighbors and with themselves, then it becomes, ipso facto, a soteriological problem.

Bonhoeffer's soteriology, then, addresses both the problem of destructive social power and the problem of the powerful ego. It is in the latter realm, however, that the deepest autobiographical dimension of his theology is most evident. This is seen in the movement from attempted ego suppression in *Discipleship* to a theological affirmation of ego autonomy in the *Letters and Papers from Prison.* However, this movement is not a private, individualistic pilgrimage. For, I shall argue, it was through his confronting the social problem in the resistance movement that he was fully freed for an 'existence for others.' In realizing this freedom he was enabled and obliged to affirm the strengths of the ego as necessary to a Christian life of free responsibility in society. In the course of this movement the soteriology, like the anthropology, is clarified. In the *Discipleship* period (1932–1937) the Christology vacillates between the power and weakness of Christ, the former being predominant. In the prison theology the paradoxical understanding of the strength of Christ in his weakness and suffering is clear and uncompromised.

> Before and with God we live without God. God allows himself to be
> pushed out of the world on to the cross; God is powerless [ohnmächtig]
> and weak [schwach] in the world and that is precisely the only way that

he is with us and helps us. Matt. 8.17 makes it quite clear that Christ does not help by his omnipotence [Allmacht] but by his weakness, his suffering![73]

These summary and anticipatory statements will be documented by examining Bonhoeffer's personal "turning" in 1932, and then analyzing its theological expression in *Discipleship*. This illuminates not only the autobiographical dimension of that book, but also the development of his theology as a whole.

B. 1932: BONHOEFFER'S PERSONAL COMMITMENT

The problem of the powerful ego highlighted in Bonhoeffer's theology was also the major personal problem for the theologian himself. When he wrote in the prison letter of his turning "from the phraseological to the real," he referred to the two passages in I and II Timothy which speak of one who "formerly blasphemed" but later served God "with a clear conscience." Bethge has documented that this is a quite personal allusion on Bonhoeffer's part.[74] The "turning," or "break," occurred in the latter half of 1932. In examining what Bonhoeffer described as "a great liberation," we see that the personal problem is, indeed, the problem of the ego and its power. This correspondence allows us better to understand the autobiographical dimension of his theology and is therefore indispensable for interpreting Bonhoeffer's theological development.

Bonhoeffer kept hidden the personal change of 1932.[75] Had it been otherwise he would have succumbed to that insidious temptation so deftly diagnosed in T. S. Eliot's drama of Thomas à Becket: "The last temptation is the greatest treason, To do the right deed for the wrong reason."[76] Had Bonhoeffer publicized his own spiritual struggle and the new commitment of faith and obedience which issued from it, he would have invalidated it; self–reflection would have deflected faith, and vanity and self–righteousness would have subverted obedience. For reasons intrinsic to the nature of the case, therefore, he kept it hidden. Understandably, he confided in a few intimate friends and members of his family, mentioning the change in a very few letters to them.

---

[73]   WE 534, LPP 360f.

[74]   DB 246, DB-E 203.

[75]   DB 250, DB-E 206,

[76]   "Murder in the Cathedral," (New York: Harcourt, Brace and Company, 1935), 44.

The most explicit and frank reference is in a letter to a girlfriend written on January 27, 1936; its text proves that he is speaking of his experience prior to 1933. Describing his early career, and the transition "from the phraseological to the real," he writes:

> I plunged into work in a very unchristian way. An...*ambition* [Ehrgeiz] that many noticed in me made my life difficult....

> Then came something else, something that up to this day has changed my life and turned it sharply around. For the first time I came to the *Bible*. Previous to this I had often preached and seen a great deal of the church...*but I had not yet become a Christian*....

> I know that to that time I had made the cause [Sache] of Jesus Christ into *an opportunity for my own advancement*.... I had never, or hardly ever, prayed. Despite all my abandonment *I was very pleased* [ganz froh] *with myself. The Bible, especially the Sermon on the Mount,* liberated me from that. Since then everything has been different.... *It was a great liberation* [Befreiung]. It became clear to me that *the life of a servant of Jesus Christ must belong to the church* and step by step it became clearer to what extent this must be so.

> Then came the crisis of 1933. That confirmed me in it.... *All that matters to me now is the renewal of the church and the pastorate*....

> Christian pacifism, which I had recently combatted passionately, ... suddenly became self–evident to me....

> My calling is clear to me. What God will make of it I do not know....[77]

This letter is perfectly candid that the motivation for his previous theological work had been ambition and self–advancement. The Bible, and especially the Christ of the Sermon on the Mount, shattered this self–satisfied egotism and for the first time leads the theologian to a serious commitment to personal discipleship in the church.[78]

---

[77]   DBW 14 112ff., DB-E 204f., italics mine. (There are several direct connections between this letter and *Discipleship*: the polemic against self–made plans of discipleship; the centrality of the Sermon on the Mount; the experience of the great change; the notion of proceeding "step by step"; the importance of "call" and "calling"; and the advocacy of non–violence. Bonhoeffer was, of course, working on *Discipleship* at Finkenwalde at the time of this letter.)

[78]   I shall show below that it is characteristic of Bonhoeffer's personal and theological concern with the problem of power that he turns to the Sermon on the Mount for a solution. Again the difference from Luther is notable. The Reformer found the problem of the negative, guilty conscience resolved in the *sola gratia, sola fide* of the doctrine of justification. Without rejecting this

A year earlier he had written a letter to his eldest brother, the agnostic physicist Karl–Friedrich, about this experience of finding his calling and himself for the first time. Noting that his brother may think him "somewhat fanatical" and might prefer him to be "more reasonable," he writes that he is very happy to feel that he is on the right track for the first time in his life. He is now taking the Sermon on the Mount seriously; his life now means something totally different from when he began with *"theology ... as a more academic affair."*[79]

In another letter to his brother–in–law Rüdiger Schleicher, he also mentions the Bible as his source of inner simplicity and security. Above all, the Bible is his protection against his worst temptation: "I am afraid... of running into a divine counterpart [göttlichen Doppelgänger] of myself."[80] This is, of course, the central theme in those consistent passages on the soteriological problem. Fallen Adam "is his own creator and lord" who "makes himself God and God his creature." He is Adam *"sicut deus."* The powerful ego is alone in "naked self–lordship" dominating "that world which his ego interprets and devises for itself." For fallen Adam, "God is man himself." In 1932 Bonhoeffer finds the Christ of the Sermon on the Mount to be a genuine 'other' who stands where the divine "Doppelgänger" previously stood.

Bonhoeffer's personal liberation in 1932, and its relation to his theology, is given indispensable clarification by the biographical insights Bethge has provided. Bonhoeffer acknowledged his personal "ambition," his initial view of theology as an "academic affair," his use of theology and the church as "an opportunity for self–advancement,"

Bonhoeffer tries to resolve the problems of the powerful and self–satisfied ego by a doctrine of absolute, obedient discipleship to the commanding Christ of the Sermon of the Mount.

[79] Letter of January 14, 1935; DBW 13 272f., DB-E 205f., italics mine. "Theology...as a more academic affair" certainly fits Bonhoeffer's description of his earliest work as "phraseological." (Incidentally, since so many interpreters regard *Discipleship* as an apolitical product of an ecclesiastical ghetto, it is significant to note that in this letter, written two years after Hitler came to power, Bonhoeffer connects his new faith and commitment to political–ethical responsibility. He relates himself to his agnostic brother by saying that peace, social justice, and Christ brook no compromise, and that seriousness about the Sermon on the Mount is the only explosive to blow the Nazi phantasmagoria sky high. It was not till later, however, that he became a partner of an elder brother and his brothers–in–law in active political resistance.

[80] DB 249f., DB-E 206.

and his self–satisfaction with his own success. What were the personal factors in Bonhoeffer's decision to become a theologian?

Bethge shows convincingly that the established church, the local congregation, and his confirmation class did not significantly contribute to Bonhoeffer's boyhood decision to become a theologian.[81] Rather, it is the family context which is decisive. I refer not only to the precedents of ministers and theologians among his ancestors and relatives, nor only

---

[81] DB 62ff., DB-E 37. Bethge's judgement on this point calls into question the heavy weight he himself gives to Bonhoeffer's experience of the Catholic church in Rome (1924) as formative for the early theology. The Rome experience was certainly significant, especially in giving Bonhoeffer his first taste of the human and temporal catholicity of the church, in contrast to its rather parochial and homogeneous appearance in Germany. The Rome experience, however, did not lead him to an existential faith committed to the church. This commitment is first made in 1932. In the letter of January 27, 1936, quoted above, Bonhoeffer says that the Bible, and particularly the Sermon of the Mount, led him to believe "that the life of a servant of Jesus Christ must belong to the church," and that after Hitler's advent in 1933 this commitment made "the renewal of the church and the pastorate" his whole concern (DB 249, DB-E 205). Further, the fact that his commitment to the church is not made until 1932 is a biographical confirmation of my judgment, argued above, that it is erroneous to read *Sanctorum Communio* as an exclusively ecclesiological book, not recognizing that there Bonhoeffer intends to inform the whole of theology with sociality. To relativize the Rome experience, therefore, is to disagree with Bethge's opinion "that the origins of the theological themes of [Bonhoeffer's] early period can be discerned" in that experience (DB 93, DB-E 65; cf. DB 91). To say this is indeed "to say too much," if for no other reason than the fact that the strong impression of St. Peter's leads to no necessary and programmatic commitment to develop the complex and sophisticated theology of sociality which begins in *Sanctorum Communio*. If Bethge believes, and quite rightly so, that the motivation to become a theologian comes out of various aspects of the life of the family, it is natural to ask: in addition to intellectual and cultural stimuli for Bonhoeffer's concern with sociality, might not the life of the family itself also be the experiential matrix for this same concern? There are, I believe, good reasons for answering the question affirmatively. For example: the family embodied and cultivated qualities of individual independence in common solidarity; relations between individual persons were like those described in Bonhoeffer's theological concept of the person existing in socio–ethical relations; a sense of corporate responsibility for society and history was highly developed in the family as a whole and its individual members; and an impressive array of strengths of mind and will were expected and nurtured. The family was, in short, both a laboratory and a model of sociality as Bonhoeffer presents it. Additional investigation here of this experiential, social matrix would involve undue digression from the main argument, but I note it briefly as a fruitful area for further study.

to the important influence of his mother. His biographer attributes decisive, though not sole, importance to the gifted young man's determination to carve out an independent sphere for himself amidst the "bourgeois–empirical atmosphere" of the world of his elder brothers and his father.[82] Bonhoeffer, Bethge writes, had "an elemental drive to independence," which meant that "his life was governed by a craving for an invariable self–realization." Consequently, the precedents of ancestors and contemporary relatives were not decisive, but

> What was in many respects [his] isolation in the grouping of brothers
> and sisters[83] is far more likely to have nourished *the desire to accom-*
> *plish something himself which all of them had not achieved.*[84]

---

[82]   DB 60; DB-E 34; cf. DB 42, DB-E 20, where Bethge explicitly relates Bonhoeffer's rivalry with his elder brothers to his choice of a career in theology as well as to his surpassing them in musical accomplishment. This is in line with what was just noted: *independence* within common solidarity was encouraged in the Bonhoeffer family.

[83]   In the family grouping, Dietrich was in the middle of the girls at the younger end of the family. He had a twin sister, and a sister three years younger; two older sisters separated him from his elder brothers who were, respectively, five, six, and seven years older than he.

[84]   DB 62, DB-E 37 cf. 20, italics mine. In my judgement, Bethge has quite rightly given considerable weight to the influence on his "inner motivations" of Dietrich's place as the youngest, isolated boy in the family. But should one go on to say, as Bethge does: "One could say, oversimplifying somewhat: because he was lonely he became a theologian—and because he became a theologian he was lonely"? It seems, rather, that what the biographer is documenting is ambition and competitiveness. To be sure, we have seen that loneliness and solitude have a significant place in Bonhoeffer's portrait of the man whose powerful ego excludes him from community with God and his neighbors. But Bonhoeffer's writings make loneliness the *consequence* of egotism, not egotism a compensation for loneliness. I do not wish to engage in psychological speculation here. What is theologically important, and biographically clear, is the indisputable correlation between the soteriological problem of the powerful ego in Bonhoeffer's theology, and the ambitiousness, the drive to independence, and the craving for self–realization that his biographer has documented.

For the same reason, Bethge must be asked whether the experience of his brother Walter's death, his mother's deep grief, and the deaths of relatives and friends in World War I was a "deeper" motivating impulse [tiefergehende Wirkung: DB 62] at this stage than his relation to his elder brothers and father. In support of this view, Bethge cites first a recollection of the twin sister Sabine about their childhood meditations and fantasies on death; then he quotes Bonhoeffer's *own* 1932 autobiographical memoir on that childhood experience (DB 62ff., DB-E 38ff.). The sister's recollection indeed puts the emphasis on meditation about death. But Bonhoeffer's memoir, written about the same time

Bonhoeffer grew up in a family which nurtured and expected great personal strengths in its members.[85] At the same time, this obliged each member of the family to find an independent sphere and identity within the solidarity of the family. In this family Bonhoeffer indeed developed an impressive array of personal strengths. Most conspicuous was his outstanding intellectual competence and achievement in theology and philosophy. To write *Sanctorum Communio* at the age of twenty–one was a formidable accomplishment! But he also excelled in music, surpassing at an early age his elder brothers in this art;[86] he was active and successful in competitive sports such as sprinting, jumping, and tennis; and he loved

---

as the schoolroom memoir, emphasizes egotism, competitiveness, and vanity, and notes that even as a child he was "disgusted with his theatrical fantasies." (Quite possibly his sister never knew of this vanity which infected her brother's meditations.) Bethge, however, does point to the permeation of vanity throughout Bonhoeffer's 1932 memoir on his boyhood fantasies about death (DB 63, DB-E 38). Therefore, whatever significance for his motivation to theology might be given to the exposure to death, it seems apparent that Bonhoeffer himself saw egotism and ambition as the most decisive influence. He confirms this in the letter we have discussed above when he speaks of the time prior to 1932 as one when he "had made the cause of Jesus Christ into an opportunity for [his] own advancement" (DB 248f., DB-E 205). In any case, it is obvious that the soteriological problem for Bonhoeffer is not death, but the power of the dominating ego.

[85] In addition to Bethge's biography, the revised translation of which contains fuller information on the family, see the following literature on the Bonhoeffer family: Karl Bonhoeffer's "Lebenserinnerungen" in *Karl Bonhoeffer zum 100. Geburtstage,* ed. J. Zutt, E. Strauss, and H. Scheller (Heidelberg: Springer–Verlag, 1969); Sabine Bonhoeffer Leibholz "Dietrich Bonhoeffer: A Glimpse into Our Childhood," *Union Seminary Quarterly Review,* vol. XX, no. 4, May, 1965, pp. 319–331 [a less successful translation of the same piece under the title "Childhood and Home" is found in *I Knew Dietrich Bonhoeffer,* ed. Wolf–Dieter Zimmermann and Ronald Gregor Smith (New York: Harper & Row, 1966), pp. 19–33; see also the piece by Emmi Bonhoeffer in the same volume]; the "Memoir" by his brother–in–law, Gerhard Leibholz, CD 13–39; Sabine Bonhoeffer Leibholz, *Vergangen, erlebt, überwunden: Schicksale der Familie Bonhoeffer* (Wuppertal–Barmen: J. Kiefel, 1968); and also Bonhoeffer's highly autobiographical "Dramenfragment" and "Romanversuch" written in prison and partially published in GS III 478–512 (partial translation of the former may be found in *I Loved This People,* ed. Hans Rothfels, trans. Keith R. Crimm [Richmond, Virginia: John Knox Press, 1965] as "from a Fragment of a Drama," pp. 49–50, and of the latter as "Happiness and Power," trans. Hilda M. Bishop in *The Bridge,* magazine of the German–British Christian Fellowship, April, 1955, pp. 4–15); see now full publication and translation in FT and FP.

[86] DB 47f., 43; DB-E 25, 20.

chess and bridge, competitive games of intense intellectual concentration. He brought to sports and games a will to win, and required his partners in recreation to do likewise.[87] His father encouraged his children to think and speak precisely, and showed his pleasure and approval when they produced clear and precise definitions for him.[88] His mother was a stimulating, energetic, strong–willed, and independent woman; being rather critical of the state schools, she gave the children their early education herself, providing them with an excellent start and putting them ahead of their peers.[89] Since the father was an agnostic, it was the mother who provided the religious education of the children, though independently of the church.[90] A better context than this family for developing the strengths and skills of a strong and healthy ego would be difficult to imagine.[91]

Within the solidarity of this strong family Bonhoeffer had to actualize his "elemental drive to independence"; he desired "to accomplish something himself which all of them had not achieved." As Bethge has shown, this was a major—if not the decisive—motivation in his decision to become a theologian. Although he may have felt that this decision was consistent with the Christian upbringing given by his mother, there is no doubt that from the outset his vocational choice was made over against the discouragement of his brothers and sisters. The less seriously they took him, the more resolute he became. His brothers told him he was taking the road of least resistance. Compared with the aristocratic family tradition and the distinguished professional accomplishments of the father and brothers in psychiatry, physics, and law, they argued that the church was a miserable, petit–bourgeois institution. Bonhoeffer's reply, at the age of fourteen, was typically independent, if not defiant: "Well, I will reform that church!" Bonhoeffer's father shared the view voiced by the brothers, though, not wishing to curb his son's independence, waited more than a decade before he revealed to Dietrich what he had originally thought; but by 1934 the father saw an importance in his son's church activities which his scientific outlook previously could not imagine.[92]

---

[87]　DB 20, DB-E xx (Portrait).

[88]　DB 37, DB-E 15.

[89]　DB 38ff., DB-E 16ff.

[90]　DB 59ff., DB-E 34ff.

[91]　The term 'ego' here is used with the meaning given in the working definition at the beginning of this chapter.

[92]　DB 61f., DB-E 37.

By 1932 Bonhoeffer was well established as a brilliant young theologian. His outstanding intellectual gifts and achievements were acknowledged by senior colleagues at the University of Berlin, his teaching as a young professor was attracting considerable student attention, and he commanded positions of leadership in the ecumenical movement. Only twenty–six years of age, he had conspicuously established his independence and accomplished for himself a very great deal indeed.

Yet for some time, as the personal letters confess, he had been troubled by his ambitiousness, his 'academic' approach to theology, and using the cause of Christ as an opportunity for self–advancement. The problem of the powerful ego[93] which he had discussed in his theology for several years now became an existential crisis. The crux of the crisis is simply formulated: it is the clear contradiction between his vocational profession to be a servant of Christ, and his actual, conscious use of his vocation to serve his own ambition. "I had not yet become a Christian."

---

93   In speaking deliberately of the power of the ego, I want to guard against a misunderstanding. Bonhoeffer's soteriological passages speak of egocentricity, selfishness, dominance, autocracy, violation, and so on. To regard these words as a simple or complete description of his personal relations with family, friends, and associates during his early life would be a travesty. Their testimonies to his character speak of sensitiveness, generosity, fairness, cooperation, helpfulness, considerateness, and other appealing traits (see the biography and the writings of family and friends cited above). To be sure, one can find signs of a an attitude of superiority, and of aggressiveness, competitiveness, and ambition. (Note how he criticized American theological students in 1931 for showing "little intellectual competition [geistige Konkurrenz] and little intellectual ambition [geistige Ehrgeiz]"; GS I 85f., CW I 87). But these attitudes were channeled chiefly into *intellectual and professional pursuits,* especially theology. That is, they are found in the realm of the ego, as defined above. This is why Bonhoeffer's personal crisis which came to a head in 1932 was centered on his vocation and his professional life. It is also the reason for the critique of boundless intellect, self–glorification in thought and philosophy, and the violation of a "self–interpreted world" which features so prominently in the passages on the anthropological problematic. For the same reason *Discipleship* is replete with polemics against false Christianity as following self–chosen ideas, principles, and beliefs; the true disciple must get away from theology as an "academic affair" into concrete obedience of life—the word of Christ in the Sermon on the Mount must be *obeyed,* not manipulated by human thought and self–interest. To avoid misinterpretation then, a relative distinction must be made between activities in the realm of ego's powers, and personal behavior in relating to others.

As Bethge has shown, several influences over two or three years
contributed to his "great liberation" in 1932.[94] But above it all was "the
Bible, especially the Sermon on the Mount," that finally united his
professed calling and his actual life, and convinced him "that the life of
a servant of Jesus Christ must belong to the church." From this personal
commitment to the Christ of the Sermon on the Mount[95] came the

---

[94]   See, for example, DB-E 457: his American experience leads him to
question the conventional Lutheran interpretation of the Sermon on the Mount;
DB-E 153f.: the Union Seminary friendship with the French pacifist Jean
Lassere; DB-E 138: his friendship with Franz Hildebrandt, especially the latter's
influencing him toward more biblical thinking; DB-E 184f.: his personal
meetings with Karl Barth; DB 176f., DB-E 139f.: the profound personal
encounter in 1930 with the novels of Georges Bernanos, of which Bethge writes:

> He was disconcerted to find again here his most personal problems: the
> priest and saint as the chosen target of the tempter, the man who can
> scarcely endure the alternating assaults of *desperatio* and *superbia*....

> The renegade priest is the intellectual sceptic whose 'wilful thought
> is the best weapon against grace'; he writes theological books,
> 'treacherous wilful work, scintillating, unfruitful books with a tainted
> heart, masterpieces.'

> Bonhoeffer's encounter with these early works of Bernanos [*Sous le
> soleil de Satan,* 1926, *L'Imposture,* 1927; German translations 1927
> and 1929 respectively] is the most revealing personal sign we know of
> in this period. The question of his life commitment was more burning
> than ever. The discovery of Bernanos so disturbed him that he did
> something he very seldom ventured, namely, tried to interest his father
> in what he was reading.

See also DB-E 562f., GS III 43. A thorough study of Bernanos in light of
Bonhoeffer's spiritual pilgrimage would be a useful contribution. Because of the
similarity of personal concerns in Bernanos' characters and Bonhoeffer himself,
it is obvious why the French novelist had such an impact on him.   But a
preliminary comparison of the respective resolutions of these concerns suggests
a significant difference between the approaches of the French Catholic and the
German Protestant. The Christ of Bernanos comes out of the Catholic sacrificial
and sacramental tradition; in *Nachfolge* Bonhoeffer presents the un–Lutheran
commanding Christ of the Sermon on the Mount, though, to be sure, a Christ who
encounters one in the Word.   Bonhoeffer continued to read Bernanos as his
writings came out and recommended *The Diary of a Country Priest* to his
Finkenwalde students when the German translation appeared in 1936.

[95]   In the 1931 Catechism the will of Christ had been linked to obeying the
Sermon on the Mount (DBW 11 234f., GS III 255, CW I 147); in the summer
semester 1932 seminar on ethics the question about knowing the will of God

theology of *Discipleship*: "Discipleship" is Bonhoeffer's personal commitment before and behind the book on that subject.

Before discussing *Discipleship*, however, a concise review of the autobiographical dimension of the theology of sociality and its soteriological problem in the pre–1932 writings is necessary.

I have already demonstrated the striking connection between the soteriological problem of the powerful ego in Bonhoeffer's theology and his autobiographical memoirs and correspondence. Without suggesting for a moment that personal concerns were the only factors influencing the shape and direction of his theology, this connection is quite apparent. In *Sanctorum Communio* Bonhoeffer portrays human beings created in communities of mutual love, freedom, and responsibility for one another. To be human is to be essentially social, in its interpersonal and corporate aspects. This essential sociality is turned against itself by individual and collective egotism. Self–seeking, egocentricity, the dominant will, using the other as a means to the ends of the self—these destroy the primal community. The sinful person is now alone, a "solitary lord and creator," in the solidarity of egocentric individualism. Since being human is essentially being a person in sociality, the crisis of the self and the crisis of sociality is one and the same. From this loss of true humanity in sociality people are delivered by Christ. Christ is the reality of the new humanity, personally present in the social community of the church; by his Spirit of love people are freed from the isolation of their individual egocentricity and domination of others, and bonded together in a new social community characterized by "active being for one another." Both the individual person and human community are, in the church, in the process of being made over and renewed.

There is no evidence I am aware of to show that Bonhoeffer realized the extent to which his own personal concerns were involved in the theology of *Sanctorum Communio*. No sooner had he completed that book, however, than the questions of reason, consciousness, self–consciousness, reflection on the self, and conscience form the point of departure for *Act and Being*. Conscience and self–consciousness (together with thought and reason as a primary instrument by which the ego glorifies and justifies itself, dominating a self–interpreted world and being in the center of its own thinking as a closed circle) are fundamental issues in the book as well as consistent components in the series of passages on the soteriological problem, including the autobiographical

from the Sermon on the Mount had been discussed (DBW 11 306; cf. 312).

memoir. I have shown, in Chapter 3, that his concern with the soteriological problem of the knowing ego heavily informs the whole argument
of *Act and Being*. After Bonhoeffer finished the book in February, 1930,
it is no wonder that the two Bernanos novels which he then read disturbed
him profoundly and confronted him existentially. After that experience
he could hardly avoid noticing some connection between this theological
and existential concerns. When he wrote the 1932 autobiographical
memoir he clearly described his own concerns in the identical categories
and words he had been using in his theology.

It is not necessary to my argument, however, to hold that Bonhoeffer
was fully self–conscious of the inter–relation of his theology and his
existential concern with the powerful ego. It would not be surprising if
this was quite limited. The point which was introduced by the passages
on the soteriological problem of the ego, and which is reinforced here is:
sociality and its problems was both an existential and a theological
concern for Bonhoeffer.

In *Discipleship* Bonhoeffer deals with this problem in full self–
awareness. A powerful new element is *added* to his theology of sociality.
Obedience to Christ in the church is the resolution which he attempts to
work out in his life and writing for the next five years.[96]

C. Obedience as Liberation: *Discipleship* and the Autobiographical Dimension of its Theology

The fundamental themes of *Discipleship* were present in 1932;[97] the book
grew to completion during the London pastorate and the directorship of

---

[96]   This is not to say that the idea of obedience is totally new in 1932. See,
for example, the point in *Act and Being* that reason, including its function in
theology, must be taken into obedience to Christ (AB 45, 130ff.). In the
Catechism, written in 1931 with Franz Hildebrandt, it is said that a person in his
calling [Beruf] owes God obedience (DBW 11 231, GS III 251, CW I 144). In
the lectures on "The Nature of the Church" in the summer semester of 1932,
Bonhoeffer repeats the *Act and Being* point that "theology should serve the
church in concrete obedience" (DB 1059). None of these statements—except
perhaps the last—imply, however, the radical, total and existentially urgent
obedience which comes to full expression in *Nachfolge*.

[97]   See below, and also DB-E 458. Hence Bethge cogently dismisses the
view of Müller (and, by implication, Phillips) that the political events of 1933
diverted Bonhoeffer's development and distorted his theology (DB-E 457ff.,
210). It would be safer to say that the theological problems of *Discipleship* are

the Confessing Church seminary at Finkenwalde.[98] Its context of writing in the church is a direct expression of Bonhoeffer's "becoming a Christian" and discovering "that the life of a servant of Jesus Christ must belong to the church." In his personal experience as in his book, discipleship and commitment to the church are synonymous.[99] Bethge has already given several broad hints about the autobiographical dimension of this book.[100] This must now be examined in some detail, clarifying the new element of discipleship in Bonhoeffer's theology at his juncture. In doing so I will demonstrate that the *addition* of the theology of discipleship does not cancel or leave behind the theology of sociality. *'Discipleship'* is an addition; it *requires* and *presupposes* quite explicitly the theology of sociality.

That the theological foundations of *Discipleship* were laid in 1932 can clearly be seen from an address on "Christ and Peace," given to the Berlin Student Christian Movement. The best date for this address is November, 1932.[101] The theological basis for the discussion of peace is essentially the teaching of *Discipleship*. The address began with the commandment of wholehearted love to God and neighbor in the version of Matthew 22:37–39,[102] and continued with the following interpretation of discipleship: Jesus Christ is the one "absolute authority" over and

---

more related to personal dynamics than political events; cf. Bonhoeffer himself, LPP 369, and the discussion of this below.

[98] A definitive study of *Discipleship* would need to examine its text alongside the sermons and other writings which accompanied its growth; cf. DB 523ff. Essential for this research is not only the material available in the first four volumes of *Gesammelte Schriften*, and the 1933–35 London sermons which were published in GS V, but also the new material now available in the relevant DBW volumes.

[99] Here "church" means, naturally, the Confessing Church and particularly that highly specific form of it which bore Bonhoeffer's personal stamp: Finkenwalde. That this commitment to the church is an existential appropriation of the theology of sociality is a point argued below.

[100] DB-E 456, 457f.; cf. 174, 185, 210, 233, 677, 862f.

[101] This is the date given by Jürgen Winterhager in his communication to me of May 29, 1971. Bethge's summary in the biography (DB 253f., DB-E 209f.) is based on Winterhager's notes of the address. Winterhager's date is consistent with Bethge's deduction that the address was given after July, 1932. It is also consistent with the winter, 1932 date given by Glenthøj who first published the fuller version in MW V 69ff. See now DBW 12 232ff., where the address is dated December, 1932.

[102] It is found in *Discipleship* in the version of Luke 10:27; cf. CD 84.

above all human authorities; discipleship is simple, unreflective faith, and faith is genuine only in discipleship, i.e., *following*—simple *obedience* to the commandment of Christ; the Sermon on the Mount speaks unmistakably to the single–minded reader; the understanding of law and gospel which offers grace without requiring obedience offers "cheap grace"; faith replaces self–reflection on the self, as simple obedience knows nothing of good and evil; the world lives in enmity to the Kingdom of God proclaimed by Jesus; no unmediated human fraternization is possible, for access to the enemy is through prayer to Christ, the Lord of all peoples; Christians renounce war and violence, and seek the peace grounded in God's reconciliation, their weapons being faith and love refined by suffering; any attempts to organize peace out of human possibilities are sin, the "lordship of self–glorifying man." As this address shows, and *Discipleship* confirms, the *authority* of Christ and obedience to his command is the essence of discipleship.

The most obvious sign of the autobiographical dimension of this book's theology is the role of the Sermon on the Mount in Bonhoeffer's view of discipleship. His intimate letters not only spoke of the Bible as the main thing that had liberated him from his ambitious egotism; they explicitly singled out the Sermon on the Mount as decisive for clarifying his 'calling' and commanding his commitment to Christ in the church. Almost two–thirds of *Discipleship* is given to a detailed exposition of the Sermon on the Mount and related passages. Indeed, Bonhoeffer's design for the book, which was obscured in the original English translation, was that Part I on the Sermon and Part II on the Pauline corpus would be shown to be in complete harmony with each other.[103] This deliberate departure from traditional Lutheranism is a direct consequence of the importance of the Sermon for Bonhoeffer himself. There he heard the authoritative Word which spoke to his condition. Not Luther's message that grace alone justifies the person enmeshed in guilt, futile works, and hatred of God, but the command that the successful, self–satisfied, wilful man must abandon his own ambitions and singlemindedly follow Christ—

---

[103] See N 219, CD 229: "We rupture the unity of Scripture if we say that Paul proclaims the Christ who is present to us now in just the same way, while the synoptic writers speak of a presence of Jesus Christ which we can no longer know. Such a view indeed commonly passes for Reformation and historical–critical thinking; but in fact it is the opposite of that, namely the most dangerous enthusiasm [Schwärmerei]." See also Godsey's discussion of the structure of the book, "Reading Bonhoeffer in English Translation: Some difficulties," *Union Seminary Quarterly Review,* XXIII. 1, (Fall 1967), 82f.

that was the message Bonhoeffer heard in the Sermon. He must no longer use theology and church as an opportunity for personal advancement; he must become a disciple of Christ who serves the church and devotes everything to its renewal.

The title of the book therefore states in one word exactly what Bonhoeffer himself had done: he had become a disciple, a Christian, one who followed along after Christ. The title communicates the personal and existential character of Bonhoeffer's own commitment to obedience, as well as the message of the book. No longer is theology what he had described to Karl–Friedrich as an "academic affair"; it is an existential matter of obedience of life. It is not 'phraseological,' but 'real.'

This intense emphasis on the obedient commitment of life in following Christ, as well as the book's astringent and timely challenge to the German church in the battle with Hitler, has obscured, however, the *underlying continuity of the theology of sociality in Discipleship*. While the book has new theological motifs—some of them, indeed, in strong tension with the theology of sociality—the theology of sociality is by no means repudiated. Although it is in the background and is presupposed, it is still *intrinsic* and *indispensable* to Bonhoeffer's interpretation of discipleship. Discipleship is the *existential* dimension which is *added* to the theology of sociality. Few readers of *Discipleship* in 1937 had even read the earlier writings, and the situation has not dramatically altered in the decades since then. But Bonhoeffer's statements about earlier 'academic' or 'phraseological' theology should not be misread as a repudiation of his theological foundations.[104] The phrase, "from the phraseological to the real," must be understood as adding existential reality to the conceptual structure of the theology of sociality. I will demonstrate this by showing the presence of the basic concepts of sociality in *Discipleship*, and indicating how they are intrinsic to and necessary for the existential interpretation of discipleship which is added. Then follows a detailed analysis of the autobiographical dimension of the book, and its unresolved theological and personal problems.

---

[104] The situation is analogous to his later attitude toward *Discipleship*; he had reservations about it, and saw it as the end of a stage, but still stood by what he wrote.

1. SOCIALITY AND DISCIPLESHIP

The theology of sociality in *Discipleship* is most obvious in Part II, especially in the sections on "The Body of Christ," and "The Image of Christ." This is to be expected because these sections discuss the Pauline corpus, on which Bonhoeffer drew heavily in formulating the theology of sociality in *Sanctorum Communio* and *Act and Being*. In *Discipleship* the synoptic gospels, and above all the Sermon on the Mount, are joined to the Pauline corpus. This already provides *prima facie* evidence that the existential impact of the Sermon is added to the theology of sociality. But precisely because of this synthesis, the theology of sociality is found throughout the whole book, and presupposed by the logic of its argument.

The concept of 'person,' in its individual and corporate use, is still fundamental. "Person" used of Christ and human beings still involves the historical, socio–ethical concept of person in sociality. A disciple is "bound to the person of Jesus Christ."[105] A human being is never human alone, but always in relation to others. The 'other' is "the living claim on my love and service,"[106] the 'Grenze' to the will of self.[107] Christ is present in the messengers, who are "like Christ"; in their word, people encounter the Word of Jesus.[108] Encounter with this Word makes people responsible individuals; while they hear the Word and call [Ruf] in relation to others in the community, each must answer and decide themselves.[109] Yet precisely in deciding as an individual a person is incorporated into the community which is the body of Christ.[110]

Bonhoeffer continues to speak also of the existence of both human beings and Christ in corporate communities, and this includes a heavy reliance upon the 'Kollektivperson' concept with respect to humanity generally and to the church. Adam is the Kollektivperson of created and fallen humanity.[111] He falls because he wants to make himself *sicut deus*.

---

[105] N 78, CD 87.

[106] N 178, CD 184; cf. CD 78.

[107] N 123, CD 127.

[108] N 210, CD 220; cf. CD 226f., 249f.

[109] N 87, CD 94.

[110] N 232ff., CD 241ff. Cf. "Einheit" and "Vielheit" in Gemeinschaft (N 234), the exact terms Bonhoeffer had used in *Sanctorum Communio*.

[111] N 297f., CD 237f.; cf. CD 265f. The actual term 'Kollektivperson' is not used of Adam, though it is clearly presupposed. When Bonhoeffer says that Christ present in the church is to be understood not as an institution but "as a living *person,* though a person in a quite unique sense" (N 232, CD 241), he obviously means Kollektivperson but does not use the technical term.

"He made himself god and now had God no more. He ruled alone as a creator–god in a godless, subjugated world."[112] Since Adam 'personifies' all human beings both individually and collectively, this means that genuine humanity is destroyed in personal and corporate life.[113] The sociality of created human existence is now in contradiction with itself.

Christ is the Kollektivperson of the new humanity of all humanity and of every human being.

> In the Incarnation of Christ all humanity received back the dignity of the image of God…. In the community [Gemeinschaft] of the Incarnate our true humanity is given back to us. We are delivered from the individualistic isolation of sin and simultaneously given back the gift of the whole human race. In so far as we participate in Christ, the Incarnate, we share in the whole humanity which he bore.[114]

Even in *Discipleship*, his most ecclesiastical and 'anti–world' book, Bonhoeffer continues to insist on this key premise of the theology of sociality: Christ 'personifies' the new humanity of all human beings corporately and of each individual personally. In this capacity Christ is the Stellvertreter[115] and Mediator.[116]

The church, as previously, is consistently understood as the concrete, social form of the new humanity of Christ. It is regularly described as a Gemeinschaft[117] in the distinctive way Bonhoeffer had appropriated and modified the concept in *Sanctorum Communio*. Christ is present in the Gemeinde as Gemeinschaft; he is the head of the community, and the community is really his body.[118] The community is the Gestalt Christi in the world.[119] It is an end in itself, since it is the place where people receive

---

[112] N 298, CD 299. Note the summary of the soteriological problem in terms identical to the seven detailed passages discussed above.

[113] N 301, CD 301f.

[114] Ibid. CD 239ff.

[115] N 84, CD 92; N 216, CD 244; cf. CD 150f., 301f.

[116] CD 59, 95ff., 100ff., 162, 183, 231.

[117] N 94, CD 100f.; cf. 75, 92, 110, 120, and *passim*. Note that the original English version usually translated 'Gemeinschaft' as 'fellowship' or 'communion,' or both, and 'Gemeinde' as 'community'; this obscured the sociological import of the former and the ecclesiastical significance of the latter, and so further disguised the presence of the theology of sociality in this work.

[118] See especially N 227ff., CD 236ff.

[119] N 234: "Der gekreuzigte und auferstandene *Christus existiert* durch den Heiligen Geist *als Gemeinde*, als der 'neue mensch'…" (italics mine); this repeats the well-known formula of *Sanctorum Communio*, Christ existing as church-community.

the gift of their true humanity; and it is a means to an end, since it is commissioned to proclaim and live Christ's word and action for all people. Christ is present by his Spirit;[120] Bonhoeffer clearly implies the view (first developed in *Sanctorum Communio*) of the Christian community as a Geistgemeinschaft in which the Spirit 'actualizes' what is already 'real' in Christ as the Kollektivperson of the new humanity.[121] It is the Spirit who creates love in the community.[122]

After studying the early theology, this is a thoroughly familiar conceptuality. I have documented its presence in *Discipleship* because Bonhoeffer's continued use of the theology of sociality in this work has been consistently overlooked. But certain as it is that discipleship is a powerful new element added to Bonhoeffer's theology in 1932, it is just as certain that the theology of sociality is essential for Bonhoeffer to present his understanding of discipleship. *Discipleship* infuses the whole conceptuality with the dimension of *personal obedience;* sociality continues to express Bonhoeffer's understanding of the presence and purpose of Christ in the world. In brief, he still sees human beings as essentially social persons whose personal and corporate relationships have become self–contradictory through egotism and destructive power. Christ is the 'personification' of the new humanity who is present in the concrete, social form of the Christian community, restoring the true being of humanity. What is *added* to the theology of sociality is the overriding emphasis on the *obedience* Christ demands of his disciples. Yet in order to argue that Christ is present among us today with the same call to obedience which the first followers heard, Bonhoeffer employs his theology of sociality to articulate the presence of Christ.

The argument of *Discipleship*, in more detail, runs as follows. Part I of the book sets forth discipleship as faithful obedience and obedient faithfulness: *"only the believer is obedient, and only the obedient believes."*[123] This is the discipleship of "costly grace."[124] It is spelled out by exegesis of synoptic pericopes on the call to discipleship, on obedience, on the cross, and above all through exposition of the Sermon on the Mount. In the earthly life of Jesus, the disciples heard him person-

---

[120] N 223f., CD 233; cf. CD 242, 247, 255.

[121] See particularly N 234f., CD 243ff.

[122] N 189, CD 194f.

[123] N 52, CD 63, Bonhoeffer's italics.

[124] CD 43ff.

ally and followed him bodily. The situation is identical, Bonhoeffer argues in Part II, for people today.

> Jesus Christ is not dead, but is living today; he still speaks to us through the testimony of Scripture. He is present to us today; present in bodily form and in his word. If we would hear his call to follow, we must listen where he himself is present. The call of Jesus Christ is promulgated in the church through his Word and sacrament. The sermon and sacrament of the church is the place of the present Jesus Christ.... Here he is, fully, the same one who encountered the disciples. Yes, here he is already—glorified, victorious, living. Nobody else but he himself can call us to discipleship.[125]

As Jesus gave his first followers an unambiguous command, so he speaks now. The command of Jesus demands the faith of an undivided heart; it demands the love of God and neighbor with the whole heart and mind. This command of Christ is heard where Christ is personally and bodily present: in and as the church.[126]

Having argued the unity of the message of discipleship in the Gospel of Matthew and in Paul, Bonhoeffer elaborates this in two following chapters on "The Body of Christ" and "The Visible Congregation" [Gemeinde, i.e., church-community].[127] Here the theology of sociality is most conspicuous. The essence of the argument, then, is this: in his earthly life Jesus is the Incarnate one who is present bodily and calls together a community of disciples who follow him obediently; he is the Kollektivperson of the whole human race who, by his death and resurrection, bears to death the whole of the corporate old humanity and creates the new humanity which is real and 'personified' in him; as the Incarnate Christ was present bodily, uniting his disciples to himself, so the community of the church is nothing other than the contemporary, bodily presence of Christ—"die Kirche is die gegenwärtige Christus selbst";[128] in the *Word* and *sacraments* of this *community* people are united bodily to the person of Christ, entering individually and collectively into his new humanity, so that "Christ is the new humanity in new

---

125 N 215f., CD 225f.

126 N 216ff., CD 227f.; cf. CD 229ff., 233, 235, for the equivalence of Synoptic "discipleship" and Pauline "baptism" as both involving the call of Jesus and the follower's "visible act of obedience."

127 CD 236ff.; cf. 234.

128 N 232, CD 241; cf. N 243f. for Bonhoeffer's insistence that Christ is Lord of the church. In the 1932 summer semester lectures on the church, Bonhoeffer developed this point, first enunciated in *Sanctorum Communio*, in

human beings"; thus people today are Christ's disciples.[129] As it was in
the earthly life of Jesus, so it is now: God comes to a person not as an
idea, a philosophy, a religion, but as a human being in the Christian
community of the new humanity.[130]

In this argument Bonhoeffer gives theological expression to his own
personal commitment. He becomes a Christian, a disciple, and discovers
that "the life of a servant of Jesus Christ must belong to the church." His
personal commitment, in response to the command of Jesus in the
Sermon on the Mount, adds the existential dimension of discipleship to
his previous theology. In explicating discipleship as adhering bodily to
Christ who is personally present in the Christian community, he employs
his theology of sociality. The phraseological has now become the real.

2. THE AUTOBIOGRAPHICAL DIMENSION OF THE THEOLOGY

To keep the autobiographical dimension of *Discipleship* in perspective,
the other concerns of its theology must be mentioned briefly. I have
already mentioned the claim of the biblical text as providing the
exegetical basis of the new theological element in the book; note,
however, that the personal significance of the Sermon on the Mount for
Bonhoeffer himself accounts for its prominence and structural significance in the book. Two other dimensions must be underlined: the
ecclesiastical and the *political.*

The opening attack on "cheap grace" purveyed by the churches, and
Bonhoeffer's accusation that that the churches in Germany had distorted
their Lutheran heritage, both clearly show his ecclesiastical concern. So
too does the opening sentence of the book, which states that times of
church renewal occasion a richer understanding of Scripture.[131] There
are also several allusions to the conflict between the Confessing Church
and the Volkskirche infected by the German Christian mentality.[132]

---

the direction of *Nachfolge*: the Gemeinde of Jesus' earthly followers lived and
died in his life and death; in the death of Jesus the old Adam triumphed and was
defeated; after his resurrection and ascension, Jesus recreates and lives in the
Gemeinde; by his presence he is the Grund of the church (DB 1062, DBW 11
269ff.).

[129] N 227–39, CD 236–47; particular attention should also be given to the
following pages (CD 248–71) for the amplification of this argument.

[130] N 299ff., CD 300ff.

[131] N 21, CD 35.

Allusions to the German political situation of the 1930s are equally evident. The voice of the Holy Spirit is not heard in the call of blood and nature. The church looks on as an outsider at the idolatrous celebrations of the nation. In clashes between the church and civic authorities, Christians may have to leave their secular professions. Christians, who know the unity of Jew and Greek in Christ, will not support the State's tearing asunder what God has joined together; "open your mouth for the dumb" will be their watchword—the saying from Proverbs 31:8 that Bonhoeffer used repeatedly when speaking on behalf of the Jews.[133]

Together with these exegetical, ecclesiastical, and political dimensions, the autobiographical dimension pervades the whole book. Indeed, it is even more evident than the ecclesiastical and political concerns. The following discussion shows its influence on three parts of the argument: Bonhoeffer's interpretation of becoming a disciple, his exegesis, and his portrait of Luther.

Becoming a disciple. "Understanding cannot be separated from the existence in which it has been won."[134] Verifying this statement, Bonhoeffer interprets becoming a disciple just as he had experienced it in his own personal existence. To say this is not to deny the obvious fact that *Discipleship* intends to be, and is, exegesis. Bonhoeffer's interpretation of Scripture, however, does not occur in a vacuum. Exegesis has a concrete ecclesiastical and political occasion; it also has in this case an urgent, existential import for the theologian himself, and this informs the way Bonhoeffer's exegesis interprets 'becoming a disciple.'

Discipleship is replete with criticism of the "slavery of a self-chosen way."[135] Christ does not want followers who volunteer on their own terms; Christ wants disciples who obediently follow his call. The self-willed life, piety rooted in the self, insistence on choosing one's own way—these are repeatedly and vehemently repudiated as absolutely contrary to Christian discipleship.[136] Genuine discipleship,

---

[132] See CD 105f.: the distinction between the disciples and the people of the Volkskirche (N 99); CD 192: the separation of real and nominal Christians; CD 201f.: the religious leaders lead the people astray; CD 252: the church claims space in the world for its own order; CD 208: Christ's followers are not to expect privilege and status in society.

[133] CD 214, 108, 215f., 265f., 258.

[134] N 38, CD 51.

[135] N 35, CD 49.

accordingly, is not a career for an ambitious man.[137] Nevertheless, there are in the church men who—perhaps quite unconsciously—seek not Christ but power, influence and fame through their intellectual ability or prophetic insights.[138] Not only so, such would–be disciples may be quite untroubled by the contradiction in their lives; indeed, Bonhoeffer points out, the depth of their contradiction against God is seen precisely "the more convincing and proud their apparent success."[139] They are not defeated or guilty, but self–confident and pleased with their own performance.[140] Perhaps the most successful way to avoid the call to obedient discipleship and to achieve self–chosen ambitions is this: treat Christianity as a matter of ideas, opinions, principles, abstract questions—an intellectual enterprise, a "phraseological" and "academic" affair; that is precisely the way of "cheap grace."[141]

Here is ample documentation of Bethge's point that in *Discipleship* Bonhoeffer was dealing theologically with his own very pressing existential problem. These numerous statements throughout the book correspond intimately with what Bonhoeffer revealed of his early life. *Discipleship* repudiates ambition, Christianity as a career for self–advancement, self–centeredness, faith as ideas, intellectual achievement and personal programs, and the self–satisfaction of the powerful ego glorying in its own success. But how does the theology of discipleship resolve the problem? How does one move from the phraseological to the reality of true faith?

Bonhoeffer's answer is categorical: *obedience.* In the concrete situation Jesus calls for single–minded obedience "because he knows that a person is freed to believe only in concrete obedience."[142] *"Only the believer is obedient,* and *only the obedient believes."*[143] The first proposition cannot be separated from the second. If obedience presupposes faith, faith equally presupposes obedience. One can believe "only in this

---

[136] CD 59, 61, 72, 84, 90, 93, 142, 206, 214, 215, 225, 279.

[137] CD 60, 62, 67, 113, 167, 171, 191.

[138] N 185f., CD 191. Cf. the remark in the 1932 summer semester lectures on the church: "even the unbeliever can preach" (DB 1064).

[139] N 298, CD 299.

[140] CD 78., 163f.

[141] CD 43, 59, 72, 78f., 184, 191, 197, 206, 225, 238, 248ff., 300.

[142] N 73, CD 83.

[143] N 52, CD 63. Cf. CD 47, where Bonhoeffer says that in the monastery Luther learned obedience to Christ and his church because he knew that "only the obedient can believe." Whether this is, in fact, what Luther learned in the

new existence created by obedience.[144] The whole person must be refashion-ed, not just one's ideas or isolated acts. So God comes to people as person, as a human being and not an idea, and encounters them with the call to obedient faith.[145]

This radical interpretation of faith as obedience to the command of Christ had an obvious social impact, and it is no wonder that Bonhoeffer was known during his lifetime as the author of *Discipleship*. In the context of the Kirchenkampf and the life or death struggle with Nazism, it called Christians out of ersatz religious mythology and into a critical engagement with the demonic powers of that time. It was an uncompro-mising challenge to the church. Bonhoeffer surely would have agreed with Albert Camus' formulation: "Christians should get away from abstraction and confront the blood–stained face history has taken on today. The grouping we need is a grouping of men resolved to speak out clearly and pay up personally."[146]

But, in addition to this, it was above all Bonhoeffer's personal resolution of his own spiritual conflict. The theme of costly grace as obedience to the 'absolute authority' of Christ's command was formu-lated first in 1932 when Bonhoeffer found in the Sermon on the Mount the word which spoke to his condition. Yet why this particular resolu-tion? The answer must be understood in relation to the existential crisis of the theologian who gave it.

Bonhoeffer is exegetically quite right in reading the synoptic gospels and the Pauline epistles as calling people into a new life, not just teaching them new ideas.[147] But this had a quite special significance for Bon-hoeffer himself, and this strongly influences his interpretation. First, obedience necessarily involves the whole of a person's life, and so Bonhoeffer found it to be the way out of an academic and phraseological approach to Christianity. Second, if the heart of the personal problem was the hiatus between the professed vocation and the actual manner of life, only a change of *existence* could integrate the two; the vocation, as ideal, must become reality, and the actual life must be changed to enable the

---

monastery is a question discussed below.

[144] N 53, CD 64, italics mine.

[145] CD 299f., 59.

[146] *Resistance, Rebellion and Death,* trans. Justin O'Brien (New York: Alfred A. Knopf, 1961), p. 71.

[147] This was a crucial point in the resistance to gnosticism in Paul's time and in later centuries.

vocation to be real in life—obedience is the catalyst. Third, and catching up both these points, obedience was Bonhoeffer's answer to the power-ful, ambitious, successful, self–confident, autonomous ego. Here is the heart of the matter. If the ego is living by its own autonomous power, that power must be overcome and made obedient to the authority of Christ.

This explains the most characteristic tone of the whole book, in its Christology and its anthropology. Christ is above all the *authority* who *commands* his followers and *demands obedience* from his disciples.[148] The disciple must make a complete *break* [Bruch[149]] with his former way of life, and this involves the complete surrender, mortification and renunciation of his own will.[150] Bonhoeffer, to be sure, speaks of the grace, love, and forgiveness of Christ, and of the disciple being justified by faith; he speaks, too, of the joy, confidence, and freedom of the disciple. But these are set strictly within the context of the *authority* of Christ's *commands* and the *obedience* these *demand*. In short, the theology of *Discipleship* presents Christ as a mighty *power* who defeats the strong self–will of the powerful, autonomous human ego.

The book, then, interprets discipleship in a way that joins together the biblical text and Bonhoeffer's own experience. Ambition, intellec-

---

[148] The statements on this point are copious; selective documentation follows. On the *authority* of Christ: Jesus has "unbedingte, unvermittelte und unbegründbare Authorität," "Vollmacht zu rufen und auf sein Wort Gehorsam zu fordern," and Jesus can demand this obedience as "totally devoid of content [schlechthin Inhaltloses]": N 45f., CD 58; cf. 74f., 81f., 210. On the *command* [Gebot] of Christ: CD 37, 44, 46, 61, 64, 73f., 80, 138, 209f., 226f., 253, 297. On the *demand* [Forderung] of Christ: CD 57f., 124, 138, 231, 296. On the *obedience* [Gehorsam] of the disciple: 44, 47, 49, 54, 57f., 63f., 67, 70, 73f., 78, 80, 83ff., 124, 158f., 194, 197, 214, 226, 228, 233, 253, 262, 267, 295, 304. (In each case the German words indicated lie behind the texts cited in the English translation.)

[149] As noted at the beginning of this chapter, Bonhoeffer recalled in prison an earlier time when he longed for a "break" in his life, though later he stressed the continuity. In *Nachfolge* the idea of a "break" with the former manner of life is decisive in the theology of discipleship; cf. N 37, CD 50; N 87ff., CD 94ff.; N 221ff., CD 231ff. Note particularly the statement that one learns about the personal 'Bruch' "from the Bible and *experience*" (N 94, CD 100; italics mine).

[150] These statements are also copious. On the *mortification of self–will* see: CD 164, 170, 231. On the complete *surrender* of self–will see: CD 164, 166. On *self–renunciation* [Selbstverleugnung, Verzicht] see CD 47f., 88, 106f., 109ff., 119, 131ff., 153; note that while renunciation is chiefly concerned with self–will, Bonhoeffer also includes a physical asceticism which he later re-nounced (CD 131ff., 169ff.). On *submission* [unterstellen] see: CD 87.

tual success, and self–centeredness are encountered by the omnipotent authority of Christ. The disciple hears the command of Christ to obey, submits to the power of Christ, and renounces his self–will, his career, plans, and autonomous thinking. He dies to his old life, binds himself to Christ present in and as the church, and gives his whole life as a servant of Christ to the service of the church. Obedience leads to liberation from a self–willed life. It brings him out of isolation into the Gemeinschaft of Christian brothers. He no longer dominates but serves others. Conscience and self–reflection are put behind him, for his eyes are now fixed solely upon Christ.

Exegesis. Bonhoeffer's exegesis also reveals the autobiographical dimension of his theology in *Discipleship*. The second chapter, "The Call to Discipleship," begins the exegesis. After a brief exposition of the call of Levi[151] as Jesus' demand for obedience to his absolute authority, Bonhoeffer comes to a highly personal discussion of the volunteer disciples and conditional disciples of Luke 9:57–62.[152] It is the first long passage exegeted in the book. The first man is a volunteer, and Jesus tells him he does not know what he is doing; discipleship is not a *self–chosen way*. The second man is called, but wishes to follow within the conditions prescribed by religious law; the command of Jesus opposes the law. The third man interests Bonhoeffer most of all and receives the longest exposition: he both volunteers and "sets his own conditions." In Luke's text this third man only requests permission to say farewell to his family before setting out to follow Jesus. Bonhoeffer's elaboration of this shows that he has applied the text quite directly to himself, and interprets it out of his own experience. This third man, he informs us, viewed discipleship as his "own, self–chosen career [Lebensprogram]," a "human program" arranged to suit his own judgement. This fits exactly with the fact that Bonhoeffer had chosen theology as a career for himself during adolescence, that he had pursued it as "an opportunity for self–advancement," and that he came in 1932 to see that this was not a Christian life of discipleship. As this *Discipleship* passage puts it, such a course involves one "in contradiction not only with Jesus but also with himself." Bonhoeffer's personal involvement in his exegesis, and this influence of his own experience upon it, is quite clear at this point.

---

151 Mark 2:14.
152 N 48ff., CD 60ff.

The second piece of exegesis interprets the story of the rich young man in Matthew 19:16–22;[153] it is given even lengthier discussion, but is treated in the same way as the Luke 9 passage. The young man wants to hold an interesting intellectual "discussion" about eternal life with the "good master," and thus avoid obedience to the "unconditional, binding divine order" which he already knows in the command of God. Jesus exposes his question as rooted in a "self–conceived and self–chosen piety." He tried to avoid Jesus' order to obey the commandments by making them questions for further discussion; then he adds that he has indeed kept all the commandments from his youth. The biblical text at this point moves directly to Jesus' command that the way of discipleship for the young man is to sell his possessions and follow. But Bonhoeffer elaborates on the young man's motivations before coming to this. The young man, Bonhoeffer says, thought that the revealed commandments were not enough for him; what he wants to do is "something extraordinary and unique." This ambitious desire is the height of obstinate defiance of Jesus, and "his final effort to retain his autonomy [bei sich selbst zu bleiben]." Jesus calls this man to die to *"his own will."*[154] Once again we have a correlation between the exegesis and Bonhoeffer's own early ambitious urge to an independent, impressive self–realization. This correlation is all the clearer since it follows a discussion of how a man can gain freedom not just from bad habits or possessions, but *from himself.*[155]

As a third example, consider Bonhoeffer's view of the "break" with the world which is either "hidden" or "open," or both. In the section on "Discipleship and the Individual," Abraham is discussed as one in whose life there is both an *open* and a hidden break. The first break is the open one when he follows the call to leave his friends and his father's house. Then comes the call, not known to Abraham's servants and *hidden* even from Isaac, that the son should be offered as a sacrifice. Abraham has to make a inner, *hidden* break with his unmediated relationship to his son; that he obeys to the point of sacrifice is his willingness to let the hidden break come into the *open.* Yet he comes down from the mountain, with Isaac, just as he had gone up; everything appears the same, but everything has changed.

---

153 N 60ff., CD 70ff.
154 N 81, CD 90, italics mine.
155 N 54, CD 65.

Outwardly everything seems to remain as before. But the old has gone—behold, everything has been made new. Everything had to pass through Christ [the Mediator].[156]

What is the inspiration for this striking interpretation of the Abraham story?[157] Bonhoeffer reveals the answer when he says that the outward break is easier than the hidden break, and that this must be learned "from the Bible and from *experience*."[158]

His own pilgrimage closely follows the course of his Abraham interpretation. Vocationally he leaves "his father's house." Then comes the hidden "break" with his own self–will. He continues in the university for over a year; everything has changed, though everything appears the same.[159] Then comes the time when the hidden break must be made open, and he leaves the university for the church; his allusion to the Kirchenkampf is unmistakable when he says that clashes between the claims of the world and the church may call a Christian to leave his secular vocation.

The Christian then enters upon open suffering. He, who died with Christ in baptism, whose secret suffering with Christ was unknown to the world, is now publicly expelled from his vocation in the world. He enters the visible suffering community and brotherly help of the church-community.[160]

---

[156] N 93, CD 99.

[157] The "two call" motif, including the notion of the "break," is also found in Bonhoeffer's interpretation of Luther, though without the hidden and open dialectic; cf. CD 50. By taking together Mark 1:17 and John 21:22, Bonhoeffer also interprets Peter in terms of the 'two call' schema (CD 45). There are some similarities between Bonhoeffer's account of Abraham and that given by Kierkegaard in his *Fear and Trembling*, and I am grateful to Tom Driver for reminding me of this. But the two are not identical, and one cannot say that Bonhoeffer simply took over his Abraham interpretation from Kierkegaard. For discussions of other relationships between Kierkegaard and *Nachfolge*, see Geffrey B. Kelly, "The Influence of Kierkegaard on Bonhoeffer's Concept of Discipleship," *Irish Theological Quarterly* XLI.2 (April,1974), 148–54, and Ernst Feil, *The Theology of Dietrich Bonhoeffer*, 224 n. 45.

[158] N 94, CD 100, italics mine.

[159] In his "Memoir" of his brother–in–law, Gerhard Leibholz makes a pertinent and perceptive observation: "Bonhoeffer always acted spontaneously, *'in hiding,'* far from all publicity,...considered *self–righteousness* and *complacency* great sins against the Holy Spirit, and regarded *ambition* and *vanity* as the start of the road to hell" (CD 23f., italics mine).

[160] N 262, CD 266; cf. CD 233f.

It is experience and the Bible, or, the engaging of experience by the Bible, which leads Bonhoeffer to his Abraham exegesis.

To point out the degree to which Bonhoeffer's exegesis is informed by his personal experience is not to argue that the biblical interpretation is arbitrary. Exegesis that confines itself to exact, historical explication of the text is a necessary discipline, which functions to protect theology from excesses of speculation and from naive literalism; but a purely academic exegesis lacks that 'concreteness' which Bonhoeffer sought so passionately. His exegesis in these passages is not arbitrary, but it is *specific* to his own personal concerns. Since his own concerns also involved issues pertinent to the church in his historical situation, the words which spoke to his own condition also spoke to many of his fellow Christians in Germany when *Discipleship* was published.

Bonhoeffer's portrait of Luther. In the earlier discussion on the soteriological problem, I distinguished the problem of the power of the ego in Bonhoeffer's theology from the problem of the guilty conscience in Luther. Bonhoeffer's portrait of Luther in *Discipleship* confirms this distinction. By what he says, and particularly by what he omits to say, Bonhoeffer paints Luther as virtually a modern man. The sixteenth century Reformer, in fact, emerges not at all unlike Dietrich Bonhoeffer himself.

What was the crux of Luther's problem according to Bonhoeffer? "Luther taught that a man cannot stand before God even in his most pious efforts, because everything he did was basically self–seeking."[161] Understood as Luther's repudiation of justification by works, this statement is historically correct. The *cor curvum in se* is trapped in the effort of self–justification by religious works. But Bonhoeffer gets more specific.

> The knowledge of grace was for him the final, radical break [Bruch] with *his besetting sin*.... Laying hold of forgiveness was the final, radical refusal of a *self–willed life*.[162]

That Luther's soteriological problem is, according to Bonhoeffer, essentially the egotism of a wilful, ambitious man is spelled out further. Luther, Bonhoeffer tells us, went into the monastery leaving "all behind, except for himself, his pious self." The apparent renunciation, however, was in fact "the ultimate, spiritual self–assertion [Selbstbehauptung] of

---

161 N 36, CD 49.
162 N 37, CD 50, italics mine.

the religious man."[163] The theological problem here, Bonhoeffer implies, is that monasticism was a form of elitist self–assertion by wilful men. Accordingly, when Luther received the gift of costly grace as comfort in his Angst, it was forgiveness and "liberation from the slavery of a *self–chosen* way."[164] This, as we have seen above, is precisely the phrase which Bonhoeffer uses to describe his own becoming a disciple; it fits perfectly with the soteriological problem he himself wrestled with, and reflects accurately his own autobiographical confessions.

From this account one gets the impression that Luther entered the monastery like a knight storming the gates of heaven.[165] His besetting sin, we are asked to believe, is his egocentric wilfulness. The historian must object, however, that while Luther indeed acknowledged an intensity and scrupulosity in performing his monastic works, he never made out that he was trying to serve himself and his own ambition by this. He wanted desperately to serve and love God. In his statement quoted above Luther did not suggest that his besetting sin was ambition: rather, it was that, for all his effort to serve God, he *hated* the God who called for his love, and thereby compounded his own guilt. Bonhoeffer has left this completely out of the picture, and so his portrait of Luther begins to resemble quite closely what Bonhoeffer has revealed of himself.

That Bonhoeffer's Luther interpretation is informed by a hermeneutic other than the canons of historical scholarship is demonstrated by none other than the great Luther scholar who was his own teacher: Karl Holl. A comparison of Holl's scholarly and historically balanced picture of Luther with the portrait painted in *Discipleship* proves the extent to which Bonhoeffer's own existential concern acts as a principle of selection and interpretation. This existential involvement accounts for the omissions and historical distortion in Bonhoeffer's interpretation.

In 1921 Holl published in his *Gesammelte Aufsätze zur Kirchengeschichte, I, Luther* a profusely documented study entitled "Luthers Urteile über sich selbst."[166] Much of it had been public since

---

[163] N 34, CD 47.

[164] N 35, CD 49, italics mine.

[165] Contrast Bonhoeffer's 1944 observation about how people today usually forget about dangerous crises as soon as they are over, whereas "with Luther a flash of lightning was enough to change the course of his life for years to come" (LPP 203). We might add to this Luther's repeated reference to the ability of a mere rustling leaf to strike terror into the human heart.

[166] See the translation by H.G. Erik Midelfort, "Martin Luther on Luther," in *Interpreters of Luther: Essays in Honor of Wilhelm Pauck,* ed. Jaroslav

1903; in any case, it was certainly available when Bonhoeffer worked in Holl's seminars in 1925 and 1926. Holl's portrait of the Reformer is in striking contrast to Bonhoeffer's at several crucial points. The contrasts to Bonhoeffer's picture of Luther, and the omissions, are notable.

Luther, Holl writes, displayed a "sort of natural timidity...in the event which led him into the monastery." Further,

> compared to other religious leaders, Luther had a fundamentally more difficult time attaining self–confidence, especially religious self–confidence. He was not like those men whose strong will, like a natural force, compels them to speak.

Again,

> he lacked everything that usually encourages gifted men to step forward. He had to confess correctly that he lacked ambition.... He had none of that "German aggressiveness" which finds fighting joyful in itself.

Holl, of course, points out that Luther acted vigorously as a Reformer, that he could show great determination, and that he attained a certain dialectical form of confidence, self–assertion, and even boasting. Yet he felt his office to be more a burden than a source of pride. Contrary to the man described in Bonhoeffer's writings, Luther "found no joy whatever in ruling and commanding. 'I don't like to govern. It doesn't agree with my nature.'" Growing fame made him anxious. So did the praise of his friends; he rejected their respect for him as an authority. He was "utterly devoid of envy at the talents he saw in others," whom he praised, while he "downgraded himself." Such were the dynamics of conscience and grace in his life that his confidence and self–affirmation were always paired with self–accusation, doubts, and anxieties; it was in a lifelong struggle with his Anfechtungen that he turned again and again for solace to the doctrine of justification. These 'attacks,' he confessed, were thus meat and drink to him, gifts of God as much as temptations of the devil; were they to cease, that would be the most distressing trial of all.[167]

Pelikan (Philadelphia: Fortress Press, 1968), pp. 9–34, from which the following quotations are cited.

[167] Holl concludes with the following balanced historical judgment. "Luther lived in this contradictory double attitude all his life." "And yet, this aspect of Luther too has a liberating significance. Since he knew how to bind together self–negation and self–affirmation, Luther transcended the inner contradiction which dominated contemporary feelings of personality. In the waning Middle

If Holl's portrait is historically balanced, Bonhoeffer's is highly selective. As he tells us nothing of the fear and trembling in which Luther entered the monastery, neither does he mention that what plagued Luther most sorely was the accusation of his guilty conscience. Because he omits this from Luther's original problematic, he can attribute even to Luther his own view of discipleship: grace comes in the command to obedience. Hence he can also make quite problematic statements about Luther's evaluation of the monastic endeavor. Luther, he says,

> did not reject the fact that in the monastery heavy demands had been made, but that obedience to the command of Jesus was understood as the achievement of the individual.[168]

Luther did indeed repudiate works as achievement. But he also rejected the demands, since they intrinsically expressed what he found to be a distortion of the righteousness of God and human salvation. At best their function was that of the *secundus usus legis:* they brought one to the point of simply accepting the 'passive righteousness' of God as sheer, forgiving acceptance.

What is happening here is not new in the history of theology. We are familiar with the New Testament Paul, the Augustinian Paul, the Lutheran Paul, and the Bultmannian Paul; likewise there is the original Augustine, the Thomistic Augustine, and the Lutheran Augustine. Here we find Bonhoeffer's Luther.[169] Just as his theological forebears appropriated from the tradition and brought it to life in the context of their own particular situations, so Bonhoeffer did with Luther.[170] As in his

---

Ages the ideals of humanity were either the absolute self–rejection of the monk or the equally absolute self–affirmation of the strong man of the Renaissance. There was no bridge between them. Luther was able to unite the truth of both because his faith in God encompassed them both."

[168] N 260, CD 265.

[169] Further detail on Bonhoeffer's understanding of Luther can be found in his two graduate seminar papers on the Reformer written for Holl: "Luthers Stimmungen gegenüber seinem Werk in seinen letzten Lebensjahren, nach seinem Briefwechsel von 1540–1546" (cf. DB 108f., 116); "Luthers Anschauungen vom Heiligen Geist nach den Disputationem von 1535–1545 herausgegeben von Drews" (cf. DB 108f., 116). Not transcribed from Bonhoeffer's difficult handwriting when this study was first written, these two papers are now available in DBW 9 271ff. and 355ff.

[170] For a similar phenomenon in the relation of Bultmann and Luther, see Roger A. Johnson, "Is Bultmann an 'Heir' of Luther? Reflections on Historical Continuities and Particularities," *Dialog,* 6.4 (Autumn, 1967), 265–275.

exegesis, this is not simply an arbitrary process. But it is not an academic historical appropriation; it is existential. It is heavily informed by Bonhoeffer's own personal and social history.

The liberty which Bonhoeffer takes with the historical Luther, however, leads to some problematic results. Had Luther foreseen what Bonhoeffer was to write four centuries later, he would surely have filed away a set of theses to be nailed to the Bruderhaus door at Finkenwalde. (Whether these questions would have been angry, friendly, or simply instructive Bonhoeffer can decide for himself in his later theology.) I refer particularly to the discussion of the "first step."[171]

That it is crucial to the theology of discipleship is clear when Bonhoeffer says that it is "qualitatively different" from everything that follows, that it is this which gets the wilful rich young man out of his academic discussions, and that it initiates the new existence of obedience in which faith is possible. This "first step" which carries such weight, however, is "a purely external act"; it "is and remains a dead work of the law, which never of itself leads to Christ." Bonhoeffer, *pace* Luther, can even invoke in this discussion what was to the Reformer an infamy, a teaching of the very devil: the *facere quod in se est* (do what is in oneself to do) of the Roman theology.[172]

The portrait of Luther in *Discipleship* further substantiates what we have seen in the understanding of discipleship and the exegesis. There is an autobiographical dimension to Bonhoeffer's theology that is particularly influential in this book which grew out of an intense spiritual experience at a critical stage of his life. Without understanding this it is impossible fully to understand the book itself, and its place in Bonhoeffer's theological development as a whole. This autobiographical dimension, however, illuminates not only the significance of the book but also its problems.

3. *THEOLOGICAL AND PERSONAL PROBLEMS IN* DISCIPLESHIP

This evaluation of *Discipleship* is selective, focusing upon the central problem of the work, and its significance for Bonhoeffer's theological

---

[171] N 53ff., CD 64ff. He relates this, but does not ascribe the explicit teaching, to Luther. He also claims support from the Lutheran confessional writings, though chides them for not being as clear and forceful about the matter as he was himself.

[172] N 55, CD 66.

development. To make this critical evaluation is not to detract from the integrity and genuine contribution of the book. Bonhoeffer's stringent interpretation of discipleship was most timely in the German church situation during the 1930s. In addition, *Discipleship* remains a sharp challenge to all who complacently distort the Christian gospel into a pallid, self–serving abstraction. Furthermore, it continues to remind theologians of acute problems in the Protestant heritage, keeping on the agenda the crucial issues of justification and sanctification, faith and ethical life, and the responsibility of the church in society.

Nevertheless, the critical problem of *Discipleship* for Bonhoeffer's theological development is its treatment of power in the anthropology and Christology. Bonhoeffer's anthropology in the early 1930s does not clearly distinguish between dominating power and mature strength. This lack of clear distinction leads to problems. If strength is indiscriminately negated together with the rejection of dominating power, then the converse can follow: weakness can be indiscriminately affirmed. Now it is one thing to point out the special concern of Christianity for weak and vulnerable people, and to remind Christians about the occasions of helplessness and suffering which accompany their service of the gospel. But it is a quite different matter to do so by trying to suppress the mature strengths of the healthy autonomous ego. In fact, however, Bonhoeffer unwittingly tends to negate strength as well as self–serving power, and to affirm weakness in an indiscriminate and undialectical way; the two sides of this anthropological problem are highlighted retrospectively by the dramatic contrast of his "non–religious Christianity," where strength— especially ego strength—is vigorously affirmed, and the weakness of Christian suffering is sharply differentiated from that weakness and dependence which is the root of "religion."

These problems der. ve, largely, from Bonhoeffer's personal struggle with the problem of power. But they are reflected in the Christology as well as the anthropology. Just as he does not clearly treat the anthropological power–strength–weakness syndrome, so his Christology vacillates between a power Christ and a dialectical interpretation of the weakness of Christ in the *theologia crucis* tradition; the former, the power Christ, is predominant in *Discipleship*.[173]

---

173 More discussion of the whole problem is found in the next chapter. The problem already appears in 1932–34, though it is more apparent in the anthropology than the Christology at that time. The Christological side of the problem seems to intensify during the mid 1930s and comes to fullest expression with the

When all is said and done, the Christ of *Discipleship* is an over-whelming power of "absolute authority" who demands total submission to his commands and the complete renunciation of any independent human will. The power of Christ is set over against the power of the self; the self–centered man renounces the ambition of his autonomous ego and is obedient to Christ in the service of the church.

However, in making this critical observation, it should be recalled that Christ is not only a counter–power to the power of the individual ego. He is also, in the historical situation of Nazi Germany, the counter–power to the power of Hitler's regime. Hitler is the Antichrist, a false messiah whose power literally destroys humanity. The Christ of the Confessing Church calls his community into radical, militant, and uncompromising opposition to Hitler; obedience to Christ, in whom the old humanity is crucified, gives the possibility of authentic humanity. There can be no question that this theology of Christ as the true power and authority offered a way of redemption to German society and posed the crucial spiritual issue of the time.[174] Furthermore, in view of the long and deep German social tradition of authority and obedience, it spoke an indigenous language which confronted people with this theological issue. The commanding Christ of the Sermon on the Mount, therefore, had an appropriateness to the social context of Christian theology as well as a liberating, personal significance for the theologian himself.

While the Christology of *Discipleship* ultimately rests on the power and authority of Christ, we do find in the theology of discipleship ambivalent and even contradictory statements about power, strength, and weakness. In the Christology, Bonhoeffer vacillates between the pre-dominant theme, the power Christ, and a form of *theologia crucis* which stresses the weak Christ. Corresponding to this ambivalence, the anthro-pology vacillates between, on the one hand, a combative power in the disciples and a downright weakness which Christians must learn to accept, and, on the other hand, a strength in Christian action and suffering whose source is the Christ of the *theologia crucis*.

---

publication of *Nachfolge* in 1937. Further work on this issue is necessary, particularly in the London sermons and the writings from the Finkenwalde period. See now DBW 13 311-421. See also the meditation on Luke 9:57-62, entitled by Bethge in GS IV 171ff. "Drei Nachfolger" ["Three Disciples"], which was given in London on New Year's Day 1934 (DBW 13 344-346).

[174] Bonhoeffer continues in *Nachfolge* his critique of dehumanizing power in society in accord with the political aspect of the theology; cf. CD 108f., 142, 202, 258.

In the predominant Christology, even the discussions of the power of Christ disclose two meanings. There are valid statements about the power of Christ, the Word of God, and the cross, in the sense of power as that which really accomplishes something, power as effectiveness and capacity; usually Bonhoeffer uses the word "Kraft" in these statements.[175] But he also goes beyond this, speaking of the power of Christ in an authoritarian, combative, and frequently violent language. Discussing, significantly, the "break" with the old self–centered life he asks: "why does this angry power [ärgerliche Macht] intervene between a person and the God–given orders of one's natural life?"[176] Again he says: only in "simple obedience" does the Word of Jesus have its "honor, power [Kraft], and might [Macht]" among us.[177] Obedient discipleship involves the disciples in a power struggle with the world. For this fight Jesus gives his disciples a conquering power [Macht] greater than the power of the devil in the world; this power is Jesus' "greatest gift" to his followers.[178] Hence the church "breaks into the world and tears away its children...[by] the power of the Lord who dwells in it."[179] These statements are by no means synonymous with those at the beginning of the paragraph; they have a spirit which is nothing less than violent and which recurs throughout the book.

In the subordinate Christological motif, Bonhoeffer can appropriate the Lutheran theme of the *weak* Christ. The Christian has neither right nor power [Macht] to force salvation upon people. Fanaticism

> confuses the Word of the gospel with a conquering idea. The idea demands fanatics, who neither know nor heed opposition. The idea is strong [stark]. But the Word of God is so weak [schwach] that it allows itself to be despised and rejected by people.... The Word is weaker than the idea. Likewise, the witnesses of the Word, like the Word itself, are weaker than the propagandists of an idea.... The disciples...do not want to be strong [stark] where the Word wants to be weak [schwach].... Disciples who do not know this weakness have not perceived the secret of God's lowliness. This weak Word, which suffers the resistance of the sinner—only this is the strong [stark], merciful Word which converts

---

175 Cf. CD 232, 245, 250, 285, 298; in each case the German word is "Kraft."

176 N 88, CD 95, italics mine.

177 N 191, CD 197.

178 N 196, CD 204.

179 N 249, CD 255. I think that the metaphors here require "Kraft" to be translated as "power."

sinners in the depths of their hearts. Its strength [Kraft] is veiled in weakness.[180]

This is pure *theologia crucis*. This paradoxical understanding of the divine strength in weakness, which has strong New Testament foundations, is also found elsewhere. The disciples "must acknowledge in fear and amazement the simultaneous strength [Kraft] and weakness [Schwachheit] of the divine word."[181] Hence the Word is not a 'manifest power' at their disposal, and they are not engaged in an "heroic conflict" [Kampf] or the fanatical imposition of a great idea or good cause.

In the Christology, then, there is a conflict. It is between a form of *theologia crucis* which understands the strength or power of Christ in the dialectical manner of I Corinthians 1:25,[182] and a Christ with dominating, authoritarian power often expressed with considerable violence. The latter is predominant in *Discipleship*; the former comes to fruition in the prison letters.

The same tension, or contradiction, is found in the anthropology. The disciples, we have heard, can have a 'manifest power' just like the authoritarian and combative power of Christ: Jesus gives his disciples a power by which they combat the world,[183] though this does not allow them to acquire worldly power [Macht] and privilege.[184] Yet the reverse can also be found, namely a 'manifest weakness,' so to speak, in submission before the 'manifest power' of Christ. Peter, for example, has to learn his own powerlessness [Ohnmacht] and the almighty power [Allmacht] of his Lord.[185] Similarly, Bonhoeffer can also say what he would never permit in the theology of "religionless Christianity": that with respect to their material needs in the world people are "completely powerless" [völling ohnmächtig], cannot alter the conditions of the world, and any attempt to do so is a wish to usurp the control [Regiment] of God.[186]

---

[180] N 180ff., CD 186f.; cf. CD 237f. which actually quotes Isaiah 53, only alluded to in this passage.

[181] N 203, CD 211; cf. N 162f., 167 for the same usage.

[182] "For the foolishness of God is wiser, and the weakness of God is stronger, than any human being"; cf. I Cor. 1:26–31, and I Cor. 15:43, II Cor. 12:9–10.

[183] Cf. also N 201: "Kampf mit den Mächten des Satans."

[184] N 200, CD 208.

[185] N 51, CD 63.

[186] N 172, CD 179.

On the other hand, there are discussions of strength and weakness in the disciples which express the dialectic of the *theologia crucis*. The suffering witness of the disciples, for example, has a paradoxical strength.[187] The word of Jesus strengthens [starken] them when they are defenseless and powerless [ohnmächtig].[188] In the same vein Bonhoeffer says that the love of the enemy is born out of strength [Kraft], not of weakness [Schwachheit].[189]

Awareness of the autobiographical dimension of *Discipleship* helps to clarify these Christological and anthropological conflicts, especially the non–dialectical statements about the power of Christ and the weakness of the disciples. Viewed in the light of Bonhoeffer's own struggle with personal power, we must conclude: the statements which either describe the disciples with a combative 'manifest power,' or which subordinate the disciple in weakness to the powerful Christ, both reflect Bonhoeffer's internal conflict. He is over–reacting against his own past. Because his strengths had existed in the mode of autonomous power, he is trying to subject all autonomy to Christ's "absolute authority" and power; hence the statements about weakness. But since he has not distinguished between mature and healthy ego strengths and selfish, dominating power, he is involved in the attempt to suppress the strengths of his ego—strengths which theologically and psychologically should be affirmed. There is thus a power struggle within himself. To a significant degree, this struggle is reflected in the statements about the authoritarian and combative power of Christ.

In contrast to this predominant spirit there is the *theologia crucis* whose Christological and anthropological resources could have helped Bonhoeffer to avoid these problems. The *theologia crucis* could provide Bonhoeffer with a way to affirm the healthy strengths of the ego—including its autonomy—in the service of others, and to acknowledge the suffering and weakness which may accompany the service of the gospel—a weakness which is not at all incompatible with strength, as Bonhoeffer was later to discover. But at this stage of his personal and theological development Bonhoeffer has not clearly apprehended this possibility, and it remains a subordinate theme.

The contradictory attitudes in both Christology and anthropology, then, reflect a battle in the theologian himself. This, in turn, illuminates

---

[187] See, for example, CD 215, 244f. [Kraft]; cf. N 182, CD 188.
[188] N 204, CD 213f.
[189] N 143, CD 148f.

the significant phenomenon of *violent language* in *Discipleship*; the metaphors are usually those of warfare and combat, robbery and plunder, and tearing and rending.

Christ comes like an "angry power" between people and their natural life.[190] Human beings are "subdued" [überwinden] by grace.[191] The call of Jesus means that those called must be the salt of the earth or else be "annihilated" [vernichten].[192] Christ "invades" the realm of Satan's power, "tearing asunder" past and future.[193] The church, likewise, "invades" the world and "conquers territory" for Christ;[194] it "breaks into" the world and "tears away" its children.[195] Christians remain in the world to make a "frontal attack" [Angriff] upon it.[196] They are engaged in "combat" with the powers of Satan;[197] indeed, it is a "hand–to–hand combat."[198] The Christian loves God and "hates" the world.[199] The same violence is found in language about the body: the will of the flesh must be "broken" by an "assault" [Angriff] in continual "battle" [Kampf]; the flesh must be "chastised" and "humiliated."[200]

How are we to understand this authoritarian power language with its recurrent violent spirit? Probably the violent rhetoric and conflicts of the political situation are part of the explanation. The situation in Germany in the 1930s, furthermore, should probably be seen as intensifying the expression of those feelings of anger and violence—usually repressed— which are found in societies with a conspicuous stress on authority and unqualified obedience. But there is also a deep personal reason which belongs in a full explanation. In this book Bonhoeffer is expressing the obedient submission of his own will to the authority and command of Christ; all autonomy of will, ideas, and personal goals are totally renounced. There is a complete 'break' between the old life of ambition and self–seeking, and the new life of service to Christ in the church.

---

[190] N 88, CD 95.
[191] N 43, CD 55.
[192] N 112, CD 117.
[193] N 252, CD 258; cf. CD 272, 278.
[194] Ibid.
[195] N 249, CD 255.
[196] N 260, CD 264.
[197] N 201, CD 209.
[198] N 34, CD 48.
[199] N 170, CD 176.
[200] N 164f., 169ff.

Now, insofar as this expressed the New Testament message that people must die to the old life of sin and be born to the new life of following Christ in faith, it is theologically valid. But it involves more than that. It does so because Bonhoeffer has not yet clearly distinguished—theologically or personally—between the dominating, self–centered ego as *power,* and the *strength* of the strong, healthy, mature ego. The former should, indeed, be renounced. But the latter should be affirmed. Strength of will and mind, as Bonhoeffer later came to see, are precisely necessary for the service of Christian love and responsibility in a complex, problematic world where numerous forms of power wreak destruction and exploitation upon human life. This was his whole purpose when he gave in the prison letters a theological affirmation and Christological interpretation to the 'adulthood' and 'autonomy' of modern people.

But the distinction between dominating power and a mature strength which is free to love and serve others has not yet been made in *Discipleship.* Bonhoeffer sets the authority and power of the commanding Christ over against the wilful and self–serving autonomy of his own strong, successful ego. Because of the contradiction between his professed theological vocation and his ambitious personal life, he attempts to suppress and deny his own independence and ego strength.[201] He does this in such a way, however, as to do unnecessary violence to himself; he has not yet fully found the way to affirm and free his strength for the service of the gospel. So intense is the wrestle with strong self–will that it would be unrealistic to expect the distinction to be made at this time. The most urgent existential concern must be dealt with first.

However, a price has to be paid for this singularity. The effort totally to submit his will and mind to the power of an authoritarian Christ involved an unnecessary self–denial. The attempted suppression of his own ego strength and independence was a self–violation.[202] The

---

[201] In his actual life, of course, Bonhoeffer did not practice the ego suppression advocated in *Discipleship.* He mobilized the German congregations in England against Hitler, was a leader in the ecumenical movement and active in church politics, and creatively directed the Finkenwalde seminary; the ego strengths he so notably possessed were actively employed. To be sure, these strengths were serving Christ and the church, not personal ambition; this change is important, even though it did not involve the posture of total submission propounded in *Discipleship.*

[202] Paul Lehmann pointed to an aspect of Bonhoeffer's character which supports this interpretation. Writing with a light touch he said that Bonhoeffer,

conflict within the theologian is reflected in two main ways: the contradiction between the *theologia crucis* and the power Christ, and its anthropological corollaries; and the violent language which repeatedly surfaces in the book.

When he later expressed reservations about *Discipleship*, Bonhoeffer was aware of this problem. While most interpreters emphasize the contrasting attitude to 'the world' in *Discipleship* and the prison letters, they fail to observe the personal significance of the comments. In a quite intimate letter, Bonhoeffer wrote:

> For a long time...I thought I could *acquire faith by trying to live a holy life,* or something like it. I suppose I wrote *Discipleship* as the end of that path. Today I can see the dangers of that book, though I still stand by what I wrote.
>
> I discovered later, and I am still discovering up to this moment, that it is only by living completely in this world that one learns to have faith. *One must completely abandon any attempt to make something of oneself,* whether it be a saint, or a converted sinner, or a churchman....[203]

One of the "dangers" of *Discipleship* is that it involves an "attempt to make something of oneself." It was written out of an intense, internal struggle, and bears in its theology the marks of the conflict. The "attempt to make something of oneself," on the one hand, and, on the other, submission to authority as power which involves an indiscriminate and harsh self–renunciation (expressed in violent language)—these are two sides of the same coin. For all its creativity and pertinence, *Discipleship* nevertheless replicates—albeit unwittingly and understandably—the problems of power and authority in the tradition of Bonhoeffer's German society.

Theologically and personally, therefore, *Discipleship* represents only a *partial resolution* to the soteriological problem of personal power. Bonhoeffer nevertheless stood by what he wrote, even when he later saw the dangers of the book. In his theology of discipleship he articulates a form of liberation from a "self–willed life" and a "self–chosen way"; his

---

as a university student, "had no problem with military service except that he found it difficult to bend his will to external claims upon it" (*Union Seminary Quarterly Review,* XXIII.1 (Fall, 1976), p. 99).

[203] LPP 369f, italics mine; cf. LPP 361f., which rejects the effort to be a Christian by making something out of oneself on the basis of some *method* or other. (The last word of the quote is, incidentally, "Kirchenmann.")

commitment to the service of Christ and the church was from that point wholehearted and unqualified. It led eventually to his personal freedom for the supreme act of discipleship: "Every call of Christ leads to death."[204] He stepped, indeed, "from the phraseological to the real." But in making that step he was already on the way to the time when he could affirm the strength and autonomy of his own ego in a theology where the weak Christ is truly the freeing Lord of a person who has "come of age."

In the interim the new understanding of discipleship had several consequences for his theology.

D. PERSONAL DISCIPLESHIP: ITS INFLUENCE ON BONHOEFFER'S THEOLOGICAL DEVELOPMENT

Since *Discipleship* was Bonhoeffer's major writing in the middle and later 1930s, we have therefore already met the main theological consequences of his turning in 1932 "from the phraseological to the real." It remains only to specify them briefly in a systematic form.

1. BIBLE AND CHURCH

Personal commitment added the existential dimension to the original theology of sociality, and brought it from the intellectual, verbal level into the reality of life. Since it originated in a discovery of the *Bible* as a personal word to himself, it is natural to find Bonhoeffer's theology taking a more exegetical form during the 1930s. *Discipleship* is the cardinal example. But it is not the only one. Immediately after his summer experience of 1932, Bonhoeffer lectured on Genesis 1–3. Partly this was a result of current theological concern with the doctrine of "orders of creation," and Bonhoeffer's awareness of how this would be used under National Socialism. But it also expressed the new role of the Bible in his own thinking. The lectures on "Creation and Sin" began with a sentence not retained in the published version: "in these three chapters God speaks to us as we are today, as sinners who are crucified with him."[205] This existential tone, and Christological method, is found

---

[204] N 81, CD 89. This is the actual translation of the sentence made famous by Bishop Bell's opening to his Foreword for the book, "When Christ calls a man he bids him come and die."

[205] DB-E 216.

in numerous biblical studies over the next several years. In 1935 he wrote a piece on "Christ in the Psalms," and addressed himself to the problem of New Testament hermeneutics.[206] In 1936, studies on King David and on Ezra and Nehemiah appeared.[207] In 1937 a New Testament study on church discipline preceded the completion of *Discipleship* in November.[208]

In June, 1938, a biblical study of temptation was written;[209] in October came the piece, "Our Way according to the Witness of Scripture."[210] In 1939–40 Bonhoeffer wrote meditations on his favorite psalm;[211] in 1940 came a small book on the whole psalter.[212] Many other smaller biblical studies may also be found in the *Gesammelte Schriften.*

Although Bonhoeffer shifted his emphasis to a biblical orientation from philosophy and related disciplines as discussion partners for theology, this did not mean that henceforth he ignored philosophy, or that he stopped thinking systematically. Analysis of *Creation and Fall* in the next chapter will make this quite evident.

If the Bible, and particularly the Sermon on the Mount, brought Bonhoeffer to personal discipleship, it also led him into the *church*. The church is the social form of the present Christ who makes the biblical word come alive and speak to his people. The theoretical role of the church in the earlier theology of sociality now was transformed into a genuine Lebensgemeinschaft for Bonhoeffer. He left the university for the church, becoming a leader of the Confessing Church in the Kirchenkampf. After his service in the London pastorate he returned to lead the Confessing Church seminary and Bruderhaus at Finkenwalde. Here Bonhoeffer actually gave reality to his understanding of the church as it had first been formulated in *Sanctorum Communio* and then made existentially personal in this theology of discipleship, where sociality and discipleship are joined together. *Life Together,* written in September,

---

[206] DBW 14 369ff., GS III 294ff.; "Vergegenwärtigen Neutestamentlicher Texte," DBW 14 399ff., GS III 303ff.

[207] DBW 14 878ff., GS IV 294ff., DBW 14 930ff., GS IV 321ff.

[208] DBW 14 829ff., GS III 369ff.

[209] *Temptation,* published with *Creation and Fall* (New York: Simon & Schuster, 1997).

[210] DBW 14 407ff., GS II 320ff., CW II 173ff.

[211] "Meditationen über Psalm 119," DBW 15 499ff., GS IV 505ff.

[212] *The Prayer Book of the Bible: An Introduction to the Psalms,* in DBWE 5 (Minneapolis: Fortress Press, 1996).

1938, and published the following year, was one theological reflection on the experience of the Finkenwalde community.[213] The *Gesammelte Schriften* contain many other pieces from the 1930s, dealing with the theology of the church in both its communal and ecumenical forms.[214]

2. CHRISTOLOGY AND ANTHROPOLOGY

In addition to the theme of the authority of Christ who commands obedience—a problem Bonhoeffer will later rework—two motifs appear in his Christology at this time which have enduring significance for his theology: incarnation and mediation.

The theme of Christ as Mediator was implicit in the 1932 address on "Christ and Peace" summarized above. It has a major role in the 1933 Christology lectures, as Chapter 5 will show. It is easy for Bonhoeffer to unite this with his previous understanding of Christ as Stellvertreter. By saying henceforth that Christ mediates between people and their own selves, their relations with others, their dealings with society, and their relations to nature, Bonhoeffer finds a way to overcome the problem of the self–centered, powerful ego enclosed in its own ideas, ambitions, will and desires. Christ as Mediator also has great political importance in his theology. The conception not only develops the point made in *Sanctorum Communio* that the I can never know the

---

[213] DBWE 5 (Minneapolis: Fortress Press, 1996).

[214] For the years 1932-33 see, for example, *Das Wesen der Kirche,* ed. Otto Dudzus (Munich: Chr. Kaiser, 1971), first published by Bethge in a shorter form (DB 1050-72) and now in DBW 11 239-303. See also DBW 11 317-357, 363-366, GS I 121-132, 140-170, 175-181; DBW 12 349-358, 408-415, 362-407, GS II 44-53, 62-69, 90-119; DBW 12 235-239, 508-509, GS III 286-293; DBW 12 423-431, GS IV 93-101. For the later 1930s see, for example: "Die Kirche und die Welt der Nationen" (DBW 13 295-297, GS I 212-215); "The Church and the Peoples of the World" (CW I 289-292, DBW 12 298-304, GS I 216-219); "The Confessing Church and the Ecumenical Movement" (CW I 326-344, DBW 14 378-399, GS I 240-261); "The Question of the Boundaries of the Church and Church Union" (CW II 75-96, DBW 14 655-680, GS II 217-241); "Das innere Leben der deutschen evangelischen Kirche" (DBW 14 714-720, GS IV 385-390); "Konfirmanden-Unterrichtsplan. Zweiter Katechismus Versuch" (DBW 14 786-819, GS III 335-367); "Bonhoeffer's Lectures on Preaching" ("Finkenwalder Homiletik," DBW 478-530, GS IV 237-293) in Clyde E. Fant, *Bonhoeffer: Worldly Preaching* (Nashville: Thomas Nelson, 1975), 123-180; see also the material on the church in the biblical studies mentioned above.

other as I, but only as You: in *Discipleship*, it becomes a sounder Christological basis for the anthropology.

That incarnation now comes to the fore along with the original kerygmatic stress on cross and resurrection is also related to the personal experience of 1932, though this is easier to see retrospectively than in the texts of that period. As with the theme of Christ the Mediator, so the Incarnation of Christ (which is indispensable to the theology of discipleship) has an essential place in the 1933 Christology lectures.[215] Of course, Bonhoeffer found the theme of incarnation central in the classical Christological texts as he prepared for these lectures, and this also obliged him to deal with this aspect of Christology. But again, incarnation had always been implicit throughout the theology of sociality: Christ is present in human form—in the "other" as the form of revelation and transcendence, in the community of the church as the body of the present Christ (Christus als Gemeinde existierend).[216] But in *Discipleship* it is stressed and explicitly related to the cross and resurrection of Christ more forcefully than ever before. By his becoming human, Christ vicariously dies the death of every sinful human being and of sinful humanity corporately, and liberates people to the new life of resurrection and grace; the new humanity has its concrete social form in the church, and there people are incorporated into Christ and reunited with each other, having been freed from the egocentricity, domination, and isolation of their own power. Since this view of the incarnation is crucial in the theology of *Discipleship*, and since it is found in the 1933 Christology lectures only a year after the experience which was formative for that book, there is good reason to see this theological development as growing out of Bonhoeffer's commitment to personal discipleship.

With respect to the relationship of Christology and anthropology, I have argued that the development of Bonhoeffer's Christology cannot be understood in abstraction, nor in terms of unresolved internal tensions in the Christology itself. It must be understood in relationship to the anthropology. The analysis which is now complete provides dramatic

---

[215] Incarnation was briefly mentioned in the seminar paper on "The Theology of Crisis" in the spring of 1931; cf. DBW 10 434-449, GS III 113.

[216] This point had been repeated in the 1932 summer semester lectures on the church: "As the one who became fully human, Christ is our brother"; because he is the true brother, his presence in the community allows the brother in faith to become "Christ to me" (DB 1062f.; cf. 1066f. on the priesthood of all believers; cf. DBW 11 273f., 287ff.).

confirmation of this point. It is evidence of a relationship between Christology and anthropology which in this case is not simply theoretical, but which is rooted in the existential, spiritual pilgrimage of the theologian himself. Why does Bonhoeffer, contrary to Luther and the Lutheran heritage, set forth from 1932 to 1937 the commanding authority of the Christ of the Sermon on the Mount as crucial to his theology at that point? The answer is plain: it grew directly out of his own spiritual struggle with the problem of the powerful ego which was his own personal problem as well as the soteriological problem in his theology. Without understanding this anthropological and existential correlation with Christology it is impossible to explain this radical, new development in his thought. But in seeing this we do not discover something for which we are unprepared. The concern with theological anthropology has been with him from the beginning of his theological work; his Christology and anthropology have always been related, above all at the point of the anthropological problem. Now we see that this aspect of Bonhoeffer's theology is also involved in the "turning from the phraseological to the real."

Finally, to complete this chapter a retrospective and prospective overview is appropriate. From Chapter 2 onwards I have documented the argument that Bonhoeffer has a programmatic concern with the sociality of human existence, involving the articulation of all theological concepts in this perspective. Pre–eminent among these doctrines is Christology. Christ is interpreted as present in human form in the matrix of social relationships; his presence is the reality of the universal new humanity, in its corporate and individual dimensions, and the Christian community is the community of persons where the reality of the new humanity of Christ becomes actual in the social world.

In this chapter I have argued that the anthropology and Christology both deal with a specific—and characteristically modern—soteriological problem: human power. Viewed from the perspective of the individual self, Bonhoeffer diagnoses the way the strengths of the ego can operate in the mode of dominating power and destroy the true sociality of existence: in the domination of others, the isolation of the self, and the inner division manifest in conscience, the individual subverts relations of love and mutuality and is cut off from others. Viewed from the corporate perspective, forms of power such as class oppression, ruthless economic competition, warfare and militaristic imperialism, and the anti–human use of technology are equally destructive of the relations of peoples and nations.

The intensity of his involvement with the personal problem of the power of the ego heavily influenced, and indeed compromised, Bonhoeffer's attempt to find the Christological and anthropological resolution to this soteriological problem in *Discipleship*. Despite the problematic and incomplete resolution, however, the powerful Christ of the theology of discipleship offered him and his society a way to meet real and present crises. Bonhoeffer himself took the step of obedience, overcoming—to a significant degree—inner conflict, ambition, vanity, and self–centeredness; his society, for the most part, sought salvation in demonic myths of its own devising, and unleashed upon the world a display of destructive power scarcely rivaled in human history.

Yet in *Discipleship*, even the theological and psychological ambivalence of the Christology and anthropology hints at Bonhoeffer's way forward. For the *theologia crucis*, which conflicts with the power Christ, and which also conflicts with the vacillation between postures of power and weakness in the anthropology, was ultimately to bear fruit in the theology of "non–religious Christianity." By that time Bonhoeffer will have found a theological way to rehabilitate the strong ego in the service of others. The weak Christ as "the one for others" shapes and forms the strong and autonomous ego of modern people into Christian life as "existing for others." This development in Bonhoeffer's theology simultaneously involves the full affirmation of ego strengths and autonomy in himself and his contemporaries, and the liberation of these strengths for the life of free responsibility in personal and corporate relationships of human society. Though fragmentary in its literary formulation, Bonhoeffer's initial purpose thus comes finally to fulfillment.

Chapter 5

CHRIST AND HUMANITY IN BONHOEFFER'S THEOLOGY, 1932–33

This chapter deals with the last year of the period which comprises Bonhoeffer's early theology. Its two chief writings derive from lecture courses in the winter semester of 1932–33[1] and the summer semester of 1933.[2] Since Bonhoeffer's approach to the anthropological subject matter of creation is Christological, and since the form of his Christology in the 1933 lectures is anthropological, the prima facie rationale for the title of this chapter is apparent.

This chapter shows that, while Bonhoeffer's personal liberation in the summer of 1932 introduced new notes and concepts in his thinking, his theology of sociality continues to characterize his writings; it remains the basic conceptuality in which he deals with Christology, theological anthropology, soteriology, and ethics. His continued concern with the problem of power will be analyzed, particularly the unresolved tension between *power, strength, and weakness* as anthropological and Christological issues. In addition to interpreting the new writings of this year, therefore, this chapter reinforces the argument of Chapter 4 that the

---

[1]   The lectures were entitled "Schöpfung und Sünde," and were published as *Schöpfung und Fall*. See DBWE 3, *Creation and Fall*.

[2]   The reconstructed lectures were first published posthumously in GS III 166–242. A paperback edition was published under the title *Wer ist und wer was Jesus Christus. Seine Geschichte und sein Geheimnis* (Hamburg: Furche–Verlag, 1962); this title is misleading. See now DBW 12, 279-348.

theology of sociality continued to function in *Discipleship*, and that unresolved problems remain in that work. It also prepares the way for discussing, in Chapter 6, the concepts of sociality and its central soteriological problem in the prison writings.

The first part of the chapter will focus on *Creation and Fall*, the second on the Christology lectures; analysis of these texts will be related to shorter, occasional pieces from the same period. The third part of this chapter will discuss and summarize the developments in sociality, theological anthropology, and soteriology, thereby showing that the Christology lectures are a culmination of the theological path which Bonhoeffer began to open up with *Sanctorum Communio* in 1927.

A. CHRIST AND CREATION

Bonhoeffer's lectures on "Schöpfung and Sünde" are his first approach to doing theology in the mode of Biblical exegesis;[3] this may be seen as a direct consequence of the new role the Bible had come to play in his life and thinking. But he does not cease to think systematically, as seen in his

---

[3]   A detailed discussion of Bonhoeffer's Old Testament exegesis is not possible here, but the following is briefly noted. On the one hand he quite defensibly ascribes to the Bible the theological status of the church's Scripture, expounding it as a contemporary address of the Word of God and interpreting it Christologically for this reason. On the other hand he rejects verbal inspiration, and readily acknowledges that the ancient worldview of the biblical text is scientifically naive, that it contains "undisguised mythology," "fairy tales" belonging to a "world of the magical"; since the biblical writers were limited by their own time and knowledge it could not be otherwise (cf. CF 50, 75, 82).

Here Bonhoeffer is not so far from Bultmann. He insists that there must be a theological "translation" from the images of myth and magic to the "new picture language of the technical world" in order for the hearer to be personally encountered by the Word as address. But, unlike Bultmann, he does not feel the necessity to reject "myth" in order to make way for "God's Word" since human speech about God is always in "pictures" (82f.). There are other important differences from Bultmann, but this lack of anxiety about the conflict of faith and the scientific worldview (which is repeated in the prison letters; cf. LPP 285, 329) suggests that Bonhoeffer is moved by a different concern from Bultmann, even if his later charge about Bultmann's liberal reductionism is problematic.

What needs further clarification is the role played by Bonhoeffer's unquestioned acceptance of the findings of historical and scientific criticism of the biblical text in his "theological interpretation." To raise this question, however, is not to accept Harrelson's criticism that Bonhoeffer's Christological interpretation is "gratuitous" any more than his characterization of this interpretation as

use of many concepts developed earlier, and the systematic pattern of thought which informs his interpretation of the Genesis texts. For this reason, Bonhoeffer quite accurately described his approach to the biblical text in the subtitle to the published version: "Theologische Auslegung von Genesis 1 bis 3."[4] The present analysis cannot go into every interesting question which arises in studying this text, but will concentrate on Bonhoeffer's main points and their relation to my overall argument.

1. THE CHRISTOLOGICAL FOUNDATION OF THE DOCTRINE OF CREATION

In *Sanctorum Communio* Bonhoeffer argued that the "primal state" could only be discussed in light of the revelation in Christ. In *Act and Being* he likewise contended that a theologically legitimate Daseinsverständnis followed from the encounter with the revealing Christ present in his Word in the Christian community.[5] In *Creation and Fall,* also, the point of reference for the anthropology and the doctrine of creation is Christological.

"existentialist philosophical theology which [he] later abandoned"; cf. "Bonhoeffer and the Bible," *The Place of Bonhoeffer,* ed. Martin E. Marty (New York: Association Press, 1962), pp. 120f. Not only does Harrelson's view of exegesis beg the theological question of the Bible as the Scripture of the church; he also seeks to foist upon Bonhoeffer a non–theological, historical interpretation of exegesis, and then proceeds to charge him with inconsistency! For two of Bonhoeffer's own discussions of theology and exegesis, see the 1925 seminar paper "Lässt sich eine historische und pneumatische Auslegung der Schrift unterscheiden, und wie stellt sich die Dogmatik hierzu?" (DBW 9 305-23) and the 1935 discussion of hermeneutics: "Vergegenwärtigung neutestamentlicher Texte," DBW 14 399-421, GS III 303–324, CW I 308–325. A dissertation has been written on this question: Martin Kuske, *The Old Testament as the Book of Christ. An Appraisal of Bonhoeffer's Interpretation,* trans. S.T. Kimbrough (Philadelphia: Westminster, 1976); cf. also R. Grunow, "Dietrich Bonhoeffers Schriftauslegung," MW I, 62–76.

4   Dumas, *op. cit,* p. 145, correctly states that *"Creation and Fall* is a commentary that is philosophical in its formulation... and biblical in its subject matter...."

5   *Creation and Fall* at several points echoes the discussions of the 'primal state' in *Sanctorum Communio* and the creature in *Act and Being.*

"We can know about humanity in the beginning only from Christ."[6] "Jesus Christ is the name of God."[7] Here Bonhoeffer is not proposing a unitarianism of the second person[8] but insisting, as he has done from the outset, that "after the fall" we do not have direct access to God, and that we only rightly know about our creatureliness where the creator has come to us in our fallenness, i.e., in God's revelation in Christ the Mediator. Bonhoeffer is just as much an opponent of natural theology as Barth. God creates by the Word, with the result that there is no continuum between God and world nor identity of substance, essence, and nature of creation with that of God. Hence any natural theology—*"via eminentiae, negationis, causalitatis"*—is ruled out.[9] In following this approach, it is also significant that Bonhoeffer does not take the doctrine of incarnation from Christology as the basis for his interpretation of creation; we have seen that incarnation, which will be discussed further in the next section of this chapter, plays a major role in the Christology of *Discipleship,*[10] but it has not yet come to the fore by 1932. Here the Christology is kerygmatic.

The resurrection of Christ is the ultimate revelation of God's living freedom. It is therefore Bonhoeffer's theological basis for interpreting the *creatio ex nihilo.* God, whose name is Jesus Christ, is the beginning, and it is out of God's own freedom that creation comes into being.

> The God of creation, of the utter beginning, is the God of the resurrection.... Indeed it is because we know of the resurrection that we know of God's creation in the beginning, of God's creating out of nothing.... By his [Christ's] resurrection we know about the creation. For had he not risen again the Creator would be dead and would not bear witness to himself.
>
> In the beginning–that is, out of freedom, out of nothing–God created heaven and earth. That is the comfort with which the Bible addresses us who are [now wrongly] in the middle [Mitte] and who feel anxiety before the spurious nothingness, before the beginning without a beginning and the end without an end. It is the gospel, it is Christ, it is the resurrected One who is being spoken of here. That God is in the

---

6 SF 58, CF 62; cf. CF 22, 26.

7 SF 70, CF 75; cf. CF 96, 145f.

8 See the various background references to the Trinity in this work: CF 29, 64; the same phenomenon is found in most of his books.

9 CF 41.

10 In the *Ethics,* incarnation in Christology is repeatedly used in relation to creation.

beginning and will be in the end, that God exists in freedom over the world and that God makes this known to us–that is compassion, grace, forgiveness, and comfort.[11]

Creation is not the theological presupposition of resurrection any more than the death of Christ is its possibility; that would be to place grace under necessity. The fact that the God of the resurrection is the Creator constitutes the world as a realm of the freedom, livingness, and grace of God.

Bonhoeffer discusses the other side of the kerygma, the cross, in relation to the primeval deep, the *tehom:* the dark 'deep' is the first sound of the power of darkness and therefore of the passion of Christ. Bonhoeffer interprets this primeval deep as power [Macht] and force [Gewalt] which is given form in creation. In formlessness it simultaneously bespeaks complete submissiveness and unsuspected force [Gewalt]. In receiving form it is simultaneously shaped and released; by its form it is increased in power [Macht]. The original condition of the unformed creation in its power and force is a "sound" of the passion of Christ since, ex post facto, it becomes revolt [Aufruhr] and rebellion [Empörung] when torn away from God as its origin and beginning.[12] Without going into historical question of the primitive associations of the "primal waters" in Babylonian and Hebrew thought, what is significant for our purposes is to see Bonhoeffer speaking of the elemental "stuff" of creation in terms of power. He is not trying to make some connection with concepts of energy in physics or with any scientific theories about the origin of the cosmos. Fundamentally he is concerned with the human realm. The reference to the rejection of created form in "revolt" and "rebellion" points forward to the Fall of Adam, where the encounter of human beings and serpent is interpreted as a power struggle; where Adam even after the Fall and the divine curse is a Promethean figure, whose life is a continuous assault on the lost kingdom guarded by "the powers" (cherubim) with the flaming sword; and whose son, finally, imbued with a greater passion for life and hatred of God than his father, makes into actual fact what was only darkly hinted at in the primeval power—Cain, the murderer, lays violent hands on human life.[13]

---

[11] SF 33f., CF 34ff.

[12] SF 35, CF 37f.

[13] This is further discussed below. Note that in the interpretation of Cain (CF 145), Bonhoeffer moves directly from the destructive violence of the murderer to the final paragraph on the cross of Christ.

The most emphasized Christological note in this interpretation of creation, however, is the connection between the freedom of God and the freedom of the creatures. As we have seen from the discussion of God's freedom in *Act and Being*, it would be highly artificial and at variance with Bonhoeffer's theology of sociality to discuss this subject in isolation from anthropology.

2. *IMAGO DEI* AS *ANALOGIA RELATIONIS:* THE FREEDOM OF THE CREATOR AND THE CREATURES IN SOCIALITY

In his interpretation of the *imago Dei* Bonhoeffer introduces a long overdue and far–reaching revision into the whole theological tradition. The image of God is understood not as an individualistic attribute but as a particular social relationship between persons, based on the relationship of God to humanity.

Classically the theological tradition had regarded reason as the human image of God. In addition to the exegetical problem this entails, two chief objections must be raised to this view. First, by so emphasizing reason it cannot do justice to the *wholeness* of the human being as the image of God.[14] Second, it permits an *individualistic* theological anthropology, since every person is endowed with reason as their own possession; the fact that the common possession of reason has been used as the basis for human social relatedness and for ethics does not overcome the essential individualism of this interpretation. Accordingly, it is noteworthy that nowhere in these lectures does Bonhoeffer use the *logos* doctrine with which classical theology had related Christology and creation. He does not take this opportunity which the combination of the biblical text and the tradition offered him. Rather he expounds the *imago Dei* as *analogia relationis,* analogy of relationship; sociality, not rationality, is the key to his interpretation. When, in the Christology lectures, Bon-

---

14   This is a consequence of a faulty theological method, which sought to define the image of God in terms of that which human beings alone possessed in distinction from the non–human creation. But this is a method of natural theology, historically conditioned by the impact of Greek *logos* on the formation of Christian thought. Without oversimplifying the complex causal factors involved, one may observe that psychologically the exalted status of reason was normally accompanied by asceticism with regard to bodily life in general and sexuality in particular, and that sociologically the primary status of intellect was a doctrine taught by a class of Christian intellectuals.

hoeffer discusses Christ as *logos,* and his relation to human reason, sociality is again the key to his interpretation.

Bonhoeffer expounds the *imago Dei* as an *analogia relationis* under the rubric of the freedom of God and human freedom. The exposition is a direct development of the interpretation of God's freedom given in *Act and Being*, and a clear anticipation of the statements about the freedom of Christ and humanity in the *Letters.* The message of the gospel is that God in freedom is bound to us, that God's free grace only becomes real for us in this relationship since

> God does not will to be free for himself [für sich] but for humanity. Because in Christ God is free for humanity, because he does not keep his freedom for himself, it follows that we can only think of freedom only as a "being–free–for...."[15]

In the light of the resurrection of Christ we know that the freedom of true humanity is being–free–for. In the grace of the resurrection humanity is free for God. In being free for God we are simultaneously free for our neighbors. The relation to God and to others is vividly expressed in the following statement where, once again, Bonhoeffer interprets 'being' in terms of sociality.

> Freedom, in the language of the Bible, is not something that people have for themselves [für sich] but something they have for others. Nobody is free 'per se' ['an sich'] as if they lived in a vacuum, or in the way that they may be musical, intelligent, or blind per se. Freedom is not a quality a person has; it is not an ability, capacity, or attribute of being.... *Freedom... is a relation and nothing else–a relation, indeed, between two persons.* Being free means *'being-free-for-the-other'* ['frei-sein-für-den-anderen'], because the other *has bound me to himself.* Only in relation to the other am I free. We cannot think of freedom as a substance or as something individualistic. Freedom is just not something I have at my command like an attribute of my own; it is simply something that comes to happen, that takes place, that happens to me through the other.[16]

Since God's freedom is relational, in being free for humanity, so human beings are the image and likeness of God in being in relations of freedom—free for God and free for others. The *imago Dei* is therefore

---

15   SF 59, CF 63. Anticipating what follows shortly, note that "being–free–for" God and other people does not contradict humanity's being free "from," or better, over, the natural world.

16   SF 58f., CF 62f., italics mine.

a relationship, *analogia relationis.* But the *imago,* the likeness, is not just relationship per se. It is not as if the analogy could be expressed in the statement: just as God is related to humanity, so the image and likeness of God is seen in the relation of human beings to God and to neighbors. It is a *particular* relationship which constitutes the *imago:* just as the true Lordship of the Creator is God's being free for the creation, so the true humanity of God's creatures is co–humanity in being free for others on the basis of their freedom for God through Christ. Most specifically, this social freedom of the Creator and humanity is the freedom of love.[17]

Analogous to the freedom of the Creator, the freedom of the creature is nevertheless *creaturely* freedom. The creatureliness of human freedom consists in its sociality, being related to the other: human being is a being together with, directed to, and in encounter with the other person.

> The creature is free in that one creature is related to the other creature, in that one human being is free for another human being. And God created them man and woman. The human being is not alone. Human beings exist in duality, and it is in this *dependence on the other that their creatureliness consists.* The creatureliness of human beings is no more a quality or something at hand or an existing entity than human freedom is. It can be defined in simply no other way than as co-humanity–the existence of human beings over-against-one-another, together-with-one-another, and in-dependence-upon-one-another.[18]

Creaturely freedom is not the freedom of aseity but of relation, that is, of sociality.

Without mentioning Barth by name, or referring to his concept of the *analogia fidei,* Bonhoeffer clearly stands with him here in the rejection of an *analogia entis.*

> God is the God who in Christ attests to God's 'being-for-humanity'. The likeness, the analogia, of humanity to God is not analogia entis but *analogia relationis....* The analogia ...has its likeness *only* from the prototype.... Analogia relationis is therefore the relation which God has established, and it is analogia only in this relation which God has established. The relation of creature with creature is a relation established by God, because it consists of freedom and freedom comes from God.[19]

---

[17]   CF 62f; cf. 46.

[18]   SF 60, CF 64.

[19]   SF 60f., CF 65f. *Schöpfung und Fall* was the first of Bonhoeffer's books which Karl Barth read (DB-E 180, 217). Although Barth had reservations about some of the exposition, he appropriated Bonhoeffer's concept of the *analogia*

Analogia relationis is the form in which *analogia fidei* appears in Bonhoeffer's theology of sociality.

The *analogia relationis* in *Creation and Fall* is not only a revision of the theological tradition which appears naturally in Bonhoeffer's interpretation of Genesis 1:26f.; it is also a formulation which expresses afresh a fundamental part[20] of his theology of sociality—the concept of the person in the I–You relationship. The chief aspects of his concept of the person are treated in this work as follows.

The *relatio* among human beings is an *analogia* of the relation of God the Creator to humanity. In connection with the interpretation of the two trees in the center of the garden of Eden, Bonhoeffer introduces a favorite metaphor: the center [Mitte]. This concept has been used before, chiefly in discussions of the anthropological problem of a man by his

---

relationis; cf. *Church Dogmatics* (Edinburgh: T. & T. Clark) III/1 especially pp. 194ff., III/2, III/3. Barth used the *analogia relationis* to develop his formulation of the *analogia fidei* with which he had replaced the *analogia entis* of natural theology. A detailed comparison is not possible here. (For discussions of Barth's concept of analogy cf. George Hunsinger, *How to Read Karl Barth. The Shape of His Theology* [Oxford University Press, 1991]; Hans Urs von Balthasar, *Karl Barth: Darstellung und Deutung seiner Theologie* [Cologne: J. Hegner, 1962]; Henri Bouillard, *Karl Barth* [Paris: Aubier, 1957], 3 vols.; and Jung Young Lee, "Karl Barth's Use of Analogy in his Church Dogmatics," *Scottish Journal of Theology* 22.2, June 1969, pp. 129–151.) Here I simply note two points. First, Barth was perfectly correct in seeing the complete compatibility of Bonhoeffer's *analogia relationis* with his own *analogia fidei*. Second, Barth's use of the *analogia relationis* in his discussion of man and woman departs from Bonhoeffer's exposition at this point. Bonhoeffer interprets the relation of Adam and Eve as one of self and other, I and You, without making any theological significance of a distinct sexual identity of the two persons. Where Barth imports sexual difference as a theologoumenon into his argument he runs into difficulties which are all the more striking since they conflict with his notable desire to interpret sexuality as a sphere of genuine freedom unhampered by confining stereotypes.

20 The word "part" is used advisedly. While Bonhoeffer in this work continues to regard Adam as the prototype of everybody and the solidarity of all people (i.e., Kollektivperson), he does not develop the *analogia relationis* in terms of human communities, as he had previously done by using 'person' as a conceptuality to describe both communities and humanity as a whole. The reason for his discussion of the *analogia relationis* here in terms of individual, personal relations is the biblical text. No theological change has occurred which has weakened his concern for the corporate dimension of sociality; the concept of the Kollektivperson is explicit and implied in later texts such as the Christology lectures, *Discipleship,* and *Ethics.* Had the occasion encouraged it, the *analogia relationis* could easily have been applied to the corporate as well as the individual dimension of human sociality.

power trying to make himself the center, source, and ground of reality and life; this theme continues in *Creation and Fall*. But now "Mitte" becomes a metaphor expressing the sovereignty and primacy of God the Creator, the giver of the true life of humanity.[21] The two trees are "pictures" which communicate the relationship of God to humanity. It is in fact God who is the Mitte, the giver of life, the Lord who in the freedom of love gives human beings their own freedom in love for others and in their own dominion over nature.

> The life that comes from God is at the center; that is to say, God, who gives life, is at the center.... Adam has life in the unity of unbroken obedience to the Creator precisely because he lives from the center of life, and is oriented toward the center of life, but he himself does not live in the center.... *The limit of the person is at the center of our existence,* not at the margin; the limit that is sought at the margin of human life is the limit of the human condition, the limit of human technology, the limit of human possibility [Möglichkeit]. The limit or boundary that is at the center is the limit of our *reality [Wirklichkeit],* of human *existence as such....* The very God who gives life *is at once the limit and center of our existence.* [22]

As the Mitte, God is simultaneously the human creature's Grenze. In the primal state Grenze does not mean any deprivation or restriction of the creature's humanity. On the contrary, it is that which guarantees the creature's genuine human identity. Like the red light blocking off the road to death, it is the sign to the way of life; like the marker indicating the reefs that cause shipwreck, it is the pointer to the wide open seas of freedom. Hence prohibition in this context is not negation, but gift; it is pure grace.[23]

---

[21]   In the Christology lectures, Mitte is a Christological concept related to Christ as Mittler, i.e. Mediator. The same metaphor is found in LPP in the Christology, the critique of religion, the soteriology and ethics, and the ecclesiology. (Like Grenze, it is another example of Bonhoeffer's use of spatial terms as metaphors for socio–theological concepts.)

[22]   SF 78f., CF 83ff. Note the direct connection of the passage with the contrast in LPP between 'religious' people who, at the end of their possibilities and technology, call upon a peripheral power God, and the non–religious Christian who lives from the 'weakness' of God at the center of life. Cf. also the previous discussions of Grenze, Möglichkeit, Werk, etc. in *Act and Being* and the inaugural lecture.

[23]   CF 87.

But God is the Mitte and Grenze only in the sociality of human existence.[24] God remains the Mitte, but the person—Eve in the Yahwist creation story—is the form or bearer of the divine Grenze. While the two persons are bound together in the unity of the primal Gemeinschaft,[25] they are distinct individuals. As independent, willing persons they encounter one another, each being an "other" to one another. But each person as Grenze to the other in the primal Gemeinschaft has a special meaning which no longer obtains after the Fall destroys the primal simplicity of created humanity and the unity of relation between self and other; in the primal community, the other person as Grenze is nothing but the one to whom Adam's love is directed.

> The Creator knows that this free life as a creature can be borne within its limit [Begrenztheit] only if it is loved, and out of unfathomable mercy the Creator creates a helper who is a partner suitable for a human being, one who is simultaneously the embodiment of Adam's limit [Grenze] and the object of Adam's love. …By the creation of the other person freedom and creatureliness are bound together in love. That is why the creation of the other person is once again grace to the first person, just as the prohibition against eating from the tree of knowledge was grace. In this common bearing of the limit by the first two persons in community, the character of this community [Gemeinschaft] as the church is authenticated.[26]

In the context of the primal state, the other is Grenze not as a judgment, a demand, or a restriction; indeed, the other is only a claim on the self in being there as one whom the self loves in freedom, so that 'claim' means only opportunity. Bonhoeffer is describing a simple and unambiguous mutuality of love. What, then, is the point of the word

---

[24] Bonhoeffer's subtitle for this part of the interpretation "Die Kraft des anderen," merits attention. It does not mean the power or force, but the *strength* of the other. This strength is the free being of the other for me in love, and constitutes a guarantee of my humanity in being a Grenze (see below). While Bonhoeffer does not exegete his subtitle, I believe that it is appropriate to see this as a foreshadowing of the combination of strength and freedom in love which comes to fruition in the *Letters*.

[25] CF 99f.

[26] SF 92, CF 98f. Note that the other is Grenze in bodily form (see below). In the reference to the church, it would have been more exact of Bonhoeffer to speak of "primal church," or to say that created community and pure Christian community are identical; as he has sufficiently stressed, the actual church lives by the grace of forgiveness and justification which do not apply in the primal state.

'Grenze' in the primal state? It expresses human creaturely freedom as creaturely, as a freedom with and for others.

It is a promise and guarantee to Adam that the fulfillment of his humanity and the realization of his identity precisely consist in being a person in the free community of love with others. Its only negative connotation is that it contains the warning that he should not try to be boundless, unlimited, infinite; that he should not pretend to *aseitas;* that he should not be tempted to become *sicut Deus.* To do so would be to forfeit his true humanity as co–humanity rooted in the free love of his Creator. This warning, therefore, is a simple promise to the creature that he should have every confidence and hope in his humanity, which is the same thing as trusting and praising his Creator who looked upon his creation and saw that it was "very good."

Here in the interpretation of the primal state are Bonhoeffer's basic concepts first met in *Sanctorum Communio* when the Christian idea of person was described in terms of sociality: self and 'other,' being as *being–for* in relation, Grenze, the individuality of persons in the related-ness of Gemeinschaft, love as the social basic–relation in the primal state, and the socio–historical, ethical encounter of persons. It is clear, therefore, that the *analogia relationis* embraces the anthropological side of Bonhoeffer's theology of sociality. In addition, by means of the *analogia,* it concisely grounds the anthropology in the Christological understanding of God's freedom and love which was so strikingly and cogently presented in *Act and Being.* Even so, this does not exhaust all the implications of the *analogia relationis.*

There is another side to Bonhoeffer's exposition of the *imago Dei.* The first note in the theme of *imago Dei* is the human being's likeness to God in being for others in the free relationship of love; created freedom is like, and originates from, this freedom of the Creator. Its second note is that just as God is Lord over the whole creation in free love, so humanity is given lordship in relation to nature. Vis–à–vis other human beings, freedom is freedom to be for the other; vis–à–vis the rest of the creation, human freedom is freedom *from* and over nature.[27] Two forms of freedom—serving and ruling—characterize the relationship of the creatures to their human companions and to nature respectively; in both these forms of freedom, the creature exhibits a likeness to the freedom and lordship of God.

---

[27] SF 61f.

It is appropriate to continue this aspect of the discussion in the next section which explores the dimensions of 'Geist' and 'Natur' in human nature and in the relationship of humanity to nature.

3. THE FREEDOM OF HUMANITY AS GEIST AND NATUR

That human being is both Geist and Natur, spirit and nature, is a view found in Bonhoeffer's previous writings.[28] In them it was discussed briefly; here it receives a fuller treatment. It is important to analyze this subject because of its intrinsic anthropological significance in his interpretation of creation, and because of its role in the Christology lectures.

Bonhoeffer describes the status of humanity in relation to nature—the whole nonhuman animate and inanimate world—as that of lord [Herr] and its function as lordship and ruling [Herrschaft, herrschen].[29] But this does not mean humanity has a license to dominate the earth in destructive and irresponsible exploitation. It is God's creation which is ruled, and human ruling is done by God's commission and as service to God. Humanity is, so to speak, the junior partner of God in caring for, shaping and using nature. While Bonhoeffer gives no explicit critique here of the ruthless and wanton exploitation of nature which has characterized the technology and capitalist economics of the modern industrial era, he alludes to this in two brief references to technology as a sign of humanity's loss of primal, created relation to nature consequent upon losing authentic humanity in the sociality of God and other human beings.[30] Fundamentally, his interpretation of humanity as lord of nature

---

[28] Consistent with the position he adopted in *Sanctorum Communio*, Bonhoeffer made the following statements in his Barcelona lectures. "The concept of the soul is Greek–the Jew thinks of the human being as the unity of spirit-and-body, who is created by and fallen away from God" (DBW 10 317, GS V 151). He describes as follows the life of a man or woman before God: "There nature and spirit are married in the beauty and harmony of a well-created being, neither violating nature nor spirit, but both are ordered and irradiated by the spirit of God" (DBW 10 343, GS V 177).

[29] SF 61f.

[30] CF 66f, 48f. There could also be some romantic, anti–technical bias here which would need rethinking in light of the affirmation of reason, science, and technology which emerges in the prison letters. One may also question, in the context of the present environmental crisis, whether the terms 'lord' and 'lordship' are the most suitable to interpret the 'dominion' of Genesis 1:26, though see Mark 10:42ff. At least in principle, however, Bonhoeffer has theologically guarded his position against the misinterpretation of 'dominion' as

means that nature is a realm of human freedom, for the freedom of love is the essence of the divine rule in Christ. There is no divine or demonic substance in the world, so nature is neither to be worshipped nor feared. Humanity therefore, is to live in nature as a natural realm, to be at home in the world as the environment of creativity, art, imagination, knowledge, and work. Further commentary on the relationship of humanity and nature is given in the relationship of Geist and Natur in Bonhoeffer's anthropology.

In his earlier references to human being as Geist and Natur, Bonhoeffer related them in a mutual interaction: Geist has priority but bodiliness is essential; in human life, Natur as body is therefore embraced and humanized in the social–historical being of Geist. This position is elaborated here. Humanity's "being–free–from–nature" is not some sort of Platonic or idealistic floating above the natural and bodily realm; ruling over nature is precisely the bond which involves the human creature intimately in the natural world.

> It is my world, my earth, over which I rule. I am not free from it in the sense that my essential being, my spirit [Geist], has no need of a nature [Natur] which is alien to spirit. On the contrary, in my whole being, in my creatureliness, I belong wholly to this world; it bears me, nurtures me, holds me.[31]

In the same vein Bonhoeffer continues emphatically:

> The body belongs to a person's essence. The body is not the prison, the shell, the exterior, of a human being; instead a human being 'is' body and soul. The human being in the beginning really is the body, is one being—just as Christ is wholly his body, as the church is the body of Christ. People who reject their bodies reject their existence before God the Creator.... Flight from the body is as much flight from being human as is flight from the spirit. The body is the form in which the spirit exists

---

exploitative domination; cf. CF 96 where he speaks of the animals in the world of nature as the brothers (sic!) whom Adam loves.

[31] SF 62, CF 66. It is necessary to observe that while he insists on bodiliness as integral to human beings, Bonhoeffer does not define creatureliness as bodiliness per se, but as co–humanity; sociality, not a spirit–matter dualism, provides the conceptuality for interpreting creation. For some sparkling polemics against the weak, escapist, religious otherworldliness of "the disloyal sons of the earth" see "Thy Kingdom Come" in John Godsey, *Preface to Bonhoeffer.*

[Existenzform von Geist], as the spirit is the form in which the body exists [Existenzform von Leib].[32]

Human bodiliness, as our most intimate way of being in nature and nature's being in us, is not a dimension of our being which is uninvolved in sociality. The personal being of Geist has body as its Existenzform, and personal being is only found in sociality. For this reason our relations to others are always relations to persons who, like ourselves, are only encountered and loved in their bodily presence. The other as Grenze is the *telos* of a person's free love in bodily form. Hence Natur qua body belongs to the *imago Dei* in the *analogia relationis*.

> Human beings are the image of God ...not in spite of but precisely in their bodily nature. For in their bodily nature they are related to the earth and to other bodies; they are there for others and are dependent on others. In their bodily existence human beings find their brothers and sisters and find the earth. As such a creature the human being of earth and spirit is 'like' God the Creator.[33]

Bodiliness, furthermore, does not conflict with the fact that human Geist is a special manifestation of the divine Geist in the world. God creates the cosmos, the inanimate and animate world, by the Word. Human beings are created with God's own Spirit of freedom and love, and this Spirit is the very life of humanity.[34] So God's divine life—God remaining as distinct from the world as individual persons remain distinct in their very relatedness in Bonhoeffer's theology of sociality—is truly reflected in the earthly, bodily world of the creation which glorifies its Creator. "'The end of the ways of God is bodiliness.'"[35]

Everything said thus far refers to humanity and creation in the primal state, that is, it describes the human creature from the perspective of Christ who reveals both God the Creator *and* true humanity. But this can be said precisely and only from Christ, apart from whom the creatures do not truly know either their Creator or themselves. We turn now to Bonhoeffer's interpretation of sin, and meet a familiar presentation.

---

[32] SF 71ff., CF 76f.; cf. CF 46 and the criticism of Kant.

[33] SF 74, CF 79. At this point in his exposition Bonhoeffer mentions the coming of Christ in the body, and speaks of the Eucharist as the sacrament in which the present Christ meets one in bodily form; I will discuss this in the analysis of the Christology lectures later in the chapter.

[34] CF 78f.

[35] CF 78, n. 17, quoting Oetinger; the aphorism is to be read, of course, in Bonhoeffer's context, and not in terms of Oetinger's mystical 'theosophy'.

4. SIN AND SOCIALITY:
FALLEN RELATIONSHIPS 'IN ADAM'

For Bonhoeffer, the story leading to the fall is the drama of a power struggle fought with the weapon of knowledge in the arena of creature-hood and divinity which surrounds the tree of knowledge. The consequence of the fall is that Adam gains power—a pseudo–divine *sicut deus* being—and he gains knowledge—of his own alienation from God, from others, and from nature. The interiorized form of alienation is the self–accusing knowledge of conscience.

As with the English world "subtle" describing the serpent, so the German word "listiger" suggests a cunning, and, in this case, deceitful intelligence. The serpent's power [Kraft] is the offer of a life without limits [Grenze] in a self–established knowledge of "a better, prouder God," appealing to Adam's own "idea, principle, [and] ...knowledge of God."[36] The serpent's 'powerbase' [Machtstellung] is his claim to be himself the ultimate power [Kraft]—behind the given Word of God— from which God's power is drawn.[37]

Adam grasps the opportunity to "be more intelligent... than God" in order to be without limit and become godlike.[38] Armed with his knowledge of the "better, prouder God" he storms the gates of heaven in revolt—and loses his humanity and the whole world as a result.

Bonhoeffer explicitly compares Adam to Prometheus who, by robbing Zeus, bestowed the power of fire and knowledge upon humanity.[39]

---

36   Note Bonhoeffer's typological descriptions of Eve as the first "knower" [Wissende], the intelligent [kluge] primal–mother of "knowing" children [die Wissenden] and God; SF 128. Cf. CF 141: the tree of life is only endangered by the tree of knowledge.

37   SF 98ff., CF 105ff.

38   CF 112; cf. previous references to Adam's intelligence.

39   CF 137; but see also in "Thy Kingdom Come" (November, 1932) on the eternal right of Prometheus to love the earth (DBW 12 269, GS III 274). Bonhoeffer also quotes from Goethe's Faust (CF 132). Whereas the Faust of Spiess and Marlowe in the   sixteenth century was a scoundrel deserving damnation, Lessing's Enlightenment interpretation made him a symbol of human heroic striving for power and knowledge; for Lessing, Faust is like a German counterpart to Prometheus. Goethe took up Lessing's basic reinterpretation and developed it. So while Goethe laments the destruction of paradise "with mighty fist," he still urges the "mighty one of the sons of the earth" to rebuild paradise in his heart. Bonhoeffer protests: "This does not at all apply." The lament and the exhortation are both less than serious; "heroes" will not solve this problem. (Cf. SF 123f., CF 132f.).

Adam's revolt is supposed to be "the great, proud, liberating act."[40] It comes as no surprise, however, to learn that Adam emerges as a power figure himself from this power struggle with the serpent. His being *'sicut deus'* is a *self*–determination of his 'being–for–God, it is disobedience in the form of obedience, it is the will to dominate disguised as service. In violating the Word of God he necessarily violates the other person. In living not from the center but from himself he exercises an arbitrary and unlimited self–will; he does not acknowledge other persons in their own right but robs them of it, dominating and claiming to possess the other.[41] Adam now has his power, but he no longer has the other in the mutuality of love.

The dominating, knowing ego of fallen Adam is described in words which, having appeared so regularly, now sound like a liturgical chorus. *Sicut deus* Adam

> is himself creator, the source of life, the origin of the knowledge of good and evil. He is only for himself [für sich], he lives out of himself, he no more needs others; he is the lord of his world, but now of course the solitary lord and despot [Despot] of his own mute, violated, silenced, dead ego–world.[42]

As the very nature of sin is a violation of the sociality of love in which human beings live with God and with each other, so its consequences are the violated social relationships in the asocial solidarity of powerful, individualistic, dominating, self–centered people. Adam's conflict with God is seen in the loss of simplicity and peace in relation to the divine Word; he is caught up in and assailed by the wrong questions of religious godlessness.

In human community, the sexual relationship first expresses the isolation which now separates people. In the demandingness, possessiveness, and shame which permeate fallen sexuality, we see that "the knowledge of *tob* and *ra* [good and evil] is not primarily abstract knowledge of ethical principles, but [fallen] sexuality, i.e., a perversion

---

40   CF 121.

41   CF 115ff., 124f.

42   SF 131f., CF 142; cf. CF 113, 143. It is quite in line with this, though rather imaginative exegesis, when Bonhoeffer describes Adam's naming of Eve as an act of exultation, defiance, insolence, and conquest (CF 138); likewise at the birth of Cain, so briefly narrated in the biblical account, Bonhoeffer ascribes to the primal parents the pride of being creators (CF 145). This 'inventiveness' is consistent with what was found in the exegesis in *Discipleship*.

of the relationship of one human being to another."[43] Sexuality in the love of the primal community should be a primary expression of being for the other.

> Nakedness is the essence of unity, of not being torn apart, of being for the other, of respect for what is given [Sachlichkeit], of acknowledging the other's right, of recognizing the other as my limit, of affirming the other's creatureliness. Nakedness is not even knowing the possibility of robbing the other of this right. Nakedness is revelation; nakedness believes in grace.[44]

Here is the authentically natural freedom and unselfconsciousness of love. But when unlimited power, demanding, self–centered passion, and arbitrary, possessive claims enter in, then the self–consciousness and inhibition of shame appear: "human shame is the involuntary allusion to revelation, the limit, the other, and God."[45]

From sexuality in the realm of human community there is an easy transition to the relation with nature. Since nature for human beings is embraced by the historical character of their existence in sociality, so their being in nature is not unaffected by their conflict with God and neighbor. In expounding the Genesis text Bonhoeffer has occasion to mention a point pertinent to his own distinctive concerns. The primal relation between humanity and nature is destroyed, and so "a man's *work*... expresses the estrangement of fallen humanity from nature."[46]

One cannot live without God, without others, without nature. Such life is the living death of the despotic ego. Conscience, Bonhoeffer argues in characteristic fashion, is the flight from God in which a person asserts his own power; in his isolation and inner division he judges himself, thereby seeking "to feign the presence and reality of another in his life."[47]

---

43   SF 117f., CF 125; cf. CF 100: "Sexuality is nothing but the ultimate realization of our belonging to one another.... Here the community of man and woman is the community derived from God, the community of love glorifying and worshipping God as the Creator."

44   SF 116, CF 124.

45   SF 117, CF 124; cf. CF 101. This is a consequence of self–assertion in the form of denying the other as God's creature.

46   SF 126, CF 134; see the discussion at the end of this chapter of the sermon criticizing the bourgeois work–ethic. (Here, in an unusual usage, Bonhoeffer writes "die *Arbeit* des Mannes"!)

47   SF 132, CF 142; cf. CF 129.

Adam has power, but is alienated from God, from others, from nature, and from himself. Having the appearance of life, power and knowledge, he is in fact living in death. He lives only because the Creator is the Preserver; the created world is now the preserved fallen world.[48]

5. PRESERVATION TOWARD CHRIST

In *Creation and Fall* Bonhoeffer published a major revision of the Lutheran theological tradition. He set a concept of "orders of preservation" [Erhaltungsordnungen] in place of the traditional Lutheran doctrine of "orders of creation" [Schöpfungsordnungen].[49] While it can be argued that the impending political and theological emergency involved in the rise of the Nazis gave urgency to his revision in 1932,[50] the revision simultaneously expresses Bonhoeffer's theological method which related every question to the revelation in Christ. Bonhoeffer stood with Barth in rejecting natural theology, even though he made serious criticism of Barth's early theology. A theology which developed "orders of creation" gave, at the very least, an opportunity for reading off from nature, history and society the divine will for the state, family, economic organization, and so on. The advent of the Nazi religious mythology resulted in the most demonic exploitation of this opening to the right which Christian theology had ever witnessed. By the end of 1932 Bonhoeffer had anticipated the implications of the first article of the 1934 Barmen Confession for the doctrine of creation after the fall.

The concept of orders of preservation is explicit in the November, 1932 address "Thy Kingdom Come!"[51] given during Bonhoeffer's lecture course on "Schöpfung und Sünde." The relationship of church and

---

[48] SF 129.

[49] He first introduced the concept at an ecumenical conference in Berlin, April, 1932, and also used it subsequently in addresses and similar meetings, cf. DBW 11 324, 337, 345; GS I 129f., 150ff., 160; DBW 12 350, 375, 380; GS II 45, 88, 99, 102; DB 1074.

[50] The National Socialists won 230 Reichstag seats in the July election, and held 196 seats in November; Hindenburg called Hitler to be chancellor on January 30, 1933; cf. Bethge, Zeittafel, GS II appendix. On the relation of the political situation to the interest in "orders of preservation" in these lectures, see DB-E 215.

[51] Translated by John D. Godsey in *Preface to Bonhoeffer*.

state is discussed in the conceptuality of the theology of sociality. Church and state are the "twofold form" of the presence of God's kingdom in the world which God preserves after the fall.[52] They encounter each other as do persons in the social basic-relation of I and You, but here as 'collective persons' who simultaneously limit each other and call each other to their distinctive responsibilities. The role of the state is not to be the creator of life as it disastrously attempted to do in the Third Reich,[53] but to *preserve* the life which the Creator continues to affirm as Preserver. The authority of the state is qualified: it is a form of God's kingdom in so far as it acknowledges and protects the order of preservation of life by preventing destruction, restraining the breakdown of human communities through arbitrary, individualistic action, and protecting people by civil law from lust for power.[54]

In addition to the state, Bonhoeffer mentions three orders of preservation in his address: marriage, family, and nation [Volk].[55] In view of his discussion of *work* in *Creation and Fall* it is safe to assume that this would have been included in any systematic theological exposition as it was later in the scheme of the 'mandates' in his *Ethics;* but "Thy Kingdom Come!" was an invited public lecture, not a systematic theological treatise. *Work* in fact appears in the list given in the draft for the Bethel Confession of August, 1933, where the orders mentioned are: sexes, marriage, family, nation, property (work and economic order), occupation, and government.[56]

---

52   DBW 12 272f, 276; GS III 278f., 282. This relationship will be further considered in the context of the 1933 Christology lectures; here the concern is with the question of preservation.

53   In a prophetic and pregnant utterance Bonhoeffer states that because the Kingdom of God's rule among us has this twofold form, it is not "one visible, powerful [machtvolle] *imperium,* the 'new' Reich of the world."

54   DBW 12 273-75; GS III 279–281.

55   DBW 12 274; GS III 280. The concept of orders of preservation and the specification of these particular human communities is clearly a transition between the thinking of *Sanctorum Communio* and the idea of 'mandates' in the *Ethics,* though the latter involves a further change in his view of the church–state relationship than that given here. In 1933, however, any talk of 'orders' was dangerously vulnerable to National Socialist ideology and its theological allies, so Bonhoeffer dropped the 'Erhaltungsordnungen' terminology altogether in the latter part of the year.

56   DBW 12 375; GS II 99.

What is more significant than the catalogue of orders, however, is the basic theological idea. In estrangement from God, neighbors, self, and nature, the sinful creature has no unmediated relationships to the primal creation nor any access to truth and liberation except through the revelation in Christ the Mediator.

> All orders of our fallen world are God's orders of preservation that uphold us and preserve us for Christ. They are not orders of creation but orders of preservation. They have no value in themselves; instead they find their end and meaning only through Christ.[57]

Consequently, Bonhoeffer argues that any order, no matter how sacred it may be, can and must be dissolved when it prohibits the proclamation of the gospel.[58]

---

[57] SF 129f., CF 140.

[58] CW I 166f., 180. Here a note on Bonhoeffer's view of church and state is appropriate. At the same time as he was lecturing on "Schöpfung und Sünde" he gave a course on "Jüngste Theologie" (DBW 12 153ff; DB 1077ff.); its content would be more clearly described as "Theology, ethics, and contemporary politics." His sharp criticism here of Gogarten's *Politische Ethik* (1932) shows that he was self–conscious and deliberate in his criticism of the prevalent Lutheran doctrine of church and state (cf. DBW 12 162-68; DB 1082-85). He finds Gogarten's church–state doctrine preoccupied with the church's role in condemning sin and supporting the state's containment of evil. This, Bonhoeffer objects, is a restatement of Christian conservatism which is probably in agreement with Lutheran doctrine but is not New Testament teaching. The latter sees the ambiguity of the state, knowing its capacity not only to restrain evil but also to take the form of evil itself and thus perpetrate the greatest wickedness. Therefore, the church must continually call the state into question, remembering that "in no case is the church there only to prop up the state." The church knows the "better righteousness" of God's kingdom, and this "establishes a relative, revolutionary Christian right" of the new which opposes the existing order in a radical way (the "better righteousness" is important in *Nachfolge*). Since Gogarten ignores this "better righteousness," and forgets that the gospel of the cross and resurrection proclaims the breaking through of worldly orders, he is victim of an orthodox conservatism. By his Christology, Bonhoeffer wants to affirm and relativize the claims of both order and revolution in the name of the God who is Lord of the state and "who alone can create order and revolution." Added to this are several points which show that Bonhoeffer's doctrine of the duality of the church and state is not uncritical repetition of the "two realms" teaching, but a deliberate criticism and reconstruction of such teaching. (1) Church and state are not two autonomous, isolated realms, but mutual 'limits' [Grenzen] for each other; thus each is related intrinsically to the other on the model of the corporate use of the person concept in historical, ethical encounter. (2) As an 'Erhaltungsordnung,' the state is not autonomous but made accountable

In unfaith Adam anticipates death as nothingness. But God's merciful affirmation of the fallen world preserves Adam toward Christ. In Christ's death the fallen, dead humanity of Adam dies. In his resurrection Christ is the second Adam, the Mediator of the new humanity. This theme leads naturally to the Christology lectures.

B. CHRIST THE MEDIATOR: THE 1933 CHRISTOLOGY

In the summer semester of 1933 Bonhoeffer delivered his last full course of lectures in the University of Berlin.[59] The subject was Christology. While his manuscript has not been found, a very careful reconstruction has been made by Bethge from several sets of student notes. While Bonhoeffer's complete, original materials would presumably add detail to the reconstruction, the congruity of its contents with the texts previously analyzed enable us to have every confidence in the editor's work.[60] (A different version of the reconstructed text is found in the *Dietrich Bonhoeffer Werke*, volume 12, published in 1997; and yet another set of

---

to Christ who is the criterion of the relative validity of any order of preservation as also the source of a command to overthrow a given order. (3) Bonhoeffer's relentless concern with the "concrete command," which the church must speak at appropriate times as a corporate act done with the same concreteness as it preaches forgiveness of sins, commits the church to specific political positions on issues such as socialism and war. (4) The *one* Christ personifies the new humanity of all people, and he is present in the two modes of church and state. This Christology prevents either church or state being considered as separate, autonomous entities; they are, to be sure, distinguished, but the distinction is within a dynamic relationship. (Further discussion on Christology and politics and the church–state relation is found later in this chapter.)

[59]   At the same time he gave a seminar on Hegel's philosophy of religion. One set of student notes survived from this seminar and has now been published; see *Dietrich Bonhoeffers Hegel Seminar 1933*, ed. Ilse Tödt (Munich: Christian Kaiser, 1988).

[60]   *Pace* T. F. Torrance who, in a review of the work, made the astounding and completely unfounded charge that Bethge had "systematically suppressed" all mention of Barth throughout the lectures; cf. *The Scotsman*, May 28, 1966, and Bethge's letter in reply, June 10, 1966. Having seen the student notes, I can vouch for the care and faithfulness of Bethge's reconstruction. Further, the exposition which follows will dispel Torrance's contention that "the first of them [i.e., the two main sections] on the Present Christ is the most difficult to follow, probably because it has become twisted in the editorial reconstruction."

student notes was found after that volume was completed. Because I have retained the wording from the Christology lectures in the *Gesammelte Schriften,* and the English translation based on that version, I have not given in this section the citations to DBW 12 as well as to GS III. While I am confident of the main lines of interpretation, it is possible that nuances of wording may be required after future comparison and analysis of the texts.)

The lectures were designed to have an introduction and three main parts.[61] The introduction deals with methodological prolegomena, first considering the relation of Christology to other intellectual disciplines, and then discussing the connection between the doctrine of the person of Christ and soteriology. The three main parts were to treat the present Christ, the historical Christ, and the eternal Christ. Part Three was not reached before the semester concluded. Part Two, although placed second in order, in fact discloses the historical and systematic presuppositions of Bonhoeffer's own Christology. It examines the classical Christological formulations and heresies, and their modern counterparts, under the rubric of "critical Christology." It thus prepares the way for Bonhoeffer's own position. I will therefore examine the presuppositions Bonhoeffer establishes in Part Two, and then concentrate on his "positive Christology" which is formulated in the Introduction, Part One, and section IV of Part Two. The discussion has three sections: Bonhoeffer's approach to the Christological question, his treatment of the sociality of the present Christ, and his view of Christ as Mediator.

1. THE CHRISTOLOGICAL QUESTION

Bonhoeffer takes the Christology of the Chalcedonian definition as his point of departure.

> The starting point is the given: the human being Jesus *is* the Christ, is God. This 'is' cannot be deduced. It is the presupposition of all thought, and cannot be constructed subsequently. After Chalcedon the question can no longer be 'How are the distinct natures and the one person to be thought?' but strictly: 'Who is this person, of whom it is testified that he is God?'[62]

---

[61]   GS III 166, 242.

[62]   GS III 227, CC 102; cf. GS III 215, 217f.

No abstract notion of God apart from God's revelation in the human Jesus is permitted; no abstract idea of the humanity of Jesus apart from his unity with God is acceptable. In Jesus Christ we meet, at one and the same time, the "God Christ" and the "human Jesus" in an inseparable unity.[63]

Furthermore, Bonhoeffer insists, when we are dealing with the revelation of God in Jesus Christ we are encountering God fully and wholly, not merely an *idea* of God.

> Everything depends on the fact that God in his wholeness and almighty glory is this Incarnate One who encounters us in Jesus. It must always be a basic theological proposition that where God is, he is completely there.[64]

> In the concept of revelation it is presupposed that God in his revelation is identical with himself. Otherwise it is not strictly a question of revelation but of manifestation [Erscheinung] or idea.[65]

But Bonhoeffer wants to go beyond Chalcedon. With good historical reason he treats the conciliar Christological formulations as "critical or negative Christology"; their intent was chiefly to exclude heretical theological content and unsuitable forms of thought and expression.[66] It is the responsibility of individual theologians, however, to produce a positive Christology, but always with reference to the limits established by the conciliar decisions.[67]

While accepting the basic Christological affirmations of Chalcedon, Bonhoeffer notes a major problem in the conceptuality of the definition. The Chalcedonian definition uses the concepts of 'nature' and 'substance' in such a way as to disqualify them. The paradoxical statement that Christ is one person in two natures, shows that the concept of 'nature' is an unsuitable one.[68] The problem posed by the Chalcedonian language is the problem of *reification*. The paradoxical formulation of Chalcedon that Jesus Christ is to be understood as one person in two natures discloses the fact that in Christology 'natures' cannot be understood as "reified entities" [dingliche Gegebenheiten].[69] Reified categories

---

63 GS III 182, CC 47; cf. CC 81.

64 GS III 226, CC 100.

65 GS III 228, CC 102. Cf. the critique of ancient docetism and modern liberalism, GS III 207ff.

66 GS III 229, CC 104.

67 GS III 205f., CC 77f.

68 GS 218f., CC 91f.; cf. GS III 227.

69 GS III 218, CC 91.

are not only inappropriate to describe the unity of divinity and humanity in Jesus Christ; they also involve a "theoretical, spectator attitude" toward Christ.[70] This means that the wrong question is asked. In reified thinking people ask "how" questions, such as "How can a divine and a human nature be united in one person?"[71] But 'how' questions are questions of cognitive reason, not questions of faith; they are the means by which reason seeks to master a problem, not questions in which people are encountered by their Lord.

For his own positive Christology Bonhoeffer proposes a way forward in his conceptuality of sociality. "The relation of God and human beings cannot be conceived as a relationship of things [Dinglichkeiten] but only in the relationship of persons."[72] It is persons who ask of other persons the question: 'who?'

Two categories are used to develop Christology under the rubric of person: Personstruktur and Existenzweise. If the proper question of Christology is "who is Jesus Christ?" this is a question which can only be asked to the Christ who is *present.* Christology is not concerned with an ideal of Christ nor with the historical influence of Christ, but with the resurrected Christ, the living God, who is really present.[73] Furthermore, Christ is present as person not in isolation but *only in relation to persons.*

> The Personstruktur must be... developed as the *pro–me*–structure of the divine–human Jesus Christ. Christ is Christ not as Christ for himself [für sich] but in his being related to me. His being–Christ is being-related to me. His being–Christ is being–*pro–me.* This being–*pro–me...* is meant to be understood as the essence, as the very being of the person himself.... This *pro–me*–being of Christ can never be thought of in his being–in–himself, but only in his being related to me. That means, further, Christ can only be thought of in the existential relation, or in other words, in the church-community.... Every Christology condemns itself if it does not put at the beginning the statement: God is only God *pro–me,* Christ is only Christ *pro–me.*[74]

---

70 GS III 230, CC 105.

71 GS III 227, CC 101.

72 GS III 230, CC 105, italics mine.

73 GS III 178ff., CC 434ff., cf. GS III 178, CC 40.

74 GS III 182, CC 47f.; cf. GS III 172 on the Christological question as the "ontological structure of the who." It is significant to observe that in the same paragraph he repeats his position from *Act and Being* that by understanding the presence of Christ in terms of personal presence in community, theology can unite act and being, contingency of revelation and freedom–for–humanity, *Dir*–dasein and Dir–*dasein, actio Dei* and *praesentia Dei.* (For other themes from *Act*

When the Personstruktur of Christ is understood as *ontologically* related
to humanity, this means that Bonhoeffer must articulate his Christology
so that it has a necessary anthropological component. It is for this
reason that Personstruktur is developed in the pattern of the threefold
Gestalt of Christ as Word, sacrament, and church-community and that
these, in turn, are related to the anthropological categories of history,
nature, and society.

The Christ who is present in this Personstruktur is present in a
distinct mode of being [Existenzweise], namely, as the humiliated and
exalted one.[75] This is an intrinsic and necessary qualification of his
Personstruktur, for the Christ who is present among *sinful* humanity is the
One who is humiliated and exalted. The humiliation consists in the fact
that Christ is present "in the likeness of sinful flesh," and this means that
revelation encounters us as concealed and as an offense.[76] Humiliation
is not correlated to incarnation, being present in human form, for "God
glorifies himself in humanity"; "the incarnation is the message of the
glorification of God who sees his honor in being human."[77] The doctrines
of incarnation and humiliation, therefore, must be carefully distinguished from one another, because "the incarnation is relative to the first
creation, the humiliation to the fallen creation."[78] Bonhoeffer does not,
of course, wish to isolate the person of Christ from his Existenz by
making this distinction. But he does want to shift the focus of the
Christological problem. The real issue of Christology is not *how* two
natures, divine and human, conceived in isolation and abstraction may be
cognitively united; it is rather, *who* encounters us in this human being
among other human beings—merely a sinner among sinners, or the holy
God become human for humanity? As with his insistence that Christology
deals with the Personstruktur of the *pro–me* Christ, so this relocation of
the Christological issue indicates the soteriological character of
Bonhoeffer's Christology.

Soteriology is, implicitly, the concern of the second section of Part
One on "the place of Christ." Bonhoeffer argues in the introduction that
the Christological question of the person of Christ cannot be inferred

---

and Being around this time, see Bonhoeffer's review of Karl Heim's *Glaube und
Denken,* DBW 12 213-31; GS III 138–159, esp. 158.)

75   GS III 235ff., CC 110ff.; cf. GS III 181f., CC 46f.
76   Romans 8:3.
77   GS III 234, CC 109.
78   GS III 236, CC 111.

from the work but must interpret the work. Christology therefore deals primarily with the personal being of Christ, not with his deeds. But at the same time Bonhoeffer acknowledges that this is only a methodological distinction, and not a division of reality. It is therefore consonant with this recognition of the unity of person and work that, having discussed the Personstruktur of the present *pro–me* Christ, Bonhoeffer considers Christ as the Mediator in the second section of Part One.

It is the Personstruktur of Christ present in the Existenzweise of humiliation and exaltation that Bonhoeffer articulates in his Christology. The following section will show how he understands the present Christ in the form of human sociality: the transcendence and revelation of Christ are operative in the social relationships of the Christian community as these are informed and shaped by Word and Sacrament.

2. THE SOCIALITY OF THE PRESENT CHRIST

Sociality, as we have seen, involves corporate human life as well as relations between individual persons in communities. Bonhoeffer uses the concept of person to interpret both dimensions. Christology is described as the theological discipline concerned with the Personstruktur of Christ, and this enables him to continue using both the corporate and relational aspects of his concept of person as previously worked out.

To understand the Christology lectures fully it is necessary to recognize that Bonhoeffer still employs here the concept of Kollektivperson. As first in *Sanctorum Communio*, so here too, he presents Christ as the Kollektivperson of the new humanity. Only in this context does he consider the presence of Christ in the church. To be sure, the actual term is not found in the reconstructed lectures. But the idea, as the following quotation shows, is unmistakably present.

> The *pro–me* structure has threefold significance for the relationship of Christ to the new humanity.
>
> 1. Jesus Christ is *pro–me* as the pioneer, head and firstborn of the brothers who follow him. The *pro–me* structure is thus related to the historicity [Geschichtlichkeit] of Jesus. He is *pro–me* in that he is the pioneer for the others.
>
> 2. Jesus Christ is for his brothers by standing in their place. Christ stands for his new humanity before God. But if that is so, he is the new humanity. Where humanity ought to stand, he stands as representative [stellvertretend] by virtue of his *pro–me* structure. He is the church-

community. He not only acts on its behalf [für sie] but is the church-community since he goes to the cross, bears sin, and dies. So, in him, humanity is crucified, dead, and judged.

3. Because he acts as the new humanity, it is in him and he is in it. Because it is in him, God is gracious to the new humanity.[79]

The old humanity of Adam is judged and dies in the cross of Christ. The risen Christ is the representative and 'personification' of a new corporate life of humanity. The Christian community is the concrete, social form in which this new human reality is actualized. Because of this, Christ who is present in the church-community is the Mediator of the new humanity for all people, and the life of the church is thereby intrinsically related to all the life of the whole human race.

Before examining further how Bonhoeffer understands the relationship of the present Christ to all humanity, the sociality of transcendence and revelation in the church must be explicated.

The Personstruktur of Christ is articulated in the threefold Gestalt of his presence *pro me:* Christ is personally present as Word, sacrament, and Gemeinde. These three cannot be separated from each other, for just as there is no sermon or sacrament in itself but only in the congregation, so neither is there any church-community apart from the Word and sacrament which makes it the community of Christ. Here Bonhoeffer is insisting on the essential sociality of the word and sacrament; the presence of Christ is his presence in sociality. There is an explicit anthropological correlation to these three components of the form of Christ. "The One who is present in Word, sacrament, and congregation is in the center of human Existenz, of history, and of nature."[80] These anthropological categories can no more be isolated from each other than the three components of the form of Christ. The distinction can only be made in the abstract for "in actuality, human existence is also always both historical and natural."[81] This statement presupposes and implies

---

[79] GS III 183, CC 48f.; Bonhoeffer's Kollektivperson concept almost certainly lies behind the statement in the first version of the Bethel Confession (August, 1933) concerning the unity of humanity in its origin (Adam) and its goal (Christ). Cf. DBW 12 376; GS II 99; Bonhoeffer's hand is clearly evident at many points.

[80] GS III 195, CC 52; the three headings in each of the two sections of Part One thus correspond to each other, though not in the same order. This correlation of Christology and anthropology is discussed in the section on "Christ the Mediator," below.

[81] GS III 199f., CC 67.

Bonhoeffer's constant theme of the sociality of human existence, without which the anthropological correlation to Christ existing as Gemeinde would be lost. The sociality of the present and revealed Christ has the personal structure of Word, sacrament and church-community.

Word. Christ is present as Word in the form of living address between persons. If "address [Anrede] and idea are the basic structures of the word,"[82] it must be said of Christ that "the Logos is not an idea."[83] Christ is person, and he encounters us in the word of address from another human person, that is, in the sermon. Word in the form of address requires a hearer and a responsible answer. But this means that the Word is an event in community. "Truth is not something static in and for itself, but an event between two persons. Truth happens only in community [Gemeinschaft]."[84] As address in community the Word is embodied and present in human form; coming *from* the other person, the Word is *extra me;* coming *to* me the Word is *pro–me.* To understand the presence of Christ as Word of address is simultaneously to express revelation as contingent *(extra nos)* and revelation as bound to human beings *(pro nobis).* The sociality of the Word in the address–encounters between persons in community means that the other person, as an ethical subject in community, is the form of both the otherness and the presence of Christ.

Precisely in its sociality the Word has an historical character. The Word as living address is an event which happens, not a timeless, ahistorical idea which is always in principle available to the human *logos.* "Christ as Word in the sense of address is thus not timeless truth. He is the truth spoken in the concrete moment [Augenblick], the address which places one in the truth before God."[85] Since the gospel encounters me and obliges me to answer in responsible decision, this gives to my Existenz an historical character. This historicity, however, is not understood individualistically but as intrinsic to our socio–ethical existence in community.[86]

---

82 GS III 185, CC 50.
83 GS III 167, CC 28.
84 GS III 185, CC 51.
85 GS III 185, CC 51.
86 Contrast the individualistic understanding of historicity as *self–relatedness* in Bultmann; see, e.g., his *Theology of the New Testament,* vol. I (London: S.C.M. Press, 1952), pp. 191ff., esp. pp. 195ff., 204f., 209f., 219, 227.

Bonhoeffer's continued polemic against idealism is quite apparent in this discussion of the sociality and historicity of the Word. His critique is the same as previously; in the realm of the idea, the human *logos* has unlimited power of self–assertion; it has an unchallenged dominion [Herrschaft] but is self–imprisoned; because ideas are generally accessible to its power of classification, they cannot function as a genuine Grenze nor encounter human Existenz, and so are unable to free the self from its isolated egotism.[87]

The positive assertion of the social–historical character of the Word of Christ, and his criticism of Word as idea, both express Bonhoeffer's characteristic understanding of transcendence and revelation. Significantly, he discusses the transcendence of Christ as person in explicit contrast to an anthropology in which a human being is understood as *logos* qua reason, subjecting the world, other people, and Christ to its classifying power.

For Bonhoeffer, then, transcendence does not refer to an inaccessible otherness or beyondness of God; it refers to the present Christ. But the present Christ is 'other,' 'outside' the self, in such a way that he cannot be drawn into the dominating power of the self–sufficient ego. It is as *person* that Christ is 'other,' 'outside' the self. Christology states its presupposition about "transcendence, namely, that the Logos is person. This human being is the transcendent."[88] Concretely this means that Christ is present in the other person who encounters me in the church with the Word. If the Word were merely an idea it would be subject to the dominion [Herrschaft] of the human *logos*. But the Word embodied in another person stands over against the self; each person, as an independent willing subject, is a *Grenze* to the other.[89] Word in the form of person

---

[87] GS III 167ff., 184ff., CC 28ff., 50ff.

[88] GS III 167, CC 28.

[89] That this discussion is still quite consciously using the concept of 'person' in the I–You relation as worked out in *Sanctorum Communio* may be seen from the sharply critical review of Karl Heim's *Glaube und Denken* which Bonhoeffer wrote in December, 1932. (Cf. DBW 12 213ff.; GS III 138ff., esp. 143ff.; the abridged translation in CW I 347–59 omits most of the material pertinent to this issue.) (For Heim's response to Bonhoeffer's critique, see the English translation by E. P. Dickie of the third edition of *Glaube und Denken* under the title *God Transcendent. Foundation for a Christian Metaphysic* (New York: Charles Scribner's Sons, 1936), pp. 235–39; it is quite apparent from Heim's reply that he is unfamiliar with the sense in which Bonhoeffer uses 'Grenze' in his phenomenology of the I–You–relation in sociality.

means a personal address which encounters and challenges the self from without. Just as freedom is not an attribute of God's aseity but of God's way of relating to humanity, so transcendence is not an attribute of Christ–in–himself but a relationship of Christ whose Personstruktur is a *pro–me*–Sein. He is *pro–nobis* as *extra nos*. The form of transcendence is therefore human sociality: the Word embodied in the other person and addressed to me as person is simultaneously *extra me* and *pro me*.

As soon as transcendence is presented in this way it follows that the transcendence question is not epistemological, but a question of my existence as a person who is related to others. The appropriate question to ask of the One who encounters the self is not the 'how' question but the 'who' question. Yet in asking about the person of the other, the Existenz of the self is implicated.

> The 'who' question is the transcendence-question.... The who question expresses the strangeness and otherness of the one who is encountered, and exposes itself as the Existenz–question of the questioner himself. He asks about the being which is foreign to his own being, [and therefore] about the limits [Grenzen] to his own Existenz. Transcendence places his own being in question.... So the transcendence–question is the Existenz–question, and Existenz–question is the transcendence–question. Theologically expressed: human beings only know who they are from God.[90]

> The who question is *the* religious question.[91] It is the question about the claim of the other, about the other being, about the other authority. *It is the question of love for the neighbor. The transcendence–question and the Existenz–question become the person–question.*[92]

Jesus in fact turns our who–question around, and we find ourselves addressed by the question:

> Who are you then, to ask thus? Are you then in the truth, posing this question? Who are you, that you can only ask about me if I reinstate you, justify you, and give you grace?[93]

---

[90] GS III 170, CC 31.

[91] Although a critique of religion is found in his early writings, Bonhoeffer occasionally uses the word 'religion' in a non–polemical sense. Its meaning here is of course quite different from the specific usage of the prison writings; in this instance the meaning is very similar to 'theological.'

[92] GS III 170, italics mine.

[93] GS III 173, CC 34.

The phenomenology of transcendence in sociality is that Christ present as person in the other encounters me in the Word; the Word questions my existence by asking me about my love for the neighbor. As Christ is person *pro–me*, so he encounters me with the question of my being–for my neighbor. Transcendence is therefore operative in the sociality of relations between persons in community. The present Christ encounters the self whose false social existence is within a solidarity of isolated selves, each being a *cor curvum in se*, heart turned in upon itself (Luther).[94] His Word of judgment and grace liberates the egocentric self for the love of the neighbor, thus creating the mutuality of freedom and love for one another in the community of the new humanity.

The Word in which Christ is present is most specifically the sermon. "The proclaimed Christ is the real Christ."[95]

> Christ's presence is his being–there [Dasein] as sermon. In the sermon the whole Christ, humiliated and exalted, is present. His presence is not any power of the congregation or its objective Geist, ...but his being there as sermon.[96]

That Christ is present as sermon sharply illustrates Bonhoeffer's point that the presence of Christ always involves his humiliation. That God's word is spoken by a human being is not humiliation; that it is spoken by a *sinful* human being is the presence of Christ in the Existenzweise of humiliation and exaltation. Nevertheless, even though this humiliation is a veiling of the Word, the human word of the sermon is the Word of God since God is freely bound to the human word. Adapting Luther's words about Christ, Bonhoeffer says: "You shall point to this human word and say: 'that is the Word of God.'"[97]

The content of the Word of address Bonhoeffer summarizes in three aspects: judgment; justification, grace, forgiveness; and command.[98] The Word does not consist of hidden truths which are unveiled, new ideas of God, or new ethical teachings. Not novelty, but the fact that the address existentially encounters the hearer as an event and places one in the truth—that is what matters. This view of the Word of God is identical with the interpretation of the freedom of God found in *Act and Being*.

---

94   GS III 170f., CC 31.
95   GS III 181, CC 46.
96   GS III 186, CC 52.
97   GS III 187, CC 53.
98   GS III 187, CC 53; GS III 173, CC 34; GS III 186, CC 52.

Sacrament. We have seen that Bonhoeffer's anthropology, within its assertion of the essential sociality of the human person, includes two main categories. First, human being as Geist, Dasein or Existenz: this refers to people as willing, conscious, knowing beings who are constituted by their decisions in time in relations with others, that is, a human being is an historical, social–ethical being. Second, human being as nature: people are bodily creatures who are part of their natural, material world. Although he gives priority to the former, Bonhoeffer insists that the whole person is essentially an interrelation of these two aspects of being. In accordance with this essential place given to bodily nature in his anthropology, Bonhoeffer now interprets Christ's presence as sacrament in explicit correlation to this anthropological schema. "The Word of the sermon is the form in which the Logos reaches the human *logos*; the sacrament is the form in which the Logos reaches the human being as Natur."[99]

As previously, the category of the Word is the prior one. Like the sermon, "the sacrament is the Word of God for it is the proclamation of the gospel";[100] it is the *one* Christ who is present both in sermon and sacraments—eucharist and baptism. While the one, whole Christ is present in the sermon as in the sacrament, yet the sacrament is a specific form of Christ, for here the Word is enacted in corporeal form. Like the sermon, the sacrament is both judgment and "the promise of the forgiveness of sins," "clear revelation";[101] but it is so in the form of natural elements—water, bread, and wine—which God names and sanctifies in the creaturely world.

At a time when Nazism was elevating nature in the myth of 'blood and soil' and consecrating it on the altar of racist nationalism, Bonhoeffer is quick to assert that creation or nature in general is not revelation. This is consistent with his rejection of the doctrine of the orders of creation being taught by theologians of the German Christians. Natural theology, whether it takes its point of departure from individual self–understanding, Volk, history, or nature, is ruled out.[102] But when that has been done, Bonhoeffer insists on stressing the sacramental form against any attempt to volatilize and sublimate Christ into doctrine, idea, or general truth.[103]

---

99 GS III 188, CC 54; cf. GS III 192, CC 58.

100 GS III 187, CC 53.

101 GS III 187f., CC 53f.; GS III 192, CC 58.

102 GS III 188, CC 54.

103 GS III 188, CC 54.

> In the sacrament Christ is beside us as creature, in our midst, brother
> with brother. Since he is creature, he is also the new creature. In the
> sacrament, he breaks through the fallen creation at a definite point. He
> is the new creature. He is the restored creation of our spiritual–bodily
> existence [geistleiblichen Existenz].[104]

As in the Word spoken by sinful people, so Christ's presence in the
elements of fallen creation involves his humiliation.[105] The humiliation
does not consist in the fact that Christ is present in the form of natural
elements of creation, any more than the incarnation as such was a
humiliation or concealment of God. It is rather that, in the world after
the fall (as Bonhoeffer had argued in *Creation and Fall*), nature is mute
and no longer speaks with unequivocal directness of its Creator.[106] In sin
humanity is estranged from nature.

But since the crucified Christ is resurrected and present, the humiliated Christ is also the exalted One. Therefore when he wills to be
present in the form of these particular elements of nature, the mute is
made to speak and out of concealment and humiliation comes new
creation and revelation. Christ shows himself to be the Creator of his
new creation. Present as creature, he makes us new creatures. Further,
in the sacrament nature is restored to humanity by receiving the *pro–me*
being of Christ: "as elements of the new creation they are of course
nothing for themselves, but for humanity. This being-for-humanity
[Für–den–Menschen–sein] is their being–new–creation."[107]   As by
Christ's being–for–humanity, people are freed for one another, so Natur,
too, is freed for humanity.

Christ's presence as nature in the sacrament which reaches human
nature cannot be separated from the fact that it is a form of his being in
the church-community, i.e., in sociality.   His being–sacrament
[Sakramentsein] is a being in the church which unites being and act,
being–there [Dasein] and being–*for–you* [Dir–Sein].   In the concept of
person in community, as Bonhoeffer had argued in *Act and Being*, both
the reality and independence of being and the contingent encounter of
that being, as act, on the self can be simultaneously affirmed. Because
the sacrament is celebrated in the Christian community of persons, it is
a form of Christ's being which is independent of the self yet impinges

---

[104] GS III 192, CC 59.
[105] CC 55f.
[106] CC 56; cf. CF 84.
[107] GS III 192, CC 59.

existentially on the self—it is both *extra–me* and *pro–me*. As person in the church "Christ exists such that he is existentially [existentialiter] present in the sacrament."[108]

A sermon preached during the Christology lectures further demonstrates that, while he relates Christ's sacramental presence to the category of Natur, for human beings Natur cannot be isolated from human sociality. The eucharist in primitive Christianity, Bonhoeffer says, is a joyful meal of the community [Gemeinschaft] of brothers whose love for one another is built up by the presence of the heavenly Lord.[109] In the sacrament, Christ is present in the form of Natur *in* the community. The social character of baptism is again evident in the August argument against the Aryan clause in the church. The Jewish Christian is received into the *one* church of Christ by baptism, so any exclusion of Jewish Christians is a violation of the sacrament. Baptism is not a mere ceremony; it is the corporate act in which the baptized and the church are joined together in an indissoluble bond of solidarity.[110]

The recognition that Christ's presence in Word and sacrament is a presence in sociality leads naturally to an analysis of the third aspect of the Gestalt Christi: Christ present as Gemeinde.

Church-community. It is imperative to recognize that when Bonhoeffer speaks of the church-community as the third aspect of the Gestalt or Personstruktur of Christ, he is stressing the *social nature of Christ's presence in Word and sacrament;* he is not speaking of a third form autonomous from Word and Sacrament. It is not as if Word and sacrament, after what has already been said, could be understood individualistically. Christ as Gemeinde is not an autonomous third form which adds something lacking in Word and sacrament, such as, for example, a mystical or activistic togetherness. On the contrary, to speak of the Christian community as the form of Christ is to highlight the sociality of Christ's presence in Word and sacrament. That is the meaning of the statement that his "presence in Word and sacrament is related to his presence in the church-community as reality [Realität] is related to form [Gestalt]."[111]

---

108 GS III 192, CC 58.
109 May 25, 1933: DBW 12 457; GS IV 120.
110 DBW 12 411; GS II 64.
111 GS III 193, CC 59.

As he has held from the outset, so here Bonhoeffer asserts that the Christian community is "Christus als Gemeinde existierend."[112] Christ is the Lord of this community created by his presence; yet he is not only its head and Lord, but is so as the reality of the congregation itself and every member. This means that while the congregation only exists because of the revelation of Christ, this revelation takes temporal–bodily–social form: in the relations of persons shaped and formed by Word and sacrament, revelation is socially present in space and time.[113]

To say that the church-community not only receives but also *is* the Word of revelation, that it does not represent but is the body of Christ, is not to overlook that the *sanctorum communio* is also the *peccatorum communio*. It is to assert that the exalted Christ is present in humiliation, and to acknowledge the offense in revelation. But this is to say that the *pro–me* being of Christ is a being for people who are sinners.

The reconstructed lectures do not record the explicit use of the idea of Christ as the Kollektivperson of the Christian community which is the concrete social form of the new humanity. But it is clear from everything said above on this subject that Bonhoeffer's understanding of Christ as the new humanity and his *corporate* presence in the church presupposes this concept. This is significant because the Kollektivperson concept is a corporate one, and prevents the understanding of sociality from being limited only to interpersonal relations. Attention must be drawn to this, because in the next section I deal with the way Bonhoeffer relates the messianic function of Christ as Mediator to collective human life in the political history of society.

3. CHRIST AS MEDIATOR

Nowhere is the catholicity of Bonhoeffer's early theology more evident than in these Christology lectures. This, however, is no surprise, since it is quite consistent with his position in *Sanctorum Communio*: it is the Christ who is the new humanity for the whole human race who exists in and as the church. In these lectures, the Christ who is present in the church-community is the universal Mediator: he is present for humanity, for history, and for nature.[114] The fact that these lectures begin with the

---

[112] Cf. GS III 193.
[113] GS III 193f., CC 59ff.
[114] GS III 195, CC 62.

presence of Christ in the church should not obscure the fact that the One who is present is not confined to the church but is the Lord and Mediator of all reality.

Bonhoeffer is quite explicit on this point. In a discussion of the state he says: "Christ is present to us in a twofold form [zweifacher Gestalt], as church and state."[115] This does not mean that Christ is present partly in the Christian community, and partly in the state. It is the whole Christ who is present. But Christ's presence can be viewed in terms of two concentric circles. In the inner circle, the church, Christ's presence is revealed and confessed in faith; in the outer circle, the state, Christ is not revealed. Yet even though political authorities, and people generally, may not know the presence of Christ in all the life of society, the church affirms it nevertheless.

By linking the Christological concept of *Mittler* with the metaphor *Mitte*, Bonhoeffer further articulates his Christology. We have met this metaphor previously, most recently in *Creation and Fall* where it is a metaphor of God's lordship as the creator and giver of life. To be sure, since Bonhoeffer's approach to creation is Christological, we may say that the concept of Mitte was then, at least implicitly, a Christological concept. In these lectures Mitte becomes an explicit and major Christological concept. Here Bonhoeffer lays the solid theological foundation for the concept "Christ the center of life" which is found in the new context of the *Letters*. Its role in the Christology lectures demonstrates that its later use is not an accidental metaphor or a mere novelty; it is a fundamental Christological concept.

Bonhoeffer's discussion of Christ the Mediator highlights the anthropological pattern of his Christology. This is the necessary consequence of insisting that the being of Christ is a *pro–me*-being. When he structures the Gestalt of the present Christ as Word and sacrament in the congregation, there is a definite anthropological correlation to each of these three Christological elements. Several explicit statements establish this judgment.

---

[115] GS III 198, CC 66. This "twofold form" should not be confused with the "threefold form" of Christ's presence in the church. The latter is the *Struktur* of revelation; the former—Christ's presence outside the church—is a presence which is not revealed but is known in faith.

> The One who is present in Word, sacrament, and church-community is in the center [Mitte] of human existence [Existenz], of history [Geschichte], and of nature [Natur].[116]

> Christ is Mediator as the One who is being–there–for–me [*pro–me–Daseinde*].... He is in the center in a threefold way: in being there for [Dasein für] humanity, in being there for history, in being there for nature.[117]

Additional statements also express this interrelation of Christology and anthropology.[118] But since Bonhoeffer uses several anthropological categories—Existenz, *logos*, Geschichte, state, Nature—it is necessary to clarify how these relate to the three basic Christological categories.

Consistent with the usage of his theology of sociality, Bonhoeffer understands both Christ and human beings from his comprehensive concept of "person." Christology deals with the Personstruktur of Christ who is the Mediator of all human Existenz. A human being, we have seen, is a social person whose life is understood in two basic interrelated categories, Geist and Natur. The three categories of the Personstruktur of Christ are Word, sacrament, and Gemeinde; the three dimensions of human existence of which Christ is the Mediator are Existenz, Geschichte (specifically, the political history of the state), and Natur. But the correlation of the three Christological categories and anthropological dimensions is somewhat subtle.

In Bonhoeffer's anthropology the human being, in whom Geist and Natur interact, is an individual person who essentially belongs to corporate communities and institutions of humanity as a whole. The material on the Mediator is organized in this anthropological pattern.[119] The first paragraph focuses on the individual person in treating "Christ as the center of human Existenz," while the second paragraph treats human corporate life in the political history of the state under the heading of "Christ as the center of history"; here the two reciprocal sides of sociality, the individual person and corporate human life, serve as structural

---

[116] GS III 195, CC 62.

[117] Ibid.

[118] For the relation Word–human *logos,* sacrament–human Natur, see GS III 188, CC 54 and GS III 192, CC 58f.; for the relation of Christ as Geschichte and Natur and human Existenz as Geschichte and Natur, compare GS III 188, CC 55 with GS III 200, CC 67; for the relation Gemeinde–state, compare GS III 193f., CC 59f. and GS III 196ff., CC 63ff.

[119] Part 1, section 2.

principles in the lectures. These two paragraphs, then, highlight the sociality of human *Geist*—or Existenz, to use Bonhoeffer's most usual term in these lectures. The third paragraph treats Bonhoeffer's other basic anthropological category, *Natur,* in a discussion of "Christ as the center between God and nature."

The correlation between the three aspects of Christ's Personstruktur and these three dimensions of human life is as follows. The correlation between Christ as sacrament and human bodily existence in the natural world is straightforward: here the category "Natur" links the anthropology to the Christology.[120] Again, the correlation between Christ as Gemeinde and human political history in the state is clear; the corporate side of the social category is common to both of these.

Further clarification, however, is needed about the correlation between the Christological category of Word and the anthropological concepts, Existenz and historicity. The historicity of both the Word and human Existenz provides the clarification, provided we remember that historicity and sociality are intrinsically linked together in Bonhoeffer's Christology and anthropology. Accordingly, Bonhoeffer understands the Word of Christ to be historical, in the sense that it encounters people, calling for responsible decision; this encounter occurs in human social relations, and, since the historicity of human Existenz consists of decision in this social–ethical encounter with others in community, historicity and sociality are intrinsic to each other. This is the individual side of the sociality of Christ and humanity. Sociality also has its corporate, or collective, side. Hence Bonhoeffer discusses the state under the rubric of history. The Word of Christ is directed to the corporate, political history of the state, as well as to the historical decisions of the individual's personal existence; furthermore, the historicity of the individual and of corporate political life are inseparable in human sociality, since ethical persons must assume the role of deputy in acting with responsibility for the collectivities to which they belong.

As early as *Sanctorum Communio* Bonhoeffer had related both the historicity of the individual person and corporate, political history to the Word.[121] In these lectures, as previously, the historicity and sociality of

---

[120] It should be noted, as pointed out below, that the actual paragraph on Christ as the Mediator has little direct anthropological discussion of Natur; this is found elsewhere in Part 1.

[121] *"When peoples are called, God's will for their purpose in history is at work,* just as where individuals are called, they experiences their history" (SC 74, SC-E 119).

the Word belong together. Likewise, the historicity and sociality of human Existenz belong together.[122] When Christ is described as the "center of human existence," this draws particular attention to the *historicity* of both Word and individual life—but precisely in their sociality. When Christ in the corporate form of the church is described as the "center of a history which is made by the state,"[123] this draws particular attention to the *sociality* of the Word in the political life of society—but with explicit reference to the historical character of Word and social life.

While Bonhoeffer insists that human Existenz is always both historical and natural,[124] the very word 'Existenz' gives priority to the historical aspect of human being. In these lectures 'Existenz' is the philosophical term in Bonhoeffer's anthropology which is interpreted by his consistent theological understanding of 'person.' Previously, other philosophical terms were interpreted by 'person' in his anthropology—in *Sanctorum Communio*, 'Geist,' in *Act and Being*, 'Dasein.' The movement from Geist to Dasein to Existenz—while all interpreted as 'person'—reveals Bonhoeffer appropriating terminology from the growing existentialist movement. While there are notable points of disagreement with basic premises of existentialism, Bonhoeffer does agree with the existentialist position that historicity is essential to the existence and definition of human life.

The three fundamental anthropological categories, then, are sociality, historicity, and nature. The three are not isolated but interrelated, for just as human historical character is constituted by one's decisions in sociality, so *human nature* is embraced in and shaped by one's social historicity. These three anthropological categories are correlated to the Christological categories. Christ as Gemeinde, as Word, and as sacrament—similarly inter–related—constitute the Gestalt, or Personstruktur, of the Mediator in his *pro–me*-being. There is a correspondence, therefore, between the Personstruktur of Christ and the whole being of the human person.

While Bonhoeffer delineates the Gestalt of Christ in these anthropological categories, it is imperative to notice the movement of the correlation. The order is Word–Existenz, sacrament–Natur, Gemeinde–state (political history), not the reverse. The method is Christological; but the form

122 CC 51.
123 GS III 197, CC 65.
124 GS III 200, CC 67.

of the Christology is anthropological. The reason for this correlation and for its order is Bonhoeffer's fundamental Christological premise: in Christ *God* becomes *human* for humanity; it is *God* who becomes human, but God truly becomes *human*. Methodologically this means that the movement is from the particular to the general, from revelation to reason, from church to state. This movement is built into the structure of the lectures, the first section of Part One dealing with the Gestalt of Christ, the second section treating Christ as Mediator of human historical existence, of political life, and of nature.

In turning to examine the actual role of Christ as Mediator we are at the point where Christology becomes soteriology. What is of special interest here is how the soteriological implications of the Christology relate to the anthropological problem of power and the theological answer of freedom and love which we have considered in the previous writings.

The Mediator and new humanity: from power to love. The being of Christ as person is his "Dasein für den Menschen," his "*pro–me*–Sein." "He stands *pro me*. He stands in my place [Stelle] where I should but cannot stand."[125] Here the idea of Christ as Stellvertreter is quite evident, though the actual term is not found in the reconstructed lectures. As the representative or 'personification' of true humanity, Christ encounters the self. Person confronts person. The person of Christ is the Grenze for the self. As such, Christ who is 'other' and 'outside' the self is both the judge of one's false humanity and the promise of one's new humanity. Christ stands between the old self and the new self; as his judgment negates the old self, so his justification affirms and establishes the new self. If Christ is thus the Mitte between a person's old and new existence, he is the Mittler who frees the self–imprisoned ego from its self–imprisonment to find a new center of being in Christ.[126]

What does this mean concretely? How is new human being understood, if one's new existence has its source and center in Christ whose being is '*pro–me*–Sein,' 'Dasein für den Menschen'? If Christ is the 'personification' and Stellvertreter of true humanity, is his being–for–humanity in fact a prototype of the true humanity of every human being?

---

125 GS III 194, CC 61.
126 GS III 194f., CC 61ff.

This crucial soteriological question receives a tantalizingly brief and traditional answer in *this* part of the reconstructed lectures. Christ is described as the fulfiller of the law which humanity has but does not fulfill, and therefore Christ is at once the judgment and justification of humanity.[127]

Without minimizing the significance of this traditional statement, we find it interpreted by Bonhoeffer's own characteristic answer in the Introduction to the lectures. This has already been mentioned in the discussion above on sociality and transcendence. When people understand themselves ultimately as *logos,* as scientific, classifying reason, they exist in the dominion [Herrschaft] of autonomous and self–established power [Macht]. From this center the self operates not only in the academic disciplines but also in personal relations. Even Christ himself, the person par excellence, is subjected to the efforts of the knowing ego to bring everything into its power. Christ, who has been subjected to humanity's power in the crucifixion, encounters the human power as the Resurrected One who is not idea but person. He is the Counter–Logos [Gegenlogos].[128]

As the Counter–Logos, who, in the person of another human being, encounters the knowing and classifying ego from without in the relationship of transcendence, Christ judges the dominion of the powerful self. The old self, who seeks to bring everything under its control by always asking the 'how?' question, is contradicted and dies.[129] The "inordinate claim" of human reason encounters its Grenze in Christ as person,[130] is ultimately compelled to ask 'who' Christ is, and finds the question

---

[127] GS III 198; CC 62f.

[128] GS III 167ff., CC 28ff.

[129] GS III 172f., CC 33; cf. GS III 169f., CC 29f.

[130] GS III 172, CC 33; cf. CC 62: in the fallen world, 'Mitte' is simultaneously 'Grenze.' It must be stressed that Bonhoeffer does not react to reason as an instrument of the ego's power by advocating irrationalism—as is suggested by translating "Gegenlogos" with "Anti–Logos." The point is not to reject reason but to transform and re–establish it so that it is not an instrument of domination. Hence "the old *logos* is judged by the transcendence of the person of Christ and learns to understand its new relative right, its limit and its necessity" (GS III 172). The last part of the sentence is as important as the first; the Mediator does not destroy human reason but transforms and renews it. Hence Bonhoeffer claims that Christology is "Wissenschaft kat' exochen," and that "Christology is the unrecognized and hidden center of the *universitas literarum*" (GS III 167f.).

returned to the sender: now the question is, "Who am I as I am exposed and revealed in encounter with Christ?" The Transzendenz question becomes my Existenz question. But this question cannot be answered by the *cor curvum in se.* The transcendence–existence question "is the question of the *other person* and their claim, of the *other* being, of the *other* authority. It is the question of *love for the neighbor.*"[131]

The soteriological meaning is clear. Christ is the Mediator of human existence in that he negates the unlimited, self–established, isolated power of the dominating ego and justifies a person for a life of love for others. The gospel, in other words, frees one from egocentricity to Christocentricity; but since Christ is present for us in the neighbor, freedom for Christ means freedom for the other, the love of the neighbor. Since the being of Christ is a being–for–humanity, a *pro–me*–being, true human being is being–for–others. Admittedly, we do not yet find in these lectures the Christological formula of the *Letters,* Christ "the one for others," or the explicit description of Christian existence as "existing for others." But the whole direction of the Christology lectures, building on the previous theology, points toward these formulations. They are present in intention, if not in actual words.

In the Christology lectures we not only find a restatement of sociality as the form of Christ's presence. We also see that the anthropological problem is the problem of the self who is isolated from others and perverts human sociality by the egocentric exercise of power. The soteriological function of the Mediator is to free people for true humanity in being with and for others in love. Christ the Mediator is not only present in the form of human sociality, but is present in such a way as to diagnose its perversion by sin and to liberate people into the promise of the sociality which is the essence of human being.

The messianic Christ: Mediator of political history. As he is the Mediator of personal, historical existence, so Christ is also the Mediator of corporate, political history in the state.[132]

Political history, Bonhoeffer argues, has a messianic character. Through law, the state seeks to create an order which will fulfill the life of the people. The divine promise informs the expectation that the coming of a Messiah is the meaning of history. But, in fact, history is

---

[131] GS III 170, CC 31, italics mine.
[132] GS III 196–198, CC 63–66.

precisely not the glorification of God through the coming of the divine kingdom in political life. History is the story of rulers setting themselves up as the center of history, a process of human *self*–glorification in the succession of self–proclaimed messiahs. The promise of human politics is thereby corrupted, and its expectations are unfulfilled.

As the humiliated Messiah who is not lionized but crucified, who is hidden and not publicly acclaimed, Christ is at once the destroyer and fulfiller of the messianic expectations of history, the judge and justifier of the state. The Messiah is really present in human politics, and thus history's promise is fulfilled. But his presence as the true center of history is the Grenze and negation of all the false messianic pretensions that history spawns. As politics is not the kingdom of God, the Messiah known in the church points ahead to the future consummation of the eschatological kingdom. Since the coming and crucifixion of Christ, we should no longer seek for political messiahs.

Bonhoeffer insists, as noted above, that not only the church but also the state is a form of Christ's presence. But his presence in the state is not revealed, and he is not Mediator in that form. Bonhoeffer quotes Luther's formulation: "The state is 'God's rule with the left hand.'"[133] It is the community of faith which acknowledges his presence in the form of the state, and it is in the form of the church that Christ is the Mediator of political life. "Christ as the center of history is the Mediator between the state and God in the form of the church."[134] In his presence in the church Christ is revealed as the true Messiah; he is the Mediator in this form because the Christian community is party to the messianic secret of his cross and resurrection which disclose to faith both the divine judgment on the false messianic pretensions and the fulfilling human possibilities of politics and history.

Bonhoeffer makes clear the concrete implications of this view of Christ as the messianic center of history, the Mediator between the state and God in the form of the church, in several pieces and addresses around the time of his Christology lectures.[135]

---

[133] GS III 198, CC 66, citing WA XXXVI, 385, 6–9 and WA LII, 26, 20–26.

[134] Ibid.

[135] In addition to the three pieces discussed in the text, see also the sermons "Die Furcht" (January 15: DBW 12 439f.; GS IV 101ff.), "Gideon" (February 26: DBW 12 447ff.; GS IV 109ff.), "Moses–und Aarons–Kirche" (May 28: DBW 12 459ff.; GS IV 123ff.), the first version of the Bethel Confession (August: DBW 12 363ff.; GS II 90ff.), and "Der Arierparagraph in der Kirche" (August: DBW 12 408ff.; GS II 62ff.), all in 1933.

In the address "Thy Kingdom Come!" ("Dein Reich komme!" —a pregnant title in November, 1932), Bonhoeffer also speaks of church and state as two modes of the presence of Christ in the world, and of Christ as the center of the state in the form of the church.[136] In this address we see, first, the political responsibility laid upon the church as the revealed form of the Mediator present in the world. To assert that the Mediator has the church as the form of his revealed presence is not to encourage among Christians that other–worldly escapism which the opening of the address so roundly castigates. On the contrary, it commits the church to political responsibility. Praying for the kingdom of God is not praying for private salvation.

> The hour in which the church today prays for the kingdom constrains it, for better or worse, completely to identify itself with the children of the earth and the world. It binds it in loyalty to the earth, to misery, hunger, and death. It makes the church stand in complete solidarity with evil and with the guilt of the brother.[137]

Second, as a crucial part of this responsibility, there is the sharp Christian polemic against all false messianic pretensions.

> The kingdom of Christ is God's kingdom, but God's kingdom in the form appointed for us. It does not appear as *one, visible powerful empire*[138] [machtvolle Imperium], not as the 'new' kingdom of the world.... It appears simultaneously as the *powerless, defenseless gospel of the resurrection,* of the miracle; and as the state with authority and force [Gewalt] to keep order. The kingdom of Christ is a reality only when both are genuinely related and mutually limit each other.[139]

---

[136] In this month the German Christians gained one third of the seats in the government of the Church of the Old Prussian Union; cf. PB 37, "Christianizing of culture, politics, and education."

[137] GS III 274; trans. Godsey, PB 33.

[138] Without using the exact word, this statement is surely a polemic against the National Socialist concept of 'Gleichschaltung.' This notion called for the 'coordination' of all social institutions and regional organizations into a unified Reich, 'integrated' according to Nazi ideology; cf. DBW 16 590; GS II 433, 113ff. Because of this particular and highly problematic political context, Bonhoeffer's discussions of church and state should not be read simply as orthodox repetition of the traditional Lutheran 'two realms' doctrine. His break with that tradition in the concept of Erhaltungsordnungen is additional evidence of this point; see further discussion of this point below.

[139] GS III 282, cf. Godsey, PB 44, italics mine; note the theme of the powerlessness of Christ in the gospel, and the implicit reference to church and state as ethical Kollektivpersonen encountering each other.

The state is, as we have seen above, an order for the preservation of life, resisting destruction, protecting human communities, regulating inordinate human desires; it is not an order of salvation with a messianic destiny. God destroys those who don divine masks. It is not God's will that human beings should take over the world by their own "sheer, superabundant power [Kraft]."[140] If politics should overstep its limit and the state become a messianic pretender with imperial ambitions, then it is the responsibility of the church—which Bonhoeffer here undertakes— to encounter and limit the state in the name of Christ.[141]

This view had clear implications for Bonhoeffer's response to the Nazi state, as is apparent in the second address, first given on the radio on February 1, 1933, two days after Hitler became chancellor; the subject was the Führer concept. After tracing changes in the view of leadership in the Youth Movement, Bonhoeffer comes to the contemporary situation of his address. Now the Führer is a "political–messianic" figure. He embodies the immanent divinity of the Volksgeist, and his function must be described as religious. He is hailed as the messiah whose appearance fulfills eschatological hopes, and in whose coming the eternal kingdom draws near.[142]

The response Bonhoeffer makes to this ideology clearly shows the meaning and ethical consequences of his view that the Mediator of political history is the Messiah present in the form of the church. In a public address to the new government and its disciples, he speaks the encountering word on behalf of Christ and the church; it is recognized as such in the fact that his address was cut off before the end of the broadcast. He attacks the idolatry of the Führer, through the abdication of individual responsibility by citizens, who, by giving unquestioned obedience, seek unlimited [Grenzelose] freedom by the transference of their wishes to the Führer.[143] This is the messianism of imperialism, whose inner logic quickly became military aggression in the Nazi Reich. The type of authority embodied in the Führer is unlimited and is a self–justification of the Volk; it does not acknowledge that the authentic authority of a state

---

[140] DBW 12 267; GS III 272.

[141] Bonhoeffer takes the same attitude in his August, 1933 article on "Der Arierparagraph in der Kirche." The church is not a counterfeit copy [Nachahmung] of the state. Its service and loyalty to the state consist exactly in standing over against the state and encountering the state in the integrity of its own identity as the church of Christ; cf. DBW 12 413f.; GS II 67f.

[142] DBW 12 255.; GS II 32f., CW I 199.

[143] DBW 12 256; GS II 34, CW I 200.

derives from God and is accountable to God. Here, by allusion rather than explicit theological language, Bonhoeffer is speaking the word of the cross. If there is a word of justification to be heard, it depends on the Führer radically repudiating the idolatrous messianic role and acknowledging the divine authority which limits his office. He must not be a messiah but a servant of his office, cultivating a mature responsibility in the citizens and preserving those forms of community willed by God in which the distinctness and mutual responsibility of I and You are affirmed.[144]

The third piece was the article on the church and the Jews written April 15, 1933, in response to the April 1 boycott of Jewish shops and the April 7 legislation prohibiting non–Aryans from the civil service.[145]

---

[144] DBW 12 255ff.; GS II 33ff., CW I 200ff. For further discussion of several themes in this address, including criticism of the church's conformity to worldly notions of power and messianic glory, see the sermon "Moses–und Aarons–Kirche" (DBW 12 459ff.; GS IV 123–129), preached while the Christology lectures were being delivered. See also "Gideon," Bonhoeffer's first sermon after Hitler came to power. The proclamation of the cross throws down human self–deification, and reduces to dust all the gods, idols, and lords of the world. The critique of human power, military and personal, is central in the sermon. To say that God is the "Waffe" and "Panzer" of the church, means that the cross—the symbol of powerlessness, defenselessness, dishonor—is the place of divine strength, defence, honor, glory and victory. In the gospel God says: "my strength is powerful in the weak" (2 Cor. 12:9; see the discussion below on the 1934 sermon on this very text). We are victorious because God is victorious, and when God is victorious, people are humbled and freed from destructive messianic ambition (DBW 12 447ff.; GS IV 109–117).

[145] The Aryan clause was not introduced into the church until September 5, 1933. Bethge makes the important point that in this April statement Bonhoeffer was opposing the racist legislation of the state against all Jews, and was not only concerned about the church status of Christians of Jewish descent. When Christians concentrated on the latter and neglected the former, he repeatedly urged: "Open your mouth for the dumb" (Proverbs 31:8); cf. DB-E 273. To see this piece, and its problems, in a wider context see also Bethge, "Dietrich Bonhoeffer and the Jews," in Godsey and Kelly, eds., *Ethical Responsibility: Bonhoeffer's Legacy to the Churches* (New York & Toronto: Edwin Mellen Press, 1981), 43–96. For a July statement on the Jewish–Christian question, which anticipates "Der Arierparagraph in der Kirche" of August, see Bonhoeffer's "Appeal to the Ministers of the Old Prussian Union: The Jewish–Christian Question as Status Confessionis" in Charles S. Macfarland, *The New Church and the New Germany* (New York: Macmillan, 1934), 69–71; reprinted in J. Glenthøj, MW V: *Dokumente zur Bonhoeffer–Forschung* (Munich: Chr. Kaiser, 1969), pp. 103f., esp. p. 103 n. 1 for the evidence of Bonhoeffer's authorship. This is now found in DBW 12 359-61.

Bonhoeffer argues that the first duty of the church toward the state is to address it, calling it to its legitimate function as an order of preservation. Beyond this, the church must aid the victims of state action. But if the state deprives citizens of their rights or oversteps its limits by forcing the church to exclude baptized Jews, then the church must be prepared for direct political action in active opposition to the state. Here Bonhoeffer is referring to, but not yet advocating, the possibility that the church may have to demand the dissolution of a government which has forfeited its legitimacy. As we have seen above, an order of preservation is directed to and relative to Christ. When the state defaults on its responsibility, the church "can demand the most radical destruction precisely for the sake of the One who builds up."[146] Because it is the community of the crucified and resurrected Messiah, the church knows that times for breaking up in order to build up occur in the history of political life; the church is the center of political history as the form of the present Messiah who speaks his living Word to the state with prophetic voice.[147] For those who have learned from Bonhoeffer's whole thought and life, and have been instructed by the profound theological conflicts of Germany in the 1930s, this piece as a whole now appears unduly cautious. Yet it does reveal that the Christology of the Berlin lecture room was not an academic abstraction; it was directly connected to crucial ethical issues of contemporary politics. From this theological foundation Bonhoeffer moved into the direct, radical opposition of the political resistance movement.

The freeing of creation: Christ and Nature. After humanity's sin, nature is under the curse. This means, Bonhoeffer had argued in *Creation and Fall,* that it is no longer free unambiguously to proclaim the Word of God and glorify its Creator. Unlike humanity, it is not under guilt, and therefore does not need reconciliation; but it does need to be delivered from its bondage so that it is "freed to a new freedom" for God and for humanity.[148] As the Mediator between God and nature, Christ liberates nature to this freedom.

This is revealed by Christ's presence in the sacrament as Natur. Here Christ is seen to be "*the* new creature," and as such the liberator [Befreier]

---

146 DBW 11 337; GS I 151.
147 DBW 12 349-58, esp. 350-54; GS II 44–53, esp. 45–49.
148 GS III 199, CC 67.

of creation.[149] Here nature is freed for its Creator. In the sacrament God's Word is proclaimed, and nature is freed to sing the praise of the Creator.

Simultaneously, the sacraments speak of nature's being freed for humanity. In fact, Bonhoeffer argues, the new creation of nature is its "Für–den–Menschen–sein."[150] It is interesting to see that the liberation of nature is interpreted on the same model as human redemption; nature, like humanity, finds its true being when it is freed from isolation in itself to being–for the other creatures of creation.

But the freeing of nature in the sacraments is not restricted to nature apart from and outside of human life. As human existence is that of spirit–body [Geist–Leib], so the sacrament is the form in which Christ reaches people in their nature, i.e., their bodily existence.[151] However, the reconstructed lectures do not spell out the *anthropological* implications of Christ as Mediator between God and nature in the form of sacrament. While Bonhoeffer speaks of nature being freed to proclaim its creator, and of Christ reaching people in their bodily nature, he does not elaborate on the human soteriological significance of this. One would expect that elaboration to follow the same lines as the earlier discussion of reason, human *logos:* after negating the inordinate pretensions of reason, Christ is presented as affirming its new relative rights and its necessity within the limits of its own proper sphere. In the Christology lectures there is an implicit foundation for a theology of bodily life. The suggestion is that the *one* Christ, who is the reconciler and liberator of "human existence [which] is always both history [Geschichte] and nature [Natur]," re–establishes a proper interdependence of spirit and body in an integrated person.[152]

In view of his discussion of the impact of sin on human sexuality in *Creation and Fall,* it is natural to expect that Bonhoeffer would return to the question of bodily life in his treatment of Christ and nature. But in fact it is not until the *Ethics* and the prison writings that he seriously begins to explore the anthropological import of his 1933 Christological thesis: Christ the Mediator between God and nature. His later reflections on the natural, bodily life, pleasure, and sexuality are significant contributions to an aspect of Protestant theology which, as Bonhoeffer notes here, had long been neglected.

---

[149] GS III 199, CC 66.

[150] GS III 192, CC 59.

[151] CC 54.

[152] GS III 200, CC 67.

C. THE CHRISTOLOGY LECTURES AS THE CULMINATION OF BONHOEFFER'S EARLY THEOLOGY

The conclusion of his 1933 Christology lectures marked the de facto termination of Bonhoeffer's academic career. Although his official relationship with the University of Berlin was not severed by government action until August, 1936, he had already during 1933 unreservedly committed himself to the Kirchenkampf. He continued this opposition to the Nazi regime during his work with the German congregations in London, which he began in October, 1933, then as director of the Finkenwalde seminary of the Confessing Church, and finally in the political resistance movement and the conspiracy to assassinate Hitler which led to his own imprisonment and ultimate death.

This termination of his academic career, however, is a culmination of his theological work from 1927 to 1933. By "culmination" I do not mean that Bonhoeffer restates and summarizes in the Christology lectures every detail of his earlier theology. There is a continuity of fundamental convictions and approach, though the subject matter of Christology focuses and delimits the subjects treated. Given this appropriate selectivity, however, these lectures articulate the Christology which is the center of Bonhoeffer's theology with a concentration and clarity not seen before; and they relate his anthropological concerns—sociality, anthropological structure, and soteriology—to the Christological center of his thinking with a systematic consistency never before attempted. The lectures, therefore, draw together his characteristic themes and concerns from the previous writings, and also point forward to the later writings, especially *Discipleship*, the *Ethics*, and the *Letters and Papers from Prison*. The next chapter will examine the creative continuity between the early theology and the prison writings. This chapter concludes by discussing three points which are central to interpreting Bonhoeffer's early theology: sociality, the anthropological pattern of Christology, and soteriology.

1. SOCIALITY

The sociality of Christ and humanity is the basic vision which informs the pattern and content of the 1933 Christology. It is a measure of the consistency of Bonhoeffer's early theology that the Christian concept of person—as a Christological and anthropological category—which is formative for these lectures is precisely the basic concept which Bonhoeffer had used to establish his theology of sociality, including his ecclesiology, in *Sanctorum Communio*. By the social concept of Christ as "person," Bonhoeffer attempts to overcome the problem of objectified, metaphysical categories in classical Christology. The same concept informs his whole discussion of the presence of Christ: as Kollektivperson of the new humanity; as revealed in his existing "als Gemeinde"; as existentially encountering the individual in the church; and as the Mediator of corporate history in the encounter of church and state—these two engage, limit, and challenge one another on the model of the historical, socio–ethical encounter of persons.

Understood as person, it is essential to the ontological structure of Christ that he is *Christus pro nobis*. This means that, while Bonhoeffer is emphatic about the *extra nos* of Christ, the Christ who is not identical with us is always encountered in relation to us, and in his being-for-humanity. In the Christology lectures, the description of the *Christus pro nobis* clearly restates Bonhoeffer's crucial affirmation in *Act and Being* that God's freedom is freedom *for* humanity, "*his-having-freely-bound-himself* to historical humanity."[153] This concept of God's freedom was, to be sure, an explicitly Christological one in the earlier book; in the Christology lectures Bonhoeffer brings to the fore and makes explicit the Christological presuppositions of his previous interpretation of God's freedom. It is this view of Christ's being-for-humanity which informs all Bonhoeffer's treatment of the form of Christ's presence and his soteriological role as Mediator; as the freedom of the Mediator is his being for humanity *(pro nobis),* so his presence frees people for God and one another.[154] In other words, Christ is Christ in his social relation with humanity, and by his presence creates a new social community and new social relationships among human beings. Christ is truly Christ and human beings are truly human in the sociality of Christ and humanity.

We have seen that Bonhoeffer continues to presuppose in these lectures the understanding of Christ as the Kollektivperson of the new humanity first set forth in *Sanctorum Communio*. In the latter work

---

[153] Cf. above, Chapter 3.

[154] This soteriological function of the Mediator also recapitulates the anthropological themes of the 'Füreinander' of the Christian life in *Sanctorum Communio*, and the mutuality of love which is Bonhoeffer's exegesis of the *imago Dei* as *analogia relationis* in *Creation and Fall*.

Christ is seen as the Stellvertreter who 'stands for' and 'personifies' the new humanity which is actual in him and is realized among us by the Holy Spirit. The very passage in the Christology lectures which expresses the Kollektivperson concept explicitly speaks of Christ as Stellvertreter.[155] However, the idea of Christ as Mittler—while clearly very close to Stellvertreter—is the normative one in the Christology lectures. This change of terminology is significant in light of the role 'Mitte' has come to play since *Creation and Fall,* and will continue to play in the *Letters.* It therefore represents a strengthening of the theology of sociality, not a departure from it; it enables Bonhoeffer to relate his Christology more concretely to history, politics, and nature, and in doing so he makes Christ a more active, present agent. For the same reason it gave Bonhoeffer a Christological concept which could serve as the hub of a theological wheel in which he could integrate his intensifying concern with questions in ethics, politics, and the doctrine of creation.

Christ is the Mediator in the concrete social form of the church. The conceptuality and formulation of *Sanctorum Communio* and *Act and Being,* "Christus als Gemeinde existierend," is explicit, and is fundamental to the Christology lectures.[156] Revelation, transcendence, and salvation are presented as having both their Christological and anthropological reality and form in the social community of the congregation. They are at once bound to the community of faith as a corporate reality and, precisely because they occur in community, they involve the encounters of individual persons whose existence as ethical–historical subjects is constituted in relations with others.

Being in the community of the church necessarily relates the Christian to the civil community since the state belongs to the Gestalt of the present Christ. The exposition above showed how Bonhoeffer interprets the church–state relation on the model of the encounter of ethical persons. The church as such has a responsibility to the corporate order of the state, though this responsibility is fulfilled by means of persons acting individually—not individualistically—on behalf of and for the sake of the political order; one acts in the name of the true Messiah of history, revealed in the church, whose judgment and promise as the 'personification' of the new humanity makes him the Mediator of the political history of the state.

This brief review of central themes is sufficient to demonstrate that Bonhoeffer's statement in the Preface of *Sanctorum Communio* about

---

[155] GS III 183, quoted above.
[156] GS III 193f.

sociality and Christian theology has continued to hold good for his Christology lectures in 1933. Retrospectively, the statement must be seen as programmatic not only for his first work but also for the whole of his early theology.

2. THE ANTHROPOLOGICAL PATTERN OF CHRISTOLOGY

The Christology of the 1933 lectures has two distinctive characteristics: the first is that it is informed throughout by the conceptuality of sociality; the second is that it is structured by anthropological categories. This is not to say that Bonhoeffer presents anthropology as Christology. It means, rather, that he takes seriously the fundamental contention of classical Christology: God in human form. Bonhoeffer begins with the legacy of Chalcedon. But he criticizes any attempt to appropriate that legacy in reified and objectified concepts. Not a Christology of a *Christus an sich,* to whom 'how' questions of essence and nature are posed, but a Christology of *Christus pro nobis* who encounters people by his personal presence—that is his achievement. But in order to present the Christ *pro–nobis,* whose ontological structure essentially relates him to humanity, it is necessary to join together theological and anthropological concepts to construct such a Christology. This is what Bonhoeffer does.

We have seen that Bonhoeffer articulates the Personstruktur of the present Christ in the Gestalt of Word, sacrament, and Gemeinde. These three aspects are then correlated to human existence understood in three categories: society, history, and nature. Bonhoeffer discusses the role of Christ as Mediator in terms of these anthropological categories. The anthropological pattern of his Christology thus operates on two levels: Christ is present in the form of human speech, acts, and relationships in the Word and sacraments of the Gemeinde; Christ's mediatorial function is interpreted in relation to the anthropological categories of human history, human being as and in nature, and human sociality.

On the first level Bonhoeffer is innovating on the Lutheran tradition. To speak of the presence of Christ in Word and sacrament is traditional Reformation teaching; this, of course, presupposed that Christ's presence in these forms was in the church-community. Bonhoeffer's innovation derives from his thinking in terms of sociality: he makes the personal relations of preacher and addressed in the community *intrinsic* to the nature of the Word as the *personal* presence of Christ. The other person who is *extra* me is the form of Christ as Other who is *pro* me; the Word is *essentially social* and cannot be separated from this relationship and encounter of persons.[157]

If this articulation of the Personstruktur or Gestalt of Christ on the first level already emphasizes the social, human form of Christ's presence, the anthropological pattern of his Christology is even more striking on the second level. Bonhoeffer describes Christ as Mediator in terms of precisely those anthropological categories which he has consistently employed throughout his early theology. A human person is an historical–ethical, natural, social being; Christ the Mediator is the center [Mitte] of human life in its dimensions of personal history [Existenz], political history [State], and nature.[158] This means, further, that he is Mediator for all people, since all human life has these anthropological dimensions.

It is quite conceivable that a Christology could be presented without any such anthropological pattern. Bultmann, for example, has a quite elaborate theological anthropology, but his Christology—in so far as he would allow the word—is expressed in one term: the kerygmatic Word. Barth's Christology is presented in terms of the dynamics of the natures, states, and offices of Christ. Of course, both Bultmann and Barth have their own ways of relating Christology and theological anthropology. But in comparison with both of these alternatives, the anthropological pattern of Bonhoeffer's Christology is striking. How should it be explained?

Two points need to be made. The first is that the inner dynamics of Bonhoeffer's Christology itself propel him in this direction. The Christian God is revealed in humanity, in a human being; Christ is the *Christus pro nobis*. Here we see Bonhoeffer appropriating from his Lutheran heritage. He is at once critical and appreciative of Melancthon's celebrated dictum: *"Hoc est Christum cognoscere, beneficia ejus cognoscere; non quod isti* (i.e. die Scholastiker) *docent: ejus naturas, modos incarnationis contueri."*[159] While Bonhoeffer holds that the person must

---

[157] Note the criticism of Luther's doctrine of ubiquity in his eucharistic Christology on the basis of Bonhoeffer's concept of personal presence: GS III 190f., CC 56f.

[158] To be sure, the category of 'Natur' also requires discussion of Christ's role as Mediator of the natural creation independently of human life, i.e. Natur is not only an anthropological category. But I have shown above that it is also an anthropological category; human being is a particular mode of the natural creation.

[159] GS III 176, CC 37.

interpret the work, and cannot be deduced from it, he agrees with the soteriological–anthropological thrust of Lutheran Christology.

> Luther says: 'So it is one thing if God is there, and another if he is there for you' [WA 23, 152]. It is not only useless to meditate on a Christ in himself, but even godless. Hence we can understand Melancthon's resistance in the *Loci,* which ends up a resistance to every Christology. Every Christology condemns itself if it does not put at the beginning the statement: God is only God *pro me,* Christ is only Christ *pro me.* Given this presupposition, then specific Christological work, of course, begins.[160]

But this impulse toward soteriology and anthropology in the Lutheran tradition is not, of itself, enough to give a full explanation.

The second point of the explanation, therefore, comes from what we have previously discovered. Theological anthropology has a major role in Bonhoeffer's thought. It was systematically articulated in *Sanctorum Communio*, it was his chief preoccupation in *Act and Being* and the inaugural lecture, and it features consistently in the courses he taught— particularly those on "Creation and Sin" and the seminar on "Problems of a Theological Anthropology," both given in the semester before the Christology lectures. It is no accident, therefore, that the anthropological categories which Bonhoeffer employs in his exposition of Christ the Mediator are exactly the categories he has consistently used throughout his theological anthropology. For Bonhoeffer, Christology is never found in isolation. The movement of his theology is always found in the *interaction of Christology and anthropology.* The structure and content of the 1933 Christology can only be fully understood when the important status of theological anthropology in his thought is acknowledged.

In this context one must remember that, while Bonhoeffer was a 'Barthian' in Berlin, he was nevertheless a 'Berliner.' He described himself as having been educated in a Ritschlian ethos.[161] He voluntarily took extra study with Harnack in addition to his official courses; on behalf of Harnack's students at his funeral, Bonhoeffer spoke of the pride and responsibility for the future with which he and his fellow students inherited the legacy of Harnack.[162] It is not in the least surprising,

---

160 GS III 182f., CC 48.
161 DBW 10 442; GS III 118.
162 DBW 10 346ff.; GS III 59ff., CW I 29ff.

therefore, that later in prison Bonhoeffer should describe himself as combining the influences both of Barth and liberal theology.

> I feel obliged to tackle these questions ["Mündigkeit," "religionless Christianity," etc.] as one who, although a 'modern' theologian, is still aware of the debt he owes to liberal theology. There will not be many of *the younger people in whom these two trends are combined.*[163]

Nor is it accidental that in the *Letters* an anthropological insight is what causes Bonhoeffer to pose the Christological question yet again.[164]

Before considering the relation between the early and later theology, however, the present discussion must be completed by summarizing the soteriology of the Christology lectures.

3. SOTERIOLOGY

To advance the previous discussion, I will draw together the material in these lectures and in related texts on Christ and the soteriological problem of power. Bonhoeffer's Christology in these lectures is a *theologia crucis*. This is clearly documented by his relocation of the Christological question: it is not the 'how' question about two isolated natures, one divine and the other human; it is the question of the relation of the one divine–human person to his existence for us "in the likeness of sinful flesh."[165] To use Bonhoeffer's technical terms, the Personstruktur of Christus *pro nobis* must be expounded in the Existenzweise of humiliation and exaltation.

Like Luther before him, Bonhoeffer now accords the *weakness* of Christ a special place in the *theologia crucis*.

> Jesus the human being is believed in as God.... If Jesus Christ is to be described as God, then we may not speak of... divine essence, nor of his omnipotence [Allmacht] and omniscience, but *we must speak of this weak* [schwachen] *man* among sinners, of his crib and his cross. When we discuss the divinity of Jesus, *we must speak of exactly this weakness* [Schwachheit].[166]

---

[163] LPP 378, italics mine. This positive estimate of liberal theology does not prevent Bonhoeffer from criticizing it sharply and fundamentally; cf. LPP 285, 327.

[164] See Chapter 6.

[165] GS III 181, CC 46.

[166] GS III 232f., CC 108, italics mine; cf. GS III 236, CC 111.

It is very important to observe that, while Bonhoeffer here appropriates a celebrated Lutheran theme, he also finds it contradicted in Luther and his followers. Thus he criticizes the *genus majestaticum* in the doctrine of the *communicatio idiomatum,* notwithstanding the fact that he considers it "the principal item of Lutheran Christology."[167] Bonhoeffer is thereby not only *appropriating* the theme of the weakness of Christ in the *theologia crucis,* he is *intensifying* it.

There is no explicit statement by Bonhoeffer that this intensification is related to his concern with the soteriological problem of human power. But there are reasons to believe that the two are intimately connected.

The evidence is clearest in several sermons preached in the months before and after the Christology lectures. The most striking statements are found in two sermons given in English to his London congregations in 1934. The second sermon takes II Corinthians 12:9 as its text: "My strength is made perfect in weakness."[168] Bonhoeffer gives several examples of human weakness: "poor people, old people, insane people… a man exploited by society, a coloured man in a white country,[169] an untouchable…." When the Christian message gives a new meaning to the weak, then the charge is made that, in Nietzsche's words, "Christianity is a religion of slaves." The vehement "protest by an aristocratic philosophy of life… glorified strength and power and violence as the ultimate ideals of humanity." Moreover, "Christendom has adjusted itself far too easily to the worship of power."

> Christianity stands or falls with its revolutionary *protest against violence, arbitrariness and pride of power and with its plea for the weak....* Christians should give much more offence, shock the world far more, than they are now doing. Christians should take a stronger stand in favour of the weak rather than consider the possible moral right of the strong.[170]

When Bonhoeffer concludes the sermon with the theological reason for this rejection of power and the Christian commitment to the weak, we find not only a restatement of his Christology but also a passage which could almost have come straight out of the prison letters a decade later.

---

[167] GS III 220ff., CC 94ff.; cf. CC 56ff., 115.

[168] DBW 13 409-12; GS IV 179–182.

[169] Clearly an allusion to his experience among African–Americans in the United States; cf. DB-E 151f., 154ff.

[170] DBW 13 411; GS IV 180f.; Bonhoeffer's English, italics mine.

What is the reason for this new explanation of the meaning of weakness in the world? ...Because God suffers in the world through man and whenever he comes he has to suffer from man again. God suffered on the cross. Therefore *all human suffering and weakness is a sharing in God's own suffering and weakness in the world....* "My strength is made perfect in weakness," says God. Whenever a man in a position of weakness—physical or social or moral or religious weakness—is aware of his existence with God, he shares God's life, ...God's grace, God's love.... God glorifies himself in the weak as he glorified himself on the cross. God is mighty where man is nothing.[171]

"Sharing in the sufferings of God at the hands of a godless world" is a theme in the prison theology to be discussed in the next chapter.[172] For

----

[171] DBW 13 412; GS IV 181f.; Bonhoeffer's English, italics mine.

[172] Here I must anticipate that analysis in relation to the discussion in Chapter 4 about the unresolved conflicts in *Discipleship* on power, strength, and weakness as Christological and anthropological motifs; Bonhoeffer was working on *Discipleship* at the time of this 1934 sermon. In the sermon there is no distinction between power and strength, nor any suggestion that there are some forms of weakness which Christianity cannot encourage. (Indeed, he makes statements here which would later be rejected in the *Letters*.) "Christian love and help for the weak means humiliation of the strong before the weak, of the healthy before the suffering, of the mighty before the exploited.... Weakness in the eyes of Christ is not the imperfect over against the perfect, rather is strength the imperfect and weakness the perfect" (DBW 13 411, GS IV 181). See also the statement quoted above which says indiscriminately that in all forms of weakness one shares in God's life; one of the main reasons why 'religion' is so vehemently attacked in the prison theology is precisely because it is rooted in weakness and serves to reinforce it. That Bonhoeffer has not yet resolved the dynamics of weakness, power, and strength can be further seen by comparing this sermon with the November, 1932 address, "Dein Reich komme!" To otherworldly weaklings Bonhoeffer says: "be not otherworldly, but be strong." Christ does help the weak person, though "Christ does not will or intend this weakness; instead he makes the person strong." Secular Christians, on the other hand, love nothing more than a good fight in worldly power struggles under a divine banner of their own hoisting; to them Bonhoeffer says, "Become weak in the world and let God be the Lord" (trans. John Godsey, PB 28–31). This position is much closer to the prison letters than the 1934 sermon; but it does not yet move out from the weakness of Christ to affirm the strengths of secular people, as the letters do. While this ambivalence is apparent, however, it should be noted that the main point of the 1934 sermon is a polemic, based on the weakness of Christ, against oppressive power in society; *this* conviction is certainly not retracted in the later theology. The same lack of distinction between power and strength is found in the January, 1933 sermon, "Die Furcht." In a criticism of the human search for false securities, Bonhoeffer includes the statement that all security and freedom from fear derives from faith in the crucified Christ alone, and not from one's strength or the strength of other people (DBW 12 446; GS IV 108; there is some

the present the clear connection of the Christological theme of Christ's weakness with the soteriological problem of human power should be noted. Bonhoeffer's *theologia crucis* is directed not primarily to the problem of the guilty conscience, as in Luther, but to the modern problem of power—power used arbitrarily and violently to dominate and exploit the weak.

If that sermon is oriented more to the critique of power in social exploitation,[173] the other is directed more to individual life. It has several highly autobiographical allusions. The text is, "A man's heart deviseth his way: but the Lord directeth his steps."[174] While many factors influence people's lives, they exert "an extremely strong, inflexible, incomparable will-power" to attain their ambitions. "Everyone forges his own luck,"[175] as the old German proverb has it. "Our fate depends entirely on our will-power, our work, our sacrifices..." it is commonly believed. Here is the fighting spirit of the proud, individualistic drive for success, the ethos of the competitive work–ethic. So a man pursues his dreams and the imaginations of his heart. But sooner or later this powerful, ambitious, and successful man finds his way crossed by the cross of Christ. God, like a superior chess player ostensibly giving ground before the bold moves of the other player, retreats to the cross where divine victory and human defeat are strangely and unexpectedly revealed.[176] Only through the death of self–will and power at the cross of Christ does one enter the divine kingdom and find life. In this sermon we again find striking confirmation of power as the soteriological problem, and the weakness of God in the crucified Christ as the divine strength which liberates people to true life from their own egotistical and individualistic ambition.

With such clear evidence only brief reference is needed to other material which confirms this point. Bonhoeffer continues to focus his definition of sin on the problem of power. Thus in the Bethel Confession

----

ambiguity in the statement itself, since "Kraft" here may have the connotation of power rather than strength). In the prison letters Bonhoeffer would certainly not argue that all human strengths are to be discounted or that faith and natural human securities are inevitably in conflict.

[173] In addition to the reference to aristocratic disdain of the poor and weak, see the discussion of bourgeois paternalism on DBW 13 411; GS IV 181.

[174] Proverbs 16:9; DBW 13 404-408; GS IV 174–179.

[175] "Jeder ist seines Glückes Schmied."

[176] Chess was one of Bonhoeffer's favorite games; cf. DB-E xx.

he asserts—with a clear allusion to the lust for power in the Nazi movement—that the meaning of the gospel is repentance, not the will to victory.[177] Again, he states that the orders of preservation are to protect people from the self–destructiveness of licentious egotism and selfishness [Selbstsucht].[178] Further, the "Gideon" sermon, Bonhoeffer's first after Hitler came to power, proclaims that the divine strength, glory and victory is revealed in the weakness of Christ's cross, over against the Reich's search for might and glory through military power; Gideon, who hears God's Word, not Siegfried the warrior–hero, is faith's paradigm for the true creature of God.[179] Finally, the sermon "Moses–und Aarons–Kirche,"[180] given during the Christology lectures and just after a major victory of the German Christians, is a potent proclamation of the crucified Christ over against the deification of worldly power. While Moses waits for the Word of God on Sinai, the people clamor for manifest deity and sacrifice their dearest possessions in a veritable religious orgy; Aaron presides over their deification of human thoughts and values and leads them in usurping the divine omnipotence [Allmacht].

> The worldly church celebrates its triumph, the priest has proved his power [Macht], and now he himself stands in the center [Mitte][181] in his purple robe and holy crown and worships the creature of his own

---

[177] DBW 12 391; GS II 109.

[178] DBW 12 375; GS II 99.

[179] DBW 12 447-54; GS IV 109–117. For the cult of the hero in the Third Reich, including discussions of Siegfried, see Alfred Rosenberg's *Der Mythus des 20. Jahrhunderts* (Munich: Hoheneichen–Verlag, 1930); after Hitler's *Mein Kampf,* Rosenberg's was the most popular book of the Reich. Its 1939 edition (149.–159 Auflage!) is dedicated to the "heroes" of the German armies. Konrad Heiden wrote: "The decisive factor in human society was, to Rosenberg, the outstanding personality, the great lone wolf, the creative superman. This idea was not new, but it well fitted Hitler's purpose...."; see Heiden's "Introduction" to Ralph Manheim's translation of Hitler's *Mein Kampf* (Boston: Houghton Mifflin Company, 1943), p. xvi. Strange as it now seems, Rosenberg's book was never translated into English until 1982; but see Albert R. Chandler, *Rosenberg's Nazi Myth* (Ithaca, New York: Cornell University Press, 1945), esp. p. 123 for Rosenberg's 1942 proposal that *Mein Kampf* and a sword should replace the Bible and the cross on church altars.

[180] DBW 12 459-65; GS IV 123–129, CW I 243–248.

[181] This is surely a deliberate use of the term 'Mitte,' its contrast to the meaning in the Christology lectures heightening Bonhoeffer's picture of the political and religious perversion of Christianity in National Socialism and the German Christians.

hand. And all around him the people [Volk] bow down happily, looking up at the god they have made with their own power [Kraft] and their own sacrifice.[182]

In opposition to this unbridled glorification of destructive human power, Christ is clad in purple robe, crowned with thorns, and enthroned on a cross—the end of all idolatry.

The examination of the Christology lectures in relation to other courses, addresses, and sermons of the period indicate that Bonhoeffer's concern with the soteriological problem of power extends across the whole range of human experience. We have seen how, in the academic context of the lecture room, Bonhoeffer reiterates his long–standing critique of *logos* as an instrument of power and dominance in the self's relations to the world and to other persons. He still speaks of sin as willfulness [Eigenwille],[183] of the human *logos* in its Kraft, Herrschaft and Macht making inordinate claims for the self,[184] of people's resisting the "other" (Christ, the neighbor) who is a Grenze to their own self–assertion;[185] this exercise of egocentric power imprisons the self in its own authority as a *cor curvum in se* who must be liberated by the *pro–me* being of Christ in order to love others. In more political material he sets the crucified Christ in critical contrast to the glorification of power and military might in the Third Reich. In broader social and historical observations he takes his stand with the weak Christ against the aristocratic glorification of "strength and power and violence" and Christendom's too easy adjustment to the "worship of power"; Christians should identify with the weak and oppose the "violence, arbitrariness and power" of those who oppress the weak. In the pastoral context he urges his congregation to let their lives be ruled from the cross and not dominated by the bourgeois, individualistic, competitive work–ethic with its formula: ambitious will–power equals success.

The cross of Christ is the ultimate sign of Christ's being *pro–nobis*. The weakness of the crucified Christ is not only a critique of destructive power. It is also the way for a person to enter into the being of Christ as being–for–others. In the Word of the cross the Transzendenz question is intrinsic to the Existenz question; self–centered power gives way to

---

[182] DBW 12 463; GS IV 127, CW I 247.

[183] GS III 236.

[184] GS III 169, CC 29f. Note that no distinction is made between Kraft and Macht in this passage.

[185] GS III 170f., CC 31.

love for others, and we are freed for that personal and corporate existence in love for which we were created and toward which we move in the kingdom of God. The Mediator frees people from power over others, and its attendant self–isolation, to freedom for others in the co–humanity of love.

Here we see in 1933 that *theologia crucis* which is subordinated to the power Christ by the time *Discipleship* is published in 1937. The 1933 Christology, however, does not disclose the contradictions later found in *Discipleship,* even though the foundations for that book were laid several months prior to the Christology lectures. But the anthropology is more ambiguous in 1932–33, as we have just seen; the ambiguity is at the point of the relations between power, strength and weakness. This anthropological ambiguity will continue and be intensified in *Discipleship.* All of this we have seen in Chapter 4.

In the *Letters* these problems are resolved. But the *Letters* have much more significance for the early theology than this resolution. The relation of the theology of sociality and the theology of "religionless Christianity" is therefore the subject of the next chapter.

Chapter 6

THE PRISON LETTERS AND THE THEOLOGY OF SOCIALITY

The theology of the prison letters, Bonhoeffer's most discussed and most influential writings, not only confirms this analysis of his early theology; it also gains indispensable illumination when seen in the light of his theology of sociality. Indeed, the substance of these informal theological reflections cannot properly be appreciated without reference to the three focal concerns of the early theology: sociality, Christology and anthropology, and soteriology.

The exposition is shaped by this two–way relationship. A comprehensive analysis of every important question which is discussed in the theology of "religionless Christianity" cannot be presented here, any more than the examination of *Discipleship* could evaluate every detail of that book. Nor is a full account possible of the development—in its intellectual and biographical aspects—which brought Bonhoeffer to the position articulated in his final writings. In short, a comprehensive and definitive interpretation of Bonhoeffer's theology from 1933 to 1944 remains to be written. Within the limits appropriate to this book, however, I contend that the heart of the prison theology is presented here. Accordingly, I also believe that the basic dynamics of the development from *Sanctorum Communio* through *Discipleship* to *Letters and Papers from Prison* are clearly disclosed here. What remain to be expounded further are the details of this development.

This chapter has two parts. The first section discusses three topics: Bonhoeffer's anthropological category, "Mündigkeit" or "Autonomie"; his critique of "religion"; and his "non–religious interpretation" of Christianity. In this exposition the concerns with sociality, anthropology

247

and Christology, and soteriology connect the early theology and the prison writings. The second section of the chapter concludes the work with some suggestions about Bonhoeffer's contribution to contemporary theology.

A. THE THEOLOGY OF RELIGIONLESS CHRISTIANITY

There are three inter–related subjects under discussion in the prison letters: the "coming of age" of modern people, the critique of religion, and the proposal for a "non–religious" Christianity. The first is the anthropological question, the second is a polemical clarification of the question and the answer, and the third is the Christological and anthropological answer.

1. MÜNDIGKEIT: THE NEW ANTHROPOLOGICAL QUESTION

When Bonhoeffer begins to articulate his new stage of theological reflection in the letter of April 30, 1944, he raises the issue: "what Christianity really is, or indeed who Christ really is, for us today."[1] This issue is posed by the conviction that "we are moving towards a completely religionless time; people as they are now simply cannot be religious any more."[2] The positive category by which Bonhoeffer describes the non–religious, or post–religious, condition of modern people is that of Mündigkeit; this anthropological observation raises the issue of Christ and the nature of Christianity and leads to the answer which is given in the following letters. Mündigkeit is the one quite new ingredient in Bonhoeffer's thought at this time; it is the yeast which ferments in his prison theology. The distinctive, and to some extent, new emphasis in the Christology of the prison letters is intrinsically related to this anthropological question. In the prison letters also, then, is found the interaction of anthropology and Christology which was demonstrated at earlier stages of Bonhoeffer's theological development.

The essence of the category Mündigkeit is human *autonomy.* More particularly, this autonomy is one which involves the strength and

---

[1] LPP 279.
[2] Ibid.

competence of all those human activities of the unified and conscious self specified in the working definition of the 'ego.'[3] The person who has "come of age" is, above all, someone with a healthy, strong, and well developed set of ego skills. This is obvious in Bonhoeffer's account of the historical development of increasing human autonomy, humanity's "coming of age."

Like other contemporary theologians such as Bultmann and Tillich, Bonhoeffer in the *Letters* works with a historically developmental anthropology. Religion is seen as *"a historically conditioned and transient form of human self–expression,"* depending upon *"temporally conditioned presuppositions";* it is "one particular *stage"* in human history.[4] Growing out of this former stage, Bonhoeffer traces the movement to a human condition where people are "radically religionless"; the process has reached an "undoubted completion" by the middle of the twentieth century.[5] The movement towards human *autonomy* [6] [menschliche Autonomie] begins, roughly, in the High Middle Ages of Europe. The Renaissance and the Enlightenment mark two decisive steps along the way.[7]

In the Renaissance, Montaigne taught an ethic of independent moral principles whose validity did not rest upon the Decalogue; Hugo Grotius

---

[3]   See Chapter 4.

[4]   LPP 280, 327, italics mine.

[5]   LPP 280, 325.

[6]   WE 476, LPP 325; cf. WE 530, LPP 359: "Autonomie der Welt"; italics mine.

[7]   In a valuable article, Ernst Feil has proved that Bonhoeffer's historical perspective on the development of autonomy and Mündigkeit, and a number of major concepts ("Autonomie," "Mündigkeit," "Innerlichkeit," "religiöse Metaphysik," "Weltlichkeit"), are taken over from Wilhelm Dilthey. Bonhoeffer read in prison three books by Dilthey which provided him with this perspective and these concepts: *Das Erlebnis und die Dichtung, Von deutscher Dichtung und Musik,* and *Weltanschauung und Analyse des Menschen seit Renaissance und Reformation.* Feil also points out where Bonhoeffer departs from Dilthey, e.g., the latter valued "Innerlichkeit," whereas Bonhoeffer included it in his criticism of religion (see below). To Feil's illuminating contribution on this intellectual impulse to Bonhoeffer's prison theology, I add the insistence that the *autobiographical* significance of the affirmation of Autonomie and Mündigkeit cannot be ignored; on this point, see below. For Feil's precise and persuasive argument, see his "Der Einfluss Wilhelm Diltheys auf Dietrich Bonhoeffers 'Widerstand und Ergebung'," *Evangelische Theologie,* vol. 29, December, 1969, pp. 662–674; now included in his *The Theology of Dietrich Bonhoeffer* (Philadelphia: Fortress Press, 1985). The same discovery of Dilthey's influence was made

spoke of international law as grounded in the law of nature, not divine sanction; Machiavelli, with his doctrine of "reasons of state," established politics as an autonomous realm; in natural science Nicolas of Cusa and Giordano Bruno taught the infinity of space, which presupposes that the cosmos is self–subsisting; Descartes and Spinoza gave philosophical expression to this—in the one case deistic and the other pantheistic; but both regard the cosmos as self–subsisting. Precursors of the Enlightenment Deists, such as Lord Herbert of Cherbury, based theology itself in human reason rather than divine revelation.[8]

In the Enlightenment, the Newtonian cosmology viewed the world as an independent mechanism. The anthropological self–understanding which accompanies the scientific and intellectual developments is, significantly, expressed in terms of stages of human growth to autonomous adulthood. Humanity, Bonhoeffer says, has "come of age." He might well have cited Lessing's periodization of human history as passing through three stages: childhood, adolescence, and adulthood. Or he could have noted that Kant described the Enlightenment as humanity liberating itself from tutelage and immaturity [Unmündigkeit] by the courageous and independent use of reason.

Mündigkeit and *autonomy*, then, are interchangeable terms.[9] In the historical development Bonhoeffer sketches, he refers particularly to various intellectual developments in science and philosophy. But by the middle of the twentieth century, human Mündigkeit and autonomy characterize not only "the scientific [wissenschaftlich] field" but also "human affairs generally."[10] The movement of increasing human *knowledge, power, and control* has now come to pervade the whole life posture. Nature is controlled by technology, the application of the scientific discoveries of the past several centuries.[11] In medicine, farming, transportation and communications, and other fields, human independence of

---

independently by Christian Gremmels; see his "Mündigkeit—Geschichte und Entfaltung eines Begriffs" in *Die Mitarbeit* 18 (1969), pp. 360–72.

  8   LPP 359.

  9   See the interchangeable usage particularly in the letter of July 16, 1944, LPP 359ff. Note that the phrase in this letter, "the autonomy of humanity and the world," is equivalent to that in the previous letter of July 89, 1944, "die Mündigkeit der Welt und des Menschen" (WE 511, LPP 346). These two phrases also make it quite clear that when Bonhoeffer speaks of "the *world* come of age," this is an *anthropological* statement; see also WE 476f., LPP 325f., where "menschliche Autonomie" and "mündig gewordenen Welt" are equivalents.

  10   WE 477, LPP 326.

and control over nature is documented by numerous and often spectacular achievements. Society, similarly, is also organized by the same attitude of analysis, knowledge, planning and organization. Bonhoeffer mentions insurance[12] as one example of planning which makes social life more secure. He could also have instanced government social security programs, economic planning, medical care, retirement plans, population control, sociological research, and efforts at world organization as further examples. To be sure, Bonhoeffer is aware that social organization has been far less successful than control of nature, for in society human beings come face to face with themselves and their own organization. Here is the real problem: *human beings themselves.*[13] Nevertheless, the attitude of independence and autonomy, of taking responsibility for shaping the future of society, of finding new and effective methods for dealing with problems, is as characteristic of the modern approach to society and history as of the modern attitude toward nature.

This initial outline of the meaning of humanity's coming of age clarifies several points on which Bonhoeffer has been misinterpreted. First, it is clear that the judgment that modern people have come of age, and are therefore radically without religion, is not a judgment about world history. It refers to those people who have shaped and been shaped by the Western development he describes. "Humanity come of age" is chiefly found among the people of the contemporary West in Europe and America; the phrase particularly applies to that social group to which Bonhoeffer and his own family and friends belonged. That portion of humanity has come of age whose psychic and social life has been decisively shaped by the intellectual tradition of the Renaissance and the Enlightenment and their practical consequences. They are the people whose thought embraces the scientific view of the cosmos; whose science and technology understands and controls nature; and whose social organization provides them much more security and confidence in the world than their ancestors enjoyed. In short, modern people have much more *knowledge, power, and control* over their lives and destiny than medieval or ancient people ever had.

This leads to the second clarification. Bonhoeffer employs a metaphor, Mündigkeit, from the process of human maturation to describe a new

---

11 LPP 380.

12 LPP 380.

13 Ibid.

stage of human self–understanding and a new historical style of acting in the world. It is important to note that the metaphor refers to the point of transition from adolescence to adulthood. Literally it means reaching the stage of independence of, and autonomy from, parental control. Those who are mündig are no longer children, *dependent* upon their parents. They are *independent,* and responsible for themselves. They must think for themselves and make their own decisions. They are accountable for their own actions before the law. They have rights and freedoms which were not theirs as children. They are not expected to be continually running back to their parents to solve their problems. Bonhoeffer applied this metaphor to the growth of human powers and the corresponding decay of "religion" as depending upon God to be a *"deus ex machina,"* "stop–gap," and "working hypothesis." It should be obvious, though many have misunderstood Bonhoeffer on this point, that to speak of increasing human knowledge, power, and control as a "coming of age" which involves a greater independence and autonomy than previously in history is *not* to imply that modern people are necessarily better, more moral, or more Christian than their ancestors. To turn twenty–one is no guarantee of moral goodness; it is not an automatic door to increased care and responsibility for one's neighbors.

Mündigkeit, then, does not imply a doctrine of human ethical progress or an optimistic doctrine of history, even though it does involve a change in psychic posture.[14] The prison letters contain numerous criticisms, which many readers have carelessly ignored, of contemporary people and society. Bonhoeffer was, after all, painfully aware of the brutalities of the Nazi regime in whose prison he wrote! A person "can insure against everything, except against human beings." People can cope with everything, except the menace of themselves and their own organization.[15] Efficiency experts, demigods and lunatics know nothing about human relationships; for many the experience of the *humanum* is unknown, and human beings are merely things.[16] Irrational forces have great power in the world, as evidenced particularly in the world war.[17] Cities are often places of death; bureaucracy invades a person's proper privacy, and huge organizations frustrate people's needs for personal

---

[14] See below.
[15] WE 557, LPP 380.
[16] LPP 386.
[17] LPP 298.

relationships in manageable communities.[18] Culture is generally impoverished, and a shallow and banal secularism knows nothing of faith or discipline.[19] Envy, greed, suspicion, fear, and hate continue their evil deeds as of old.[20] Such things are what Bonhoeffer has in mind when he speaks of "God's sufferings at the hands of a godless world"; this is why "the world must be understood better than it understands itself."[21] But the Mündigkeit of modern people is better understood not by religious polemics and subversion, but "on the basis of the gospel and in the light of Christ."[22] His awareness of the godlessness of the modern world, however, did not lead Bonhoeffer to deny or undermine the very real strengths possessed by contemporary humanity.

This leads to the third clarification. Mündigkeit, *in the first instance,* is a *general anthropological category,* not a theological concept. To be sure, in his proposal for a non–religious interpretation of Christianity, Bonhoeffer's chief concern is to give a theological affirmation and a Christological shape to the new strength and autonomy of modern people whose origins and manifestations he has described. But initially, Mündigkeit (and its corresponding non–religiousness) is simply a new human phenomenon in history. Bonhoeffer describes the historical development as resulting from various human achievements. It has not been sponsored by the church; indeed, the church has more often opposed it, and Bonhoeffer's most scathing criticism is reserved for those religious apologists who continue their pointless, ignoble, and unchristian tactics of subversion.[23] Mündigkeit and autonomy, further, are not categories derived from the Bible and the theological tradition; rather, precisely the historical novelty of this human phenomenon leads Bonhoeffer to examine Scripture and Christology to see what light may be cast upon it. Nor does he claim that secular autonomy is the logical outworking in history of certain Christian perceptions about humanity and the world; it is a development which has proceeded according to *autonomous* principles—empirical research, technical experimentation, philosophical presuppositions, and so forth. To ask "how can Christ

---

[18] LPP 296; cf. 299, 380.

[19] LPP 369.

[20] LPP 390.

[21] LPP 328.

[22] LPP 329.

[23] LPP 327.

become Lord also of the religionless,"[24] how to "claim for Jesus Christ a world that has come of age"[25] is to acknowledge that, in the first instance, Mündigkeit is simply a general human phenomenon whose relationship to Christianity requires investigation. It is when Bonhoeffer sketches his "non–religious Christianity" that the general anthropological category of Mündigkeit first receives specific theological status and content. This theological appropriation of Mündigkeit is discussed below.

As a general anthropological category, and prior to its theological interpretation, Bonhoeffer makes it plain that Mündigkeit is not a positive theological norm; the secular attitude does not become an independent source for the content of Christian thinking. Accordingly, he argues that

> the weakness of liberal theology was that it conceded to the world the right to determine Christ's place in the world; in the conflict between the church and the world it accepted the comparatively easy terms of peace that the world dictated. Its strength was that it did not try to put the clock back....[26]

Although it is not a positive norm of content, Mündigkeit does have a critical function. Bonhoeffer indicates two interrelated aspects: the development of human autonomy "clears away a false conception of God" and clarifies the human situation before God.[27] Mündigkeit, in the first instance, has a negative, critical function. By clearing away false concepts of God and humanity, it enables the Bible to be read in a new way. In describing a new human phenomenon in history it poses the theological question: how is God properly understood, and what is the true human situation before God? Before these questions can be answered in the non–religious interpretation, the error in the "religious" answer must be exposed.

---

24 WE 404, LPP 280.

25 LPP 342.

26 LPP 327; the reference to Barth in this context further strengthens my point. At the end of the letter Bonhoeffer makes the statement that Mündigkeit is better understood "on the basis of the gospel and in the light of Christ," not out of the autonomous, secular attitude itself (LPP 329). Cf. also LPP 362: the godlessness of people who have come of age must not be concealed but exposed in a new light.

27 WE 534f., LPP 361.

Before turning to the critique of religion, however, we must consider the significance of Bonhoeffer's affirmation of human autonomy and strength in relation to his previous theological development.

First, there is a clear differentiation between strength and power. Bonhoeffer now gives unreserved affirmation to all forms of human strength, without diminishing his critique of power. We have seen above how his criticism of the Nazi regime remained uncompromising. Similarly he insists that the church must particularly rid itself of the vices of "hubris and power–worship" [Anbetung der Kraft].[28] When he had made exactly the same point in the 1934 sermon, criticizing the church for its easy adjustment to "the worship of power," there was no indication that power, domination, and exploitation could be negated while simultaneously affirming both personal and social strengths. Here in the letters the distinction is clearly made. To refer back to the two main themes in the definition of power,[29] Bonhoeffer continues in the prison theology to criticize power as authoritarian superiority and domination, while simultaneously affirming power as "capacity necessary for self–fulfillment"; it is the latter which he refers to in the terms Mündigkeit, autonomy, and strength.[30]

Second, it is striking that the human strengths which Bonhoeffer affirms in the development of autonomy and Mündigkeit are strengths of the *ego*. The working definition of the ego listed such functions of the conscious self as rational analysis and organization of the natural world and human society; projecting and willing specific activities and goals; calculating consequences; problem solving; and intellectual analysis, perception, judgment, and evaluation. Precisely these ego skills have been developed and proved effective in the various fields of problem–solving which Bonhoeffer discusses and implies: scientific research, industrial and farming technology, medicine, social and economic planning, insurance, and so on. The activities of reason have taken over the solving of problems formerly in the province of religious ritual.

---

[28] WE 560, LPP 383. In the context of saying that the church should be serving and helping, not dominating or ruling [herrschend], "Kraft" is properly translated as "power."

[29] See the beginning of Chapter 4.

[30] The two terms used throughout the letters are 'Stärke' and 'Kraft.' The latter term can have in German the same two sets of meaning as the English 'power'; it is clear from the many contexts where is it used in the letters that it is power in the positive sense of 'strength' which is meant. Cf., for example, WE 407, 455, 471, 478, 504, 548, 551, 574.

This affirmation of ego strengths is all the more notable in that Bonhoeffer makes it in terms of the historical development of human *autonomy*. This affirmation of the strengths of the healthy, human ego is quite evidently more than a general theological celebration of certain salient characteristics of modern people. It is also a personal affirmation of precisely those strengths and gifts which Bonhoeffer himself so notably possessed and which his family had nourished. This explains the sense of personal excitement and discovery which no perceptive reader of the prison letters can overlook. This theological stage, too, has for Bonhoeffer its "autobiographical dimension." What he wrote to his godson and grandnephew about the legacy inherited by the child, applied equally to himself.

> The urban culture of the bourgeois tradition embodied in the home of your mother's parents[31] has created in its bearers the proud conscious-ness of a calling to high public responsibility, to intellectual achievement and leadership, and the deep–rooted sense of obligation to be guard-ians of a great historical legacy and cultural tradition; it will give you, even before you realize it, a way of thinking and acting which you can never lose without being untrue to yourself.[32]

Citing the same passage, Charles West correctly observes:

> His nonreligious man in the 'world come of age' was precisely this bourgeois humanist, as he knew him in his father, his relatives, his friends, and his co–conspirators in the plot to assassinate Hitler and reestablish responsible government in Germany. They were heirs of a long tradition of expanding science and of coping with society 'without calling for the help of the "working hypothesis: God."'[33]

The "bourgeois humanist" and "nonreligious man" was also, of course, Dietrich Bonhoeffer himself;[34] not least among the "relatives" with whom he was profoundly reunited in the resistance conspiracy were his own two elder brothers, as well as his father. Bonhoeffer was not untrue

---

[31] Rüdiger and Ursula Schleicher; Ursula was Bonhoeffer's own elder sister.

[32] WE 429, LPP 294f.

[33] *The Power to be Human: Toward a Secular Theology* (New York: Macmillan, 1971), 262f.

[34] Cf. LPP 295, the paragraph following the sentences just quoted: "Your great–uncle [i.e., Bonhoeffer himself] ...is striving to keep up the spirit—so far as he understands it—which he sees embodied in the home of his parents and your great–grandparents." For other reflections on the importance of Bonhoeffer's family to him, see LPP 165, and especially 40; here, almost a year before he

to himself, to his intellectual achievements, his gifts of leadership, and his sense of responsibility for a great cultural heritage.

Biographically, then, the context of the prison theology is this. Bonhoeffer, as a Christian, had now truly found freedom from the ambitiousness of self, and the competitiveness it entailed. This was true freedom because it no longer had to take the form of submission, renunciation, and self–denial; it now had the form of serving and self–giving. In the resistance movement he entered into an authentic freedom for others. This fulfilled freedom then allowed him to affirm his own strengths, now with the confident knowledge that they were no longer self–serving; the suppression of the ego strength and autonomy advocated in *Discipleship* was no longer necessary. Obedience had led to freedom, but a freedom greater than he had earlier understood. In the same social situation he was also bound together, as never before, with his elder brothers and his father, from whom he had earlier found it necessary to distance himself. In them, and their associates, he found the responsible exercise of human strengths.[35] United in this partnership, he was able to affirm in himself the strengths which they all possessed.[36] He was also obliged to rethink the Christian message, so that it could engage

---

speaks of the "existing for others" of Christ and the Christian, he describes the common life of the Bonhoeffer family as "füreinander tun und denken" (WE 72). Further, as in *Sanctorum Communio* he said that the patriarchal family was the most similar social form to the church as a distinctive social structure (SC-E 263), so here he says that the earthly family is a Gemeinschaft which is a reflection [Abglanz] of God's fatherhood over all people (WE 79, LPP 46). These comments confirm my suggestion in Chapter 4 that his experience of his family was a formative contribution to Bonhoeffer's theology of sociality.

[35] Three observations by Bethge say a lot in a few words about Bonhoeffer's relationship to his family and its significance for his theological development. In the face of the predominantly scientific attitude in the family and the disdain of his elder brothers for the church, Bonhoeffer found it "more worthwhile to become a theologian than a parson and to deal in that way with other people's philosophies and agnosticism." Later he left the brothers of the Finkenwalde Bruderhaus to join a different circle of fellow workers. "He again joined his own brothers in their political efforts and found himself among comrades who knew little of his Finkenwalde associates." A new turn was made. "The enthusiastically rediscovered church [expressed in *Discipleship* and the Confessing Church] turned out to be sterile in its conception, and liberal brothers and friends turned out to do the necessary Christian deeds. This situation had to be penetrated and theologically verbalized in a way that expressed the true character of Christ and the true character of those worldly, secularized men. It was to serve this purpose that Bonhoeffer set out to rewrite his theology under the rubric of 'non–religious interpretation of the Gospel in a world come of age.'" Cf. "Turning Points in

such strong, autonomous, non–religious people. The problematic status of religion, and the question of true Christianity, then, had as much existential urgency for Bonhoeffer as the affirmation of Mündigkeit.

2. THE CRITIQUE OF 'RELIGION'

In analyzing Bonhoeffer's critique of religion, three initial observations should be made.[37] First, Bonhoeffer completely separates Christianity and 'religion.' While he allows that in the past Christianity had a religious form,[38] there is no sense in which his contemporary reinterpretation of Christianity involves any rehabilitation or justification of religion as he defines it. In this his position is different from Barth who, after his attack on all religion (including Christianity) as unbelief, presents a view of Christianity as "true religion" under the rubric of the doctrine of justification by grace.[39] Although Bonhoeffer claims that Barth began the theological critique of religion which he is extending, there is a significant difference between their respective definitions of religion.[40] Barth uses

Bonhoeffer's Life and Thought," *Union Seminary Quarterly Review,* XXIII.1 (Fall, 1967), pp. 9, 12f., 19.

[36] Bethge describes Bonhoeffer's friendship with Oskar Hammelsbeck in the early 1940s in terms related to my interpretation. Hammelsbeck, a student of Jaspers, had worked in adult education and socialism, and then became a member of the Confessing Church; the general course of his life was rather similar to Bonhoeffer's. Bethge writes: "Hammelsbeck was trying to keep together his new church service and the secular sphere of life, which had once been his own, and not at all leave it to its own devices. In so doing he found a partner in Bonhoeffer who had once tried to leave his earlier sphere of life behind him *both inwardly and outwardly, but who was now newly relating secular and Christian* [literally: kirchliche] *existence to each other* " (DB 802, DB-E 714, italics mine).

[37] In the following argument, as in the preceding discussion of Mündigkeit, I am drawing upon my previous research. See *Bonhoeffer's Concept of Religion. An Essay in Interpretation,* S.T.M. thesis, (New York: Union Theological Seminary, 1964); "Bonhoeffer's Concept of Religion," *Union Seminary Quarterly Review,* XIX.1 (November, 1963), pp. 11–21; "Sociality and Church in Bonhoeffer's 1933 Christology," *Scottish Journal of Theology,* 21.4 (December, 1968) esp. pp. 432ff.

[38] LPP 280.

[39] *Church Dogmatics* I/2, "The Revelation of God as the Abolition of Religion," p. 280–361 (Edinburgh: T. & T. Clark, 1956). The translation of "Aufhebung" as "abolition" is misleading in that it does not take account of the negative and positive meanings of the German word, and thus distracts the reader from Barth's point that revelation "abolishes" religion and also establishes Christianity as a "true religion" of God's grace.

more general, theological categories such as "idolatry" and "self–justification" in his critique of religion. While Bonhoeffer's position is compatible with this, he formulates the phenomenon of religion in a much more anthropological way and describes it in terms of a quite specific historical form. He is describing the particular ways in which "religious" people actually behave in the present situation, rather than proposing a general theory of religion which would hold good for all times and cultures. The reason both for Bonhoeffer's complete separation of Christianity from religion, and for his difference from Barth, is found in his own distinctive definition of religion.

Second, when Bonhoeffer speaks of the 'religious' posture he sees some people still adopting, he is referring to a phenomenon which flourished in a previous historical stage. If the development of human autonomy and Mündigkeit simultaneously means the dying of religion, then people who continue to act in a 'religious' way are the last survivors of a dying life–style; if religion is not completely dead—and Bonhoeffer is not concerned with absolute judgments—it is certainly moribund. What he finds to be more typical is that even people who honestly describe themselves as 'religious' do not very often behave in a religious way; they therefore mean something quite different by the word.[41]

Third, and amplifying these two points, it follows that when Bonhoeffer defines religion in his own particular way, he is describing a form of religion which has been decisively affected by the process of growing human knowledge, strength, and autonomy. As Ebeling points out, such religion is a product of relatively recent historical developments.[42]

Bonhoeffer's position on religion can now be discussed under two heads: its essence and manifestations, and his critique.[43]

---

[40] LPP 280, 286, 328; cf. the comparison of Barth and Bonhoeffer in my *Bonhoeffer's Concept of Religion,* cited above, note 37.

[41] LPP 279.

[42] See "The 'Non–religious Interpretation of Biblical Concepts,'" *Word and Faith* (Philadelphia: Fortress Press, 1963), pp. 133f. While Ebeling is basically correct, his stress on the specific historical locus of Bonhoeffer's description of religion should not obscure the possible fruitfulness of using Bonhoeffer's model to analyze the nature of religion in previous historical periods and in different societies and cultures. A particularly fruitful study would be a comparison of Bonhoeffer's critique of religion with that of Freud with his thesis that religion is rooted in anxiety, regression, and projection. An earlier historical figure who began on the line which Freud sophisticated psychologically was David Hume; he argued that religion was based in anxiety, ignorance, and imagination. Bonhoeffer, however, does not draw upon or even discuss

The essence and manifestations of religion. The essence of 'religion' which Bonhoeffer portrays has two main components. Anthropologically, religion is rooted in human weakness: danger, ignorance, fear, sickness, and so on. Corresponding to this human weakness, and indeed compensating for it, is the religious view that the essence of God is *power.* God is the power upon whom people call in times of weakness, usually emergencies and crises. The relationship of a weak person to the power God in religion, then, is one of *dependence;* dependence links human weakness and the power of God. *Weakness,* human *dependence,* and the *power God,* therefore, are the essence of the religious posture.[44] Several statements and examples quickly verify this summary.[45]

> Religiosity makes people look in their *distress* [Not] to the *power* [Macht] of God in the world: God is the *deus ex machina.*[46]

> Religious people speak of God when human knowledge runs out (often because they are too lazy to think), or *when human strengths* [Kräfte] *fail*—it is really the *deus ex machina* they trot out, either to seemingly solve insoluble problems or as *strength* [Kraft] in human

---

Hume and Freud; he arrived at his own position independently. Further discussion of Bonhoeffer and Freud is found later in this chapter.

[43] In the following I am presenting my own systematic organization. Bonhoeffer did not offer a comprehensive definition of religion, though he makes occasional summary statements of a general kind. For example, he links religion to "the temporally conditioned presuppositions of metaphysics, inwardness, etc. etc." (WE 405, LPP 280). In the following letter he says that a religious interpretation speaks "metaphysically and ... individualistically" (WE 414, LPP 285f.). In my article, "Bonhoeffer's Concept of Religion," cited above, I have suggested how these summary statements relate to the essence and manifestations of religion considered here. To my earlier discussion I would now add that Bonhoeffer's early distinction between social and epistemological thinking is probably in the back of his mind when he uses the word "metaphysical"; cf. LPP 381, and Bethge's discussion at DB 979f., DB-E 873f. See also Feil's article on Dilthey and Bonhoeffer (esp. pp. 666 and 671), cited above, where the appropriation of 'metaphysics' and 'inwardness' from Dilthey is discussed; I doubt whether Bonhoeffer had really integrated these ideas into his own distinctive view of religion when he first borrowed them from Dilthey at the beginning of his own discussion.

[44] The implicit human paradigm here is the child and the parent, particularly in Bonhoeffer's time the father. 'Non–religiousness,' then, is quite appropriately described as 'coming of age' to 'autonomy.'

[45] See the fuller documentation and argument in my thesis and article on "Bonhoeffer's Concept of Religion," cited above.

[46] WE 534, LPP 361.

failure—always, that is, exploiting human weakness [Schwäche] and human boundaries: that is feasible only until people by their own *strength* [Kraft] push out the boundaries somewhat further and God as *deus ex machina* becomes superfluous.[47]

In the same vein Bonhoeffer writes that the religious mentality understands redemption as "redemption from *cares, distresses, anxieties,* and *longings, from sin and death,* into a better world beyond death [Jenseits]."[48] Again, he describes the 'God' of religion as "a working–hypothesis, as a stop–gap for our difficulties [Verlegenheiten]."[49]

> Who is God? Not first of all a general belief in God, in God's *omnipotence* [Allmacht], etc. That is no genuine experience of God; it is just a projection of the world [ein Stück prolongierter Welt]…. Our relation to God is not a 'religious' relationship to a highest, most powerful [mächtigsten], best being conceivable—that is not authentic transcendence….[50]

In all of these passages, and in others, the essential components of 'religion' are always human weakness which turns in dependence to a power God.

One vivid illustrative experience described in the letters is the case of a man in the Berlin prison during an air raid. Bonhoeffer came upon him, absolutely paralyzed with terror, as the bombs exploded nearby; all the poor fellow could do was cry out, "O God, O God." It was a perfect example of a man behaving religiously in a condition of helpless dependency. Bonhoeffer rejected the chance to pounce upon an unhappy person in a moment of crisis to force religion down his throat. Instead, he calmed him by telling him that the raid would soon be over.[51] Some weeks afterwards he asked rhetorically: "Are we to fall upon a few unhappy people in their times of weakness and, so to speak, religiously assault them?"[52] Numerous examples could be cited from personal and public life which manifest the religious posture Bonhoeffer describes. People live their day–to–day lives relying on secular techniques such as medicine, scientific knowledge, machines, insurance, and so on, but

---

47 WE 407, LPP 281f., italics mine.
48 WE 500, LPP 336, italics mine.
49 WE 557, LPP 381.
50 WE 558, LPP 381, italics mine.
51 LPP 199.
52 WE 404, LPP 280, cf. LPP 311; note again the 'religious' correlation of human weakness and divine power.

suffer a religious relapse in times of crisis: the executive who discovers he has cancer; the mother whose child is killed in an automobile accident; the urging of the nation to a veritable orgy of praying after an explosion in a spacecraft, followed by the front page article in *The New York Times* where senators and other dignitaries unanimously averred that the successful return of the crippled craft proved the enduring power of God and religion—NASA, however, kept the posture of Mündigkeit and ordered an investigation of human negligence.

From these passages and illustrations it is obvious that Bonhoeffer's concept of religion is an *operational* or behavioral one; it is not morphological or institutional. Many interpreters have misunderstood him on this point. They have assumed that when he spoke of religion, he meant the same as themselves. For them, religion meant the church institution and the forms of its life, such as worship, Scripture, doctrine, prayer, rites, and so on. But this morphological definition is not what Bonhoeffer is talking about. His definition is operational in the sense that it describes a particular way of behaving, feeling, and thinking in the effort to cope with human weaknesses and problems. In other words, it is a particular *psychic posture* with three aspects: weakness, dependence, and the power God. Because he is talking about a psychic posture, and not institutional forms per se, he can describe the secular activities of certain psychotherapists and existentialist philosophers as "religious"; they may have nothing to do with the ecclesiastical institution or with Christian content, but their approach to people involves the same psychic posture as religion.[53]

Once it is clear that Bonhoeffer approaches religion operationally as a particular psychic posture, we can understand the central intent of his argument in the letters. If religion is understood operationally, then it follows that a double possibility obtains for the church, the forms of its life, and its biblical and theological concepts: they can be understood and operate either in a *religious* or a *non–religious* manner. Given this double possibility, Bonhoeffer exposes and denies the religious interpretation of the church, Scripture, prayer, doctrines, and so on. He is repudiating their *religious* psychic posture as theologically invalid and historically inappropriate in order then to present a "*non–religious* Christianity." He wants these aspects of the Christian life to be shaped by the new posture and informed by a new spirit—one that is Christologically valid and anthropologically appropriate for people who have grown from *dependence* to *autonomy.* Hence the concise statement: "Let me just summarize

---

53 LPP 326, 341, 344f. ("religious blackmail"), 346.

briefly what I am concerned about—claiming for Jesus Christ a world that has come of age."[54] A "non–religious Christianity," therefore, is not one which repudiates the church and the elements of its common life; it is one that *changes* the psychic posture of Christianity from a religious one to another which can engage the self–understanding and life–style of people who have "come of age."

Having clarified Bonhoeffer's *operational* concept of religion, his reasons for rejecting religion as *dysfunctional* can now be examined. What are the manifestations of the essence of religion as weakness, dependence, and the power God? On what theological grounds is the critique of these manifestations made? Why, theologically and historically, is religion dysfunctional? I will first set out the interrelated manifestations of religion, and then give Bonhoeffer's critique; the latter will serve as a bridge to the discussion of non–religious Christianity.

First, religion is *episodic*.[55] It is a crisis phenomenon, an emergency device. People live most of their lives and manage their concerns by reason, knowledge, technology, organizing ability, and other secular methods. Only when a crisis appears, when they are reduced to a state of weakness which cannot yet be managed by such methods, do some people revert to the religious posture. This episodic character is consistently indicated in religious 'theology' by the role of 'God' as stop–gap, *deus ex machina,* and working–hypothesis.

A second manifestation of religion is its *peripheral* or parochial character.[56] The more knowledge increases, the more control people have over their lives, and the more they are able to cope with problems, the less they find themselves in situations of helpless dependency and the less likely they are to resort to God as a stop–gap and working–hypothesis. Hence the room where religion may operate is more and more constricted. Religion is not in the center of existence; it appears only at the boundaries; it is confined to the shadowy corners. It deals only with a small segment of life and does not provide the shape and motivation to a person's whole life.

Following from this is the third manifestation: religion is *subjective*[57] and inward. It is easier, clearly, to deal with medical problems by developing antibiotics, or to deal with many social problems by various forms of insurance, than it is to deal with concerns such as the lurking fear

---

54 LPP 342.
55 LPP 280ff., 311f., 360f., 380f.
56 LPP 281f., 311f., 325f., 336f., 341, 381.

of death, or guilt. Hence as more and more areas of life are handled by autonomous activities—such as education, science, technology, economics—religion is more and more confined to those inward, private, subjective problems. Even here, *pace* Bonhoeffer and his tirades against certain types of psychotherapy, secular psychological means of dealing with such problems are frequently effective and healing.

The fourth manifestation is related to the subjectivity and inwardness of religion, namely, its *individualism*.[58] By focusing concern upon guilt and death as the locus of soteriology, religion cultivates an individualistic self–preoccupation. Concern for 'saving one's soul', in both Catholic piety and Protestant evangelicalism, is a very individualistic concern; it is frequently accompanied in the attitudes of popular evangelists by the view that social and political issues will all be solved when each particular person has individually dealt with the issues of God and their personal 'soul'.

Related to both inwardness and individualism, as well as to the religious starting point of people's weakness in the world, is a fifth manifestation: *otherworldliness*.[59] In contrast to the biblical view, Bonhoeffer writes, religious "redemption myths have as their goal precisely the overcoming of the boundary of death.... Redemption myths seek, in an unhistorical attitude, an eternity after death." When Christianity was understood in this way "the emphasis then falls upon the Jenseits beyond the boundary of death." Salvation then means "redemption from cares, distresses, anxieties and longings, from sin and death, into a better world beyond death."[60] Religious otherworldliness looks for the off–stage refuge of the *deus ex machina*.

Another manifestation of religion is *intellectual dishonesty*.[61] To invoke God as a working–hypothesis when a limit is reached in human knowledge is simply dishonest.[62] To pray to God for the safety of astronauts whose danger is manifestly the result of human negligence may be psychologically explicable, but it is also a patent piece of intellectual dishonesty.

57　LPP 279, 304, 326, 327, 336., 341, 344ff., 361f., 380f.
58　LPP 286, 326f., 336, 344ff., 361f.
59　LPP 282, 286, 336.
60　WE 500, LPP 336.
61　LPP 280ff., 311f., 360.
62　WE 532f., LPP 360; cf. LPP 280.

A seventh manifestation is that religion is *humiliating*.[63] This is seen in common forms of apologetics and proselytism. Efforts to subvert human strengths and happiness, to undermine recently gained autonomy, and to spy out areas of weakness are castigated by Bonhoeffer as meaningless, ignoble, and unchristian.

> The attack by Christian apologetic on the Mündigkeit of the world I regard as first, meaningless, second, ignoble, and third, unchristian. Meaningless, because it looks to me like the attempt to put grown up people back into adolescence, i.e. to make them *dependent* [abhängig] on things upon which they simply are not, in fact, *dependent* any more—to push them back into problems which are no longer really problems for them. Ignoble, because here an attempt is made to exploit the *weakness* [Schwäche] of people for purposes which are alien to them and which they do not freely affirm. Unchristian, because Christ is confused with a certain stage of human religiosity, i.e. with a human law.[64]

A final manifestation of religion is one that really permeates almost all the previous criticisms. Such religion is *self–centered*.[65] It directs people to their *own* weaknesses, inner problems, and longings for the future; it does not transform and reorient human existence into a free and responsible "existence–for–others." Nor does it create a community of faith which serves the world, but one which is self–directed, which regards itself as "specially favored," and which fights for its own preservation.[66] In so doing, the religious posture only reinforces that weakness and dependency in which it is rooted. There is no authentic transcendence in religion. Its power 'God' is merely a projection from and compensation for human weakness, not a genuine 'Other'; consequently, religion cannot transform and liberate human life.

Bonhoeffer's critique of religion. Bonhoeffer's critique of religion is most fully understood on the basis of his non–religious interpretation of Christianity. It is a clearer and simpler procedure, however, to present first the negative critique of religion. We can then concentrate on the central positive affirmations of "religionless Christianity," and its relation to the early theology, without distracting the argument by constant

---

[63] LPP 280, 326f., 341f., 344ff.

[64] WE 478f., LPP 327; italics mine.

[65] LPP 286, 326f.

[66] LPP 281, 300, 381.

reference to its polemical thrust. This discussion therefore presupposes
what follows, as well as forming a bridge to it.

If religious weakness and dependence manifests itself in the episodic, peripheral, inward, individualistic, and otherworldly character of
religion, this is to be criticized on Christological and anthropological
grounds. Christologically it denies the lordship of Christ. It confines
Christ to the margins of existence, refusing his place as the 'center' of life,
and his being as the Mediator of all human experience.[67]

> God is not a stop–gap; he must be recognized in the midst of life, not
> only at the limits of our possibilities; in life and not only in death; in
> health and strength [Kraft] and not only in suffering; in activity and not
> only in sin. The ground for this lies in the revelation of God in Jesus
> Christ. He is the center of life; he did not at all 'stop by' to answer our
> unsolved problems.[68]

The corresponding anthropological criticism is that religion undermines
the wholeness of human life and militates against the integration of
existence. "The 'religious act' is always something partial, 'faith' is
something whole, an act of the whole life. Jesus calls people not to a new
religion, but to life."[69]

Secondly, the individualistic and self–directed posture of religion
denies the biblical teaching about human sociality and the ethical
responsibility of people for one another and their corporate life. Are
there not more important questions than the individualistic preoccupation with saving one's own soul?

> Does the question about saving one's own soul appear in the Old
> Testament at all? Are not righteousness and the Kingdom of God on
> earth the focus [Mittelpunkt] of everything, and is it not true that Rom.
> 3:24ff. is not an individualistic doctrine of salvation, but the culmina-
> tion of the view that God alone is righteous?[70]

Rather than cultivating this responsibility for righteousness and the
Kingdom of God on earth, religion appeals to people who regard
themselves as the most important concern in the world;[71] faith and
repentance, on the other hand, free people from self–preoccupation and

---

67   LPP 281f.

68   WE 455, LPP 312

69   WE 537, LPP 362; cf. the well–known polemics in the *Ethics* about
"thinking in two spheres," E-E 193ff.

70   LPP 286.

from taking themselves too seriously. Faith allows people to be caught up into the messianic event and the sufferings of God.[72]

Thirdly, Bonhoeffer rejects the otherworldliness of religion as contrary to the biblical view of humanity and history, understood in the light of Christ's resurrection.

> We are concerned not with the next world [das Jenseits] but with this world, as it has been created, preserved, shaped by laws, reconciled and renewed. What is above this world is there, in the gospel, *for* this world; I mean this... in the biblical sense of the creation, and of the incarnation, crucifixion, and resurrection of Jesus Christ.[73]

Similarly, in the Old Testament, redemptions[74] are "*historical*, ...i.e. on *this* side of the boundary of death...."[75] Spelling out what Christ's resurrection means for human historical life in the world, Bonhoeffer says:

> The Christian hope of resurrection, in contrast to the mythological [otherworldliness], sends people back to their life on the earth in a completely new way—this is even more sharply defined than in the Old Testament. Christians... must, like Christ, ...totally give themselves to earthly life, and only in doing so are they crucified and resurrected with Christ. Earthly life may not be prematurely written off; in this the New and Old Testaments agree.[76]

Otherworldliness is escapist; faith is responsible for humanity and history in the world.

Fourth, religious apologetics, with its intellectual dishonesty and its humiliating efforts to subvert human strengths and autonomy, are rejected on anthropological and Christological grounds. Anthropologically it is 'meaningless' to try to push mature people back into adolescent dependence, and 'ignoble' to exploit their weakness against their own wishes. Intellectual dishonesty is simply a more abstract form of the same thing; the honest approach will find God in what is known, not pretending that God is a stop–gap or working hypothesis to give pseudo–solutions to problems as yet unsolved.[77] Christologically, the error is

---

71 LPP 326f.

72 LPP 370, 361f.

73 WE 415, LPP 286.

74 Note the plural; Bonhoeffer refers to the Exodus from Egypt, and the deliverance from Babylonian captivity.

75 WE 500, LPP 336.

76 WE 500f., LPP 336f.

turning the gospel into a law. If, according to Bonhoeffer's historically developmental anthropology, religion is "a historically conditioned and transient form of human self–expression," then to give the religious posture the status of timeless, unchanging law is to deny the freedom and livingness of Christ and of human existence. It is to make Christ subservient to a particular past style of human existence, and to turn his freedom into a rigid and dominating demand. But since Christ liberates people for responsible freedom, Christianity should foster the health, strengths, and maturity which are necessary for this, and should dispense with its misguided and subversive apologetics.

Finally, the egocentric self–preoccupation which is endemic in religion is completely at variance with Bonhoeffer's whole theological development over the previous seventeen years. Christ as the Stellvertreter in *Sanctorum Communio*, as the freedom of God *for* humanity in *Act and Being,* and as the Mediator who liberates human existence in the 1933 *Christology* all point forward to Christ as the embodiment of a transforming transcendence in the prison letters. Christ, "the one for others," is the paradigm of Christian existence as "existing for others." The individualistic self–centeredness of religion is but another form of that isolated self–preoccupation which was so central in the soteriological problem of the early theology. There is, to be sure, an important difference. In the early theology, related as it was to Bonhoeffer's own existential struggle, the individualistic self–centeredness was a problem of power, whereas in religion it is rooted in weakness. Yet the phenomenon also shares a common problem with Bonhoeffer's original soteriological issue: whether based upon power or rooted in weakness, *individualistic self–preoccupation is a denial of the sociality of Christ and humanity.* Further, since religion projects a God of power as the compensation for human weakness, it tacitly involves a glorification of precisely those human forms of power which Bonhoeffer had found so problematic and dehumanizing in his society and his own life. Another starting point—neither *human* weakness nor *human* power—must therefore be found for Christian theology. This must enable Christianity to sustain and shape the strength, autonomy, and maturity of contemporary people. Here is the fundamental agenda for a religionless Christianity, requiring both Christological and anthropological answers. The several criticisms of the essence and

---

[77] LPP 311f.; cf. 282.

manifestation of religion ultimately rest upon the Christology at the center of the "non–religious interpretation."

3. RELIGIONLESS CHRISTIANITY

Bonhoeffer has several phrases to describe his new proposal. He speaks firstly of "religionless Christianity," "religionless Christians," and "religionless–worldly [weltliche] Christians."[78] Then he turns to the noun "Interpretation," as in "non–religious interpretation of biblical concepts" and "worldly [weltliche] interpretation."[79] Terminological variations are not decisive here, since the several phrases refer to the one proposal. But two observations should be made. First, while statistically Bonhoeffer spoke more often of "interpretation of biblical concepts," he is clearly after something more than conceptual alteration: he is, as stated before, trying to describe a new *psychic posture* which affects a person's whole life, and this obviously involves more than "concepts"; for this reason I highlight the phrase "religionless Christianity," instead of "non–religious interpretation."[80] Second, Bonhoeffer's several phrases clearly fall into two groups: the negative, polemical formulations which use the adjectives "religionless" and "non–religious," and the positive descriptions which speak of "worldly [weltliche] Christians" or "worldly interpretation." The latter is oversimplified when "weltliche" is translated by "secular" without further explanation. He means to emphasize, of course, over against the otherworldliness of religion, that Christians belong wholly to the world[81] "in the sense of the Old Testament and of John 1:14";[82] as Christ was incarnate in the world so "the Christian must, like Christ, totally give himself to earthly life, and only in doing so is the crucified and resurrected One with him." But we must go beyond

---

78   WE 404f.; LPP 280, 282.

79   WE 509, 512, 529, 535; LPP 334, 346, 359, 361; cf. WE 414, LPP 285f. Related to this are: "speak... in a worldly [weltliche] way about 'God'"; "speak of God without religion" (WE 405, LPP 280); "eine neue Sprache... vielleicht ganz unreligiös" (WE 436, LPP 300); and "'nichtreligiös' sprechen" (WE 537, LPP 362).

80   Bethge is right when he says that "more than a program of interpretation" is at stake; the issue is the Christian "Lebensgestalt." Hence "with Bonhoeffer, non–religious interpretation is more an ethical than a hermeneutical category...." (DB 986f., DB-E 879f.); "ethical," however, is too limiting a term, and this is why I prefer the phrase "psychic posture."

81   WE 405, LPP 281.

terminological clues to the heart of the matter and present a systematic analysis of the Chris₋ology and theological anthropology of Bonhoeffer's "religionless Christianity."

Christology: the religionless theologia crucis. Over against religion must be found a Christological center which can affirm and shape the strength of contemporary people, but which may not reflect either the immaturity of human weakness or the destructiveness of human power. This center is given in the form of a *theologia crucis* which Bonhoeffer develops. Like Luther's *theologia crucis*, Bonhoeffer's is dialectical; the dialectic is epitomized by the affirmation that the *'weak Christ'* is Lord of the world. As in Luther, this dialectic has both a polemical and a constructive function. Bonhoeffer himself does not speak of his Christology as a *theologia crucis*. But it is epitomized in the two phrases which are frequently quoted catchwords from the letters: the 'weak Christ' and "Jesus, the man for others." In two highly significant passages, where he indicates the theological starting point for the "weltliche Interpretation," this Christological dialectic is obvious.

> Human religiosity points people in their distress to the power [Macht] of God in the world; God is the *deus ex machina*. The Bible points people to the *powerlessness* [Ohnmacht] and suffering of God; only the suffering God can help. Mündigkeit... frees people to see the God of the Bible, *who through his powerlessness* [Ohnmacht] *wins power* [Macht] *and space in the world.* This is the starting point of the 'worldly interpretation.'[83]

> Who is God? Not first of all a general belief in God, in God's omnipotence [Allmacht], etc. That is no genuine experience of God; it is just a projection of the world. *Encounter with Jesus Christ gives the experience of the transformation of all human existence here in that Jesus only 'is there for others.' The 'Für–andere–Dasein' of Jesus is the experience of transcendence! Only out of his freedom from himself, his 'Für–andere–Dasein' even to death, arises his omnipotence, omniscience and omnipresence.* Faith is participating in this being of Jesus (incarnation, cross, resurrection).... Our relation to God is a new life in 'Dasein–für–andere,' by participating in the being of Jesus. The transcendent is not infinite, unattainable

---

82 LPP 286f.; cf. LPP 336f., 369f.

83 WE 534f., LPP 361; in its second occurrence in this passage, it is impossible to understand God's 'Macht' as in any way similar to dominating and exploitative human power.

tasks but the neighbor given and accessible at any time. *God in human form (!)... 'the one for others'(!), therefore the Crucified, the one living out of the transcendent....* Interpretation of biblical concepts from this perspective.[84]

The essence of the dialectic is that the power of Christ, or better, his transforming strength, is given in his weakness, his victory in his suffering, his resurrection through his crucifixion and death. "For God's foolishness is wiser than human wisdom, and God's weakness is stronger than human strength."[85] The two sides of the dialectic—the suffering and the helping, the weakness and the strength, the incarnate and the transcendent, the serving and the lordship—must never be separated. Otherwise we would have the cult of an impotent God, with no capacity to transform human life, and no way in which Christ could be Lord of people in their Mündigkeit.

As Luther's *theologia crucis* was in part a polemic against the *theologia gloriae* of scholasticism, so Bonhoeffer's "weak Christ" is a polemic against the 'power God' of religion. By emphasizing the weak Christ he demolishes in one stroke the power God of religion. The cosmic screen on which religious fantasy projects its images of compensatory power is chopped down. In religious weakness people look to God to find power; in the Bible they find not the power God, but the weak Christ. Christ sends them back to their own human strengths; precisely in these strengths—in knowledge, achievements, success, responsibilities, happiness—people should find God, Bonhoeffer argues. Also, in removing the power God he is overcoming that immature *dependence* typical of religion; if religion reinforces weakness and dependence, Christian faith builds mature strength and independence. The weak and suffering Christ, then, is the ultimate critic of religion. The transformation of human life brings people from the periphery of life to its center, from a fragmented existence to an integrated life, from otherworldliness to historical life in the world, from an episodic regression to a faith which informs their whole life, from subjective inwardness to responsibility in public life, from dishonest and humiliating apologetics to meaningful acceptance of reality, from individualistic self–preoccupation to 'existing for others.'

Christ thus not only overcomes religious weakness but also creates strength, freedom, independence, responsibility, and integration—in

---

[84] WE 558f., LPP 381f., italics mine.
[85] I Corinthians 1:25

short, maturity. Bonhoeffer's contribution here has far–reaching historical importance. If I were to select one criticism shared and repeated
by the humanist critics of religion in the nineteenth century—Feuerbach,
Marx, Nietzsche, Freud, to name a few—it would be this: religion
dehumanizes people by robbing them of their strength and creativity; it
fosters instead a weak, servile, and irresponsible dependence. In this
broad context the constructive significance of Bonhoeffer's non–religious *theologia crucis* may be appreciated for its originality and its
historical contribution.

The weak Christ who demythologizes the power God of religion
simultaneously is *the guarantee and supporter of human Mündigkeit and
autonomy*. People are no longer threatened and inhibited by an absolute
divine power standing over against them, sapping them of their own
strength, independence, and creativity. On the contrary,

> ...we must live in the world *'etsi deus non daretur.'* This is just what
> we recognize—before God! God himself compels us to this recogni-
> tion. So our coming of age leads us to a true knowledge of our
> situation before God. God lets us know that we must live as people
> who can manage their lives without God. The God who is with us is
> the God who leaves us alone [verlassen] (Mark 15:34)![86] The God
> who lets us live in the world without the working–hypothesis–God is
> the God before whom we stand continually. Before God and with God
> we live without God. God allows himself to be driven out of the world
> on to the cross. God is powerless [ohnmächtig] and weak [schwach]
> in the world, and that is precisely the only way that he is with us and
> helps us. Matthew 8:17[87] makes it perfectly clear that Christ helps us
> not by his omnipotence [Allmacht] but by his weakness [Schwachheit]
> and his suffering.[88]

The *weak* Christ calls upon *strong* people to be responsible in their
adulthood. Christ calls people to use their strengths of reason, knowledge,
science, technology and psychic health and confidence in the service of
human well–being, in this way being transformed by the paradigm of

---

[86] "And at the ninth hour Jesus cried with a loud voice, 'Eloi, Eloi, lama
sabachthani?' which means, 'My God, my God, why hast thou forsaken me?'"

[87] "This was to fulfill what was spoken by the prophet Isaiah, 'He took our
infirmities and bore our diseases.'"

[88] WE 533f., LPP 360f. The verb 'verlassen' in this passage should be
read, I think, not simply as 'forsake,' but in the sense of the trust and confidence
which God has in people to leave them alone; this is the connotation of the noun
'Verlass.'

Christ's 'existing for others.' Human Mündigkeit, far from being undermined by Christ, is shaped by him and drawn into his service for humanity.

This leads to the constructive side of Bonhoeffer's *theologia crucis*. If the weak Christ serves to demolish the power God and to support human strength and autonomy, it is Jesus as 'the one for others' who is the paradigm of true humanity with and for others. Jesus not only died on the cross, he lived in the world and is present in the world as the life–giving Lord of humanity. But he is present in his service and self–giving, not in omnipotent power. This 'existing for others' which people encounter in Jesus is nothing other than encounter with authentic *transcendence*. It is this that gives Christian shape and theological content to human Mündigkeit, accomplishing "the transformation of all human existence." This is how Christ's lordship and transcendence is at work.

At this point Mündigkeit becomes more than a general, anthropological category referring to the new psychic posture which supersedes religion as "a historically conditioned and transient form of human self–expression." Now, shaped by Christ, Mündigkeit is taken up into a contemporary Christian anthropology and given theological status. This points again to the interaction of Christology and anthropology in Bonhoeffer's theology.

The two functions of the weak Christ in relation to the human strength and autonomy in Mündigkeit and the human weakness and dependence in religion once more document the close interaction of Christology and anthropology. The anthropological insight of Mündigkeit first raised anew the Christological question in the prison letters. Then it influenced the actual form and emphasis in the Christology: the weakness of Christ functions to support Mündigkeit, just as it counteracts the weakness and dependence of religion. To show this influence of anthropology on Christology is by no means to overlook the influence of the *theologia crucis* from the Lutheran tradition in Bonhoeffer's early theology, especially the Christology lectures and *Discipleship;* nor is it to deny the continuity with this earlier theology which certainly informs the interpretation of 'non–religious Christianity.' Yet we ask: why is the *theologia crucis* of the 1933 Christology radicalized in the prison letters? Why has the 'power Christ' of *Discipleship* completely disappeared in the letters, while the compromised *theologia crucis* of *Discipleship* has come to fruition there? The answer is plain: the anthropological insight of Mündigkeit has caused Bonhoeffer to revise his Christology. Mündigkeit has obliged him to clarify both the distinction between strength and power, and to distinguish between illegitimate and legitimate forms of human weakness; these concepts were unclear, and the distinctions were not made, in the theology of the early and mid–1930s. The development from that time to his prison theology is not fully intelligible unless we see this interaction between anthropology and Christology.

The interaction, however, goes in both directions. Bonhoeffer has no intention of sanctifying the secular status quo. As a human phenomenon in a historical development, Mündigkeit exhibits an ambiguity. Along with its increase of human strength and initiative which hold great promise for good is found its evil corruption. Thus Mündigkeit poses the crucial question: *human beings themselves.* Therefore Bonhoeffer argues that the gospel of Christ is the point from which "the world must be understood better than it understands itself." Christ is the presence of transforming transcendence in the world. Christ is at once the weak and suffering Christ of the cross and the Lord who is 'the one for others.' So understood, Christ is the basis of Bonhoeffer's theological anthropology.

Christian anthropology: human strength in "existing for others." The anthropology of religionless Christianity has already been suggested in the analysis of Mündigkeit and autonomy and the critique of the anthropological presuppositions of religion. In place of the weakness and dependency characteristic of religion, Bonhoeffer affirms human strength and autonomy as indispensable in a contemporary Christian anthropology. Above all, it is the strength of the ego which is affirmed; what he had earlier tried to suppress in himself, he now rehabilitated both for himself and for others. Beyond its autobiographical importance, however, the theological and social significance of this ego affirmation must now be explored in relation to the Christology of the weak Christ as 'one for others.'

We must bear in mind the quite specific social and historical context in which Bonhoeffer wrote, though without detracting from the larger significance of his thought. To imprison Bonhoeffer in his own specific situation would make the remarkably catholic influence of his thinking unintelligible. Nevertheless, this catholic appeal originated in a definite locus, just like the appeal of Luther in the sixteenth century. Bonhoeffer was writing for himself and his partners in the resistance movement; their ego strength and their freedom for others in taking public responsibility—risking their lives, even to death—is the immediate human context of his thinking.

The *theologia crucis* themes of the weak Christ and his existing for others interpret Bonhoeffer's understanding of incarnation, cross, and resurrection. This is the content of Christ's lordship. This Christology shapes Mündigkeit and Autonomie into Christian anthropology.

Christ as the Lord is the *center* of life. This theme of Christ as the "center" pervades Bonhoeffer's theology. It is implicit in the notion of Christ as the Stellvertreter and Kollektivperson of the new humanity, and it is explicit in *Creation and Fall* and the *Christology;* it continues with the Christ who demands sole obedience in *Discipleship,* and the Christ who unites all reality in the *Ethics.* In the *Letters* Bonhoeffer renews the 1932–1933 metaphor, 'Mitte,' and gives it new concreteness in the anthropology of Mündigkeit. Christ engages the *whole* person in the midst of life, not only in sickness, helplessness, sin, and death, but above all in life, strength, health, and activity.[89]

This means that Christ blesses earthly, natural life. His cross does not deny all that the Old Testament includes under "blessing."[90] The best Christological interpretation of the Song of Songs is that which reads it as an ordinary love poem, not spiritualizing and allegorizing it but gladly accepting the "passionate, sensual love" it portrays.[91] Jesus never questioned people's health, strength [Kraft], or happiness, but restored the sick to health and the weak to strength.[92] Jesus affirms human powers and secular achievements, sustains human reason against intellectual dishonesty,[93] and now even requires people to celebrate their *autonomy* over against an immature dependence on God.

Along with the blessing of natural life goes the encountering of "unnatural" life, that is, human sin. From the beginning Bonhoeffer had emphasized that the relation to Christ was a relation of the whole person; in *Sanctorum Communio, Act and Being,* the *Christology,* and *Discipleship,* the socio–ethical concept of human persons and their being encountered by Christ in the willing of the 'other' meant an encounter of a person's whole existence.[94] But now, in the context of Mündigkeit, this encounter with transcendence which brings repentance has a new emphasis. Christ encounters people at the point of their *strength.*

---

[89] LPP 311f.

[90] LPP 374.

[91] LPP 315, 303.

[92] LPP 341f.

[93] Cf. the establishing of the "relative rights of reason" in the Christology lectures.

I want therefore to start from the premise that God should not be smuggled into some last secret place, but that we should simply recognize the Mündigkeit of the world and humanity and not run people down in their worldliness but confront them with God at their strongest point.[95]

Amplifying this, Bonhoeffer says that it is not the sins of weakness but of *strength* which are decisive. Are Napoleon and Goethe to be confronted at the point of their marital infidelities, Bonhoeffer asks. (He might have included Hitler's relation to Eva Braun in the same question.) From the viewpoint of his theology and his action, the answer is: obviously not. What then, are sins of strength? Bonhoeffer gives three examples: in the peasant, breaking the order of life; in the genius, hubris; in the bourgeoisie, *shunning free responsibility.*[96]

These illustrations are revealing and instructive. In speaking of hubris we do not know whether Bonhoeffer had in mind his own encounter and repentance of 1932; nevertheless, that was certainly an occasion of a man being confronted at his strongest point. When he speaks of the bourgeois sin of "shunning free responsibility" there can scarcely be any doubt that he is thinking of the contrast between the responsibility accepted by the resistance movement, including himself, and those whose sin consisted in the lack of faith needed for commitment to *free responsibility.*[97] The non–religious interpretation of repentance, then, focuses on those issues which are decisive for personal and public life. Here, where a person's whole identity is involved, where the life of a people is at stake, where history is being made, is the locus of the encounter with Christ. This

---

94   Recall the concept of Grenze; this is Bonhoeffer's social existentialism, so to speak.

95   WE 511, LPP 346.

96   LPP 345, italics mine.

97   Cf. LPP 298. See also the discussions on responsibility in the *Ethics,* and particularly in the piece, "After Ten Years" (LPP 3–17); this was a Christmas present in 1942 for Hans von Dohnanyi, Hans Oster, and Eberhard Bethge (WE 19), comrades in resistance. Note the references to the statement that Germans had understood freedom in terms of service to their calling [Beruf], and, not realizing sufficiently how submissiveness [Unterordnung] could be misused for evil ends, lacked a fundamental perception: "the necessity for the free, responsible deed even in opposition to calling [Beruf] and commission [Auftrag].... This derives from God who demands the free wager of faith in responsible action, and promises to those who become sinners in the process his forgiveness and consolation" (WE 24, LPP 6).

is the experience of transcendence and the act of metanoia as "the transformation of all human existence."

Faith is the positive side of repentance, and likewise "is something whole, an act of the whole life." If Jesus is "the one for others," then "faith is participating in this being of Jesus (incarnation, cross, resurrection)." For Christians, Christ's incarnation means that they totally gives themselves to earthly life; only in this way is the crucified and resurrected One with them. For the person whose faith is participating in the being of Jesus for others, the cross means willingness to share the suffering of Christ for the world;[98] it also means confidence in the forgiveness of Christ.[99] Christ's resurrection gives Christians an invincible hope in the action and suffering of their earthly life;[100] but it must be rooted in their love for historical existence. "Only when one loves life and the earth so much that without them everything would seem lost and finished may one believe in the resurrection of the dead and a new world."[101]

Against the self–centered individualism of religion, a religionless Christian existence sees "righteousness and the Kingdom of God on earth as the focus [Mittelpunkt] of everything."[102] Christian existence as 'existing for others' is not restricted to interpersonal relationships; sociality always holds together the individual and the corporate dimensions of human personal being. Most concretely, this meant for Bonhoeffer the free acceptance of responsibility for his people and church at the central point of the national crisis. He continues in the same paragraph with the statement that Romans 3:24ff.[103] culminates the biblical view that God alone is righteous, and that in the gospel God's righteousness exists for the world which God has "created, preserved, shaped by laws, reconciled, and renewed."[104] A letter two weeks later makes the same point: God's kingdom is

---

98 LPP 361f, 348f., 369ff.

99 LPP 393, 362, 349.

100 LPP 336f., 370f.

101 WE 175, LPP 157.

102 WE 415, LPP 286.

103 "...they are justified by his grace as a gift, through the redemption which is in Christ Jesus.... This was to show God's righteousness...." Interestingly, this is Luther's crucial passage; he used it to make the law–gospel distinction, whereas Bonhoeffer uses it to protest against religious individualism and inwardness, and to stress Christian *social* responsibility.

> a kingdom stronger [stärker] than war and danger, ...not a kingdom of
> the heart but one of the earth and the whole world, a kingdom that
> makes its own way and summons people to it to prepare its way, a
> kingdom upon which it is worthwhile to stake one's life.[105]

That these statements may and should be interpreted by Bonhoeffer's
own personal action in the resistance movement is beyond dispute. As
he thought about the future, Bonhoeffer continued to focus upon the
social responsibility of the Christian, as when he wrote in his "Outline
for a Book" that not nature but the threat of technical organization and
human institutions would be the decisive context for Christian faith and
action.[106]

This is an appropriate point to note the position taken on a crucial
issue of power in the time preceding and during the writing of the *Letters.*
In contrast to the near pacifism of the early 1930s and *Discipleship,*
Bonhoeffer now supports and participates in a particular act of violent
power: the plot to assassinate Hitler. This must be understood both as a
specific case and as an extreme case, an 'extra–ordinary' exercise of free,
Christian responsibility. It is not a general sanctification of violent power
struggles, like that found in the Barcelona lecture;[107] it is a historical
necessity which is not grounded in general principle. It is an act of free
responsibility in which faith and historical–political judgment are wa-
gered. As an act of vicarious representative action—'existing for
others'—it was not directed to self–advancement, to gaining and main-
taining advantage over others. This was the fatal flaw of both personal
and societal power which Bonhoeffer diagnosed in treating power as a
soteriological problem; such power is dominating, tyrannical, exploitative, and destructive. On the contrary, this use of power is a willingness
to lose all, "to stake one's life," for the sake of truth, justice, freedom, and
humanity for others. It is an act of penitence rather than an act of self–
aggrandizement and self–justification. Bonhoeffer, therefore, came to
see the necessity in a certain extreme case of using violent and destructive
power as a means of liberation; precisely in doing so he continued his
opposition to power in oppressive and exploitative forms.[108]

Finally, we must consider suffering in the anthropology of religionless
Christianity. If Christ's weakness prevents people from irresponsibly

---

104 WE 415, LPP 286.
105 WE 443, LPP 304.
106 WE 557, LPP 380.
107 See Chapter 4 above.

using God as a crutch, and his being 'the one for others' shapes human strength after his own likeness, then those who participate in his

108 The Tegel literary fragments (for many years only partially published in the *Gesammelte Schriften*) contain some significant discussions of power in relation to history, sociality, and "civic responsibility." In the novel fragment, for example, we find the major expressing Bonhoeffer's sentiments.

> It's quite another thing [from getting agitated about blunt speech] when people exploit the power they have been given over others to humiliate, debase, defile, and destroy them.... It desecrates all genuine authority and destroys all human community. You can be dead sure it will lead to anarchy. Franz, I don't know where it comes from, but there is in all of us a dark, pernicious instinct to abuse the power [Gewalt] that is given to us and thereby to destroy life—our own and that of others. Wherever we encounter this truly evil instinct—first of all in ourselves—we must counter it with the force of all the hate and passion we can muster.... It's an uncanny thing that there must be power [Macht], indeed that power is something holy, that it is from God, and yet that it so easily allows us to become devils, turning us into great or petty tormenters of others (GS III 497; FT 123f.; FP 86; following the translation of *Fiction from Tegel Prison*, DBWE 7).

The Major later resumes with the following reflection upon a lesson he had learned as a schoolboy through a bitter struggle with a classmate (Hans) which had eventually led to their friendship.

> We, too, had both thought we were demigods, until we realized—or at least sensed—that we are human beings who need each other, who must live with each other, and tolerate each other's presence. And that was our good fortune. We became friends. Demigods have no friends, only tools which they use or discard, according to whim. I distrust anyone who has no close friend. Either they're a demigod or, much worse, imagine they are. For me, the main issue for individuals and for peoples [Völker] is whether or not they have learned to live with other human beings and peoples. That's more important to me than all their ideas, thoughts and convictions.... But the decisive thing was not what we both lost, namely our claim to live alone in the world as demigods, but what we gained, namely a humane life in community with another human being. Now I believe the same thing holds true for nations as well, and fundamentally for all historical movements (GS III 506ff.; FT 176f.; FP 121f., in the *Fiction from Tegel Prison* translation).

This is a remarkable passage: it repeats the basic point of *Sanctorum Communio* that people become persons through socio–ethical encounter with one another; it applies the same analogy to peoples and historical movements, as found throughout the early writings; the sentence that human beings must live

transforming being find themselves "sharing in the suffering of God in Christ," "being caught up into the messianic suffering of God in Jesus Christ."[109] This theology should not be explained away by a psychological reductionism as merely a reflection of Bonhoeffer's own prison suffering. It is rooted in the *theologia crucis* of the Lutheran tradition which Bonhoeffer had begun to make his own over a decade earlier. Now, doubtless clarified by his own experience, it comes to fruition. The Christian knows both action and suffering, freedom and bondage, life and death. Suffering is not to be sought out and made into an abstract principle or method; it is contingent upon the divine will and action in the world.[110]

Nor is suffering submission, but "an extension of our action and a completion of freedom."[111] Suffering belongs in the 'polyphony' of Christian existence. This posture of faith, free from morbid preoccupation with suffering and death, expressing the *theologia crucis*, and simultaneously negating religious dependence, wishfulness and selfishness, is beautifully expressed in two passages.

> The God of Jesus Christ has nothing to do with what a God, as we imagine him, must and can do. We must persistently and patiently steep ourselves in the life, sayings, deeds, suffering, and death of Jesus to know what God promises and what he fulfills. It is certain that we can always live close to God's presence, and that this life is a completely new life for us; that nothing is then impossible for us, because nothing is impossible for God; that no earthly power can beset us outside of God's will, and that danger and distress only drive us closer to God. It is certain that we can demand nothing and yet may pray for everything; it is certain that our joy is hidden in suffering, our

---

"aufeinander angewiesen, miteinander und nebeneinander" is virtually identical to that in *Creation and Fall* (1932–33) where human creatureliness is defined as the "Gegenüber–Miteinander–Aufeinander–angewiesen–sein der Menschen" (SF 60); and the description of the demi–gods standing alone in the world and destroying human community is a recapitulation of the passages on the soteriological problem. While the novel fragment was being written in 1943–44, prior to the April 30, 1944 letter beginning the discussion of Mündigkeit and religionless Christianity, it shows that the conceptuality of sociality is still fundamental in Bonhoeffer's mind during his imprisonment. A heavy onus of proof would fall upon anyone who suggested that this conceptuality was dropped when the new stage of reflection began.

[109] WE 536, LPP 362; cf. LPP 337, 370, 374f., 391.

[110] LPP 374; cf. LPP 361f.

[111] LPP 375; cf. LPP 370f.

life in death, and that in everything we are in a community [Gemeinschaft] which bears us. To all this God has said Yes and Amen in Jesus. This Yes and Amen is the solid ground on which we stand.[112]

If this is a perfect example of non–religious reliance upon God, ringing with Pauline overtones, the second passage has the same polyphony of Bonhoeffer's non–religious *theologia crucis* as it related to "worldliness"; significantly, it was written on July 21, 1944, the day after the unsuccessful attempt to assassinate Hitler.

> In recent years I have more and more come to know and understand the profound this–worldliness [Diesseitigkeit] of Christianity. The Christian is not a *homo religiosus,* but simply a human being, as Jesus... was human.... I mean... the profound Diesseitigkeit which is full of discipline, and in which the knowledge of death and resurrection is always present.

> To this very moment I am still discovering that one learns faith only in the complete this–worldliness of life.... By this–worldliness I mean living in the richness of our duties, questions, successes and failures, experiences and perplexities. Then we throw ourselves completely into the arms of God, then we no longer take seriously our own suffering but the suffering of God in the world, then we watch with Christ in Gethsemane. That, I think, is faith, that is μετάνοια; in this way one becomes human, and Christian.... How can successes make one arrogant or failures lead one astray if one shares in God's suffering in such a this–worldly life?[113]

Were this a full–scale examination of the theology in the *Letters,* other important issues would need examination. Suffice it to say, on the basis of the above passages, that in Bonhoeffer's mature writings there is no dissolution of faith into humanist secularity[114] or of the Christian community into secular invisibility. In these passages he has spoken both of the 'discipline' and of 'community' which are necessary for the non–religious Christian life. Bethge has persuasively argued that the 'discipline of the secret' [Arkandisziplin] is the counterpoint to 'worldliness,' clearly warding off the former danger.[115] With regard to the Christian community, it is clear that just as Bonhoeffer wanted radical changes in

---

[112] WE 572f., LPP 391.

[113] WE 541f., LPP 369f.

[114] The two poems, "Stations on the Road to Freedom" and "Christians and Pagans" (LPP 370f., 348f.) are more than sufficient to dispel this misinterpretation. The former is really a commentary upon the meaning of being free for others; its stages of 'discipline,' 'action,' 'suffering,' and 'death' indicate that more is involved than a benign, individual altruism.

the church, so he intended a new church to come out of those changes. In his first letter beginning the critique of religion and proposing a non–religious Christianity, he asked about the significance of Mündigkeit and religionlessness for the *church* and the *congregation*. After three months of discussion, he wrote in the "Outline for a Book" that the life of the church must be reshaped by Christ: "the church is only the church when it exists for others."[116] To employ this fundamental Christological image to interpret the church is solid evidence that the Christian community is not disbanded in the theology of the *Letters*.

4. RELIGIONLESS CHRISTIANITY AND THE THEOLOGY OF SOCIALITY

Discipleship added the obedience of discipleship to the earliest form of the theology of sociality, thereby freeing Bonhoeffer from autonomous ambition, but also creating unresolved contradictions. The *Letters* add the new anthropological insight of Mündigkeit, thereby transforming an obedience of attempted ego suppression into the affirmation of ego strength in the free service of others; the Christological and anthropological contradictions of *Discipleship* are thereby overcome. Thus the theology of sociality comes to a striking fruition in the *Letters*. There is, therefore, both continuity and discontinuity in Bonhoeffer's theological development. The main connections between the early theology of sociality and the theology of religionless Christianity may be seen as follows.

Apart from the unfruitful digression into the power Christology of *Discipleship*, the connection of the early theology of sociality and that of the *Letters* is clear and direct; so much is this so that I believe it is necessary to interpret the formula, 'Christ, the one for others,' against the

---

[115] DB-E 880ff.

[116] WE 405, LPP 280; WE 560, LPP 382; cf. LPP 300. There are two main reasons why discussion, particularly in the Anglo–Saxon world, has either been distressed or gleeful—but in both cases mistaken—about the alleged disappearance of the church from the religionless Christianity of the *Letters*. First, Weltlichkeit—and that too quickly equated with 'secularity'—has been emphasized disproportionately, forgetting that Bonhoeffer's main concern was with Mündigkeit and Autonomie. Second, an institutional or morphological understanding of religion has been assumed, whereas Bonhoeffer's usage is operational and behavioral; see the discussion above on this point.

background of the early writings. This is the *underlying* unity and *continuity* of direction in Bonhoeffer's theological development.

In *Sanctorum Communio* Christ is the Stellvertreter, the embodiment of God's love for humanity. In this Christological perspective we know that "God's will to rule is his will to serve," that the divine love rules by its serving, and that the essence of this serving rule is to recreate human beings into the new humanity, the community of love. Transcendence, in its content and its form, is interpreted in terms of sociality. Christ is to be understood through a personal–social category. As the Kollektivperson of the new humanity, Christ is the personification and prototype of human sociality. The essence of Christian existence is "active being–for–one–another" [tätige Füreinander] which is cultivated in the community of faith and extended into the corporate life of society.

This line is strengthened in *Act and Being*. Everything that is focused on Christ as Stellvertreter in the first work is epitomized in the statement that since "Christ is the Word of God's freedom," God's freedom is "freedom for humanity." In this freedom, furthermore, there is a *being* of God among and for humanity which is revealed and has its form in the communal life of the community of faith. Here we find that God is freely bound to humanity. Moreover, and consistent with *Sanctorum Communio*, Bonhoeffer expressly states that God's freedom in self–revelation is not a freedom of isolated aseity in an eternal beyond, but freedom for and with humanity in history. This does not yet have the concreteness found in the attack on religious otherworldliness and the affirmation of a life derived from Christ incarnate in the world, such as we find in the *Letters;* but the retrospective continuity is undeniable.

In the writings of 1932 and 1933, particularly *Creation and Fall* and the Christology lectures, the Christology and anthropology is further developed in the direction of the *Letters*. Christ continues to be presented in the relational–corporate conceptuality of 'person' theologically interpreted as Mitte and Mittler. This catches up the idea of Christ as Kollektivperson of the new humanity and specifically relates it to the soteriological problem of power, since by their personal and corporate seizure of power people put themselves in the 'center' of life, dominating and exploiting others. The Mediator, consistent with everything since 1927, is the center of personal and political history, and of nature. The theme of Christ's freedom–*for* and being–for humanity is continued in the articulation of the Personstruktur of Christ as his being–*pro–me*. Above all, the *theologia crucis* emerges at this time; to speak of the divinity of Jesus, we speak not of an omnipotent divine being, but of his weakness and humiliation. Christ's "self–assertion" is in "his death for the brothers."

The Christian anthropology of this time follows the Christology. The *imago Dei* is the *analogia relationis:* human freedom, like divine freedom, is "being–free–for–the–other." The Christian "understands life as responsible vis-à-vis the other human being [Bruder-Mensch].... The Christian lives essentially through and for the other, coordinated to the other in responsibility." The same goes for corporate life; even the Gemeinschaft of the whole people [Volk], understood on the model of person, "lives in responsibility for the other people [Brudervolk]." Thus, if Christ's relationship of transcendence depends on his personal being in human social form, the transcendence question is the question of new human existence, the question of love for the neighbor. Human beings, furthermore, are essentially nature, body, and belong to the earth.

In the early 1930s, and through the publication of *Discipleship* in 1937, this Christology and anthropology is related to the soteriological problem of personal and corporate power. The early theology of sociality is fundamentally concerned with the liberation of individuals and communities from dominating and destructive forms of power which destroy the sociality of Christ and humanity. We have seen that Bonhoeffer's existential struggle with the power of the ego, complicated as it was by the struggle with Nazism, produced a partial resolution and a compromised solution of this problem in *Discipleship*. By his experience in the resistance movement, and his theological reflections in prison, Bonhoeffer first took upon himself that "deputyship" which had such deep roots in his theology and then discovered a freedom from the unnecessary attempt to suppress the strength of his own ego which he had earlier attempted. He looked back on *Discipleship* and saw it as the end of a necessary "station on the way to freedom."[117]

With his way now open, the affirmation of Mündigkeit and Autonomie was possible, first as a new historical phenomenon and then as essential to the non–religious Christian anthropology of the *Letters*. Without denying the genuine and decisive innovation which occurs in Bonhoeffer's last year of theological work, it is remarkable to see how all the basic motifs from the Christology and anthropology in the theology of sociality come to fruition in religionless Christianity. If Bonhoeffer's first decade

---

[117] The title of one of his prison poems, its movement being from 'Discipline' through 'Action' to 'Suffering' and 'Death'; we are surely entitled to read this as Bonhoeffer's commentary on the stages of his own life; cf. LPP 370f.

of theology possesses insights and poses problems which are fully intelligible only in light of where they eventually led, the theology of the *Letters* reveals its full substance only in light of its origin and course of development.

B. BONHOEFFER'S THEOLOGY OF SOCIALITY

It would be needless repetition to review in detail the whole course of the previous argument. Suffice it to say in summary that the analysis of Bonhoeffer's early theology has clearly demonstrated that the conceptuality of sociality which he set out in *Sanctorum Communio* is characteristic of and, indeed, determinative for his writings through the 1933 Christology lectures. A consistent set of concepts, centering on the idea of person understood relationally and communally, is employed in both the Christology and the anthropology of this period. Within this basic social conceptuality there is a refining of the Christology from the understanding of Christ as Stellvertreter in the first work to the *theologia crucis* of Christ the Mediator in the *Christology;* this refinement is directly related to Bonhoeffer's work on the soteriological problem of power. Likewise, the anthropology exhibits a consistent conceptuality: the concepts which comprise the category 'sociality' and, within this, the understanding of human life as Geist and Natur; by the former term (and its later equivalents, Dasein and Existenz). Bonhoeffer refers to human being as historical, willing, thinking, deciding, ethical being in relations with other persons and in the responsibility of corporate life. Christology and anthropology are thus intrinsically linked together in the conceptuality of sociality. Above all, the soteriological problem of power which vitiates the sociality of personal and corporate life is the point where the most intimate connection of Christology and anthropology is evident: Christ is the presence of transforming transcendence in the world, liberating people individually and corporately from self–serving and dominating power so that true freedom, love, and responsibility is a really new and present possibility in history.

This theology of sociality, furthermore, is still presupposed in *Discipleship,* even though this book contains Christological and anthropological contradictions which are rooted in the early problem of power and resolved in the mature theology of religionless Christianity. In the *Letters* the new anthropological insight and question of Mündigkeit leads to a striking consummation of the central Christological and anthropological tendency of the theology of sociality. Christ as 'the one for others' and the life of the Christian and the church as 'existing for others' are simple yet rich and pregnant formulas which epitomize in a new context the import of the early theology of sociality. At the same time, 'discipleship' is freed from the predominantly dominating Christ who demands the suppression of the ego in *The Cost of Discipleship*. The *theologia crucis* of the weak Christ who, as 'the one for others' is the Lord of the adult, secular world, transforms a discipleship of submission into a discipleship of free responsibility and free self–affirmation.

Rather than engaging in further summary, it is more fruitful to conclude with several observations about the import for contemporary theology of those aspects of Bonhoeffer's thought which are central in this study. Of necessity, such observations must be exploratory and must be made in a general form which contrasts with the detailed analysis and documentation of the previous exposition. These observations are grouped under three headings: Bonhoeffer and the Lutheran tradition; the wider import of the autobiographical dimension of Bonhoeffer's theology; and the new possibilities for theological work which are suggested by Bonhoeffer's preoccupation with sociality.

1. BONHOEFFER AND THE LUTHERAN TRADITION

Without being fully conscious of the fact himself, Bonhoeffer points toward a fundamental reconstruction of the Lutheran tradition on two critical and interconnected issues: its soteriology and its social ethics. These are interconnected because the doctrine of the 'two realms' is the theological–sociological consequence of the 'law–gospel' relationship which is the theological–psychological locus of soteriology.

In Luther, soteriology is focused on the guilty conscience. The doctrine of justification enthrones the grace of Christ in the conscience of the sinner and banishes the law to the outer realm which is ruled over by the state (God's 'left hand') through civil law.[118] Hence the state has an essentially conservative role as the divinely empowered restrainer of evil. When evil is contained by the force of the state, the church can preach the gospel of God's pure, forgiving grace, and so the 'proper work' of God's 'right hand' is done in the church. Luther, of course, insists that faith leads to good works of love in the Christian's vocation

---

[118] Historically it is instructive to observe that Luther "made the true division," as he put it, in what Anselm's *Cur Deus Homo*? had striven mightily to keep together: the mercy and justice of God. Anselm and Luther approached their soteriologies from two quite distinct basic questions.

in the world; but, in distinction from Calvinism, the Lutheran tradition is consistent with its founder in generally rejecting a *tertius usus legis*. For Lutheranism the two basic uses of the law are: first, the ordering of civil life by the state so that evil is contained and the gospel has room in which to work *(primus usus legis);* second, exposing and rebuking sin in the accusation of conscience so that the sinner will turn to the saving word of justification in the gospel *(secundus usus legis)*.

The logic of Luther's position was not only compelling to him personally, it was also persuasive to innumerable contemporaries, and his radical re–interpretation of justification by faith has remained a liberating word to succeeding generations. By creative modifications, contemporary Lutheran theologians such as Bultmann and Tillich have demonstrated the critical and liberating power of the Reformer's basic insights in the changed situation of the modern world. Further, while we can no longer naively identify Luther's exegesis with Paul's gospel in all details,[119] there is no doubt that the *spirit* of the Apostle's gospel of Christ's grace brought a faith to late medieval Europe which was as liberating then as in the Judeo–Hellenistic world sixteen centuries before. I am not suggesting that we ignore the continuing power of Luther's understanding of grace and faith. Rather, it is a matter of seeing the pertinence of the gospel as concretely in our own time as Luther did in his. In doing so we must also confront the negative side of the Lutheran tradition.

On the problematic side, Luther's theology has had substantial psychological and sociological consequences. Psychologically, this theology—along with its central doctrine of forgiveness—has also tended to reinforce various sources of guilt and anxiety. The guilty conscience and the justified conscience constitute the basic polarity in the locus of faith; Holl's portrait of Luther, as we saw, shows how this polarity was fundamental to his whole temperament. There is a symbiotic relationship between guilt and faith. One issue which arises here is whether the guilt Luther experienced is as characteristic of our situation as of his. Another problem is that forms of psychic guilt can be assimilated into the dynamics of faith when their theological status is highly dubious: adolescents and adults may wrongly feel guilty about sexuality, or

---

[119] See Krister Stendahl, "The Apostle Paul and the Introspective Conscience of the West," *loc. cit.*

conflict, while having no sense of *ethical culpability* for such blatant evils as racism, military oppression, and economic exploitation.

Sociologically, the doctrine of the two realms has had even more problematic ethical consequences. Luther's response to the peasants' revolt was revealing, in that there the gospel and radical social change were set at loggerheads. If that tragedy was an extreme situation, in more tranquil times the doctrine of the two realms has been a de facto sanction of political conservatism in government; at the same time it has tended to cultivate in the Christian an unquestioning deference to the authority of the state in an individualistic ethic of duty and 'calling' within an established order. The state is given too much authority and autonomy and the Christian too little responsibility and initiative in corporate political life, particularly as regards social change.

It is no accident that Bonhoeffer first began with a soteriological problem quite distinct from Luther's, and then ended up on a course of radical political action which a great number of his co–religionists find unacceptable to this day.

As we have seen, the guilty, negative conscience is not the starting point for Bonhoeffer. Accordingly, he questions Lutheran soteriology in his first work by stating that conscience can as easily be the point of ultimate human self–justification as the point of Christ's spiritual attack [Anfechtung] through the law; in the *Letters* he is increasingly dubious about guilt as a point of departure for faith, and he even more sharply repudiates all attempts to undermine any form of human strength and confidence in order to make a person religious. The reason for this is clear: for Bonhoeffer the crucial issue is the power of the ego, its domination of others, its attendant isolation, and its inner conflict between self–serving power and true selfhood as living in a free mutuality of love with others.

The Christological resolution to this problem is the freedom of Christ's co–humanity as *pro–humanity*.[120] Christ frees the self to love and serve others, integrating the self and overcoming its isolation; this existing for others intrinsically includes the Christian's responsible action in vicariously taking ethical responsibility [Stellvertretung] for corporate human communities.

---

[120] It is suggestive to observe that in Bonhoeffer's theology, Christ is primarily a *brother* figure, whereas in Luther he is a parental figure—though even in revealing "God's paternal heart," as Luther never tired of saying, Christ discloses maternal as well as paternal aspects in the deity.

Given this different preoccupation, neither the psychological law–gospel dynamics nor the sociological two–realms relationship are characteristic of Bonhoeffer's Christology, soteriology, anthropology, or ethics. Bonhoeffer, therefore, does not think in this sixteenth–century conceptuality, and when he sometimes uses its vocabulary, this is more conventional than fundamental; he unwittingly assimilates Luther into the modern era, thereby translating him with one stroke through four centuries of history; he cannot assimilate Luther's phenomenology of conscience into his own; and even his writings in the 1930s which approximate the two realms pattern are consciously modifying it and, less consciously perhaps, overstepping its limits.

Bonhoeffer works through the problem of the powerful self–serving ego until he comes to the *Letters* where we find a clear theological affirmation of the strengths of the mature ego which is liberated and shaped by Christ for the service of others, especially in responsibility for corporate, political life. At this point it is not only destructive human power which still concerns him, but also the problem of *weakness,* especially as manifested in religion. Central to the problem of weakness in religion is its individualistic preoccupation with interior problems to the neglect of public responsibility. Religious apologists who tried to find in guilt or fear of death a point of departure for the gospel were only, Bonhoeffer argued, reinforcing the outmoded psychic posture of religion and vainly trying to subvert the new psychic posture of Mündigkeit.

Even though Bonhoeffer's early writings do not speak of Mündigkeit, it is clear that this is his own posture at that time, as it was the posture of his family. This was the product of a historical development which had taken place over several centuries and certainly did not appear out of the blue in 1944 when the term became central in his thinking. The ego whose strengths exist in the mode of ambitious power is still the ego of Mündigkeit, even if Bonhoeffer had to be freed from the power problem before he could theologically acknowledge and affirm the value of the strong, healthy ego. The fact that Bonhoeffer had this psychic posture from the beginning explains why his thought simply cannot fit into the theological pattern which was relevant to the psycho–social conditions of Luther and his sixteenth–century contemporaries.

We cannot say that the problem of guilt as negative conscience which Luther faced is no longer found in contemporary experience, though theology must question whether such guilt should be a presupposition of faith. Nor can we claim that the posture of Mündigkeit is universal throughout the modern West, though it is becoming increasingly typical. We acknowledge that Bonhoeffer's focus on the strong ego—with its danger of power and its promise of free service to humanity—is intimately connected to his own particular familial and social context in which his anthropology and Christology developed. But we cannot imprison his theology there. To do so would be to ignore the basic validity of his analysis of the historical growth of Mündigkeit, to overlook the confirmation of this in daily observation of our contemporary experience, and to render unintelligible the remarkable appeal of the *Letters*. Mündigkeit and Autonomie, therefore, are more characteristic of the contemporary psychic posture than the anthropology either of Luther or of the 'religion' Bonhoeffer described. The crucial problems of our time are more related to what people and nations do with their powers than how they will deal with guilty consciences; indeed, an amorality and lack of guilt about heinous crimes against humanity is more conspicuous today than a sense of God's imminent wrath hanging like a sword over the heads of guilty sinners. This suggests that Christian theology and ethics should draw a clear distinction between *psychic guilt* and *ethical culpability*.

Bonhoeffer, then, in distinction from Luther, establishes a different locus for soteriology: not the guilty conscience (negative superego) but the strong ego which is corrupted by power. When Christ transforms destructive power into the strong ego which serves others, he simultaneously establishes a new relationship between the Christian and politics, the church and the state. The traditional 'two realms' doctrine is transcended. To be sure, church and state, Christian and secular existence, are not undialectically fused; yet nor are they so autonomous as in the doctrine of the two realms. The gospel and the church are given a political role: Christians cannot simply do their individual duty as defined by the authority and established order of government and society; the church and state are directly related in encounter and debate about the corporate well–being of humanity as the church understands it from the gospel; and the state is no longer envisaged in an essentially conservative role as the container of evil through law and order.

In saying this I am not, contrary to Müller, making Bonhoeffer into a revolutionary, or ignoring that aristocratic outlook which he clearly embodied in its best form. Nor am I claiming that Bonhoeffer himself saw the full implications of his departure from the traditional Lutheran position. I am suggesting, rather, that the legacy of his work requires a fundamental rethinking of the presuppositions of Lutheran soteriology and social ethics.

This is not the place to go into the many questions in Bonhoeffer himself, or all the issues which must be faced in thinking through his challenge to his Lutheran tradition. I simply want to indicate: (1) that in Luther and Bonhoeffer there is an intrinsic connection between their respective positions on soteriology and social ethics; (2) that Bonhoeffer's position is clearly distinct from Luther's; (3) that this calls into question the assumption by the Lutheran tradition of the timeless validity of a conceptuality inherited from the sixteenth century; and (4) that it requires a fresh start on soteriological and ethical questions which will take account of the new personal postures and political problems which are characteristic of our own time.

2. *"VIVENDO FIT THEOLOGUS"*

When Luther said *"Vivendo, moriendo et damnando fit theologus,"* not *"intelligendo, legendo aut speculando,"* [121] he had already done a good deal of reading and thinking—if not speculating—and continued to do so for the rest of his life. His aphorism does not recommend intellectual sloth as the royal road to theological salvation. It reminds the theologian that theology, with all its reading and thinking, is rooted in and serves human existence. Erikson's study of the Reformer discloses how true this was in Luther's own case. This study, which originated as a 'purely' theological inquiry, has demonstrated the fundamental importance of the 'autobiographical dimension' in Bonhoeffer's thought. Without risking reductionism it can safely be asserted that a satisfactory understanding of his various writings and his theological development as a whole is elusive until this dimension is taken seriously.

Heretofore, Bonhoeffer interpretation has acknowledged the interrelation of his life and theology, but 'life' usually referred so much to his role in the dramatic and critical events of German church and society from 1933 to 1945 that hardly anybody pondered the simple fact that Bonhoeffer's life was *his* life. Bethge's biography, which indicates that personal as well as public life is important for Bonhoeffer's theology, has made it possible to document the details of this intimate interaction between his theology and his personal life. From now on it is impossible to continue the one–sided interpretation which severs psyche from society.

---

[121] "Living, dying, and being damned makes a theologian, not thinking, reading, and speculating." *Operationes in Psalmos* (1519), WA 5, 163, 28; cited by Bethge, DB 996, DB-E 888.

This discovery reinforced an important lesson about the *historical* character of the *psycho–social context* of theology. Bonhoeffer himself recognized this in understanding 'religion' as "a historically conditioned and transient form of human self–expression" which had been superseded by the new psychic posture of Mündigkeit. I have explored in some detail the psycho–social dimensions of Bonhoeffer's own theology. In Bonhoeffer's case, as in Luther's, we are not dealing with ahistorical and discarnate idea systems, but with the theological thinking of a real historical person, a whole human being. What Marx and Freud long ago saw about the roots of thought in social and psychic life has now come home to roost in the nests of the theologians; this holds good even when theologians, like sociologists and psychologists,[122] rightly want to pluck the reductionist feathers from these birds.

The discovery of the autobiographical dimension of Bonhoeffer's theology ought not to be unexpected when viewed in a longer historical perspective. Even prior to the Enlightenment, but especially since then, Protestant research has acknowledged the historical character of the theological tradition, of church institutions, and even of the sacred texts and their writers. But for all the illuminating insights which have derived from the historical–critical method, the whole enterprise has remained primarily an intellectual, theoretical, and academic undertaking—even if passionate controversy has often followed in the wake of its findings. Consequently, it has been possible for much theological research to remain at the verbal and ideational level. Bonhoeffer interpretation has not escaped this oversimplification of human reality, especially at the hands of Lutheran interpreters.[123] What is now quite apparent is the historical character of the human psyche which *thinks* the theological ideas. Bonhoeffer was not Luther, and a large part of his notably catholic appeal consists in his being a twentieth–century man whose problems,

---

[122] Cf. Robert Bellah, "Between Religion and Social Science," *Beyond Belief* (New York: Harper & Row, 1970), pp. 237–259.

[123] Regin Prenter's "Bonhoeffer and the Young Luther," *World Come of Age* (Philadelphia: Fortress Press, 1967), ed. Ronald Gregor Smith, creates a virtual ideational unity between Bonhoeffer and Luther; Ebeling's "The 'Non–religious Interpretation of Biblical Concepts,'" *Word and Faith* (Philadelphia: Fortress Press, 1963) and Hanfried Müller's *Von der Kirche zur Welt* both acknowledge, in their divergent ways, the historical difference between Bonhoeffer and Luther, but still persist in reading him with *conceptual schemes,* albeit modified, which derive from the sixteenth century.

struggles, discoveries, and insights are recognized by his contemporaries as their own problems and possibilities.

What this connection between theology and psyche may be in any given case—even how relatively important or unimportant it is in any particular theologian—cannot be predicted in advance, precisely because we are dealing with an historical phenomenon. But the days of the long Platonic march of theological ideas through the sort of history narrated in the tomes of Dogmengeschichte, the days of methodological docetism, stand revealed for what they were: the heyday of university theological intellectuals. Authentic theology, however, is the faithful thinking of historical people who, as whole human beings, live concrete lives in the psycho–social reality of their own times and places.

If this perspective has critical significance for the method of research in historical theology, it has an even more existential import for constructive theology. Bonhoeffer's theology is inseparable from the *"vivendo et moriendo,"* the living and dying of his personal and public life. Those who have learned from Karl Barth the necessary lesson that language about God is not speaking about human beings in a loud voice, are now faced with a question from Bonhoeffer: must we not now regard the experience of the theologian and the Christian people in their history as the human matrix in which living speech about God is discovered and spoken?

More specifically, how shall the theologian do theology? Not without *"intelligendo et legendo,"* to be sure, especially where the Bible is the text. But such thinking and reading, even of the Bible, remains what Luther would call 'sophistical' and 'speculative' if its concern is the play of ideas rather than the life of human beings in their personal–social existence. Can theologians think, speak, and write theologically unless they really *live* in the decisive history of humanity which is now being made? Dare we speak of the *activity* of the living God in history unless we ourselves are part of that action? What will we be able to say about the ethical, political, and psychic issues of humanity today unless we live in this psycho–social reality? The Black theologian indicts American theology for its blindness and default on racism;[124] is his word even heard unless it leads to the *"vivendo et moriendo"* of the theologian in the conflict for freedom and justice? Will theologians address themselves to the doctrine of ersatz reconciliation by repression—so pervasive in the churches—unless they are actually exposed to and

---

[124] James Cone, *Black Theology and Black Power* (San Francisco: Harper & Row, 1989; 2d edn), pp. 31ff.; cf. p. 2f.

wrestling with the psychological and sociological dynamics from which such perversions of Christianity spring? Will the urgent psychic, emotional, and instinctual concerns of our present situation—which range from personal through familial and institutional to political life—be taken up by theologians unless they are involved in the pressures, perplexities, and promises which these entail?

This integration of theology and life is partly what Bonhoeffer had in mind when he wrote of finding Christ at the center of life in the world, of sharing the sufferings of God, and of learning to have faith by living completely in our history. It was his hope that prayer and right action in the midst of such living would revivify Christian thinking, speaking, and organizing and give birth to a new language which is liberating and redeeming.[125] *"Vivendo fit theologus."*

3. THEOLOGY AND SOCIALITY

Bonhoeffer's sense of history, his passion for life, and his vigorous activity in the critical history of his own times prevented his theology from becoming an abstract system. If theology today is to have a like pertinence and liveliness, we must explore ways in which Bonhoeffer's thought can stimulate our present endeavors. Of necessity, such exploration must be brief and tentative here.

Throughout the exposition we have seen that Bonhoeffer consistently developed his theology in a *social* conceptuality. In so doing, he made several deliberate reconstructions of classical theological concepts which are quite fruitful. For example, his interpretations of transcendence, revelation, *imago Dei,* and original sin are instructive contributions.

These particular contributions appeared as part of a larger effort. His early theology consciously sought to articulate concepts of sociality which would go beyond the thought patterns of elder colleagues such as Barth and Bultmann. For instance, he found the theological Neo–Kantianism of the early Barth more than problematic; had he been familiar with research of the past few years, he would also have seen that central problems in Bultmann's theology are heavily informed by Marburg Neo–Kantianism.[126]

---

[125] WE 436, LPP 300.

[126] See Roger A. Johnson, *The Origins of Demythologizing* (Leiden: Brill, 1974).

I suggest that, compared with such approaches, Bonhoeffer was on the right track in seeking to think theologically with language and insights drawn from the realm of persons, human relations, and corporate communities.

This endeavor, involving as it did a major concern with theological anthropology, kept Bonhoeffer in touch with the *concrete reality* of human existence in both his thinking and his life. To give three related examples: it led to his work on power as a specific soteriological problem characteristic of contemporary personal and corporate life, to his analysis of actual psychic and social functions of religion, and to his proposal for a non–religious Christianity. In the social matrix of contemporary historical experience, Bonhoeffer sought to understand the presence of the freeing and transforming *transcendence* of Christ.

Transcendence in the personal and corporate life of concrete human history, or "the sociality of Christ and humanity," is therefore Bonhoeffer's characteristic theme. How should this theme be taken up and pursued?

Bonhoeffer's terminology and line of thought cannot be pursued uncritically. Concepts like 'objective Geist' and 'Kollektivperson'—while expressing useful insights in Bonhoeffer's early theology—can scarcely become part of our contemporary theological vocabulary. On the contrary, Bonhoeffer's line of thought points to an area of work which he himself did not, understandably, explore. His thinking about sociality requires a much closer relation between theology and the social sciences, particularly *psychology* and *sociology,* than we find in his writings. The fruitfulness of this approach can be illustrated by a brief comparison which Bonhoeffer himself would surely have found surprising.

Bonhoeffer and Freud on religion. The similarity of the critique of religion in Bonhoeffer and Freud is striking.[127] A short comparison suggests: (1) that Bonhoeffer's critique becomes more psychologically

---

[127] Remarkably, no significant comparison has yet been written. (Possibly there is some discussion of Bonhoeffer and Freud in Paul Ricoeur's article, though the periodical is difficult to obtain; cf. "L'Interpretation non–religieuse du Christianisme chez Bonhoeffer," *Cahiers du Centre protestant de l'Ouest,* November, 1966, pp. 3–20, cited in Dumas, *op. cit.,* p. 184, n. 39.) Perhaps students have been thrown off the track by Bonhoeffer's polemics against psychotherapy, or by the erroneous view that his psychiatrist father was hostile to Freud; for a correction of this opinion see my "Two Bonhoeffers on Psychoanalysis," *A Bonhoeffer Legacy,* ed. A. J. Klassen (Grand Rapids: Eerdmans, 1981), pp. 58–75.

intelligible when related to Freud's interpretation; (2) that the theological issue of authentic transcendence is involved in the positions of both men; (3) that Bonhoeffer's "religionless Christianity" is radically different from the religion Freud rightly criticized; and (4) that Bonhoeffer is a theological ally of Freud's desire to use the adult powers of the ego in relating people to "reality" and fostering psychic health and maturity.

Bonhoeffer had not read Freud, yet their analyses of religion are basically similar. For Bonhoeffer, the essence of religion is weakness, dependence, and the power God; for Freud, the main dynamics of religion are anxiety, regression, and the projection of a cosmic Father. While Bonhoeffer offered a descriptive phenomenology of religion, he did not have a psychological model to interpret the phenomena. This is what Freud offers. In Freud's analysis, id and reality collide. Nature and society, especially the latter in modern society, threaten people and inhibit instinctual expression, especially of a sexual and aggressive kind. Anxiety is thereby generated. The defense mechanism of regression conjures the childhood model of the powerful father who protected the vulnerable infant from threats to life. This regression gives rise to the 'illusion' which is religion, the 'wish' for a powerful cosmic Father to protect people from all the threats they feel. God therefore arises out of such human need, weakness, and anxiety. But, as Freud incisively points out, a high price is paid for this defense mechanism: religion reinforces people in that essentially infantile mode of dependence from which it springs, preventing them from developing an adult autonomy which uses rational skills to deal with human problems in the world. Further, there is a tax on this price; since the father was not only the protector but also the enforcer of morality, religion reinforces the authority of society, thereby externally sanctioning the social repression which gave rise to much of the anxiety in the first place, and internally generating guilt. Religion therefore is a "universal obsessional neurosis," harmful to psychological well–being and detrimental to the growth of mature independence and responsibility.[128]

---

[128] See *The Future of an Illusion,* trans. W. D. Robson–Scott, revised and newly edited by James Strachey (Garden City, New York: Doubleday & Company, 1964). I have given here Freud's basic critical theory of religion, which is most germane to the comparison with Bonhoeffer. A full account would need to consider other aspects of his view, especially as related to his oedipal theory; other works of Freud particularly as related to his oedipal theory of religion are: *Totem and Taboo, Group Psychology and the Analysis of the Ego, The Ego and the Id,* and *Moses and Monotheism.* An excellent presentation of Freud's theory of religion is given by Ernest Wallwork in *Critical Issues in Modern Religion,* ed.

Bonhoeffer's phenomenology of religion is impressively similar to Freud's description. Freud's account—even though parts of his theory must be questioned—gives psychological intelligibility to Bonhoeffer's phenomenology. In doing so it psychologically documents Bonhoeffer's view that 'religion' offers a spurious transcendence. As Freud showed, such religion basically reflects and replicates the human condition out of which it was born; it reinforces its psychic origins, and has no independent, transforming power.

To acknowledge this is to require that a theological account of authentic transcendence must be one that brings genuinely new possibilities to the self which are healing and liberating; revelation must come 'from without,' as Bonhoeffer consistently said. Such theological work, however, cannot proceed merely in an ideational frame of reference; it must examine the psychological import of its own language, imagery, and pattern of thought. Furthermore, a theology which is concerned about the psychological effectiveness of its language must simultaneously attend to that nurturing and shaping context in which ideas and language connect with the affective life and style of relations of the community of faith; I refer here to the imagery and ethos of liturgy and to the style and pattern of relations in the common life of the Christian community.

Bonhoeffer moves toward this in his proposal for a non–religious Christianity. To discern an authentic transcendence, he cuts the umbilical cord which tied Christianity to religion. His explicit purpose is theologically to affirm human 'autonomy' and 'adulthood,' particularly that dimension of the self defined as the 'ego.'[129] He demolishes religion as infantile dependence upon a power God who merely reflects human wishes, and sets over against this Christ as "the one for others." In affirming the strengths of the healthy ego, Christ supports human maturity and frees people from a narcissistic self–preoccupation to a freedom of responsible existence for others in the social life of humanity. Here Bonhoeffer is a theological ally of Freud because the Freudian

---

Roger A. Johnson et al., (Englewood Cliffs, N.J.: Prentice–Hall, 2d ed. 1990), ch. 5.

[129] Bonhoeffer's preoccupation with the ego—first with its self–serving autonomy, then with the attempt to suppress this autonomy, and finally with its liberation for the service of others—led to neglect of the instinctual dimension of life. There are, to be sure, signs in his mature writings of increasing attention to this aspect of the self, but they are not central. Here he could have learned from Freud.

critique does not apply to a "religionless Christianity" which fosters precisely those ego skills Freud held necessary for psychological maturity and health.[130]

This brief discussion of 'transcendence beyond religion' suggests the value of developing Bonhoeffer's interest in sociality by means of a much more intimate and informed partnership between theology and psychology than he himself was able to undertake.

Sociality and Sociology. With respect to corporate life, Bonhoeffer's work is at once suggestive and in need of further development. He articulated a theological conceptuality which intrinsically related corporate life and individual personal life; he taught and exemplified in his own life the ethical accountability of the corporate communities of society and the responsibility of individuals for them; he saw Christ as the Mediator of political history as much as of the existence of the individual person; by his theology and action he sought to commit the church to political responsibility over against the individualistic inwardness of 'religion.'

Due to the exigency of his history, Bonhoeffer was obliged to pursue such theological convictions in practical action and was denied the opportunity for prolonged reflection on the actual sociological forces operative in his society. Yet, analogous to the immediately preceding discussion, I contend that theological formulations must be related to concrete sociological realities if they are to communicate effectively and to motivate effectually. For example, to describe Christ as the Mediator of political history, as Bonhoeffer did, requires an understanding of the actual sociological dynamics in any given situation.

Some obvious questions come to mind when we ask about the bearing of theology and ethics on particular situations. What were the sociological, and psycho–social, factors at work in the rise of Nazi

---

[130] I cannot go into another interesting area where Bonhoeffer is more a challenger of Freud than his ally. In his concern with the problem of repression, Freud discerned a basic antagonism between the individual and society; see especially *Civilization and its Discontents* (New York: W. W. Norton, 1962). Bonhoeffer, as we have seen, postulated a 'reciprocity' rather than an antagonism between individual and corporate life. To be sure, he did not give sufficient attention to instinctual life, and therefore did not deal directly with Freud's concern on this point. Nevertheless, there is nothing in his theological position which prevents Freud's legitimate concern from being taken up. A quite significant factor here is that Bonhoeffer appears relatively free of psychic guilt (introverted aggression, which Freud related to repression) but without minimizing ethical culpability.

dictatorship in Germany? What are the sociological dynamics of racism? What gives rise to a national neurosis of ideological anti–communism and the destructive militaristic adventures which accompany it? Why is radical social change so rigidly resisted by such a large proportion of the population? What are the operative symbols of class and national self–understanding which such postures presuppose?

The pertinence of these questions to theology, I suggest, is this. The Christian message—and the language, imagery, symbols, rites, and communities which embody it—concerns the corporate life of societies and nations as much as the individual person. Therefore, theological language and the symbols and rites of the community of faith must shape the corporate identities of peoples so that the freedom, peace, justice, and healing of the gospel concretely engage actual human life with a liberating and transforming transcendence.[131] Such engagement requires theology first to inform itself with the best sociological insights it can muster, and then to formulate the Christian message in language and symbols which speak directly to the decisive socio–political issues of its situation. Otherwise, biblical and theological terms run the gravest risk of ideational docetism and impotence.

Bonhoeffer recognized that the course of his theological development brought him finally to a new beginning. Living out his own theology also deprived him of the opportunity to pursue the new stage of work he was planning. These preliminary explorations suggest some ways to take up his legacy.

---

[131] Marx's criticism of religion, theologically interpreted, is parallel to Freud's. His fundamental critique rests on the charge that religion is an ideological reflection and mystification of a particular oppressive social arrangement, and therefore makes a spurious and self–serving claim to transcendence. See my chapter on Marx in *Critical Issues in Modern Religion* (see note 128 above), Chapter 8.

Chapter 7 ·

BONHOEFFER'S *ETHICS* — A CODA

In music, as Bonhoeffer knew, a coda is a conclusion to a composition that has an integrity of its own and a certain independence from the body of the piece. This chapter is a literary coda. It was not part of the original work but is intimately connected to it. I·invoke the liberty of the coda to give particular attention to the agenda of the *Ethics* as it grew out of Bonhoeffer's participation in the resistance movement and his hopes for the future of Germany and Europe after peace had been won. In the course of the discussion I will indicate how Bonhoeffer's theology of sociality is a continuing foundation for his ethical reflection in the crucial years 1940-1943; this is the connection to the preceding chapters.[1]

The chapter is structured by the thesis that Bonhoeffer's ethical project has two main contexts. The first had special urgency: to locate his work in the resistance movement within a theological framework and the tradition of Christian ethical reflection; this is ethics *in extremis,* the ethics of *ultima ratio,* ethical reflection in an exceptional and abnormal situation. The second is a counterpoint to the first. Recognizing that such situations are precisely extreme and exceptional, and concerned for the future of Germany and a Europe at peace, Bonhoeffer wanted to sketch the contours of a Christian ethic for more normal, everyday circum-

---

[1] An overview of the theology of sociality in relation to various works of Bonhoeffer, including the *Ethics,* is found in my essay "Human Sociality and Christian Community" in John W. de Gruchy ed., *The Cambridge Companion to Dietrich Bonhoeffer* (Cambridge: Cambridge University Press, 1999), 113-33.

stances. It is one ethic, not two. But it is focused on two different contexts. I call these for convenience the ethics of tyrannicide and the ethics of everyday life. Distinguishing them without dividing them helps to clarify Bonhoeffer's exposition and arguments.

A. EDITIONS OF BONHOEFFER'S *ETHICS*

Some explanation of the German and English texts of the *Ethics*[2] is necessary before dealing with the substantive matters. The first arrangement of the handwritten manuscripts that Bonhoeffer had composed between 1940 and his arrest in 1943 was edited by Eberhard Bethge and published in 1949. This edition was organized in two parts, the first containing an arrangement of the manuscripts in seven chapters; the second part was an appendix that contained five essays, reports, and book reviews on ethical subjects. The English translation of this edition was published in 1955.

A second German arrangement was published in 1963. In distinction from the first edition that had been ordered partly following an early outline from Bonhoeffer and partly "according to the order in which they appear to have been written,"[3] this edition attempted to order all seven chapters chronologically, according to the order in which Bethge believed they had been written. (The ordering of the pieces in the appendix—erroneously called "Part Two" in the English edition—was not changed by this new arrangement.) The English translation followed the German re-arrangement in the Collins Fontana edition of 1964, the Macmillan paperback edition of 1965, and the S.C.M. edition of 1971. Bethge's new preface explaining the new arrangement was first included in the Macmillan edition of 1969. This Macmillan edition was re-issued in 1995 in a new printing with different pagination under the Touchstone imprint of Simon and Schuster—the edition that will be cited in this chapter.

Work began in the mid 1980s on the German critical edition of the *Ethik* for the *Dietrich Bonhoeffer Werke (DBW)*, and this led to yet a third

---

2   For an early report of on-going research on this subject see my essay, "The Text of Bonhoeffer's *Ethics*" in William J. Peck (ed.), *New Studies in Bonhoeffer's Ethics,* (Lewiston, New York: Mellen, 1987), 3-66.

3   Cf. Bethge, cited in Green, "Text," 6.

arrangement of the material when the volume was published in 1992.[4] The critical edition included only those texts that the editorial committee believed Bonhoeffer intended for his book on ethics.[5] And, because Bonhoeffer had not numbered his manuscripts as a series of chapters, this book is arranged as a sequence of unnumbered manuscripts. The sequence follows the chronology of Bonhoeffer's composition of the manuscripts, as reconstructed by the editorial committee.[6]

This brief history suggests that the *Ethics* presents the most complex textual issues in the Bonhoeffer corpus, followed at some distance by *Sanctorum Communio*. Whether the *DBW* arrangement will establish itself as the definitive solution to the problems of arranging the *Ethics* manuscripts remains to be seen. Already at the 1996 International Bonhoeffer Conference in Cape Town a paper was given by Hans Pfeifer, a member of the *DBW* Editorial Board, raising issues about the arrangement and "present[ing] a new concept of the structure...."[7] This chapter cannot do more than alert the reader to the textual history, and note that questions of *ordering* the manuscripts and questions of *interpreting* the text cannot ultimately be divorced. Indeed, to what extent interpretive principles entered into the chronological ordering of the manuscripts in the *DBW* edition is certainly a legitimate question. Having noted these

---

[4] A second edition of the *Ethik* was published in 1998, and the English translation of this new edition began in the same year.

[5] It therefore omits the pieces formerly in the appendix—see DBW 16, 506-35, 550-62, and 600-29—except for the manuscript "On the possibility of the word of the church to the world" which is included in *Ethics*.

[6] The evidence for the arrangement, which was largely the work of Ilse Tödt, is contained in numerous editorial notes throughout the volume.

[7] See "Ethics for the Renewal of Life: A Reconstruction of its Concept," in John W. de Gruchy (ed.), *Bonhoeffer for a New Day. Theology in a Time of Transition* (Grand Rapids: Eerdmans, 1997), 137-54. In this important essay some of the main points Pfeifer makes are these: that "the material as a whole can be regarded as belonging to a well-constructed unity" although "we are far away from an agreement about the structure of Bonhoeffer's ethics even among those who consider the papers as different parts of a whole" (138). The ethics manuscripts are part of a larger theological agenda, which involves *both* Christology *and* a philosophy of history (142), that stretches from about 1931 right through the prison letters. So they are not to be seen as occasioned *only* by Bonhoeffer's work in the resistance and the crisis of National Socialism, the latter being the "final expression" (140) of a larger crisis in the West. For a related perspective see Larry Rasmussen's essay, "The Ethics of Responsible Action," in *The Cambridge Companion to Dietrich Bonhoeffer*, ed. John W. de Gruchy (Cambridge: Cambridge University Press, 1999), 206-25.

points I will proceed to discussing the substance and content of Bonhoeffer's ethics project.

B. CHRISTIAN ETHICS, COUP D'ETAT, AND TYRANNICIDE

Bonhoeffer made his initial personal contacts with leaders of the resistance movement in February 1938. After his short sojourn in New York in the summer of 1939, he returned home and became a civilian agent of the Abwehr, German military intelligence, in August 1939. The writing of the ethics manuscripts began most likely in March 1940. Allusions to his historical situation in a war waged by Nazi Germany are readily apparent.[8] It is not a time of stable, established orders of life, he writes, but of "villains and saints" who emerge from the primeval depths.[9] Hitler is portrayed in everything but name as a "tyrannical despiser" of humanity—in contrast to the noble few in the resistance movement.

> Fear he calls responsibility. Desire he calls keenness. Irresolution becomes solidarity. Brutality becomes masterfulness. Human weak-nesses are played upon with unchaste seductiveness, so that meanness and baseness are reproduced and multiplied ever anew. The vilest contempt for humanity goes about its sinister business with the holiest of protestations about devotion to the human cause. ...The small band of the upright are reviled. Their bravery is called insubordination; their self-control is called pharisaism; their independence arbitrariness, and their masterfulness arrogance.[10]

The Third Reich is depicted as an "idolization of death."

> There is no clearer indication of the idolization of death than when a period claims to be building for eternity[11] and yet life has no value in this period, or when big words are spoken of a "new man," of a new world and of a new society which is to be ushered in, and yet all that is new is the destruction of life as we know it.[12]

---

8   For an overview of connections between Bonhoeffer's texts and con-temporary events during the Third Reich and World War II, see the Editor's Afterword to the German critical edition, DBW 6 424-34.

9   E-E 66.

10   E-E 74f.

11   The allusion is to the 1,000 year Reich propaganda of National Socialism.

12   E-E 80.

In this situation Bonhoeffer could not write with complete candor. The risk that his papers would be confiscated was ever present—indeed, when he was arrested on April 5 1943, the Gestapo removed (and later returned) the manuscript on "The 'Ethical' and the 'Christian' as a Subject."[13] Consequently it is not surprising that we do not find treatment of the justification of tyrannicide as contained in the tradition of Christian ethics, for example in the works of Aquinas and Calvin. Nevertheless, Bonhoeffer's own interpretation of his involvement in plans for a coup d'etat and tyrannicide is unmistakably clear. Put bluntly, a Nazi prosecutor who was familiar with Bonhoeffer's theology could find plenty of evidence through a careful reading of the *Ethics* to charge him with treason—according to Nazi views of loyalty.

A good place to approach Bonhoeffer's ethic of resistance is the analysis of ethical stances he judged inadequate to the times;[14] it is found at the beginning of the manuscript "Ethics as Formation," the one from which the allusions to the Nazi regime were just quoted above. Written in autumn 1940, this analysis was included in the piece "After Ten Years" that Bonhoeffer gave as a present to Eberhard Bethge and his conspiracy colleagues, Hans von Dohnanyi, and Hans Oster, at Christmas-New Year 1942-1943.[15] The title refers, of course, to the ten years of resistance to National Socialism in the church and politics since Hitler's ascendancy in January 1933. The excerpt from the *Ethics* manuscript appears under the significant heading "Who Stands Fast?" Six ethical postures are sketched by Bonhoeffer and criticized in light of the experience of the past decade: they are based, respectively, on reason, principle (or "moral fanaticism"), conscience, duty, absolute freedom, and private virtuousness. Given Bonhoeffer's exposé of the failure of these ethical postures in the 1930s, it is surprising—and revealing—to note how he summarizes his analysis. These are not the ethics of evil people, but of "the best of men"; reason, conscience, duty, moral principle and the like are the "achievements and attitudes of a noble humanity." "It is all too easy,"

---

[13] It may be significant that these were the papers Bonhoeffer left out on his desk to be discovered, since they focus more on ethics for normal life rather than on resistance ethics. ("Subject," incidentally, is a more appropriate translation of the German "Thema" than using the English "theme.")

[14] E-E 67-69.

[15] It is the opening piece in all German and English editions of *Letters and Papers from Prison;* see LPP 4-6. Another translation appears in the Bonhoeffer excerpts edited by Hans Rothfels and translated by Keith R. Crim as *I Loved This People* (Richmond: John Knox Press, 1965), 17-38.

Bonhoeffer continues sympathetically, "to pour scorn on the weapons we have inherited from our ancestors, weapons which served them to perform great feats...."

What is wrong, then, with these noble ethical postures? What is their common failure? They are weapons *"which in the present struggle can no longer be sufficient."*[16] That is, none of these approaches to ethics can provide the moral basis—in reflection and behavior—of the coup d'etat and tyrannicide for which Bonhoeffer and his resistance colleagues are working. This is the criterion against which these ethical postures have been measured and found wanting. Rationalists cannot perceive the depths of evil. The moral fanatic, opposing evil with his principles, is trapped by his clever adversary. The person of conscience is confused by evil and "can never understand that a bad conscience may be healthier and stronger than a conscience which is deceived."[17] The person of duty ends up obeying the devil's orders,[18] for duty cannot produce *"the bold stroke of the deed* which is done on one's own *free responsibility,* the only kind of deed which can *strike at the heart of evil and overcome it."*[19] The posture of absolute freedom has the strength of valuing *the necessary deed* rather than a spotless conscience, but freedom to choose the bad in order to avoid what is worse may actually end up choosing what is worse. (This is the only option of the six about which Bonhoeffer is ambivalent, describing it as potentially tragic; the reason for the ambivalence is because this position is closest to his own position of "free responsibility.") The posture of private virtue abandons the ethical challenges of public life, and is blind and deaf to the surrounding wrongs. In short, it is because such ethics cannot provide a moral framework for the coup d'etat and tyrannicide planned by the resistance movement that Bonhoeffer judges them inadequate to "the present struggle."

How, then, does he propose to describe a Christian ethical alternative to these venerable options? What is his answer to the question "who stands fast?" What weapons are adequate to "the present struggle"? What ethical position provides for a "bold deed" which can "strike at evil and overcome it"?

---

16   E-E 69f., italics mine.
17   E-E 68.
18   Adolf Eichmann is a classic case.
19   E-E 68.

Only the person whose final standard is not his reason, his principles, his conscience, his duty, his freedom, or his virtue but who is ready to sacrifice all this when he is called to *obedient and responsible action in faith* and *in exclusive allegiance to God*—the responsible person who makes his whole life an answer to the question and call of God.[20]

"Responsible action," also called "free responsibility," as portrayed here is in fact at the center of Bonhoeffer's ethic of resistance.

Responsible action, however, cannot be separated from "exclusive allegiance to God." With this phrase Bonhoeffer reminds us of a basic premise of his ethics which is boldly stated in two different places. The very first point of "Christ, Reality and Good," which the new *DBW* edition of *Ethik* regards as Bonhoeffer's initial and programmatic manuscript of the work, states that anyone wishing to engage in Christian ethical reflection must reject as irrelevant the usual questions about being good and doing good. Instead one must ask "the utterly and totally different question, 'What is the will of God?'"[21] The question of goodness is shifted from the human subject, the Christian believer, to the will of God, to God's reality and God's goodness. But this is more than a standard 'Barthian' move—it is specifically related to the decisions confronting Bonhoeffer in the resistance movement. "All concern with ethics will have as its starting point that God shows himself to be good, even if this involves the risk that I myself and the world are not good but thoroughly bad."[22] Here Bonhoeffer is opening up the possibility that doing the will of God may not coincide with behavior that is normally regarded as "good," even by fellow Christians. Put more sharply, in doing the will of God one may become a sinner in the process.

It is precisely in this direction that "After Ten Years" continues following the section "Who Stands Fast" just examined above. The next section is called "Civil Courage." In it Bonhoeffer first argues that Germans have learned obedience, subordinating personal desires and beliefs to their vocation. But self-sacrifice and submission to authority can be exploited for evil ends, and when that happened "all the moral principles of the German were bound to totter."[23] That is to say, duty, conscience, reason, principles, and virtue all fail and are inadequate in the present struggle against National Socialism. The fundamental need in

[20] LPP 5, italics mine.

[21] E-E 186. See also "The Love of God and the Decay of the World," E-E 21: "The knowledge of good and evil seems to be the aim of all ethical reflection. The first task of Christian ethics is to invalidate this knowledge."

[22] E-E 187.

[23] LPP 6.

Germany, and the ground of civil courage, is "free and responsible action."

Civil courage, in fact, can grow only out of the free responsibility of free men. Only now are Germans beginning to discover the meaning of free responsibility. *"It depends on a God who demands responsible action in a free wager of faith, and who promises forgiveness and consolation to the man who becomes a sinner in that venture."* [24]

So far Bonhoeffer has led us up to the rarified atmosphere at the peak of an ethical Sinai. Common frameworks of ethics—duty, conscience, principles, reason, and virtue—have all been stripped away. We stand morally naked before God, knowing only that we must be ready for "a free wager of faith," a deed of "free responsibility," in exclusive allegiance to the will of God. But where shall we find ethical clothes? In other words, if Bonhoeffer is now in a position where planning for a coup d'etat and the killing of Hitler is not impeded by ethical thinking which is irrelevant to "the present struggle," where are the ethical impulses that support this course of action? If the will of God cannot be deduced from a manual or principles already in hand, what are the resources of faith which lead one to "a free wager"? The answer is found in two main places, Bonhoeffer's Christology and his discussion of "The Structure of Responsible Life."

In "Ethics as Formation" Bonhoeffer turns to Christology as soon as he has completed his analysis of the ethical postures which are inadequate to the struggle of the resistance movement. Indeed, "formation" in the manuscript title is simultaneously a Christological and an ethical category. Christology is treated under the rubric of Jesus Christ as the reconciler of God and the world, and developed under the headings of incarnation, cross, and resurrection.[25] These christological themes are

---

[24] Ibid., italics mine. Correcting the translation from a "bold venture of faith" to a "free wager of faith" is important because Bonhoeffer regularly speaks of "free responsibility." Further, "wager" is preferable to "venture" in the Neville Horton Smith translation. The German "Wagnis" and the English "wager" come from the same root, and both entail more risk than the word "venture" suggests. In speaking of a "wager of faith," [Glaubenswagnis] it may be that Bonhoeffer is alluding to Pascal's wager, now understood of an ethical decision.

[25] Compare the christological section of Chapter VII where, directly influenced by Barth, Bonhoeffer adds a paragraph on "Jesus Christ as the eternal Son with the Father" to his usual reference Christ as reconciler in the incarnation, cross and resurrection; see E-E 291-294, and compare E-E 72-83, 130-32.

loaded with contemporary ethical freight. How are they related to Christian ethical life in the resistance movement?

In Jesus Christ the world is reconciled with God—not by conscience, duty, virtue and the like, but by the lived love of God. God's love does not "withdraw from reality... but suffers the reality of the world in all its hardness."[26] More than that, God takes upon God's own self the guilt of the world and thereby "the abyss of the love of God encompasses even the most abysmal godlessness of the world."[27] Christ is the center of history,[28] who calls the Christian into the world in all its godlessness, knowing that action even in this godless world occurs within its reconciliation to God in Jesus Christ.

Spelling this out, Bonhoeffer deliberately sets the christological themes in opposition to themes of National Socialism.[29] Thus the incarnate Christ is set opposite the "tyrannical despiser of human beings"—it is in this section that the disguised portrait of Hitler, discussed above, is found; the cross is set in opposition to worldly success; and the resurrection in opposition to the idolization of death—the section where the cynical and deceptive values of the Third Reich are exposed.

Scrutinizing these paragraphs for ethical guidance pertinent to Bonhoeffer's activity in the resistance movement we find that the *incarnation* reveals the love of God for the *real world and real people*, not an ideal (that is, fantasy) world of human wishes and judgments. Furthermore, in the incarnation God takes on humanity itself, human character, real humanity. This is a judgment on the tyrant who cynically despises human beings, mistrusts them, demeans them, and scorns their rights—as also on the well-meaning "philanthropist" who deifies human beings. The *cross*, likewise, is a judgment on those who equate good with historical success. "In the cross of Christ God confronts the successful person with the sanctification of pain, sorrow, humility, failure, poverty,

---

[26] E-E 72.

[27] Ibid.

[28] Cf. 220ff. above on this theme in the Christology lectures, including its explicit political implications. Christ as the Kollektivperson of the new humanity, and therefore the center of history, is from *Sanctorum Communio* onwards a fundamental tenet of the theology of sociality.

[29] Eberhard Bethge clearly recognized this when he supplied the subheadings drawing attention to Bonhoeffer's critical themes descriptive of National Socialism: "The Despiser of Men," "The Successful Man," and "The Idolization of Death"; cf. E-E 73-79.

loneliness and despair."[30]   The *resurrection* is the good news that
"humanity has been made new in Jesus Christ.... The new human being
has been created."[31]   Christ's resurrection exposes "that idolization of
death which is prevalent among us today."[32] In its victory over the grave
and its eschatological promise the resurrection relativizes death—no
unimportant matter for those engaged in a life-risking wager.[33]

In this manuscript on "Ethics as Formation," the anthropological and
ethical correlates of these christological themes are spelled out under the
rubric of "conformation," that is, being formed according to the incarnate, crucified, and resurrected Christ.

To be formed in the gestalt of the Incarnate is to be really human
before God—not less and not more.   Contempt for humanity and
idolization of humanity are not Christian options.   In two specific
respects Bonhoeffer rejects Nazi ideology here.   The cult of the heroic,
of the demigod, is repudiated.   So is the propaganda that there is an ideal
type or "definite picture of the human character,"[34] a clear rejection of the
Aryan ideal of National Socialism which was an intrinsic part of its anti-
semitic racism.   "The rich and manifold variety of God's creation" is not
to be forced violently into a "false uniformity."[35]

To be conformed with the image of the Crucified means daily to live
under the sentence of God upon sin, to live as justified only by grace.   In
this paragraph Bonhoeffer first continues the thought of the previous one
by arguing that, also because of sin, "one cannot raise oneself up above
any other person or set oneself before others as a model...."[36]   He then
goes on to quote a poem of Karl Friedrich Harttmann who wrote that "it
is in suffering that the Master imprints upon our minds and hearts his own

---

[30]   E-E 79; cf. "The View from Below," LPP 17.

[31]   E 80; cf. *Sanctorum Communio* 137ff., 147, 158.

[32]   E-E 80, italics mine.

[33]   E 80. See the well-known passage of July 21 (the day after the last failed
attempt on Hitler's life), LPP 370, where Bonhoeffer speaks of "this-worldli-
ness" and sharing the suffering of God in the world; compare it to the affirmation
here that, in light of the resurrection, "one takes of life what it offers, not all or
nothing but good and evil, the important and the unimportant, joy and sorrow;
one neither clings convulsively to life nor casts it frivolously away."

[34]   E-E 82.

[35]   Ibid.

[36]   E-E 83.

all-valid image."[37] This anticipates the recurrent idea in *Letters and Papers from Prison* of sharing the suffering of God in the world. But that idea is so important in the *theologia crucis* of the *Letters* because Bonhoeffer had already learned that resistance to tyranny meant walking the path of suffering, including acceptance of the judgment of God.

Being conformed to the Risen One means living as a new person before God—but this is life in the midst of death and righteousness in the midst of sin. Since the glory of Christ remains hidden, so does the new life of Christ's follower—it is a "secret."[38] There are only eschatological hints of the new life that is to be revealed: "But he who knows espies already here and there a gleam of what is to come."[39] Is it reading too much to construe these "gleams" as signs and hopes for a new order after a coup, as well as referring to the final eschaton?

If these Christological and anthropological paragraphs contain regular connections to Bonhoeffer's *Sitz im Leben* in the resistance movement, when we turn to the manuscript "History and Good," and particularly to its section on "The Structure of Responsible Life," the references to the context fairly leap off the page. Here is where we can expect the most direct reflection on "doing the will of God" in relation to planning for a coup and tyrannicide.

Some background to this manuscript will reinforce my argument for its importance to Bonhoeffer's ethic of resistance. First, of the whole *Ethics* this is the only manuscript which Bonhoeffer reworked and polished into a second draft.[40]

Second, in writing this material Bonhoeffer did something that he did not do with his other ethics manuscripts—he sought special help for its topics. In the autumn of 1941 he tried to get three Swiss theologians to write articles for a Christmas pamphlet of the Confessing Church.[41] Each of the subjects he proposed are found in "History and Good." Although this plan did not come to fruition, Bonhoeffer's assignment of subjects is of special interest—particularly the theme of "responsibility."

---

[37] Ibid. Cf. E 82, editorial note 72, on the Harttmann hymn from which this comes.

[38] Cf. LPP 281, 286, and 300 on the discipline of the secret.

[39] E-E 83.

[40] Both versions are published in DBW 6 218-99. The English translation until now has contained only the second draft; the first version was formerly published only in GS III 455-77. A close analysis and comparison of the two versions would be a valuable study.

[41] Cf. Charlotte von Kirschbaum to Pastor Paul Vogt, DBW 16 207f.

This constituted the heart of the chapter, as we can see from the two main sections on "The Structure of Responsible Life" and "The Place of Responsibility."[42] This was the subject, "Christian Responsibility," that Bonhoeffer wanted to assign to the only theologian to whom he gave real authority in his work—Karl Barth.[43]

Because of the *content* of this material, plus Bonhoeffer's reworking of it and his effort to secure Barth's help, I believe that we are dealing here with the core ethical concerns which Bonhoeffer engaged in his ethical reflection on the coup d'etat and tyrannicide. Here he is most explicit about the themes that informed his thinking about "doing the will of God" in Nazi Germany. His thinking concentrated on four themes: Stellvertretung—vicarious representative action; correspondence with reality; taking on guilt; and freedom.

That the "structure of responsible life" has these four dimensions is obscured by the arrangement of the earlier English and German texts, which both list *six* subheadings: deputyship; correspondence with reality; the world of things—pertinence, statecraft; acceptance of guilt; conscience; and freedom; but in fact the second and third in this listing belong together as "correspondence with reality" and similarly the discussion of conscience is part of "acceptance of guilt." Bonhoeffer makes the fourfold division quite explicit right at the beginning of the treatment. Responsibility, he says, is composed of "two factors," *obligation [Bindung]*[44] and *freedom [Freiheit]*.[45] Each of these has two dimensions. *Obligation* entails both *vicarious representative action*

---

[42] The organization of this chapter is the same as the first part of Bonhoeffer's Christology lectures on "The Present Christ." He discussed first the *form* [Gestalt] of Christ and then the *place* [Ort] of Christ; here there is a slight verbal, but not conceptual, variation when he writes of the *structure* [Struktur] of responsibility and the *place* [Ort] of responsibility. Cf. DBW 12 279f.

[43] It is no accident that when, in the following spring of 1942, he was able to read proofs of a volume on Barth's ethics in the *Church Dogmatics*, Bonhoeffer appropriated Barth's approach in great gulps! (The other proposed contributors were Wilhelm Vischer on "History and Eschatology," and Pastor Alfred de Quervain on "Forgiveness of Sins.")

[44] Later in the discussion he returns to his usual word, *responsibility [Verantwortung]*; cf. E 283, E-E 244.

[45] These are "corresponding," or reciprocal, concepts in that each mutually entails the other; cf. E-E 244. (Here, among other things, Bonhoeffer presupposes the classical Christian understanding of freedom, namely freedom to do the good, the will of God, as opposed to the modern libertarian understanding according to which freedom has no content but is merely a matter of choice.)

[Stellvertretung] and *correspondence with reality. Freedom* involves both *personal accountability of life and action [Selbstzurechnung]* and the *wager [Wagnis] of concrete decision.*[46]

Vicarious representative action is a theme found in all of Bonhoeffer's theology; it is central to the theology of sociality, beginning with *Sanctorum Communio.* Its meaning is first of all Christological, referring

> to the free initiative and responsibility that Christ takes for the sake of humanity in his incarnation, cross and resurrection.... By anthropological analogy Stellvertretung involves acting responsibly on behalf of others and on behalf of communities to which one belongs.[47]

As early as his dissertation Bonhoeffer also noted "an ethical concept of vicarious representative action [that] signifies the voluntary assumption of evil in another person's stead." It is analogous to, but not identified with, Christ's action for humanity. In 1927, and with reference to Old Testament prophets acting on behalf of their people, he gave as an illustration "an act of human heroic love for one's country...."[48] In 1942, having defined "life" by Jesus, Bonhoeffer argues that the life of Jesus is not the isolated individual seeking personal perfection, but that of the One who lives in vicarious representative action for humanity;[49] he is "the responsible person par excellence." Accordingly, "that is why through him all human life is a life of vicarious representative action."[50]

---

[46] E 256f., E-E 220f. These two factors, each with two dimensions, yield "the [fourfold] arrangement for our discussion of the structure of responsible life," as Bonhoeffer explicitly says, repeating this point again in his summary (E 221, 249). The six subheadings in the old editions come from the editor, not from Bonhoeffer's manuscripts; see his own outline with these four subheadings in Bonhoeffer, *Zettelnotizen für eine "Ethik"* (Gütersloh: Chr. Kaiser, 1993; ed. Ilse Tödt), 105f.; the detail on page 106 evidently relates to the treatment of these four themes in the second version of "History and Good." In addition, note that the word "wager" [Wagnis] here is the same one Bonhoeffer uses in "After Ten Years" when arguing that civil courage requires "a free wager of faith."

[47] SC-E 120, editorial note 29. Note that the meaning of Bonhoeffer's term is broader than the understanding of "vicarious action" which focuses soteriology almost exclusively on the cross. The word "representative" especially means to highlight action on behalf of, and for the sake of, *communities* of people.

[48] SC-E 156, note 17.

[49] This is the content distilled into the phrase in the prison letters, "existing for others."

[50] E-E 222.

Thus far Bonhoeffer has laid this foundation for his ethics of resistance. Christ is life, and the Christian lives in the dialectic of grace and judgment of Christ's incarnation, cross and resurrection. Christ's vicarious representative action for humanity defines "responsibility" as being responsible for one's neighbor, indeed, "the complete surrender of one's life for the other person."[51] Human vicarious representative action is seen not only in individual and familial relations, such as a parents and teachers acting in responsibility for their children and students. It also involves people acting in responsibility for communities and nations, such as the biblical prophet or the modern diplomat. This includes Dietrich Bonhoeffer—and his family members and colleagues in the resistance movement—acting in responsibility for Germany.

Correspondence with reality is the second theme in the structure of responsible life. We turn to its pages to see how Bonhoeffer moves from his Christological foundation to the ethical field of resistance. This is by far the longest section in the discussion of responsible life—and it is hardly surprising that someone planning a coup would be concerned with reality. Contrary to the pragmatist, or "realist," however, Bonhoeffer continues with his Christological reflection! On the basis of the incarnation the Christian sees God and the world together in Jesus Christ, in a dialectical relation which neither affirms the situation of the world on principle nor negates it on principle. Both a servile submission to the facticity of the situation and an attempt to impose an abstract or ideal principle of action upon a recalcitrant situation are excluded. The world is loved, condemned, and reconciled by God, and the Christian acts in the world from this knowledge. Simplicity flows from this knowledge; one is not torn apart by conflicts of principle. Vicarious, responsible action [Stellvertretung], grounded in the vicarious, responsible action of Christ for the world, is the paradigm of Christian action.

This "action which is in accordance with reality is limited by our creatureliness."[52] We are limited, first, in that we are human, not gods. The situation must be analyzed; the likely results of a given action must be assessed; intermediate steps toward a goal must be considered; the limitations of human knowledge must be recognized. Finally, returning to a central and familiar theme, Bonhoeffer repeats his view that vicari-

---

[51] Ibid.

[52] E-E 230. Here one should recall that the idea of limit or boundary [Grenze, Schranke] is a key ethical concept in Bonhoeffer's theology of sociality.

ous, representative action is not justified in advance by an ideology or principle. Rather, the "deed is delivered up solely to God at the moment of its performance. ... The responsible person puts the action into the hands of God and lives by God's grace and judgment."[53] We are limited not only as creatures of God but also, second, by the responsibility of our neighbors. Christian responsibility is not unlimited, titanic, but creaturely and humble.

The next part of this section deals with *appropriateness [Sachgemässheit]*. Responsible action is appropriate to the sphere of activity in question, and to the rules that govern it—whether that sphere be mathematics, family life, industry, or commerce. But it is politics, "statecraft," to which Bonhoeffer quickly turns and on which he dwells. Statecraft is at the opposite end of the spectrum from technical rules. You can make a radio according to technical rules; but statecraft, intimately connected as it is with human existence, transcends the technical aspects that it does indeed entail. At this point a crucial statement appears:

> Indeed, precisely because the state is indissolubly bound up with human existence, its essential law extends far beyond the range of anything that can be expressed in terms of rules. *And it is precisely at this point that the full depth of responsible action is first reached.*[54]

Bonhoeffer immediately continues to discuss the *extraordinary situation* in which the *"raw necessities of human life"*[55] collide with all principles, laws, norms, and rules—the situation of ultimate necessity. Responsible action that is appropriate to reality must recognize the existence and claim of such situations. Indeed, such extreme situations of necessity, precisely because they transcend law and normal morality, "appeal directly to the free responsibility of the agent, a responsibility which is bound by no law."[56] Only "necessities of life" [Lebensnotwendigkeiten] constitute these situations of *ultima ratio;* responsible and appropriate action in these extreme situations aims to preserve and serve nothing less than life itself.

Here we arrive at an unspoken conclusion of Bonhoeffer's argument. The overt conclusion is this: "In the political field this ultima ratio is war,

---

[53] E-E 231. "Judgment" reflects a correction of the German text from "Gunst" to "Gericht"; cf. E 268.

[54] E-E 234, italics mine.

[55] E 272, E-E 234, italics mine.

[56] E 272, E-E 235.

but it can also be deception and the breaking of treaties for the sake of one's necessities of life."[57] The unspoken conclusion is this: tyrannicide and coup d'etat are equally actions called for in extreme situations by "necessities of life." Christian ethics had long recognized this by giving tyrannicide a parallel place to just war doctrine. But tyrannicide was a subject that Bonhoeffer could not commit to paper, much as he believed it was necessary to kill Hitler and was himself involved in planning the coup d'etat.

Responsible appropriate action, in such an extraordinary situation, must therefore be done in freedom. Here Bonhoeffer uses the same language as he did when discussing civil courage in "After Ten Years." In the freedom necessary to take responsible, appropriate action in the extreme situation which transcends law and normal morality, "the decision must be made in a free wager."[58] And, just as he had written at Christmas 1942, here too that free wager is placed in the context of faith: "one's own decision and deed are entrusted to the divine governance of history." Whether one regards as the ultimate authority the law, on the one hand, or free responsibility before God, on the other

> in either case a person becomes culpable and so can live only from God's grace and forgiveness. Each of these people—whether bound by law or acting in free responsibility—must hear and accept the accusation of the other. Neither can become the judge of the other. Judgment remains with God.[59]

If free responsible action which is appropriate to the situation has brought Bonhoeffer to this point—if doing the will of God brings one face-to-face with God's judgment (paradoxical though it may sound), it is understandable that his argument next takes up issues of guilt and conscience.

Readiness to take on guilt. Significantly, this section—including its treatment of *conscience*—is the next longest part of Bonhoeffer's discussion of responsible action. I emphasize the active verb in "readiness to *take on* guilt" rather than the more passive translation "acceptance of guilt."

Bonhoeffer's paradigm is Jesus. Neither concerned for being good himself (cf. Matthew 19:17) nor with realizing some ethical ideal, Jesus

---

[57] E 273, E-E 235, rev; Bonhoeffer also uses "Lebensnotwendigkeiten" in this sentence.

[58] E 274, E-E 236, rev. Consistently, the German term is again "Wagnis."

[59] E 275, E-E 236, rev.

is solely moved by love for real people. That is why, in ultimate identification with humanity's plight, the sinless Jesus takes on guilt. Indeed, his sinlessness is documented precisely in this! Not the heart turned in upon itself, concerned to advance its own cause or protect its own reputation; not the concern for self at the expense of others—no, the giving of the self, "existing for others," is why Jesus is the ultimate origin and ground of responsibility in vicarious representative action.[60] To take the opposite course, to set one's personal innocence above responsible action for humanity, is to be "blind to the more irredeemable guilt that one incurs precisely in so doing."[61] In just these terms Eberhard Bethge has explained Bonhoeffer's participation in the conspiracy. To those who asked how Bonhoeffer could become guilty by planning tyrannicide and a coup, he replied: How could he *not* do so? To fail to do so, in the face of Nazi aggression and the Holocaust, would be to incur the greater culpability.

Advocating that responsible action in circumstances like Bonhoeffer's requires one to take on guilt leads to the obvious question: what about conscience? From discussion of this subject earlier in this book we will hardly expect Bonhoeffer to equate conscience with the voice of God. A different emphasis, however, comes to the fore when compared with the early writings.[62] Formally speaking, conscience protects the unity and integrity of the self at a fundamental level. Imagine a torturer telling a mother he will let her go free if she will kill her baby; imagine someone who was offered money to betray his parents to murderers. To commit such acts would assault the very integrity of one's being. We expect such propositions to be rejected with revulsion. "I couldn't live with myself if I did that. I would rather die than do such a thing."

If natural conscience, formally, is a call to protect the unity of the self against self-destruction, the theological question then is: what constitutes the unity of the *Christian conscience?* Bonhoeffer answers: not the autonomy of one's own ego and its efforts at self-justification, but Jesus Christ. What does this mean? Invoking the Chalcedonian paradigm, Bonhoeffer argues that when Jesus Christ becomes one's conscience the

---

60 E-E 237f.

61 E 276, E-E 138.

62 That view is also repeated here: "The call of conscience in the natural person is the attempt on the part of the ego to justify itself in its knowledge of good and evil before God, before other people, and before itself, and to secure its own continuance in this self-justification" (E-E 239).

Christian is set free to serve God and one's neighbor.[63] Christ liberates
the conscience from a law of the self, and, what is the same thing, from
a Kantian formalism of principle which would lead to the "grotesque
conclusion" that a friend should be turned over to a murderer.[64] The
origin and goal of the Christian conscience is not a dead law but *the living
God and living human beings.*

Here Bonhoeffer has led the discussion of the freed conscience back
to taking on guilt, which he illustrates with the example of Jesus. Jesus
broke the law of the sabbath in order to sanctify it in love for God and for
human beings. He disobeyed his parents to serve God and thereby purify
obedience to parents. For the love of real human beings he came to be
forsaken by God on the cross.

> As the one loving without sin he became guilty. He wanted to share
> in the community [Gemeinschaft] of human guilt. He rejected the
> devil's accusation which was intended to divert him from this course.
> Thus it is Jesus Christ who sets conscience free for the service of God
> and of our neighbor. He sets conscience free even and especially when
> a person enters into the community of human guilt. The conscience
> which has been set free from the law will not be afraid to enter into the
> guilt of another person for the other person's sake, and indeed precisely
> in doing this it will show itself in its purity. The conscience which has
> been set free is not timid like the conscience which is bound by the law,
> but it stands wide open for our neighbors and their concrete distress.
> So conscience joins with responsibility which has its foundation in
> Christ in bearing guilt for the sake of the neighbor.[65]

Significantly Bonhoeffer here enters a qualification: responsible action
requires one to take on guilt "from time to time."[66] Not all responsible
action requires it, but certain circumstances do, including conspiring to
produce a coup d'etat and to kill a tyrant.

Yet there remains a tension between conscience and the free responsible action which incurs guilt. This tension arises in two ways. First, the

---

[63] Cf. Paul's "I live, yet not I, Christ lives in me" (Gal. 2:20). See also
Luther on conscience as the seat of Christ who expels from it the tyrannical law;
cf. *A Commentary on St. Paul's Epistle to the Galatians*, ed. Philip S. Watson
(London: James Clarke, 1953), 28.

[64] E-E 241.

[65] E 278ff., E-E 240f., rev. Note that the examples Bonhoeffer gives of
Jesus breaking the law refer to the third and fourth commandments of the
Decalogue.

[66] E 281, E-E 242.

Christian conscience retains its role as the self's call to unity,[67] and there are limits to what different people can bear. Bonhoeffer gives a range of examples: firing an employee who is no longer able to support a family; violating a political treaty; and declaring a war. We can add examples from Bonhoeffer's own resistance context. Colonel Hans Oster, leader of the resistance movement in the Military Intelligence [Abwehr], revealed to the Dutch in 1940 the impending German invasion.[68] Bonhoeffer certainly regarded this as an example of free responsible action. One can easily imagine, however, another career military officer who might have been unable to bring himself to do what he had been trained over a lifetime to regard as treason. Or one could imagine another officer who would be willing to do what Oster did, but would not be willing to shoot Hitler personally.

Second, conscience liberated in Christ is still the voice of the law to love God and to love the neighbor as this is articulated in the Decalogue, the Sermon on the Mount, and the ethical teaching of the apostles. Responsible action is confronted by this law, which is the law of life. But the law does not have the last word. "In the contest between conscience and concrete responsibility the free decision must be given for Christ."[69] Because Christ is the ground of concrete responsibility and also the Lord of conscience, Bonhoeffer can make the striking statement that "it is the same thing if we say that the responsible person becomes guilty without sin, or if we say that only the man [Mann] of liberated conscience can bear responsibility."[70] This section about taking on guilt concludes as follows: "Before other people [Menschen] the man [Mann] of free responsibility is justified by necessity; before himself he is acquitted by his conscience; but before God he hopes only for grace."[71]

---

[67] This is not a flaw in the argument, as if Bonhoeffer were vacillating between different roles of the "natural" and the "liberated" conscience. Rather, the 'carrying power' of the liberated conscience varies in different people.

[68] DB-E 675.

[69] E 283, E-E 243f. This statement is equivalent to the one noted earlier where Bonhoeffer said that Christian ethics is concerned with the question, "What is the will of God?"

[70] E 283, E-E 244, rev. The use of "Mann," the German for a man, rather than his usual "Mensch" (human being) is highly unusual in Bonhoeffer. I read it here as an autobiographical reference. It is used again a few sentences later in the closing sentence of this section.

[71] E 283, E-E 244, rev.

Freedom. Bonhoeffer understands freedom not in the modern, secular, and consumerist sense as contentless choice, but—in the classical Christian way which extends from Paul through Augustine and Luther to Karl Barth—as freedom to do the good, that is, ultimately, freedom to love God and neighbor. Accordingly, freedom and responsibility mutually imply each other.[72] This understanding of freedom is deeply rooted in Bonhoeffer. In *Sanctorum Communio*, existing for one another is one of the hallmarks of the Christian church-community. In *Creation and Fall* freedom is not an individual capacity but a relationship with and for the other. Theologically these are grounded, as seen in *Act and Being*, in God's freedom for humanity in Christ.[73] Consequently, "the action of the responsible person occurs in the obligation to God and the neighbor, the obligation which alone gives complete freedom, as they encounter me in Jesus Christ."[74]

Responsible action, nevertheless, must be taken in the midst of the relativities, the "twilight" as Bonhoeffer puts it,[75] of the human situation. Given the innumerable options, including the necessity of choosing between competing goods and not simply between good and evil, he emphasizes again that responsible action has the character of a "free wager." Precisely because such action is done by freely surrendering any claim to knowing its own goodness, God's good occurs.[76] Being willing to risk responsible action while surrendering any self-justification of its intrinsic goodness means both being a freely responsible historical actor and leaving the course of history in the hands of God. Bonhoeffer concludes:

> Precisely the one who acts in the freedom of his own most personal responsibility sees his action turned over [einmünden] to God's guidance. The free deed knows itself as ultimately God's deed, the decision as God's guidance, the free wager as divine necessity.[77]

---

[72] E 283, E-E 244.

[73] These interpretations of human and divine freedom are hallmarks of Bonhoeffer's theology of sociality.

[74] E 284, E-E 245. Note that Bonhoeffer speaks personally of the obligation which encounters *me,* not the generic *us* of the pre-DBWE English translation. This is yet another indication of his deep, personal involvement in the ethical urgency of this section.

[75] Perhaps an allusion to Hegel's owl of Minerva.

[76] E 275, E-E 246. Bonhoeffer notes that this is a key aspect of this manuscript's subject, "History and Good," and that it requires further discussion.

[77] E 285, E-E 245f.

This completes what Bonhoeffer calls the "structure" of responsible life. It has dealt with the ethical profile and orientation of the Christian person in the encounter with the specific historical context which was Bonhoeffer's own. Although the chapter is unfinished,[78] it continues by beginning the discussion of "the place of responsibility," and in particular vocation. After discussing some basic points about vocation, Bonhoeffer returns to the subject of responsible action and the relationship between freedom and law. Once again he picks examples from the Decalogue, taking up once more the issue of war with its killing and lying. He comments: "The suspension of the law can only serve the true fulfilment of it. In war, for example, there is killing, lying, and expropriation solely in order to restore to their rightful place life, truth, and property."[79] This was precisely the purpose of Bonhoeffer and his colleagues in the conspiracy. Here the manuscript breaks off.

C. ETHICS FOR EVERYDAY LIFE

This section must be relatively brief and can only sketch what I call the ingredients of the ethical life in more normal circumstances which are not dominated by the ethics of extremity. I do not suggest a dualism in Bonhoeffer's ethical thinking, for there are essential core elements in the everyday as well as the extreme end of the spectrum. But everyday life in a post-war situation could expect to involve social conditions that were not pertinent to a coup d'etat. I will first discuss those ingredients which have not been highlighted thus far, and then conclude this section by reviewing the core elements.

Perhaps the best starting point here is the last manuscript Bonhoeffer was working on, "The 'Ethical' and 'Christian' as a Subject,"[80] written not under the pressure of the resistance movement but under the influence of Karl Barth's ethics in *Church Dogmatics* II/2. Indeed, Bonhoeffer identifies the context as "the sphere of everyday happenings," and mocks the folly of moralists who talk as if a divine policeman has scattered signs reading 'forbidden' and 'allowed' over all human behavior, resulting in a "pathological overburdening of life by the ethical."[81] Ethical obligation

---

[78] See the outline in E 299, E-E 258, and *Zettelnotizen* 105.
[79] E 298, E-E 257.
[80] E-E 259ff.
[81] E-E 260f.; cf. 264, "the fulness of everyday life."

and reflection arise when the ongoing flow of life is disrupted or breaks down—or, one might add, when novelties such as atomic weapons, organ transplants, and genetic engineering break into settled practice.

In addition to Christology, there are four ingredients of Christian ethical life which Bonhoeffer discusses at some length in his manuscripts: scripture, offices, mandates, and natural rights and duties.

Scripture. Given the importance of the Sermon on the Mount to Bonhoeffer personally, and especially its novel prominence in *Discipleship,* we are not surprised to find that scripture has a key place in his ethics. Speaking of Jesus' summary of the law as love for God and neighbor, Bonhoeffer continues "as it is explained in the Decalogue, the Sermon on the Mount, and the apostolic parenesis."[82] The role of the Decalogue is amply displayed in the confession of guilt that Bonhoeffer wrote for the church. The behavior of the church in the Third Reich is examined by each of the ten commandments which serve as a touchstone, an indictment, and a call to confession. With the commandment against murder Bonhoeffer indicted the church for its complicity in the Holocaust: "She is guilty of the deaths of the weakest and most defenseless brothers of Jesus Christ."[83]

"The Sermon on the Mount is there for the purpose of being done," wrote Bonhoeffer, referring to the saying of Jesus quoted in Matthew 7:24ff.[84] He had long since rejected the idea that the purpose of the Sermon on the Mount was expose sin, but not to be done. His pacifism in the early 1930s and peace advocacy in his ecumenical addresses personally exemplify his attitude. Nor are there autonomous areas of life insulated from the Sermon on the Mount.[85] Furthermore, he would not permit playing off against each other the Decalogue and the Sermon on the Mount; they are not "two different ethical ideals, but one single call to obedience towards the God and Father of Jesus Christ."[86] This does not mean treating the commandments of the Decalogue and of Jesus as "absolute divine values" separate from God. Whether affirming the right to life, marriage, and

---

[82] E 282, E-E 243.

[83] E-E 113-115; the confession about the Jews is on 114.

[84] E-E 46.

[85] E-E 217.

[86] E-E 354. This comes from the manuscript "On the Possibility of the Word of the Church to the World," now included with the *Ethics* manuscripts; see E 354-64, esp. 361.

property or renouncing them, the point of the Decalogue and the Sermon on the Mount is "concrete obedience to God."[87]

Offices. Bonhoeffer frequently refers to "offices" such as those of parent, teacher, ruler, judge, and pastor which confer both ethical authority and ethical responsibility. They are constitutive of institutions and social structures such as the family, the school, the court, the church, and government. They are in part structured by relations of order [Ordnungsverhältnisse] and authority, "by concrete relation[s] between the giver and receiver of commands."[88] While he stresses the responsibility and authority by which such offices and relationships structure ethical life, Bonhoeffer is emphatic in standing with the Enlightenment in favor of the equal dignity of all people as ethical beings, and against feudalism and aristocracy and privilege.[89]

Mandates. This is intimately connected to the previous paragraph about social offices and relations of authority and responsibility. The doctrine of 'mandates', however, focuses not on the persons who hold offices but on the social spheres in which those offices and relationships are embedded.[90] Bonhoeffer earlier spoke of four mandates: work, marriage and family, government, and church; in his latest manuscript he spoke not of work but consistently of 'culture' [Kultur].[91] In *Creation and Fall* the precursor of the mandates is the idea of "orders of preservation." By refusing to use the idea of "orders of creation," which had been integrated into German Christian propaganda, Bonhoeffer negated the possibility of construing 'orders' of society and nature (such as family,

---

[87] E-E, 353f. The most extended discussion of the Sermon on the Mount in the *Ethics* manuscripts is found in the first version of "History and Good," E 218-44; see esp. 227-30, 234-43.

[88] E 375f., E-E 267f.

[89] E-E 269.

[90] The doctrine of mandates recapitulates several ideas in the theology of sociality: individual persons as members of and ethically responsible for their communities; construing communities as ethical "collective persons"; vicarious, representative action [Stellvertretung]; and the mutual limitation and ethical responsibility of persons to each other.

[91] See, for example, E-E 281f. See also E 393f., E-E 284f., where Bonhoeffer says he wants to renew the older ideas of order, estate, and office [Ordnung, Stand, and Amt]. In the 1941 essay on "State and Church" he spoke of a people [Volk] as a divine Ordnung but not a mandate; see DBW 12 526f., E-E 340f.

nation, and especially race[92]) apart from the revelation in Christ. He thus rendered theologically illegitimate the practice of Nazi sympathizers who claimed as the will of God racist and anti-semitic views of nation, and 'master race' ideas of marriage, family, and procreation. While changing his terminology to 'mandate', Bonhoeffer's theological method is the same, since the term points to its origin and purpose in God. A mandate is a concrete form of life commissioned by God for all people.

How do these mandates have ethical content which give moral shape to life? Here Bonhoeffer returns to the relations of authority and mutual responsibility discussed above under offices. People like parents, teachers, judges, and the like are "bearers" of the mandate, or commission, of God—indeed the bearer of the mandate is God's Stellvertreter, the representative who stands in God's place. But both parties—for example, parent and child, teacher and student—are mutually responsible and mutually limiting, and owe each other mutual honor; indeed, both are ultimately responsible to the commission of God which the mandate of family, or culture, or government embodies.[93]

These several spheres of social life (mandates) Bonhoeffer presents on the model of "collective persons," consistent with his theology of sociality. They are not isolated and self-sufficient but are "with, for, and in encounter with one another." Thus the commandment of God is not partitioned into segments; it is only in the interaction of the mandates that they "declare the commandment of God as it is revealed in Jesus Christ."[94]

The mandate of the church is the only one discussed in the manuscript Bonhoeffer was writing just before his arrest. Proclamation of the gospel of Christ is the commission of the church-community. In spelling out the meaning of Christ as the eternal Son, the incarnate God, the crucified Reconciler, and the risen and ascended Lord, Bonhoeffer repeats many of the points in the Christological meditation discussed

---

[92] Contrary to National Socialism, Bonhoeffer did not regard race as such an "order."

[93] E 394f., E-E 284f. In discussing mutual limitation here Bonhoeffer is still using the word "Grenze," and his discussion of authority obviously presupposes the meaning it had in describing the church as a "Herrschaftsverband" in *Sanctorum Communio*. The translation of the terms "Oben" and "Unten" as "superiority" and "inferiority" can only be described as a disaster. Bonhoeffer is talking about genuine authority in relations of mutual obligation in responsibility to God.

[94] Cf. E-E 286f., E 397f., "Miteinander, Füreinander und Gegeneinander."

earlier.[95] Christ is the mediator of all creation; because of the incarnation "divine being cannot be found other than in human form" and humanity is set free to live as truly human before God; since God's being is being-for-us, to be truly human is to live "not for self but for God and for others"; in the cross of Christ the godless world has been reconciled to God, and so people "are set free for life before God in the midst of the godless world,... set free for life in genuine worldliness"; the risen Lord sets creation free to fulfil the law of its own being of which Christ is the origin. By taking on the whole of human nature Christ created the new humanity, and so the church-community ["Christus als Gemeinde existierend"] is the personification and representative [Stellvertreter] of the world reconciled to God.[96]

The mandates give ethical shape to life insofar as they embody tasks. Work—everything from agriculture to science and art—is to create things and values. Marriage and family is for the procreation and education of children. Government is to preserve and protect through law—and force if need be—what is created through work and family life.[97]

In his discussion of mandates and offices Bonhoeffer has painted in fairly broad strokes. While the Decalogue, the Sermon on the Mount, and apostolic teaching contain a great deal of detail, there is another ingredient where Bonhoeffer goes into some quite detailed analysis.

Natural Rights and Duties. Perhaps the most novel aspect of Bonhoeffer's *Ethics* is his effort to rehabilitate the category of the natural for Protestant ethics. This should not come as a surprise, however, nor should it be attributed simply to the fact that he was writing at the Benedictine monastery in Ettal. The category of nature, along with spirit, was a central and consistent part of his theological anthropology from the beginning. That the natural is not a minor part of Bonhoeffer's ethics is suggested by the fact that the printed manuscript is over forty pages long, and far from complete—three more sections were planned but not written. One was to be on "The Natural Rights of the Life of the Spirit

---

[95] See above, 308ff.

[96] E 403ff., E-E 291ff. This repetition of sociality themes from *Sanctorum Communio* extends to using the ideas of the church as a means to an end [Gesellschaft] and an end in itself [Gemeinschaft] to create a typology and critique of Protestantism and Catholicism.

[97] E-E 204ff.; cf. 339f.

[Geist]" and another on "The Natural Right to Work and Property."[98] After that was to follow a comparable treatment of duties. The *rights* of natural life derive from the fact that creaturely life is an end in itself, and the *duties* of natural life derive from the fact that creaturely life serves the kingdom of God.[99]

By the natural Bonhoeffer means the creaturely which, after the Fall, is nevertheless directed towards Christ, while the unnatural is closed towards Christ.[100] One knows what is natural by reason, notwithstanding the fact that reason itself is affected by the Fall.[101]

The manuscript only discusses topics under the first subheading, "The Right to Bodily Life." Here Bonhoeffer treats euthanasia, suicide, reproduction (including abortion, contraception, and sterilization), and finally "bodily freedom"— from rape, slavery and exploitation, torture, and arbitrary confinement. The arguments are a combination of biblical, theological, and prudential reasons.

These ingredients of Bonhoeffer's ethical thinking about everyday life are not to be construed dualistically in relation to his ethic of resistance. In distinguishing between ethics of resistance and ethics of everyday life I am referring to two different contexts, not proposing another version of a two realms doctrine which Bonhoeffer himself repudiated. My proposal, rather, is analogous to Bonhoeffer's own distinction between ultimate and penultimate.[102] Consequently it re-

---

[98] The three projected sections of this treatment of natural rights were on body, spirit, and work; these follow the long-established categories of Bonhoeffer's theological anthropology, spirit [Geist], nature [Natur], and history [Existenz, Geschichte] as seen, for example, in *Sanctorum Communio, Creation and Fall,* and the Christology lectures.

[99] E-E 149f. Here Bonhoeffer is drawing on the typology of social relations worked out in *Sanctorum Communio* in relation to the Gemeinschaft and Gesellschaft dimensions of the church-community. See also E-E 152f. where Bonhoeffer repeats his theology of sociality thesis that individual and community are of equal weight and exist in reciprocity.

[100] E-E 143. This definition of the natural is very similar to the notion of orders of preservation: "the natural, the form of life preserved by God after the Fall, with reference to the way in which it is directed towards the coming of Christ" (E-E 148).

[101] But reason does not operate apart from Scripture. Because the Bible understands creaturely life as a gift of God, Bonhoeffer insists, against Kant, in speaking first of rights and only then of duties; cf. E-E 150.

[102] Cf. E-E 193ff., 120-42.

mains to return to the core of Bonhoeffer's ethic—his Christological contextualism—which is the center of both his resistance ethic and his ethic of everyday life.

Foundational for Bonhoeffer's one ethic is the conviction that Christian ethics is not centered on the question of being good and doing good. It is centered on "doing the will of God," which means it is centered on the person of Jesus Christ as the incarnate God in whom the world is reconciled to God. Describing Scripture, mandates and offices, and natural rights and duties as components of Bonhoeffer's everyday ethic is not to set up alternate bases of ethics independent of Christ. It is rather to point concretely to the process and ingredients of ethical formation within the church-community and society by which Christ takes form in human life.

Bonhoeffer regarded his *Ethics* as the culmination of his theological work.[103] The book is complex not only because it is unfinished but also because it is very rich. Its historical analysis, for example, has only been touched here with respect to the resistance movement against National Socialism; but Bonhoeffer thought about Christian ethics in the middle of the twentieth century also in terms of a longer historical perspective, particularly the history of the West. This chapter, then, has had a limited aim: to show that Bonhoeffer's theology of sociality remains fundamental to his thinking as he grappled with new issues in the *Ethics* manuscripts; to analyze his ethic of resistance; and to suggest that distinguishing between the ethic of resistance and the ethic of everyday life as different contexts for Bonhoeffer's Christological contextualism helps to clarify the arguments of the book. But a great deal more research is needed on this rich and complex book.[104] As the survey of writing on the *Ethics* in the critical edition concludes: "Perhaps the time has only now come in which a broader, international spectrum of research can turn its attention to these manuscripts."[105]

---

[103] See the reference, in his letter of August 23, 1944 to Eberhard Bethge (LPP 394), to the "large work" alongside the reference to the "smaller" one, namely the "book of not more than 100 pages" (LPP 380) he had begun in prison on "religionless Christianity."

[104] The critical edition of the *Ethik* (DBW 6) with its copious editorial notes and bibliography is indispensable for this work; an English translation is in process, and will hopefully be published in 2001.

[105] E 447.

Appendix

LETTERS: DIETRICH BONHOEFFER, PAUL LEHMANN, AND OTHERS, 1932-1949

Paul Lehmann was Dietrich Bonhoeffer's closest American friend. After they met at Union Seminary in 1930-31 they kept in touch over the next decade. Their theological alliance with Barth linked them together, as did Lehmann's attraction to European culture. When Lehmann studied with Brunner and Barth in Europe in 1932-33, he visited Bonhoeffer at his family home in Berlin. There, in April 1933, they planned how to get information about the intensifying anti-Semitic measures of Hitler's government to Rabbi Wise whom Bonhoeffer had met in New York. They exchanged books, Lehmann giving Reinhold Niebuhr's *Moral Man and Immoral Society* to Bonhoeffer[1] and the latter giving Herman Rauschning's *The Revolution of Nihilism* to Lehmann. In 1939 it was Lehmann, acting with encouragement from Reinhold Niebuhr, who tried to arrange a lecture tour and teaching appointment for Bonhoeffer when he came for those intense few summer weeks in New York. After the war, Lehmann, who was on the Harvard faculty at the time, arranged for Eberhard Bethge to come to the Divinity School to work on the Bonhoeffer papers and biography.[2] Friendship, letters, and regular

---

[1]   Lehmann's farewell present to Bonhoeffer after the 1930-31 year had been *Which Way Religion?* by Harry Ward, the socialist professor at Union; see DB-E 268.

[2]   See Eberhard Bethge, "Paul Lehmann's Initiative," *Union Seminary Quarterly Review* 29.3-4 (Spring & Summer, 1974), 151f.

meetings between the Lehmanns and the Bethges continued from this time up to Paul Lehmann's death in 1994.

Given Lehmann's long association with Bonhoeffer and his legacy, it was natural that Bethge and other researchers would inquire of him about the possibility of finding material from Bonhoeffer among his papers. Since Lehmann's papers were as voluminous as most academics, and probably in no better order, no discoveries came from these inquiries—including my own. After Paul Lehmann's death, in the New York apartment was found a file folder of letters between him, Bonhoeffer, and others such as Erwin Sutz from the 1930-31 year at Union. This folder had been carefully stored in a closet, separate from Lehmann's other papers. Wallace Allston, a student of Paul Lehmann and close friend of the family, published Bonhoeffer's letters to Lehmann from this folder in 1996.[3]

In the summer of 1998, the Office of Archives and Special Collections in the new Luce Library of Princeton Theological Seminary, in a generous and prompt effort of support for the *Dietrich Bonhoeffer Werke*, undertook a thorough search of the Lehmann papers which had been deposited there after his death. The seventy-two boxes yielded a group of seventeen letters[4] by and related to Bonhoeffer. Of the letters from Bonhoeffer to Lehmann, four are new finds; two are from October-November, 1932, and two from February and September, 1941, as part of Bonhoeffer's resistance work. Three other letters from Bonhoeffer have been published previously: one to his Boericke relatives in Pennsylvania for Christmas, 1932,[5] and two to Reinhold Niebuhr from February, 1933 and July, 1934 which were previously discovered by Larry Rasmussen in the Niebuhr papers at the Library of Congress.[6] In addition, this group contains the following new finds of letters from 1940 to 1949: a long letter from Lehmann replying to Bonhoeffer's request for

---

[3] "Dietrich Bonhoeffer: Previously Unpublished Letters to Paul Lehmann." *Theology Today* 55.3 (October, 1996), 289-98. They will also appear in DBW 17.

[4] The count is different from the sixteen I reported in the Bonhoeffer Society *Newsletter* (No. 68, October, 1998) since I am now counting as two (although they were mailed together) Lehmann's letter of August 2, 1941 to Bonhoeffer and its cover letter of August 4, 1941 to Sutz; see below.

[5] DBW 12 32-34.

[6] DBW 12 50-51. See Rasmussen, *Dietrich Bonhoeffer. Reality and Resistance,* (Nashville: Abingdon, 1972), 218-220. The letters in the Lehmann files are evidently copies of Rasmussen's typescript version of the originals.

information about American post-war aims; a cover letter for the latter
addressed to Sutz; two letters from Sutz to Lehmann, including one
reporting Bonhoeffer's death; a letter from Lehmann to Bonhoeffer's
sister, Sabine Leibholz; three letters from Sabine Leibholz to Lehmann,
to Mrs. Boericke, and to Dr. Paul Empie; a letter from Lehmann to the
parents, Karl and Paula Bonhoeffer; and a letter from Paula Bonhoeffer
to Lehmann.

A number of these letters will appear in volume 17 of the
Dietrich Bonhoeffer Werke.[7] In the English Edition of the *Dietrich
Bonhoeffer Works* they will be printed in the volumes where they belong
chronologically. The texts of the new letters, by Bonhoeffer and others,
are given here, along with a translation of the Christmas 1932 letter to the
Boerickes which has not before appeared in English. Also included here
is a newly-found letter of May, 1939 from Paul Lehmann to President
Samuel Press of Eden Seminary. This is the one mentioned by Lehmann
in his letter of June 28, 1939 to Reinhold Niebuhr;[8] it is a specially
tailored version of the general letter sent to some thirty or forty institutions encouraging them to invite Bonhoeffer for lectures.[9] The Lehmann
papers also contain a number of other letters between him and Eberhard
Bethge, Gerhard Leibholz, and Erwin Sutz which do not bear directly on
the correspondence published here.

DIETRICH BONHOEFFER TO PAUL LEHMANN[10]

October 30, 1932

Dear Paul,

You have written to me so nicely some time ago, but unfortunately forgotten to put the return address on the envelope, which
meant I had some trouble with my reply. For I could hardly assume
that a letter simply addressed "Paul Lehmann, Europe" would get to
its destination. However, I now gather that Mr. Sutz is somewhat

---

[7] This index volume will also contain letters and papers, like these, which
have been discovered after the publication of the respective volumes in which
they would have appeared.

[8] See DBW 15 203.

[9] See DBW 15 201f., CW II 222f.

[10] Typed, in German, on Bonhoeffer's personal letterhead with handwritten date and signature.

better acquainted with your whereabouts, and that you are perhaps even in Zurich and see him from time to time. I therefore ask him to deliver this letter. I am coming to you today with a request that is very big and very urgent, indeed almost impertinent. I have suddenly been commissioned by local church authorities to write a very brief summarizing 'paper' on the 'social gospel'.[11] It is supposed to be a brief historical outline, the essential thoughts and their development up until the present, and a bibliography. This puts me in a real quandary since I am simply not sufficiently well acquainted with the subject matter, which is why I am coming to you with the confidence that you will help me. The local church authorities intend to make the piece available throughout Germany as a resource for talks on the subject—which means it does not have to be very demanding. It is meant as an orientation for pastors. May I now simply ask you to put together such paper *as quickly as possible* for me, which I could then revise later. This is surely not very difficult for you, but for me it would mean a very big favor. Afterwards, I will do for you whatever you ask of me—up to half a kingdom—but please come to my help quickly in this difficult situation. As a matter of fact, I am so insanely busy at the moment with the university, the parish, and countless lectures that I simply would not be able to familiarize myself with the subject starting from scratch. Therefore, please be so kind and help me out! And yet another request: please let me know immediately, if at all possible, whether you want to do this. For I have to make plans accordingly, and the piece is already supposed to be done in three weeks. It is supposed to be about 4 pages long.

Now, one last request: please let me know how I can be helpful to you in some way. For such an opportunity I would be especially grateful. I am very eager to hear how you have fared thus far, what you think of Brunner, and how your own work is going. Being so close now, I might perhaps be able to assist you with it in some way after all.

In the last few weeks I had to work very hard. I had to review Heim's big book which was an enormous amount of work.[12]

---

[11] See the eventual text, DBW 12 203-212, GS I 104-112. Bonhoeffer took over this task from Herman Sasse, who had also studied in the United States at the Hartford Seminary Foundation. As of this writing it is not known whether Lehmann's papers contain his draft of the paper he sent to Bonhoeffer.

[12] See DBW 12 213-31; GS III 138-159; CW I 347-59 (abridged).

My spare time I have spent with some of my unemployed
confirmands in a small wooden cabin which I had built for myself in
a large meadow near Berlin.[13] At the time you arrived in Europe, I
was in Geneva and Zurich. When will it now be possible for us to
meet and talk about some theological questions? When do you plan
to come to Berlin? I would appreciate it if I could know soon, first of
all in order to look forward to it, and secondly to be able to keep that
time free on my calendar. Next spring, as you know, I such have a
terrible amount of travel in my schedule. Already, I am so eager to
see both of you again and to hear about New York.

How is your wife? How does Germany agree with her?

Please write soon. I too will mend my ways and write more.
Forgive my pouncing on you with this request. But I very much hope
that you will help me.

Many thanks in advance, and at any rate many greetings to
your wife and to yourself.

Most faithfully yours,

Dietrich Bonhoeffer

DIETRICH BONHOEFFER TO PAUL LEHMANN[14]

Berlin, November 29, [19]32

Dear Paul!

It is really very ungrateful of me not to write until today and
to thank you for the quick and willing help which has been so very
valuable to me. Even today, please be content with a very brief
greeting. As soon as I can I shall write, I promise. You can count on
it. Back then, the 10 dollars arrived here safely, by the way. Thus far
I have not been able to solve your tobacco troubles satisfactorily.
Please give my regards to your wife and to Mrs. Sutz; also to Brunner

---

[13] See *Dietrich Bonhoeffer. A Life in Pictures* (Philadelphia: Fortress
Press, 1986), 81.

[14] Typed, in German, on plain paper with handwritten signature.

when you have the opportunity. I also think that a meeting in the spring would be most suitable.

Sincere regards and thanks,

Yours always,

Dietrich Bonhoeffer

PAUL LEHMANN TO PRESIDENT SAMUEL PRESS[15]

May 30, 1939

President S. D. Press, D.D.
Eden Theological Seminary
Webster Groves, Mo.

Dear Dr. Press;

Were it not for the unprecedented nature of the circumstances, I should not venture to address this unprecedented request to you. It concerns a very close friend of mine who happens at the same time to be one the ablest of the younger theologians in Germany and to have been doing a solid and perilous work preparing ministers for the confessional parishes of Germany.

Last week a letter came from Dr. Niebuhr about this man whom he had seen in England. It seems to be imperative now that he find egress from Germany. Reinie has arranged a lecture appointment for him in the Union Summer Session and the hope is that he will find opportunity for further lectures during the forthcoming academic year. I am speaking about Dietrich Bonhoeffer, Lic. Theol. Berlin. He was also Union Seminary fellow, 1930-31.

I realize, of course, that the Seminary has taken on a man for the forthcoming academic year. But I wonder whether Mr. Bonhoeffer might be considered for the 1940 Convocation lectures in theology? And if not these, would it be possible for him to give a

---

[15] Written on letterhead from Elmhurst College, Department of Religion; one page, typed, single-spaced, with handwritten signature. In November, 1998 this letter was found in the Eden Seminary archives by Lowell Zuck whose help is gratefully acknowledged; it bears the Eden Seminary archive number 53-1j We 37.

single lecture at Eden some time next year? His three principal volumes are "Sanctorum Communio," "Akt und Sein," and "Gemeinsames Leben" which appeared only recently. This will give you some idea about the direction of his thought.

Mr. Bonhoeffer may be reached at Union during the summer session and thereafter through me. I shall appreciate greatly whatever consideration you may be able to give this urgent matter.

With kindest personal regards,

Paul

ERWIN SUTZ TO PAUL LEHMANN[16]

DIETRICH BONHOEFFER TO PAUL LEHMANN[17]

February 28th, 1941.

My dear Paul,

You will certainly be surprised to get a letter from me. But I must, of course, make use of the unusual opportunity of a short stay in Zürich to write to you and to many friends abroad. It is just to give you a sign of life and to let you know that I am still well. I also wish to assure you of my unchanged friendship and sympathy, and of my deep appreciation of all you have done for me last year when we met in New York. I shall never forget these hours. After the experiences of the passed [sic] 1½ year I am convinced that my decision of July 1939 to go home and to join my friends was right. I never doubted, as you know, the great difficulties we would have to pass through.[18]

---

[16] Two pages, handwritten, on paper with black borders, this letter of April 25, 1940 announces the death of Sutz' father and contains other personal news and inquiries. He asks if Lehmann's book is published, strongly supports the neutral status of Switzerland and its defense against "the revolution of nihilism" (the title of Rauschning's book), and reports that he had recently received a letter from Bonhoeffer reporting that he is very busy.

[17] Two pages, handwritten, in English, on plain paper. This letter was written four days after Bonhoeffer's arrival in Switzerland on the first of his three visits there, from February 24 to March 24, 1941; see DB-E 726ff.

[18] Ulrich Kabitz, who edited this letter for DBW 17, explains that "great difficulties" refers to the closing of the post-Finkenwalde pastoral training program [Sammelvikariat] by the Gestapo, the call up of young Confessing

But even if you hear very little about us, be sure we are still there, we work and we hope. There is not the slightest change of mind in the essential questions. The ecumenic feeling is strong and still growing. Many sacrifices are being brought by young and old people to keep up the good cause. But we realize, of course, that it must be extremely difficult for you not to loose [sic] your confidence in us. Be patient, imagine the immense difficulties which will still be greater in this year, and do not give up praying for us. We need it.

Now I must ask a great favour from you. Please, by return of post, write a letter to me—a long one!—about your view of the situation and of the future, about the activities of the churches in the present crisis, shortly about everything that is interesting to us in the present moment. We know very little and we wish to know much. What do you think will be after the war, what will be the new social and political order? What role will the church play in that order? Sometimes I think that the word of the churches might become more important in coming decisions than it has ever been before. Sometimes I think, Christianity will only live after this time in a few people who have nothing to say. Please direct your letter to Erwin Sutz, Rapperswil, Kt. St. Gallen and do not mention my name. I saw Erwin today and he sends you his best regards. Before I go home in 4 weeks I shall see him again and I hope to find a letter from you there.

How is your work going on? How is Marion? What is Reinhold doing? Please, remember me to him. Let me hear from you soon!

With all good wishes in unchangeable fellowship,

Yours ever,

Dietrich.

Church pastors into military service, and the tightening restrictions on Bonhoeffer through prohibiting him to speak in public and requiring him to report regularly to the police.

PAUL LEHMANN TO DIETRICH BONHOEFFER (VIA ERWIN SUTZ)[19]

August 2, 1941

This is the beginning of August, and I have wanted since the end of February to set down my thoughts about the times through which we are passing. But the rapidly shifting events have a way of combining with the unexpected tasks of daily life to leave one with insufficient leisure and composure to formulate impressions that ought not to go unexpressed. Perhaps the most remote and yet unmistakable sign that we too are affected by the war is the fact that letters abroad, even air mail, take more than four weeks. Who knows, therefore, when these thoughts will be read, or whether they will be related at all to this world, if they should happen to be read.

Another sign of our nearer participation in the life of a world at war is the historic departure from long established policy in the adoption of universal military training. I shall never forget the day I went to register. It seemed to me that this was a sign that we in America had come to the end of one way of life and were starting out upon another and uncertain one. Most of us, of course, could at first think only of the inconvenience of having to take a year out from civil life for military training and we were secretly troubled whether it would stop with a year. But the deeper meaning of this new order for us in America is that our democracy is not an isolationist democracy. If constitutional government survives here it will be because it survives in Europe and Asia. It was the passage of the conscription act which brought home to this country the fact of our interdependence with the destinies of all men round the world. And this was a good thing.

The conscription act has done another thing for me. It has deepened and made concrete my sense of civic responsibility on a national scale. I think it is largely true of my generation that we were divided between jingoists and internationalists, i.e., between those whose nationalism was fanatic and intolerant and those who had no

---

[19] There is no letterhead, addressee, or greeting at the head of this page. This is Lehmann's carbon copy (four pages, typed, single-spaced) of his reply to Bonhoeffer's letter of February 28, 1941.

national feeling at all. I have not realized until now how much this
lack of national feeling means that one's life and thoughts are suspended in mid-air. They have no solid roots and they are not knit into
the fabric of history. I do not disguise the danger that this innocent
sense of duty to one's country can be corrupted and become chauvin-
istic. But the alternative is not the complete absence of the sense for
the meaning of the state. Many of us see this more clearly now that
all national existence is threatened with chaos. I hope we have not
awakened too late.

It is interesting to me to discover in this connection how
much of my pacifism and socialism have been predicated upon this
lack of appreciation of the ideal and the real function of government
in the life of an individual. We believed too completely that bad
government was the obstacle to the realization of our dreams and did
not see clearly enough that the political problem is the perennial
expression of the struggle between chaos and order in sinful human
existence. In so far as our pacifism and socialism were directed at
political and economic injustice at home, they were right. They are
still right. But because they left out of account the international
problem they became alternatively romantic and doctrinaire. The best
proof of this is the current alignment of the socialist party with the
republican party in opposition to the President's foreign policy. It is
difficult to tell which is in a more pitiable state. The socialist party is
virtually impotent, whereas the Republicans have been greatly
embarrassed by Mr. Willkie's ardent support of the President. They
must now look forward to the next campaign at which time they will
have either to repudiate Mr. Willkie and be frankly oppositionist or
lose the campaign from the start because they have no issue. Of
course, they might take up a man like Lindbergh. But then, that
would be too much like Quisling.[20] Events would have to move
terribly fast for that to become a political reality by 1944.

Politically we face now what seem to me to be the two most
immediately pressing questions. One is the question whether the
Western hemisphere should surrender Europe to the Nazi tyranny and
prepare to fight its future out alone or whether we on this side of the

---

[20] Vidkun Quisling (1887-1945) was a Norwegian fascist leader who
helped Germany conquer Norway and was premier during the German occupation. The word "quisling" thus became a common synonym for "traitor" during
World War II.

Atlantic should make common cause with every effort to restrain the chaos of the new barbarism. There is still considerable appeasement sentiment in the country. But I think that on the whole the country will support the government in its determination to aid Britain until the issue on the continent has been settled and the safety of the islands is assured. There is no doubt in my mind that in the end we should be ready to send even an expeditionary force. I say this even though I know very well that the country would not be ready for such a bold act tomorrow or even this year. The main direction of our politics is and will remain away from appeasement. Lindbergh is losing rather than gaining popular support. The attack on Russia has left him too obviously on the side of the attackers and has robbed him of all support except of the incorrigible peace-at-any-price idealists and the behind-the-scenes-big-business fascists.[21] The other question is whether we in the United States shall be able to undertake this war effort with sufficient protection of the rights of labor and minorities or whether we shall submerge these vital democratic elements beneath the all absorbing international problem. There are some encouraging signs that we shall succeed in a measure in preserving democratic forms. The President has skillfully avoided any sharply anti-labor policies and has his finger on the more fundamental danger to our national life from profiteers. He wants to regulate prices, and, at the moment at any rate, not wages. This is, in my judgement a sound step in the direction of social reconstruction. The attack on Russia has also helped here. Dissident elements who had taken the Moscow line after the pact of 1939[22] were making nuisance attempts upon our industrial war effort. These are now dying down if not disappearing altogether. The labor movement itself while not being as developed politically as the British movement is showing signs of growth in statesmanship. This was evident recently when the head of the labor movement endorsed the President's occupation of a factory because labor's own prerogatives had been violated by outside influences.

I go into this little review of what is happening here because it bears directly upon my view of the future course of things. Everything depends, in my judgement, upon a British victory. But that

---

[21] This is perhaps a reference to deals between American and German companies to promote their economic interests regardless of the political and ethical issues being fought over in the war. See, for instance, Joseph Borkin, *The Crime and Punishment of I. G. Farben* (New York: Free Press, 1978).

[22] The German-Soviet non-aggression pact of August, 1939.

victory cannot come too soon. If it did, then we should have a return to capitalist imperialism for economic power would remain where it has been for too many decades already. The trend at the moment in Britain is definitely toward a reconstructed social economy. The strain of the war is leveling the tremendous distance between rich and poor and the labor movement is exercising an increasing influence upon public policy. The most significant fact for the future in my judgement is that it is this rising influence of labor and the common sense of the British people—and not British toryism—which have insisted upon the continuance of the war and indeed upon the resistance which brought the war about in the first place. If the possibilities of social reconstruction that lie here can be encouraged and developed, then I see the direction of the future course of things. Some kind of socialized economy is inescapable and indispensable. The nucleus for it is there. If this tiny germ of hope cannot be brought to birth, then frankly, I think the future is very dark indeed.

Again the uncertain quantity is Russia. It is unlikely, I think, that the course of her domestic development can be left unchanged by the war. She is fighting now by the strength of the slavic love of the fatherland and not by the power of Stalinism. Is there a possibility here of a new understanding between the Russian and the British labor movement? Or will the result of the present battle be the occasion for the bolshevist triumph over Europe? It is too early yet to say. But if the latter happens, then, the only satisfaction that can come to us for our support of Britain is that we acted in terms of our responsibility to restrain tyranny. But God in his judgement has called us to endure the terror of yet another tyranny. From this distance, at any rate, the war on Russia seems to be the first major Nazi military mistake. It has outlined real possibilities of a Nazi defeat. Though no one could wish to predict the end of the war.

So much for the political aspect of things. What about the Church? In England, the Malvern conference[23] under the leadership of the Archbishop of York is a most heartening sign. This group has come out frankly for a socialized economy and for a peace which shall not in any way be vindictive but genuinely reconstructive. On

---

[23] An Anglican conference held at Malvern in January, 1941 under the leadership of Archbishop William Temple. It was especially concerned with the church and economic life and, building on the Pope's Christmas address, put forward ten points as a basis for peace. See Visser 't Hooft's letter to Temple about this: DBW 16 161f.

this side of the Atlantic, I can say that I attended in early June the
Western Hemisphere Ecumenical conference at Toronto.[24] It was
heartening there to hear a resolution in support of the Malvern
conference; to hear from Canadians and Americans the firm desire
and resolve that there shall be no hatred of the German people and
that the Churches shall continue to be places of refuge for all afflicted
souls, where even enemies may meet and where prayers shall be said
for enemies; and to note that the Churches, in marked contrast to the
last war, were not being used as arms of the military or as recruiting
stations. I think too that at Toronto the American delegates saw more
clearly than before that the issue of participation or non-participation
in the war threatened to divide the American Church rather hope-
lessly. And they resolved there that this division should not occur. It
will be easier for both groups, I think, to keep the unity of the
household of faith.

Perhaps it is not too much to say, that the most important
religious fact of this time is the ecumenical spirit in the Church. This
spirit is doing two things: 1) keeping Christians sensitive to the fact
that there is one Lord; 2) keeping Christians sensitive to the fact that
all particular divisions among men—nation, and war, and hatred, and
race—are transcended by the unity of the household of faith. Of
course, I am troubled by the problem of the unity of faith. There is
still too much liberalism in theology over here. I get very discour-
aged at times because there seems to be no way of getting across the
barriers which spring from divergent presuppositions. One is either

---

[24] The "North American Oecumenical Conference" was held in Toronto
on June 3-5, 1941, under the leadership of John R. Mott from the USA and the
Canadian Anglican Bishop L. W. B Broughall. Two hundred and fifty delegates
attended from Canada, the United States, Mexico, and from Central and South
America, which is why Lehmann called it the "Western Hemisphere Conference." It aimed to build on the Oxford and Edinburgh conferences of 1937, and
the Madras (or Tambaram) conference of the International Missionary Council
in 1938, and was part of preparation for the World Council of Churches, the
official formation of which had been delayed by the war. The conference themes
concerned the relevance of the church to the contemporary world. Concretely
the agenda became the challenge of conserving unity among churches faced with
the divisive issues of the war—particularly pacifism vs. participation, and
especially the issue of American participation. A related issue was the relation
of the German and Japanese churches to their governments, and "whether the
church in Germany . . . has so far capitulated to the demands of the nazi regime
as to sacrifice its unity with the church universal." An article on the conference
appeared in *The Christian Century,* June 18, 1941, 798ff.

silent or talking past one another. And yet there are growing signs of understanding, particularly among students. I am encouraged too as I go about preaching how much people sense that the preaching of the last decades has no power and how eager they are for the gospel of God's judgement and forgiveness. It is not at all unlikely that the war will deepen the understanding for this gospel.

So you see, I find it possible to continue to work. Sometimes the horizon of the future seems bright with hope, at other times, very dark. But the direction is clear and the resources are clear. We must have a world of political and economic democracy, i.e. one in which the goods of life are enjoyed by all the people, in which the basic securities—employment, old age, health—are provided, in which all nations shall have access to the resources of the earth. That world can only be nourished and motivated by the Christian Church because its gospel of redemption and of responsibility is alone capable of inspiring and sustaining that world. My daily prayer is for all those who suffer and labor for the coming of that world, that that world may come in God's good time and pleasure, and that I may be faithful in whatsoever suffering and agony may yet befall me and all the children of men. 2 Cor. 3:2-11.

Your are always in our prayers, in our thoughts, and in our hearts.[25]

PAUL LEHMANN TO ERWIN SUTZ[26]

August 4, 1941

Dear Erwin,

How strange and how terrifying life is sometimes! I want to tell you in this letter both of our sadness and our joy on your account. You have been good enough to allow us to share in the passing of your father and in the knowledge of your engagement. You cannot

---

[25] There is no signature at the end of this letter. It may be that, notwithstanding the personal ending, it remained unsigned in respect of Bonhoeffer's request for anonymity. Or it may be that Lehmann signed the original with his Christian name which does not appear on the carbon copy.

[26] Two pages, typewritten carbon copy, single-spaced, on plain paper, with no signature on this copy. This is the cover letter to Sutz which accompanied the anonymous letter to Bonhoeffer.

imagine how many weeks my conscience has troubled me that I do not get a letter to you, particularly because the joys and sorrows of those who belong to one in friendship are one's own joys and sorrows. May I say for both Marion and me that we shared in your sorrow before God in prayer for the comfort and the hope which are in Christ our Lord? Will you please remember us in this way, too, to your mother? We still remember with much joy the visit with your parents that winter in Zurich. We do hope that your mother is well and carrying on in faith's own peculiar joy and strength.

And you are at last rejoicing a young lady's heart! We were overjoyed by this word for we had always felt that somehow it could not be that the dialectical theology should continue in you in vacuo and that only the piano should receive the attention of your talents. How much we should like now to meet the bride. Won't you please be sure to let us know when the wedding day will be and also send us some photos? In your joy as in your sorrow we remember you with the prayer that your ministry and your life may be deepened and enriched by the blessing of marriage. Thank you so much for your announcement.

Since the accompanying statement will give you some account of my thoughts over the long years since the famous "selbstverständlich, das bin ich selber," I shall not repeat here. You ought to know a little about ourselves and I am so ashamed by my delay that I do not want to let any more time go by before these lines go off to you.

One of these days you will get a copy of my book. It appeared a year ago in April under the title "Forgiveness: Decisive Issue in Protestant Thought."[27] The reviews have been on the whole sympathetic but it is by no means a "best seller." It was, however, a great relief to have this work done. You know that I was working on it already in Zuerich so that the time did drag out considerably. Of course, I had meanwhile also to teach. In this connection, we have had a rather disappointing experience. Last year in May, a call came to teach in Eden Seminary. Do you remember it? The Swiss one parted company there with the French one and the German and the uncertain Oldsmobile.[28] Well, we have followed the Swiss one too.

---

[27] The book was Lehmann's doctoral dissertation and was published by Harper and Brothers in 1940 with a foreword by Reinhold Niebuhr.

[28] This is a reference to Bonhoeffer's trip to Mexico in May-June 1931 with Jean Lasserre; Erwin Sutz accompanied them as far as St. Louis.

After one year, we have parted company with Eden Seminary and are
going to teach for the next few years at <u>Wellesley College, Wellesley,
Massachusetts</u>. I underline this not because it is particularly important but in order that you may not forget our address.

My going to Eden was attended by a great deal of resentment
in the faculty. This resentment was both personal and theological.
And while I must say that our life at Eden this year was not marked
by any personal disagreements, there was always an undercurrent of
uneasiness. I discovered then, in addition to this, that Eden is not
really a theological Seminary. It is not, that is, interested in theological scholarship and a cultured ministry. It is a leadership training
school, very good, perhaps, for lay workers, but very bad for training
ministers. Then, in June this year, for the second time an invitation
came to teach in Wellesley. This is a girls' school and a college. I do
not like either of these facts very much. But there is a very good
department of Bible there and they have invited me because they want
the kind of thoughts which I have emphasized there. The head of the
department has collaborated with Erminie Huntress (do you remember
her, that very strange, tomb-like girl at Union?) in translating
Bultmann's Jesus.[29] Besides, the eastern seaboard is a much more
stimulating place for theological development than the Mississippi
river. So, although I regret very much that I shall have to defer
theological teaching, I am counting on the sympathetic environment
and the leisure to enable me to study and work at theology and
perhaps even to write some more. Dei providentia et hominem
confusione, we have decided to try it.

So you have seen Dietrich? Did you ever get our card from
New York?[30] It was good news to me that he is still at work and I am
terribly sorry that I could not send the statement before now. Will
you read it and dispose of it as you think best? You see, my theological lectures this year took so much of my time that I could not get
sufficient hours together to write what I wanted to send to you. And
then, as I have said, the mail takes such a long time.

I am writing from a cabin overlooking the New Meadows
River, an arm of the Atlantic, on the coast of Maine. We are trying to

---

[29] Rudolf Bultmann, *Jesus and the Word* (New York: Charles Scribner's
Sons, 1934). Translated by Louise Pettibone Smith and Erminie Huntress
Lantero.

[30] See the postcard written the day before Bonhoeffer sailed home from
New York on July 7, 1939; cf. DBW 15 215.

get some badly needed rest here where there is only water and pine trees and no people can get to us. It is really a lovely spot and I hope that we shall be able to make good use of it. On the whole we are both in better health, although Marion gains no weight and at the end of each school year we are always worn out. It is a terrible thing though to be resting in the beauty and safety of this place when so many who like yourself are very close to us are in peril of their lives and future. We cannot be at ease for we think of you constantly.

I think I should stop now so that the letter does not weigh too much. I shall try in the near future to write again. Meanwhile, please know how much every line from you means to us and that the memories of the past and our common faith sustain us in this dreadful yet promising present in the heartening knowledge that though distant we are not separate from one another. Marion joins me in ever affectionate greeting and regard,

DIETRICH BONHOEFFER TO PAUL LEHMANN[31]

20th Sept[ember 19]41.

My dear Paul,

Thank you ever so much for your letter which I got from Erwin a few days ago. It has been most interesting for me to read this account of your thoughts and experiences. But, of course, one ought to talk about it personally and to exchange views. The development that we believe is bound to come in the near future is world domination—if you will forgive me this expression—by America. The part England will play in the coming new world order seems rather uncertain. I, personally, do not believe as most people do that she will just become the 'junior-partner' of U.S.A., and, moreover, I do not hope so. But at any rate the power of USA will be so overwhelming that hardly any country could represent a counterbalance. Now, you see, it is this idea that to a certain extent troubles us. You will not misunderstand me. USA domination is indeed one of the best solutions of the present crisis. But what is to become of Europe?

---

[31] Handwritten, two pages, on plain paper. This letter was written in the latter part of Bonhoeffer's second Swiss journey from August 28 to September 26, 1941; cf. DBW 16 202-211.

What, for instance, of Germany? Nothing would be worse than to impose upon her any anglo-saxon form of government—as much as I should like it. It simply would not work. The four liberties of your President[32] seem to indicate something in this direction. As far as I know Germany, it will just be impossible, for instance, to restore complete freedom of speech, of press, of association. That sort of thing would throw Germany right into the same abyss. I think we must try to find a Germany in which justice, lawfulness, freedom of the churches is being restored. I hope there will [be] something like an authoritarian 'Rechtsstaat'[33] as the Germans call it. I[t] will need a long process of education before the people as a whole will be in the position to enjoy all the liberties it used to have. Well, we ought to talk it over as we did in July 1939. —What has become of your friend Kalbfleisch?[34] I hope he safely arrived in USA. —Give my greetings to Reinie, please. I remember Pit[ney] v[an] D[usen] saying in 1939, if war broke out U.S.A. would take part in it within 2 months! How difficult it is to foretell the future! —I am thinking of you and of your wife with great joy and many beautiful remembrances. I am optimistic enough to hope that we shall meet again in a time not to[o] far off from now. With all good wishes

　　　I remain,

　　　　　Yours ever,

　　　　　Dietrich.

---

[32] President Roosevelt, in his New Year address of January 6, 1941, had spoken of a post-war world "founded upon four essential human freedoms" of speech, of worship, and freedom from want and from fear.

[33] A state based on constitution and law.

[34] George Kalbfleisch was a student and friend of Lehmann's who had met Bonhoeffer in Europe at Lehmann's urging; see DBW 15 205.

ERWIN SUTZ TO PAUL LEHMANN[35]

Rapperswil, June 6, 1945

My dear Paul,

Nearly four years did I make you wait for my response to your equally kind as important letter from August 4, 1941. At that time it reached us shortly before our wedding on September 23 so that I was also able to share it with our friend Dietrich Bonhoeffer who at the time stayed with us for a brief visit. But today, when the Victory Day for Europe is already behind us and we slowly catch our breath again after all the horrors that took place all around Europe and all around the borders of our fatherland, I must first of all share with you the sad news that Dietrich also has been killed in all this terrible slaughter. A week ago I met Prof. Karl Barth in Bern who himself told me the shocking news which since has also been publicized in the ecumenical news. In April or the beginning of May, shortly before the arrival of the Americans, Dietrich, together with his brother Klaus, was executed by hanging in a concentration camp near the Bohemian border.[36] And all the things he might have had to suffer beforehand! He was one of the most capable and courageous theologians of the Confessing Church, and was in contact with the best elements of the resistance movement. And for us he was simply 'the big one' without whom that year at Union Seminary would be just inconceivable. Dear, poor Dietrich. He has entered church history as one of those martyrs of whom it is written: "The saying is sure: If we die with him, we will also live with him; if we endure, we will also reign with him!" 2 Tim. 2:11.

About our dear 'French one', Jean Lasserre, I have also been without any news for years. He was (or is) pastor in Maubeuge through which the war barreled in 1940. I have tried to find out about him and his family via the Protestant Children's Aid [Protestantische

---

35 Typewritten, two pages, single-spaced, with handwritten signature, on the letterhead of "Evang. Pfarramt, Rapperswil-Jona," Switzerland addressed to Paul Lehmann at Wellesley College.

36 Dietrich Bonhoeffer was killed at Flossenbürg on April 9, 1945. Klaus Bonhoeffer, together with his brother-in-law Rüdiger Schleicher, was actually killed in Berlin on April 23, 1945.

Kinderhilfe] but thus far without success. However, I hope that some day we shall be in contact with him again.

We ourselves are also well and in good health. It is a miracle for our entire nation that, in spite of being at times under the gravest threat (especially in 1941), we have been spared the events of the war and of a German occupation with all its terror. Your bombers have caused damage several times here, and sometimes the sirens were wailing day and night. But not a single time did we have to seek refuge in bomb shelters. We maintained exemplary order in the country, and the food always remained adequate and good. The number of refugees and internees grew from year to year. Our most important task in those years was to save as many people as possible from deportation and death.[37] [. . .]

With most sincere wishes for your well-being and very sincere greetings to you and your wife—also from my wife—I remain

Your 'old little one'

Erwin Sutz

[PS] I have your letter from 1941 sitting next to me.[38] I have read it again recently. You will surely enjoy the photos.

SABINE LEIBHOLZ TO DR. PAUL EMPIE[39]

Mrs. Sabine Leibholz   Oxford, 19/5/46
née Bonhoeffer   10 Lincoln Rd

Dear Mr. Empie,
          Thank you very much for your kind letter. I am gladly prepared to give you any information about my brother Pastor Dietrich Bonhoeffer, you would like to have.

---

[37] Here follow four paragraphs of personal news about his family and parish.

[38] This is the cover letter of August 2, 1941 above, accompanying the long reply to Bonhoeffer.

[39] Four pages, typed, single-spaced, on plain paper, with C O P Y typed at the top of the first page spaced out in the German method of emphasis. Sabine Leibholz, Bonhoeffer's twin sister, is responding in this letter to an inquiry from

1.) As to your first question, my brother felt already strongly, that he wanted to study Theology at the age of 14 or 15. He was confirmed 15. III. 1921 (together with me, I being his twin-sister). Theology was somehow in his blood too. On my mother's side, Dietrich's grand-father had been a chaplain to the king and later Prof. of Theology; and Dietrich's great-grandfather was the famous Theologian and Church historian, Professor Karl von Hase, Jena.

2.) Dietrich Bonhoeffer got his exchange fellowship in the United States at Union Theological Seminary at the instigation of the Evangelischen Ober Kirchenrat, 1930.

3.) How his stay in the U.S.A. influenced his thought and activities in Germany, is difficult to say. He spoke with love and great admiration of personalities like Professor Niebuhr, Prof. Lehmann. I think he knew Dr. Leiper, Dr. Coffin, Paul Tillich and Prof. John Baillie very well. When he came back he told us how deeply impressed he was by the piety of the Christian negro-congregations.

5.) Dietrich Bonhoeffer had no Nazi friend.[40] Somehow I feel that a

---

Pastor Empie, and the numbers in her letter correspond to questions he had posed. The archives of the Evangelical Lutheran Church in America have a file on this correspondence, including the original of this letter of Sabine Leibholz, though Empie's letter to her is missing. Empie was working for the National Lutheran Council, the coordinating body for most Lutheran churches in America and their major connection to the Lutheran World Federation. In 1946 he was director of Lutheran World Action (LWA), the council's fund-raising arm. In that year LWA was preparing to make a film on Bonhoeffer to be entitled "No Greater Love." As the letter below from Paul Lehmann to Sabine Leibholz on January 1, 1947 indicates, Empie wrote to Sabine Leibholz to gather information for this film. (The ELCA archive file also contains a reply from Max Delbrück to a letter which Empie addressed to him on May 3, 1946.) While most of the information in Sabine Leibholz' letter is now very familiar, this 1946 profile is probably the earliest detailed summary of Bonhoeffer's life and work to circulate in English just a year after his death. (Two years later, when the first abridged edition of *The Cost of Discipleship* was published by SCM Press in London, it contained a "Memoir" by her husband, Gerhard Leibholz.) This letter obviously contained a lot of new information even to somebody as well-placed and well-connected to Europe as Dr. Empie. The letter also serves to highlight important aspects of Bonhoeffer's American experience, namely the impact on him of African-American congregations and piety. Some spelling, typing and punctuation errors have been silently corrected.

[40] This may seem a very incongruous comment until one learns that it is a response to a question which was asked because the film concept proposed a fictional friend for Bonhoeffer who was a Nazi and joined the Luftwaffe but later, from Bonhoeffer's example, realized he had gone the wrong way.

person having been under his influence could never have become a
Nazi. His two intimate long-time friends were Pastor Franz
Hildebrandt, with whom he studied Theology in Berlin and in later
years Pastor Eberhard Bethge; (who some years younger had been
Dietrich's pupil at the Prediger Seminar Finkenwalde, later closed
down by the Gestapo). Pastor Bethge was Dietrich's most intimate
friend during all the years of Dietrich's struggle for the Bekenntnis
Kirche and against the Nazi-regime. They lived together during the
first years of the war while Dietrich was writing his "Ethik" and
doing political underground-work. After Dietrich had been arrested in
1943, 5th of April, he managed to get many letters out of prison, by
help of a friendly guard. Many were written to his family and to
Pastor Bethge, who all to-gether did what ever they could to ease
Dietrich's imprisonment. Pastor Bethge was imprisoned himself—
after the July-plot had failed—together with my elder brother Dr. jur.
Klaus Bonhoeffer and Dr. Rüdiger Schleicher, the husband of my
eldest sister. Our brother, Klaus Bonhoeffer, and R. Schleicher were
sentenced to death by the "Volksgerichtshof" on February 3rd 1945.
On this very day the most heavy raid was made on Berlin and the
president of the "Court" Freisler, lost his life. But on the 23rd of
April our brother Klaus and our brother-in-law Schleicher were
murdered by the S.S. Pastor Bethge was liberated two days later from
the same prison by Russian troops. Pastor B. held the sermon on the
9th of April, this year, for Dietrich—on the first anniversary of his
death. I think this sermon would be most valuable to you, but I do
not know whether you would like to have it, as it is in German.

Pastor Hildebrandt left Germany for racial reasons for
England. The Bishop of Chichester, whom Dietrich met first in 1933
and with whom he held fellowship all through the years of war, held a
Memorial Service in July 1946 for Dietrich, together with Pastor
Hildebrandt. Dietrich was greatly impressed by the Bishop of
Chichester's outstanding Christian personality. In 1942 he even went
to meet him, by risk of his life, in Stockholm to tell him about the
underground movement and as the Bishop writes in a pamphlet about
this meeting "to give full information about the large underground-
movement in Germany, naming the key men who would undertake it"
(to overthrow the Nazi-government). The details about this meeting
have been published in press and radio and I think they are well
known by now.

6 & 7.) Dietrich had no direct warnings of his going to be arrested, but from his writings he seems to have anticipated it again and again. The Gestapo had closed the Seminary twice; then they[41] left the locality and opened it again somewhere else. He was then forbidden to preach or to publish anything and he was forbidden to enter Berlin. But Dietrich did not take much notice and went on with his work, working for the Brethren's council in the Confessional Church by day, and being engaged in political activities at night. His arrest took place in the house of our parents. The husband of our second sister Dr. Hans von Dohnanyi (son of the composer) was taken together with Dietrich. Then my sister Christine von Dohnanyi was arrested too, but released after several weeks. We knew of the first hearing of the Gestapo, when Dietrich was at once threatened with torture. There were many hearings and he was threatened with the arrest of his parents, his fiancée and his sisters. Then he felt that the moment had come, to say, that he was violently opposed to the Nazi regime and all it stands for and that on Christian grounds; but that was all they got out of him to save his family. Actually there was no trial. He was murdered on April 9th 1945 on special order of Himmler, shortly before the American troops advanced to the C-Camp Flossenbürg, known as "Vernichtungslager."[42] Before he was brought there he had been taken to Buchenwald, Schönberg and Regensburg. His brother-in-law, H. v. Dohnanyi, was murdered in C.-C.[43] Sachsenhausen.

8.) I do not think that he had met Bishop Wurm before 1937, perhaps later, when political work brought them together.

9.) He was not drafted for military service. Friends of the Wehrmacht, who were strong anti-nazis and underground-workers, managed that for him. When asked by a Swede before the war at a Conference in Fanö (?) "What would you do when war comes?" Dietrich answered: I shall pray to Jesus to give me the power not to "take up arms." In later years he felt strongly, that he had to stand up against the Antichrist[44] against a pagan and anti-christian government.

---

[41] "They" refers to Bonhoeffer, his colleagues, and students.

[42] Extermination camp.

[43] Here and in the previous sentence the "C" is used to abbreviate Concentration Camp.

[44] This is an interesting comment in view of Eberhard Bethge's report in the biography that Bonhoeffer did not use this term of Hitler; cf. DB-E 722f.

After he had been in London 1933/34 as a pastor to two German congregations, he got an invitation to come to India and see Gandhi. He had always longed to meet him. But at that time he felt he had to accept rather the post of a Director of the underground Confessional Church Seminary. But he hoped to go to India later. For some time he had also in mind to go abroad as a missionary.

I hope I have answered your questions herewith but I will add a few things which seem important to picture his life and ideals, and I will give you some dates in short.

Dietrich was a pupil of Harnack. When he was 17 he used to go to town with him in the morning and Harnack thought very highly of Dietrich. Later Dietrich was—for some time—strongly under the influence of Barth's Theology. He then wrote his licentiatenarbeit: "Communio sanctorum." He was then 21 years. In 1928 he was Vicar in Barcelona. In 1929 he had his first "konfirmanden klasse," boys living in the North of Berlin, a very difficult task, which he mastered admirably. He left the house of our parents where he used to live, to go to live with those boys in the same surroundings, a poor working-class district. He bought for the boys a "Wohnlaube" outside Berlin, where he went together with them in their spare-time. There he taught them and played with them, he showed them gardening, read to them and went for walks with them. The boys loved and admired him. Later he was pastor to the students of the technical College Berlin, which was a difficult task too. Dietrich was a good musician. He played the piano very well and at home—we being a large family - 4 brothers and 4 sisters—we had chamber musik every Saturday evening. Dietrich loved Bach and later on Schutz very much. He played the Beethoven sonatas very well, and he accompanied his mother and his sisters singing Beethoven, Schubert, Schumann lieder. He played the organ well too; he also had a spinet. During his imprisonment he wrote poetry for the first time; the poems have been published and have been translated into English as well. They appeared in various British periodicals. He was very fond of walking, he loved our country-house in the Harz mountains. He often went there for skiing. He liked tennis and swimming, and even in Buchenwald he played chess with his fellow-prisoner, General Lic. Theol. von Rabenau. He once had a Bernhardine dog which was overrun. During the last years Dietrich grew fond of the books of Stifter. He knew the German classics very well. He spoke English well and he spoke a little Italian, Spanish and understood French well.

In Buchenwald he was imprisoned together with Molotov's nephew, Kockovin, (?)[45] a delightful young Russian, but an atheist, to whom Dietrich brought home for the first time the teachings of Christ. Kockovin taught him Russian, and Dietrich said that he would go and visit Mr. Kockovin after the war in Moskow, if he (Dietrich) would survive. All the fellow-prisoners of Dietrich tell of his amazing courage, his unselfishness, his readiness to hope and his ability to comfort the anxious and to encourage the depressed. In his prison in Tegel he managed to get permission to minister to the sick, and to the prisoners who were condemned to death. His goodness, friendliness and charm even captured[46] some guards—not all of them were bad - so that one of them used to apologize to Dietrich for having to lock his door, after the round in the courtyard. A few months before Dietrich was arrested he got engaged to be married to Maria von Wedemeyer. Her parents and grandmother had big farms near Finkenwalde, where Dietrich had his illegal Prediger Seminary. They were strong anti-nazi Christian characters, and Dietrich was very fond of the old grandmother Frau von Kleist, who was a great personality. There he got his fiancée to know. She is many years younger and after having lost Dietrich, her home, farm, and nearly all worldly possessions in Pomerania, she is studying Mathematics in Göttingen University.

Dates:
Born 4.2.06 Breslau (father: professor, University Berlin for Psychiatry and Neurology, mother, née von Hase)
Reading Theology 1923 Tübingen, Berlin. Habilitation at Berlin University: 1929 to 1933 lecturer there.
New York 1930/31
Kibdib[47] pastor 1933
Finkenwalde Confessional College Director 1935-1940
Work for Brethren's Council, political work—1943
Arrest 5th April 1943
Executed 9th April 1945, Concentration-Camp Flossenbürg Bayern
Books: "Communio sanctorum," "Schöpfung und Fall," "Akt u. Sein," "Psalmenerklarungen," "Nachfolge," "Gemeinsames Leben," ("Ethik" unvollendet)

---

45 Wassili Kokorin.
46 Read "captivated."
47 A typing error for "London."

Hoping to have helped you in your task in giving support to the rehabilitation of the Church in Germany and asking you kindly to keep me informed about your program of relief and rehabilitation abroad.

Yours sincerely,

Sabine Leibholz

P.S.   I must add that Dietrich was given the opportunity to escape, by the help of Swedish friends after the 20th of July 1944, but that he refused it, because he feared that he would endanger our family and then the family of his friends would suffer for his escape.

The last words which reached my parents from him run as follows: "Please be not troubled about me. I am so sure of God's hand and guidance that I hope forever to be kept in this assurance. You must never doubt that I am thankful and glad to go the way which I am being led. My past life is abundantly full of God's mercy, and above all sin stands the forgiving love of the crucified. It is those who have come and been close to me for whom I am most grateful, and my only wish is, that they may never have to be sorry for me, but that they, too, may always be thankful for God's mercy and sure of His forgiveness. I wanted to say this once and for all so that you should really be glad to hear it."[48]

S. L.

SABINE LEIBHOLZ TO MRS. BOERICKE[49]

SABINE LEIBHOLZ   Oxford, 20th of June 1946
geb. Bonhoeffer   10, Lincoln Rd.

---

[48] This is a rather free translation of a passage in a letter from Tegel of August 23, 1944 actually written to Eberhard Bethge, not to his parents; see LPP 393. Sabine Leibholz also quotes this passage in German in her letter to Paul Lehmann of January 10, 1947; see below for a more precise translation and an explanation of the changes.

[49] Typewritten, on two sheets of plain paper, double-spaced, apparently with the same typewriter as the letter to Dr. Empie, with typed signature; presumably a copy.

(Karl Friedrich and
Dietrich's sister)

Dear Mrs. Boericke,

I do not know whether you have heard of the terrible tragedy, which has come over our family through the Gestapo and S.S. in April 1945! My brother Dietrich (actually my twin-brother) spoke very often of you after his return from U.S.A. many years ago. He must have had a very enjoyable and interesting time, when he was in your house then. I also remember that he spoke of a girl of about 13 years whom he admired for her riding so well. I think my cousin H. Ch. von Hase stayed in your house some years ago. Dietrich was arrested in the house of my parents by the Gestapo in 1943 April 5th, together with my sister Christine von Dohnanyi and her husband Hans von Dohnanyi. My sister was released, but Dietrich and Dohnanyi were kept in prison and Concentration camps, because they were spiritual and political leaders of the resistance movement against Hitler. Then came the plot against Hitler on July 20th 1944 and after the failure of it my elder brother Klaus, and the husband of my eldest sister, R. Schleicher, were arrested by the Gestapo too. They were tortured and held in chains by the Gestapo, and in February 1945 the "Volksgericht" sentenced them to death. They were both executed on 23rd April 1945, shortly before the Russians advanced onto the Gestapo prison. Dietrich had already been murdered on the 9th of April, and my brother-in-law Dohnanyi was executed in Sachsenhausen Concentration camp! I am sending you a memorial book, which the Churches have brought out in Switzerland for Dietrich. My father is now 78 years and my mother 70. My grand-mother Julie Bonhoeffer geb. Tafel died 10 years ago and Dietrich preached a most beautiful sermon at her funeral. My brother, Klaus and my two brothers-in-law left together 10 children between the ages of 7 and twenty-two. Prof. Niebuhr, New York Union Theological Seminary, 120th Street at Broadway, has opened a fund "in memory of Dietrich Bonhoeffer" to help the children of the Bonhoeffer family. I wonder whether you have heard of it already?

May I further ask you whether you would be good enough to send a few food parcels for my parents in Berlin? I have just heard that it is now allowed to send such parcels to the American Zone in Germany, but as the Berlin sector is excluded, it would be best to send it to my sister, Frau Christine von Dohnanyi, (she lost her

husband) who is living in the American zone She is also very short of
food with 3 children, but she would send on a part of it to Berlin. Her
address is: Windach / Post Landsberg / Ledi (64) Bayern American
Zone. By the help of British officers in the C. Commission f. Germany we help as much as we can the family in the British Zone, but
officially food parcels are still illegal to send.

Please forgive my troubling you with such a lengthy letter,
but as I still had your address from Dietrich, when he visited us here
in 1939 last, I thought I should write you. My husband, a professor
for Law released by the Nazis for racial reasons, my daughters and I
have been living in England since 1938.

Yours very sincerely,

Sabine Leibholz

née Bonhoeffer

PAUL LEHMANN TO SABINE LEIBHOLZ[50]

Room 900, Witherspoon Building
Philadelphia 7, Pa.
1 January 1947

My dear Mrs. Leibholz;
One ought to begin a year with renewed sense of direction
and responsibility. For me, this could not be more appropriately done
than by thinking and talking about Dietrich. Indeed, for many, many
weeks now, I have been wanting to write to you, and through you to
your family. For it was during this time that the crushing word came
to us of Dietrich's martyrdom. We had, of course, heard various
reports since the summer of 1945. But it was difficult to get precise
word. Then, in the late summer of 1946, Pastor Bethge's little
volume of Dietrich's poems came to me. And most unexpectedly, and
perhaps strangest of all, I was allowed to share the contents of a letter
which you wrote to Mr. Empie in connection with the film which the

---

[50] Typewritten, single-spaced, on two pages of plain paper, without
signature; presumably a carbon copy.

Lutheran Church in America is preparing and centering upon
Dietrich's life and work. The man who has written the script for that
film was directed to me by Professor Reinhold Niebuhr and it was
through his kindness that your letter to Mr. Empie came to my
attention. Your reference to my association with Dietrich, in that
letter, leads me to hope that you will understand why I write as I do,
and to you.

There simply are no words to express what Dietrich's life
and death have meant to Mrs. Lehmann and to me. We have relived
other days over and over again and with such heavy hearts that it has
seemed to us that second only to those of you who belonged to the
inner circle of his family and to his fiancée, our lives have been
completely shattered by the fact of his being so suddenly and tragi-
cally taken from us. And yet from his own heart have come to us—
and more directly and frequently to all of you, I know—words of such
remarkable power and integrity of faith and hope, that our grief has
been transformed by the strong sense of a continuing and even deeper
kinship with him. It was always so with Dietrich—this sense for the
tragic reality of life and the stronger sense of God's sure will and
purpose. And I cannot begin to tell you how vividly we live in this
companionship with him. But we do. And we now look back upon
the days at Union when he was much in our company, to the warm
hospitality with which he and your parents received us in Berlin in
1933, to the last talk I had with him as I took him to the boat in New
York in 1939 July. And it is always as if there had been no interval at
all. And when our hearts are most downcast, there is still the sense
that there has been no interval at all.

Even though this word comes to you very late indeed, will
you, nevertheless, allow Mrs. Lehmann and me to express to you, and
through you to your parents and to Dietrich's fiancée, our deepest
consolation and concern as you bear this overwhelming tragedy. We
continue to try to sustain you in our prayers and affection, desiring for
you all in your sorrow the gladness and the trust that are prepared for
all who are numbered with Dietrich in the fellowship of faith.

May I, then, make a further request? Mrs. Lehmann and I
wish to be allowed to share your suffering not in word only, but also
in deed. Although we had the pleasure of meeting your brother Klaus
during our visit to Berlin, we did not know him well nor come to
know his family. Nor have we been allowed to know your brother-in-
law and his family. Through your letter the knowledge of a tragedy

and triumph like to Dietrich's on the part of Klaus and Dr. von
Dohnanyi came to us. In all that I have said above, they and their
families have been included. But their families have continuing needs
which we should like in some small but concrete way to share in.
Would you be good enough to tell me how best we might help? There
is, of course, food. And for this, we should like so much to have the
addresses of your parents, of your brother's family and of that of your
brother-in-law; also that of Dietrich's fiancée. I should like very
much also to send a brief word directly to your parents, and to
Dietrich's fiancée. But there is also clothing, especially for the
children. Some guidance about their more specific needs would help
us so much to do what we so much wish to do, even though we
cannot do all we wish to do. I venture to hope that in the context of
my friendship with and for Dietrich, you will feel entirely free to
write me of these things.

Mrs. Lehmann shares with me every thought and every
request of this writing. She joins me too in sending to you and to Dr.
Leibholz most cordial greeting and every good wish,

Sincerely,

SABINE LEIBHOLZ TO PAUL LEHMANN[51]

Oxford,
10th of January
1947.

Dear Professor Lehmann,
Your letter about Dietrich has deeply moved me and I feel I
should have written before and should have told you all about
Dietrich. It is so good to see from all you say about him, how well
you knew him and how perfectly you understood his soul and his
mind. The poems and letters Dietrich wrote in person are indeed a
great comfort and inspiration. My parents have also written to me

---

[51] Six pages, handwritten, on plain paper, with signature; stamped date of
receipt "Jan 14 1947."

about the encouragement and strength which went out from Dietrich every time when they were allowed to visit him in prison.

An English officer, who had been together with Dietrich in Buchenwald, told me that Dietrich never worried about himself at all, but was only occupied in his mind with the well being of his fellow prisoners and with their anxieties. He was kept there in one of the worst cells, without light and heating and the water running down from the walls. But the anxiety he knew he was causing to my parents, his fiancée and all of us weighed heavily on his heart. Pastor E. Bethge, a very good friend of Dietrich's has just spent a fortnight with us and has told us about his work during the war. In the Memorial Service in Berlin held for Dietrich, Pastor Bethge began his sermon with some words Dietrich had once written home from prison:

> Please don't ever get anxious or worried about me.
> [. . .] I am so sure of God's guiding hand that I
> hope I shall always be kept in that certainty. You
> must never doubt that I am traveling along the road
> where I am being led. My life up to now is brim-
> full of God's goodness, and my sins are covered by
> the forgiving love of Christ crucified. I'm most
> thankful for the people who are close to me, and I
> only hope that they never have to grieve about me,
> but that they, too, will always be certain of, and
> thankful for, God's goodness and forgiveness. [. . .]
> I did want to say this for once, so that you would
> really hear it with a joyful spirit.[52]

I thought you would like to know these words of Dietrich's. I cannot tell you how much I miss him and my brother Claus. My

---

[52] The passage is quoted in German, and has been slightly changed from the original letter as published; see DBW 8 576, LPP 393. The letter is written to Eberhard Bethge and uses the intimate "du," whereas the version used here has the generic and formal "Ihr"; it also omits and changes wording in the final three sentences, which are pointedly addressed to Bethge and read as follows: "Forgive my writing this. Don't let it grieve you or upset you for a moment, but let it make you happy. But I did want to say it for once, and I couldn't think of anyone else but you to whom I could dare to say this and who would really take it with a joyful spirit." Other corrections to the published translation are made with thanks to Reinhard Krauss.

two sisters Christine v. Dohnanyi and Ursula Schleicher lost their
husbands also by the S.S. murderers. My brother Claus and my
brother-in-law Rüdiger Schleicher were imprisoned, sentenced to
death, and executed together and we know the place where the S.S.
buried them in a bomb crater. My parents have set a stone there
bearing the names of our four dead and the word "Blessed are they
which are persecuted for righteousness' sake: for theirs is the kingdom of heaven."

   You can imagine how much I am longing to see my parents
and sisters, but being Germans our visiting Germany is not yet
allowed, and the question of our final repatriation is so difficult to
decide at the moment as our children have not yet finished their
education, and the younger one would not be strong enough to stand
up to the terrible conditions in Germany now. My only comfort is
that I can help a little through British friends over there. It is with
much anxiety that I think of my family and friends during the present
cold. If you would send them a food parcel, as you so very kindly
offer, it would be most welcome, also clothing is badly needed,
mainly warm socks, warm stockings and shoes. They need not be
new at all. The Russians have emptied nearly every wardrobe only
leaving the waistcoats of the suits behind, which Russians not wear—
and the shops are empty too.

   I have sent you the booklet which the World Council of
Churches has published about Dietrich and the order of the Memorial
Service the Bishop of Chichester held for him in London, two
farewell letters of my bother Claus, which he wrote shortly before
his death. My husband wrote the article about Dietrich for the
Guardian.[53]

   With every good wish for Mrs. Lehmann and yourself and
with kind regards from my husband.

               Yours sincerely,

               Sabine Leibholz

---

[53] This article was probably published in the autumn of 1945. The Empie
papers of the ELCA archives contain a letter of November 4, 1945 from Gerhard
Leibholz to Reinhold Niebuhr which enclosed two of Bonhoeffer's poems and
Bishop Bell's article, "The Background of the Hitler Plot," from the October
1945 issue of the *Contemporary Review.* The same file also contains a transcript

PAUL LEHMANN TO KARL AND PAULA BONHOEFFER[54]

20 Alexander Street
November 19, 1948

Dear Dr. and Mrs. Bonhoeffer,

These lines ought to have been sent to you long ago. You cannot imagine how frequently in these last few years you have been in our thoughts, hearts, and prayers. I cannot expect that you will remember us. But perhaps you will permit me to write to you because of my friendship with Dietrich. We spent time together at Union Seminary in New York City, and subsequently in the spring of 1933 my wife and I had the wonderful opportunity to visit you in Grunewald. The last time I saw Dietrich was in 1939 at the ship on which he returned to Germany from New York.

It was not until the spring of 1946 that I received the news that Dietrich had entered the glory of his Lord. I do not have to elaborate on the depth of my personal shock over this event. However, I have to confess to you that this experience represented and still represents the most intimate loss of my life. For months I could really not find any words to express it. And then on two occasions, one shortly after the other, I had to settle into a new vocational role. In the summer of 1946 I worked at the Westminster Press in Philadelphia, and since September 1947 I have joined the faculty here at Princeton. However, what prevented me mostly from writing during these months was a heart condition which did not allow me to work any more than the minimum. It is only in the last two months that I am slowly feeling better.

In the meantime, your daughter Mrs Leibholz has been so kind as to send me the memorial brochure and the order of the memorial service that was held in England. For this kindness I am grateful to her beyond what words are able to express.

---

of a 1,000 word article by Gerhard Leibholz entitled "Dietrich Bonhoeffer" which is possibly a copy of the *Guardian* article mentioned here.

[54] Carbon copy of a typewritten letter, in German, one page, single-spaced, on plain paper, presumably with a handwritten signature on the original; written from Princeton.

But may I now rather belatedly and from afar send you this expression of condolence and comfort. The Lord who called Dietrich into his presence has been a faithful comfort for you. To this Lord I constantly offer my most ardent thanks for Dietrich's life and work. But I would also like to express my thanks to you as the parents of my dear friend whose life and death so enriched and strengthened my own work and faith, and in so doing perhaps also provide a small encouragement for you.

Please do not trouble yourself with answering this letter. It is simply meant to convey very inadequate condolences from my wife and myself. We seek to keep you always in our prayer as well in the constant memory of our friendship with Dietrich.

With kindest regards,

Respectfully yours,

PAULA BONHOEFFER TO PAUL LEHMANN[55]

December 10, 1949

Dear Mr. Lehmann!
Unfortunately I had misplaced your letter and not written down your exact address. Today, when organizing my letters, I stumbled upon your letter again, and am thus finally able to thank you for your compassionate and warmhearted letter. Yes, we too miss Dietrich very much, and so does our church! But we know that it was God's will, and we have to reconcile ourselves to it. I do not know whether you have received the news that shortly afterwards, on July 20,[56] another son (Klaus) and two sons-in-law, Rüdiger Schleicher and Hans von Dohnanyi, were also taken from us by being murdered in this terrible war. I am thus concerned about three families with children who are fatherless! A year ago, after fifty years of being happily married, I lost my dear husband who died of a stroke. As

---

[55] Handwritten in German on four sides of folded notepaper.
[56] The actual date was April 23, which was indeed "kurz darauf" April 9. The citing of "July 20" [1944] suggests that, because it was such an emotionally charged date, and the reason for their deaths, it has taken the place of the correct one.

much as I am ever and again saddened by the separation, I nevertheless know all of them to be safely in the best of hands. I assume you
know that Eberhard Bethge married my little granddaughter. I am
now already a great-grandmother for the third time. It is also wonderful that we all live only a few houses apart. Thus they all come by
every evening to say good night. Eberhard has an extensive and
successful assignment working with students from both universities.
At times things look dark all around us, but we seek to place our trust
in God. Please give my sincere regards to your dear wife also, and
accept my apologies for taking so long to thank you for your letter.
With best wishes for your well-being,

Yours,

Paula Bonhoeffer

SELECT BIBLIOGRAPHY

Bibliography

Feil, Ernst, assisted by Barbara E. Fink eds. *International Bibliography on Dietrich Bonhoeffer.* [Multi-lingual.] Gütersloh: Chr. Kaiser. Gütersloher Verlagshaus, 1998.

Floyd, Wayne Whitson, Jr., and Clifford J. Green. *Bonhoeffer Bibliography: Primary Sources and Secondary Literature in English.* Evanston: American Theological Library Association, 1992. (This bibliography contains listings and annotations of all translations and editions of Bonhoeffer's texts; it is updated annually in the February issue of the *Newsletter* of the International Bonhoeffer Society, English Language Section.)

Primary Sources

Dietrich Bonhoeffer Werke
Dietrich Bonhoeffer Works, English Edition

Sanctorum Communio, (DBW 1). Edited by Joachim von Soosten. Munich: Chr. Kaiser, 1986.

Sanctorum Communio, (DBWE 1). Edited by Clifford J. Green. Translated by Reinhard Krauss and Nancy Lukens. Minneapolis: Fortress Press, 1998.

Akt und Sein, (DBW 2). Edited by Hans-Richard Reuter. Munich: Chr. Kaiser, 1988.

Act and Being, (DBWE 2). Edited by Wayne Whitson Floyd, Jr. Translated by H. Martin Rumscheidt. Minneapolis: Fortress Press, 1996.

Schöpfung und Fall, (DBW 3). Edited by Martin Rüter and Ilse Tödt. Munich: Chr. Kaiser, 1989.

Creation and Fall, (DBWE 3). Edited by John W. de Gruchy. Translated by Douglas Stephen Bax. Minneapolis: Fortress Press, 1997.

Nachfolge, (DBW 4). Edited by Martin Kuske and Ilse Tödt. Second, revised edition. Gütersloh: Chr. Kaiser. Gütersloher Verlagshaus, 1994.

Gemeinsames Leben. Das Gebetbuch der Bibel, (DBW 5). Edited by Gerhard Ludwig Müller and Albrecht Schönherr. Munich: Chr. Kaiser, 1987.

Life Together. The Prayerbook of the Bible, (DBWE 5). Edited by Geffrey B. Kelly. Translated by Daniel W. Bloesch and James H. Burtness. Minneapolis: Fortress Press, 1996.

Ethik, (DBW 6). Edited by Ilse Tödt, Heinz Eduard Tödt, Ernst Feil and Clifford Green. Second, revised edition. Gütersloh: Chr. Kaiser. Gütersloher Verlagshaus, 1998.

Fragmente aus Tegel, (DBW 7). Edited by Renate Bethge and Ilse Tödt. Gütersloh: Chr. Kaiser. Gütersloher Verlagshaus, 1994.

Fiction from Tegel Prison, (DBWE 7). Edited by Clifford J. Green. Translated by Nancy Lukens. Minneapolis: Fortress Press, 1999.

Widerstand und Ergebung, (DBW 8). Edited by Christian Gremmels, Eberhard Bethge, and Renate Bethge, assisted by Ilse Tödt. Gütersloh: Chr. Kaiser. Gütersloher Verlagshaus, 1998.

Jugend und Studium 1918-1927, (DBW 9). Edited by Hans Pfeifer assisted by Clifford Green and Carl-Jürgen Kaltenborn. Munich: Chr. Kaiser, 1986.

Barcelona, Berlin, Amerika 1928-1931, (DBW 10). Edited by Reinhard Staats and Hans Christoph von Hase assisted by Holger Roggelin and Matthias Wünsche. Munich: Chr. Kaiser, 1991.

Ökumene, Universität, Pfarramt 1931-1932, (DBW 11). Edited by Eberhard Amelung and Christoph Strohm. Gütersloh: Chr. Kaiser. Gütersloher Verlagshaus, 1994.

Berlin 1932-1933, (DBW 12). Edited by Carsten Nicolaisen and Ernst-Albert Scharffenorth. Gütersloh: Chr. Kaiser. Gütersloher Verlagshaus, 1997.

London 1933-1935, (DBW 13). Edited by Hans Goedeking, Martin Heimbucher and Hans-Walter Schleicher. Gütersloh: Chr. Kaiser. Gütersloher Verlagshaus, 1994.

Illegale Theologenausbildung: Finkenwalde 1937-1937, (DBW 14). Edited by Otto Dudzus and Jürgen Henkys assisted by Sabine Bobert-Stützel and Ilse Tödt. Gütersloh: Chr. Kaiser. Gütersloher Verlagshaus, 1996.

Illegale Theologenausbildung: Sammelvikariate 1937-1940, (DBW 15). Edited by Dirk Schulz. Gütersloh: Chr. Kaiser. Gütersloher Verlagshaus, 1998.

Konspiration und Haft 1940-1945, (DBW 16). Edited by Jørgen Glenthøj, Ulrich Kabitz and Wolf Krötke. Gütersloh: Chr. Kaiser. Gütersloher Verlagshaus, 1996.

OTHER EDITIONS AND TRANSLATIONS OF BONHOEFFER'S WRITINGS

Christ the Center. New York: Harper & Row, 1966; London: Collins, 1966, as *Christology.*

The Cost of Discipleship. New York: Simon & Schuster, 1995.

Ethics. New York: Simon & Schuster, 1995.

Fiction from Prison. Philadelphia: Fortress Press, 1981.

Gesammelte Schriften, vols. I-VI, ed. Eberhard Bethge. Munich: Chr. Kaiser; I 1965, second edn.; II 1965, second edn.; III 1966, second edn.; IV 1965, second edn.; V 1972; VI 1974.

Letters and Papers from Prison. The Enlarged Edition. New York: Simon & Schuster, 1997.

Love Letters from Cell 92. The Correspondence between Dietrich Bonhoeffer and Maria von Wedemeyer, 1943-45. Edited by Ruth-Alice von Bismarck and Ulrich Kabitz. Postscript by Eberhard Bethge. Translated by John Brownjohn. Nashville: Abingdon, 1994.

No Rusty Swords. Letters, Lectures and Notes 1928-1936 from the Collected Works of Dietrich Bonhoeffer. Vol I. Edited by Edwin H. Robertson. New York: Harper & Row, 1965.

True Patriotism. Lectures and Notes 1939-1945 from the Collected Works of Dietrich Bonhoeffer. Vol III. Edited by Edwin H. Robertson. New York: Harper & Row, 1973.

The Way to Freedom. Lectures and Notes 1935-1939 from the Collected Works of Dietrich Bonhoeffer. Vol II. Edited by Edwin H. Robertson. New York: Harper & Row, 1967.

For a listing of occasional pieces by Bonhoeffer translated into English—lectures, essays, reviews, sermons, letters (including correspondence with Barth, Niebuhr, and Maria von Wedemeyer) and poems—see *Bonhoeffer Bibliography,* pp. 9–15; for other materials in English in the *Gesammelte Schriften,* see pp. 15–22.

SECONDARY LITERATURE

Bethge, Eberhard. *Bonhoeffer: An Illustrated Introduction.* Translated by Rosaleen Ockenden. London: Collins, Fount Paperbacks, 1979; as *Costly Grace. An Illustrated Introduction to Dietrich Bonhoeffer.* New York: Harper & Row, 1979. British edition reprinted, with different pagination, as *Bonhoeffer: An Illustrated Biography in Documents and Photographs.* London: HarperCollins, 1995.

————. *Bonhoeffer: Exile and Martyr.* Edited by John W. de Gruchy. London: Collins, 1975; New York: Seabury, 1976.

————. "Dietrich Bonhoeffer and the Jews." In *Ethical Responsibility. Bonhoeffer's Legacy to the Churches,* 43-96. See Godsey and Kelly, eds., 1981.

————. *Dietrich Bonhoeffer. Theologian, Christian, Man for his Times.* Translated by Eric Mosbacher et al., under the editorship of Edwin Robertson. Second, revised and unabridged edition. Edited by Victoria Barnett. Minneapolis: Fortress Press, 1999.

————. *Friendship and Resistance. Essays on Dietrich Bonhoeffer.* Geneva: WCC Publications; Grand Rapids: Eerdmans, 1995.

Bethge, Eberhard, Renate Bethge and Christian Gremmels, eds. *Dietrich Bonhoeffer: A Life in Pictures.* Translated by John Bowden. London: SCM Press; Philadelphia: Fortress Press, 1986.

Bethge, Eberhard et al., eds. *Die Mündige Welt,* vols I-V. Munich: Christian Kaiser, 1955-69.

Burtness, James H. *Shaping the Future: The Ethics of Dietrich Bonhoeffer.* Philadelphia: Fortress Press, 1985.

Carter, Guy Christopher. "Confession at Bethel, August 1933—Enduring Witness." Ph.D. diss., Marquette University, 1986.

Carter, Guy C. et al., eds. *Bonhoeffer's Ethics: Old Europe and New Frontiers.* Kampen: Kok Pharos, 1991.

Clements, Keith. *A Patriotism for Today: Dialogue with Dietrich Bonhoeffer.* Bristol, England: Bristol Baptist College, 1984. (Also published as *A Patriotism for Today: Love of Country in Dialogue With the Witness of Dietrich Bonhoeffer.* Second Edition. London: Collins, 1986.)

_____ . *What Freedom? The Persistent Challenge of Dietrich Bonhoeffer.* Bristol, England: Bristol Baptist College, 1990.

D'Isanto, Luca. "The Deconstruction of Metaphysics in the Thought of Dietrich Bonhoeffer." Master's thesis, International Baptist Theological Seminary of Rüschlikon, Switzerland, 1987.

Day, Thomas I. *Dietrich Bonhoeffer on Christian Community and Common Sense.* Toronto Studies in Theology, vol. 11. Bonhoeffer Series, no. 2. Lewiston, New York: Edwin Mellen Press, 1982.

de Gruchy, John W. ed. *Bonhoeffer for a New Day. Theology in a Time of Transition.* Grand Rapids: Eerdmans, 1997.

_____ . ed. *The Cambridge Companion to Dietrich Bonhoeffer.* Cambridge: Cambridge University Press, 1999.

_____ . ed. and with an intro., "The Development of Bonhoeffer's Theology," 1-42. *Dietrich Bonhoeffer: Witness to Jesus Christ.* London: Collins, 1988; Minneapolis: Fortress Press, 1991.

Dumas, André. *Dietrich Bonhoeffer: Theologian of Reality.* Translated by Robert McAfee Brown. New York: Macmillan, 1971.

Feil, Ernst. *Bonhoeffer Studies in Germany: A Survey of Recent Literature.* Edited by James Burtness. Translated by Jonathan Sorum. Philadelphia: International Bonhoeffer Society, 1997.

_____ . *The Theology of Dietrich Bonhoeffer.* Translated by H. Martin Rumscheidt. Philadelphia: Fortress Press, 1985.

Floyd, Wayne Whitson, Jr. *Theology and the Dialectics of Otherness: On Reading Bonhoeffer and Adorno.* Lanham, Maryland: University Press of America, 1988.

Floyd, Wayne Whitson, Jr. and Charles Marsh eds., *Theology and the Practice of Responsibility: Essays on Dietrich Bonhoeffer.* Philadelphia: Trinity Press International, 1994.

Floyd, Wayne Whitson, Jr., Barbara Green, Clifford J. Green, and H. Martin Rumscheidt. "Recent Bonhoeffer Scholarship in Europe and America." *Religious Studies Review,* 23.3 (July,1997) 219-21, 228-30.

Glazener, Mary. *The Cup of Wrath: The Story of Dietrich Bonhoeffer's Resistance to Hitler.* Savannah, GA: F. C. Beil, 1992.

Glenthøj, Jørgen. *Dokumente zur Bonhoeffer Forschung.* Munich: Christian Kaiser Verlag, 1969.

Godsey, John D. *Preface to Bonhoeffer: The Man and Two of His Shorter Writings.* Philadelphia: Fortress Press, 1965.

_____ . *The Theology of Dietrich Bonhoeffer.* Philadelphia: Westminster; London: SCM, 1960.

Godsey, John D. and Geffrey B. Kelly eds. *Ethical Responsibility: Bonhoeffer's Legacy to the Churches.* New York and Toronto: Edwin Mellen Press, 1981.

Green, Clifford James. "Bethge's Bonhoeffer." Review article on *Dietrich Bonhoeffer,* by Eberhard Bethge. *The Christian Century* 87.26 (July 1, 1970): 822-25.

_____ . "Beyond Individualism: From Bonhoeffer to a New Public Theology," 1986. Bonhoeffer Archive, Union Theological Seminary, New York.

_____ . "Bonhoeffer: Christian Humanist in Political Crisis," 1985. Bonhoeffer Archive, Union Theological Seminary, New York.

_____ . "Bonhoeffer, Gutierrez and American Theology." Paper presented at the DDR Bonhoeffer Komitee Tagung, September 1989. Bonhoeffer Archive, Union Theological Seminary, New York.

_____ . "Bonhoeffer in the Context of Erikson's Luther Study." In *Psychohistory and Religion. The Case of 'Young Man Luther,'* edited by Roger A. Johnson, 162-96. Philadelphia: Fortress Press, 1977.

_____ . "Bonhoeffer, Modernity and Liberation Theology." *Union Seminary Quarterly Review* vol. 46, 1993. Also in Floyd and Marsh eds., *Theology and the Practice of Responsibility: Essays on Dietrich Bonhoeffer.*

_____ . "Bonhoeffer's 'Non-Religious Christianity' as Public Theology." *Dialog* 26.4 (Fall 1987): 275-80.

_____ . "Bonhoeffer's Concept of Religion." *Union Seminary Quarterly Review* 19.1 (November 1963): 11-21. (Also published in condensed form in *Theology Digest* 13 (Spring 1965): 47-51.)

_____ . "Bonhoeffer's Public Theology and the Quest for Peace with Justice," 1986. Bonhoeffer Archive, Union Theological Seminary, New York.

_____ . "'Church and World' and 'Religionless Christianity.'" In *Bonhoeffer's Ethics: Old Europe and New Frontiers*, 42-43. See Carter et al., 1991.

_____ . "Foreword" to John D. Godsey and Geffrey B. Kelly, eds., *Ethical Responsibility: Bonhoeffer's Legacy to the Churches*. See Godsey and Kelly, 1981.

_____ . "Freedom and Solidarity: Bonhoeffer's Social Theology and our Theological Task." Paper presented at the Fourth International Bonhoeffer Congress, Hirschluch, 1984. Bonhoeffer Archive, Union Theological Seminary, New York.

_____ . "Interpreting Bonhoeffer: Reality or Phraseology?" Review article on *Reality and Faith*, by Heinrich Ott, and *Dietrich Bonhoeffer: Theologian of Reality*, by André Dumas. *Journal of Religion* 55.2 (April 1975): 270-75.

_____ . "Sharing the Sufferings of God. The Challenge of the Holocaust to Religious Faith," 1985. Bonhoeffer Archive, Union Theological Seminary, New York.

_____ . "Sociality and Church in Bonhoeffer's 1933 Christology." *Scottish Journal of Theology* 21.4 (December 1968): 416-34.

_____ ed. "Textual Research for the New Edition of Bonhoeffer's *Ethics*. Panel Discussion." In *Bonhoeffer's Ethics: Old Europe and New Frontiers*, 30-38. See Carter et al., 1991.

_____ . "The Sociality of Christ and Humanity. Dietrich Bonhoeffer's Early Theology. 1927-1933." Th.D. diss., Union Theological Seminary, New York, 1971. (Also available from University Microfilms; contains five appendices and bibliography not in the published edition.)

_____ . *The Sociality of Christ and Humanity: Dietrich Bonhoeffer's Early Theology, 1927-1933*. Missoula, Montana: Scholars Press, 1975.

_____ . The Text of Bonhoeffer's *Ethics*." In *New Studies in Bonhoeffer's Ethics*, 3-66. See Peck, ed., 1987.

_____ . "A Theology of Sociality: Bonhoeffer's *Sanctorum Communio*." In *The Context of Contemporary Theology: Essays in Honor of Paul Lehmann*, edited by Alexander J. McKelway and E. David Willis, 65-84. Atlanta: John Knox, 1974.

_____ . "Two Bonhoeffers on Psychoanalysis." In *A Bonhoeffer Legacy*, 58-75. See A. J. Klassen, ed., 1981.

_____ , ed. and with an "Introduction" to the English Edition of Bonhoeffer, *Fiction from Prison: Gathering up the Past*, vii-xiv.

Gutierrez, Gustavo. "Theology from the Underside of History." In his *The Power of the Poor in History*, 222-34. Maryknoll: Orbis, 1983.

_____ . "The Limitations of Modern Theology: On a Letter of Dietrich Bonhoeffer." In his *The Power of the Poor in History*, 169-221. Maryknoll: Orbis, 1983.

Hopper, David H. *A Dissent on Bonhoeffer*. Philadelphia: Westminster, 1975.

Hunsinger, George. "Barth, Barmen and the Confessing Church Today. (Political Apathy and Guilt)." *Katallagete* 9 (Summer 1985): 14-27.

_____ . "Barth, Barmen and the Confessing Church Today: Summary of the Original Text," with replies and rejoinders, D. Berrigan, and others. *Katallagete* 10, nos. 1-3 (Fall, 1987): 10-11.

_____ . "Karl Barth and Radical Politics: Some Further Considerations." *Studies in Religion/Sciences Religieuses* 7, no. 2 (Spring 1978): 167-91.

Johnson, Roger A. "Dietrich Bonhoeffer: Religionless Christianity— Maturity, Transcendence and Freedom." In *Critical Issues in Modern Religion*, rev. ed., Roger A. Johnson et al. Englewood Cliffs, New Jersey: Prentice-Hall, [1973] 1990.

Kelly, Geffrey B. *Liberating Faith: Bonhoeffer's Message for Today*. Minneapolis: Augsburg Publishing House, 1984.

Kelly, Geffrey B. and F. Burton Nelson, eds., and with an "Editors' Introduction." *A Testament to Freedom. The Essential Writings of Dietrich Bonhoeffer*. Revised edition. San Francisco: HarperSanFrancisco, 1995.

Klassen, A. J. ed. *A Bonhoeffer Legacy: Essays in Understanding*. Grand Rapids: Eerdmans, 1981.

Kuske, Martin. *The Old Testament as the Book of Christ: An Appraisal of Bonhoeffer's Interpretation.* Translated by S. T. Kimbrough. Philadelphia: Westminster Press, 1976.

Lasserre, Jean. "Remembrances of Dietrich Bonhoeffer." Translated by Allen Hackett from *La Vie Chretienne* (October-November 1981). *Newsletter*, International Bonhoeffer Society, English Language Section, no. 31 (February 1986): 1-4.

Lehmann, Paul L. "The Concreteness of Theology: Reflections on the Conversation Between Barth and Bonhoeffer." In *Footnotes to a Theology: The Karl Barth Colloquium of 1972*, edited by H. Martin Rumscheidt, 53-76. Waterloo, Ontario: The Corporation for the Publication of Academic Studies in Religion in Canada, 1971.

Leibholz-Bonhoeffer, Sabine. *The Bonhoeffers: Portrait of a Family.* Foreword by Lord Longford. Preface by Eberhard Bethge. London: Sidgwick & Jackson; New York: St. Martin's Press, 1971.

Lovin, Robin W. "Dietrich Bonhoeffer: Responsibility and Restoration." In *Christian Faith and Public Choices: The Social Ethics of Barth, Brunner and Bonhoeffer.* Philadelphia: Fortress Press, 1984.

Luther, Martin. *D. Martin Luthers Werke.* Kritische Gesamtausgabe, Weimar edn., 1883ff.

Marsh, Charles. *Reclaiming Dietrich Bonhoeffer: The Promise of His Theology.* New York: Oxford University Press, 1994.

Moltmann, Jürgen and Jürgen Weissbach. *Two Studies in the Theology of Bonhoeffer.* Translated by Reginald and Ilse Fuller. Introduction by R. H. Fuller. New York: Charles Scribner's Sons, 1967.

Müller, Hanfried. "The Problem of the Reception and Interpretation of Dietrich Bonhoeffer." In *World Come of Age*, 182-214, ed. Ronald Gregor Smith. Philadelphia: Fortress Press, 1967.

Ott, Heinrich. *Reality and Faith: The Theological Legacy of Dietrich Bonhoeffer.* Translated by Alex A. Morrison. London: Lutterworth, 1971; Philadelphia: Fortress Press, 1972.

Peck, William J. ed. *New Studies in Bonhoeffer's Ethics.* Lewiston, New York: Edwin Mellen Press, 1987.

Pejsa, Jane. *Matriarch of Conspiracy: Ruth von Kleist 1867-1945.* Minneapolis: Kenwood Publishing, 1991.

Rasmussen, Larry L. *Dietrich Bonhoeffer: Reality and Resistance.* Nashville: Abingdon, 1972. Originally written as "Dietrich Bonhoeffer: Reality and Resistance, Christology and Conspiracy." Th.D. diss., Union Theological Seminary, New York, 1970.

Rasmussen, Larry with Renate Bethge. *Dietrich Bonhoeffer: His Significance for North Americans.* Minneapolis: Fortress Press, 1989.

Smith, Ronald Gregor, ed. *World Come of Age.* Philadelphia: Fortress Press; London: Collins, 1967. [Selections translated from *Die Mündige Welt* I-IV (Munich: Kaiser, 1959-1963).]

Tödt, Heinz Eduard. "Dietrich Bonhoeffer's and Karl Barth's Concepts of Revelation and World," 1976. Bonhoeffer Archive, Union Theological Seminary, New York.

von Wedemeyer-Weller, Maria. "The Other Letters from Prison." In *Bonhoeffer in a World Come of Age,* ed. Peter Vorkink 103-13. Philadelphia: Fortres Press, 1968. (Originally published in *Union Seminary Quarterly Review* 23.1 (Fall 1967): 23-29. Also published in Bonhoeffer, *Letters and Papers from Prison,* 4th Enl. Ed., 412-19.)

Williams, Rowan. "The Suspicion of Suspicion: Wittgenstein and Bonhoeffer." In *The Grammar of the Heart: New Essays in Moral Philosophy and Theology,* edited by Richard H. Bell, 36-53. San Francisco: Harper & Row, 1988. (Originally presented as a conference paper at The College of Wooster, Ohio, March, 1987.)

Wind, Renate. *Dietrich Bonhoeffer. A Spoke in the Wheel.* Translated by John Bowden. London: SCM Press; Grand Rapids: William B. Eerdmans, 1992.

Wüstenberg, Ralf K. *A Theology of Life. Dietrich Bonhoeffer's Religionless Christianity.* Foreword by Eberhard Bethge. Translated by Doug Stott. Grand Rapids: Eerdmans, 1998.

Young, Josiah Ulysses III. *No Difference in the Fare. Dietrich Bonhoeffer and the Problem of Racism.* Foreword by John D. Godsey. Grand Rapids: Eerdmans, 1998.

Zimmermann, Wolf-Dieter and Ronald Gregor Smith, eds. *I Knew Dietrich Bonhoeffer: Reminiscences by his Friends.* Translated by Käthe Gregor Smith. London: Collins, 1960; New York: Harper, 1966. (Also published in paper by London: Collins, 1973; Cleveland: Collins-World, 1977.)

Index of Names

Aaron, 244
Abraham, 164f.
Adam (see Subject Index)
Allston, Wallace, 330
Anselm of Canterbury, 136, 286
Aquinas, Thomas, 47, 169, 305
Aristotle, 102
Athanasius, 136
Augustine, 51, 105, 124, 136, 139, 169, 320

Bach, Johann Sebastian, 352
Baillie, John, 28, 116, 349
Balthazar, Hans Urs von, 193
Barth, Karl, 9ff., 24, 27ff., 48, 65, 74f., 85f., 96, 105, 108, 116, 135f., 148, 188, 192f., 203, 238, 240, 254, 258f., 293f., 307f., 312, 320f., 329, 347, 352
Beethoven, Ludwig van, 352
Bell, George K. A., 179, 350, 360
Bellah, Robert N., 292
Berger, Peter, 27, 29
Bernanos, Georges, 148, 150
Bethge, Eberhard, 3, 5, 11, 14, 20, 28, 39f., 68, 74ff., 78ff., 86, 93, 95, 105ff., 119, 128, 140, 143ff., 148, 151, 160, 172, 181, 203,

206, 231, 257f., 260, 269, 276, 281, 291, 302, 305, 309, 317, 327, 329ff., 350f., 354, 356, 359, 363
Bismarck, Otto von, 129
Boericke family, 330f., 354
Böhler, D., 39
Bonaparte, Napoleon, 276
Bonhoeffer, Dietrich (see Subject Index)
Bonhoeffer, Emmi, 145
Bonhoeffer, Julie Tafel, 355
Bonhoeffer, Karl, 105, 110, 145f., 256f., 295, 331, 361
Bonhoeffer, Karl-Friedrich, 142, 153, 256f.
Bonhoeffer, Klaus, 256f., 347, 350, 355, 357ff., 362
Bonhoeffer, Paula, 146, 331, 361
Bonhoeffer, Walter, 144
Borkin, Joseph, 339
Bouillard, Henri, 193
Braun, Eva, 276
Broughall, W. B., 341
Brunner, Emil, 9, 29, 136, 329, 332f.
Bruno, Giordano, 250
Buber, Martin, 29

Index of Subjects